I, George N

The Autobiography of a Ru

By George Nepia and Terry McLean

(Stamp reproduction courtesy New Zealand Post Office)

"A great All Black fullback and also a great New Zealander"
Bob Scott

LONDON LEAGUE PUBLICATIONS Ltd.

I, George Nepia
The Autobiography of a Rugby Legend

We would like to thank the New Zealand Post Office for permission to reproduce the stamp shown on the title page and first day cover. Stamp and first day cover reproduced by kind permission of New Zealand Post Limited from their 1990 Health stamp issue. Stamps © New Zealand Post Office.

A CIP catalogue record for this book is available from the British Library.

Cover photos: Front: George Nepia just before the 1924-25 tour (photo: Courtesy Hulton Getty archive). Back: 1924-25 All Blacks team group (photo: Courtesy Museum of Rugby, Twickenham)

The original edition of *I, George Nepia* was published in New Zealand by A. H. & A. W. Reed Ltd and in Great Britain by Herbert Jenkin Ltd, with the title: *I, George Nepia - The Golden Years of Rugby*

This edition first published in Great Britain
in September 2002 by: London League Publications Ltd,
P.O. Box 10441, London E14 0SB
ISBN: 1-903659-07-8
Editors: Peter Lush and Dave Farrar
Cover design by: Stephen McCarthy Graphic Design
46, Clarence Road, London N15 5BB
Layout and design: Peter Lush
Printed and bound by: Bath Press Limited
Lower Bristol Road, Bath BA2 3BL
Distribution in New Zealand by: The Celebrity Book Company Limited
Private Box 302-750
North Harbour
Auckland 1330,
New Zealand

Foreword

On behalf of my family, I am delighted and honoured to be asked by London League Publications to provide a forward for the republishing of my father's autobiography, written by Sir Terry McLean in collaboration with my father, George Nepia.

Sir Terry is well known throughout New Zealand as one of the most travelled of Rugby Journalists of our time, covering also accounts of great tours by All Blacks, Springboks, and Lions teams, writing several books on them.

My father and Sir Terry had known one another for a number of years and through their relationship, led to the writing of this book which has become a classic of sporting literature. (Oddly enough it was Terry's father who chose Pop for his first representative match.)

In Chapter 27, my father gives an account of his turning professional league, due to the depression, and things as they were on the farm, made his decision to turn to League to help ease the burden of that time especially for my mother and family.

It was a tough decision as Pop had to make a two year trip on his own. Pop was a very spiritual and humble man, he could have been New Zealand's first "Sports Knight" but he turned the recommendation down. I believe that had mother been alive he may have accepted.

Not one of the family questioned him as you were not allowed to. As it were, I having served 34 years in the New Zealand Army declined the recommendation of an M.B.E. with respect to family protocol, that you do not supersede your father.

A marvellous man, apart from his rugby prowess, a hard worker on the farm, a great provider and dearly loved by mother and family.

Dad was made the first non-white "Honorary Vice - President" of the South African Rugby Union, by Dr Danie Craven, in 1986. Dad has a rugby record that has not been equalled and not likely to be.

George Nepia played 32 consecutive games on one tour for the 1924 All Blacks, and they won every match.

Oma Nepia
Palmerston North
November 2001

About this edition

The origins of this edition are in the research we did for our first book, *Touch and Go - the history of Professional Rugby League in London.* The story of how George Nepia signed for Streatham & Mitcham and became a key figure there for a year was a fascinating one. Then buying a second-hand copy of *I, George Nepia* added enormously to our knowledge of his life and career. Through Huw Richards we managed to contact Sir Terry McLean, and his help and support made the "nice idea" of a new, expanded edition into reality. It has been a privilege and a pleasure for a small publishing company like ours to work with a writer of Sir Terry McLean's stature. His enthusiasm, contacts and support have been invaluable. Much of our communication has been by fax, with the occasional telephone call. Sadly, our resources did not allow a visit to New Zealand to discuss the project in person. The original book is reprinted as published, as are other reprints. This has meant inconsistency in style, but we felt it would not be correct to try to have a uniform style, but to leave pieces as originally published. Inevitably, there is also some repetition and duplication - we hope this does not detract from the book and readers will enjoy it. Being thousands of miles away from our subject matter also meant problems in trying to find photos and illustrations. The selection of photos inevitably has a "British" bias, if only because that was what we could find at reasonable cost. Again, we hope they add to the book and recognise that inevitably there are gaps.

Acknowledgements

Apart from Sir Terry McLean we would also like to thank Oma Nepia for his support, for writing the foreword and for providing material for the book. Without this, the project would not have been possible.

We would also like to thank Hodder, Moa, Beckett for permission to use *Guardians of the Gate* from *New Zealand Rugby Legends: 15 reflections* and the Obituary from the *1987 Rugby Almanack of New Zealand*; the *New Zealand Herald* for permission to use the 1936 match reports, the 1986 Obituary by Terry McLean, and the reports of Nepia's death; the *Halifax Evening Courier* for permission to use *Rugby Every Time*; and Trevor Delaney for permission to use the Obituary from *Code XIII* . Thank you to everyone who provided photographs, and the New Zealand Post Office for permission to use the stamps.

We would also like to thank Huw Richards, Robert Gate, Bob Luxford (New Zealand Rugby Museum), Jed Smith & Ross Hamilton (Museum of Rugby at Twickenham), Bill Honeybone (The Celebrity Book Company), Sandra Dickinson, Kevin Vose, Stephen McCarthy, Stuart Alexander (Bath Press Ltd) and Al Ferrier for their help. However, any mistakes are the responsibility of the editors!

Contributors

Huw Richards is a freelance journalist and historian and the Rugby correspondent of the *Financial Times.* He was co-editor of *Heart and Soul - the character of Welsh Rugby* and *More Heart and Soul.* He was co-author of Robert Jones' autobiography *Raising the Dragon* and has written widely on cricket and football. He wrote a ground-breaking history of *The Daily Herald, The Bloody Circus.* He is currently working on a book on the 1953 Wales - All Blacks match, to be published next year.

Robert Gate has been following Rugby League since 1956 and writing professionally about the game sine 1984. He was a founder member of the Rugby League Record keepers' Club and was the Rugby Football League's official archivist until 1994. He has written many books on the sport, his latest works being *The Great Bev* (London league Publications), an account of the playing career of Brian Bevan, and 100 Cumberland greats (Tempus Publishing). He is currently working on *The Rugby League Hall of Fame* and *100 Halifax Greats* for Tempus Publishing.

Peter Lush was introduced to Rugby League by Dave Farrar in October 1980. 22 years later he is still enthusiastic about the game. He also has a season ticket for West Ham United FC, has a soft spot for Brentford FC, and is a member of Middlesex County Cricket Club. Apart from the books listed below, he also co-wrote *The Employment Handbook - a guide for housing co-operatives.* He writes regularly for *Our Game.* He works as a housing consultant, and for Volunteer Development England.

Dave Farrar has been watching Rugby League for 40 years. He was born in Salford and his parents watched the original Red Devils (Salford RLFC) in the 1930s. He moved to London in 1980, started watching Fulham and has now followed Rugby League in London for 22 years. Apart from the books listed below, he has also written *The Right to Vote* (with Yve Amor). He has also written regularly for *Our Game* and is vice-chairman of the London Broncos supporters club. He works as a manager in local government.

Previous publications:

Touch and Go - A History of Professional Rugby League in London by Dave Farrar and Peter Lush with Michael O'Hare
I Wouldn't Start from Here by Peter Lush and Dave Farrar
The Sin Bin by Steve Spencer, Peter Hardy and Dave Farrar
From Arundel to Zimbabwe by Robin Osmond, Peter Lush and Dave Farrar
Tries in the Valleys - A History of Rugby League in Wales edited by Peter Lush and Dave Farrar
Going to the Cricket by Robin Osmond and Peter Lush
The Rugby League Grounds Guide by Peter Lush and Dave Farrar
Our Game (Rugby League magazine) edited by Peter Lush and Dave Farrar

Sir Terry McLean

Sports journalists, we are often reminded, are 'fans with typewriters'. Some of our number possibly merit the jibe, but Terry McLean has always been much more than that. If journalism is the first draft of history, future chroniclers of New Zealand rugby will have copious reason to the grateful to him.

If you seek his monument, look in the files of the *New Zealand Herald* and in bookshops and libraries with good rugby sections. For more than 30 years, McLean was the faithful chronicler of the travels, travails and triumphs of the All Blacks, first in the columns of the *Herald* and other papers to whom his work was syndicated, and then between hard covers in a stream of books starting with his account of Bob Stuart's 1953 visitors to Britain.

Add in his years of domestic rugby coverage and other books - notably this one, an early excursion into rugby biography - and you have a remarkable body of work rewarded in 1996 with a knighthood which makes him only the second sports writer, after Neville Cardus, to be so honoured. His unique status had however been recognised long before that. In 1961 he became the first staff man in the 100-year history of the *Herald* to have all his work by-lined – creating, in deference to editor Budge Hintz's dislike of forenames, the persona of 'T. P. McLean'. One critic referred to him as "That white pointer shark among the minnows of rugby writing in New Zealand".

To read McLean is to reminded that a vital factor in New Zealand's consistent rugby success is that in addition to playing the game well, they have also analysed and explained it better than the rest of us. In 1906 Gallaher and Stead's *Complete Rugby Footballer* analysed the game with a depth and sublety far beyond any European equivalent.

McLean was similarly ahead of his European contemporaries. It was not that they did not understand the game, far from it. But McLean also brought to his work a journalistic nous honed since his days as a teenage reporter in depression-era New Zealand. Some very fine rugby writers are impossible to imagine in any other journalistic role. McLean could have turned his hand to most jobs on a paper.

This was allied to an independent cast of mind. The temptations and pressures on a reporter who spends much of his time with one team are obvious. It is only human to identify with them, to want them to win, and to allow this to transform you from objective reporter into partisan and cheerleader. Such all too human temptations are redoubled when the team are a group of your countrymen, carrying the flag far from home. Then consider further the circumstances of the 1953 tour and other early excursions when, as the only New Zealand journalist accompanying the tour, he was an official member of the tour party along with broadcaster Winston McCarthy.

Of course, McLean wanted New Zealand to win. But he never allowed this to erode his journalistic judgement, independence and duty to criticise where he felt it justified.

He was not invariably beloved of officialdom - beware the journalist who is. Today, sitting in the retirement home where he now lives in the Auckland suburb of Remuera, he explains that he doesn't get invited to games very often - one consequence, perhaps, of that flintily independent spirit.

Admittedly, in his late 80s he finds it hard to get around. There's nothing remotely wrong with his mind, but his knees are a different matter. He wields his stick with the dexterity of the fine golfer he once was, using it to open and close windows.

He can look back on a lifetime encompassing millions of words poured out in that crisp, lucid, uncluttered and apparently unhurried prose - much of it in conditions of extreme hurry as telegraph operators, sub-editors and printers waited impatiently across a 12,000 mile chain of communication.

He also had a sharp eye for a story. He has bemoaned the possibility that the anecdote most remembered from this lifetime of achievement will be of his tracing disgraced All Black Keith Murdoch to his outback fastness in Western Australia, only to be told in pungent terms that he should get back on the single-engine plane from which he had just alighted if he valued his personal safety. Exasperating as it may be that his career could be summed up in a prop forward's profanity, the story is also a reminder of the journalistic skill, tenacity and intestinal fortitude - he knew perfectly well how the intimidating Murdoch was likely to react - that have characterised his career. Other journalists might have found Murdoch. McLean went out and did it.

Few New Zealand writers can have been more widely read by their compatriots. The irony is that the one person whom we know for sure did not read the newspapers and books that contained his output was T. P. McLean himself. While taking painstaking care in composition - another New Zealand journalist recalled his making 23 attempts at the intro on a story before he was satisfied - he stopped reading himself in print in 1950.

Irritated by some of the editing of his copy from the 1950 British Lions tour, he complained to the editor of the *Herald,* Sir Leslie Munro (later Ambassador to Washington and United Nations; President in 1954 of the Security Council). Munro listened to his concerns then said "The men who made those changes are experienced journalists, chosen for their job on that basis. They have made those changes for good reasons based on their judgement and experience." His advice to McLean was that, if he did not wish to see changes in his copy, he should not read his material in the papers - a practice he has adopted to this day.

Fortunately his self-denial does not extend to the rest of us, who can continue to enjoy and appreciate his output. Gareth Williams has written of Rugby Union that it has been "a pre-eminent expression of Welsh consciousness, a signifier of Welsh nationhood." The same, without question, applies to New Zealand. That one of the most important hands in the shaping of that consciousness was T. P. McLean makes New Zealand indeed a lucky country.

Huw Richards

Huw Richards visited Sir Terry McLean in the (British) summers of 2001 and 2002, as part of his research for a forthcoming book on the 1953 Wales - All Blacks match, to be published next year.

Contents

Part of the George Nepia display at the New Zealand Rugby Museum
(Photo: Courtesy Bob Luxford, New Zealand Rugby Museum)

The original 1963 jacket text

Fourth printing, completing 19,000 copies

I, George Nepia

High on the short list of great Rugby fullbacks stands the name of the New Zealand Maori, George Nepia, and it is a tribute to his stature as a player and a man that this autobiography has been written and published almost forty years after he first burst upon the international Rugby scene.

George Nepia was only nineteen years of age and inexperienced as a fullback when he was selected as the only full-back of the 1924 All Blacks, the team that was unbeaten in its thirty match tour of England, Wales. Ireland, and France, and so came to be known as "The Invincibles". Not only was Nepia completely new to fullback play but he proceeded to distinguish himself in the position, to play in every match of a long, demanding tour and to contribute in a major way to the unbeaten record of the team. His play from first to last excited wonderment, admiration, and awe. He had total courage and upon this sure foundation he built extraordinary ability in fielding and kicking, bullet-like charges with the ball in hand through waves of advancing forwards, tackling to shake the marrow of the unfortunate opponent and an uncanny brilliance, which made the most complex of actions look disarmingly simple.

After his incredible thirty-match debut with the 1924 All Blacks, George Nepia continued a long career of Rugby which embraced forty-six appearances for New Zealand, the captaincy of various Maori teams and an important place in the record-breaking Ranfurly Shield team from Hawke's Bay.

Between times he settled on a remote East Coast farm, married and nurtured a family. To save his farm from the depression failure he signed up with a London Rugby League club and then returned permanently to New Zealand to play more League and revert to Rugby Union as player, coach and referee

All this and much else besides, is told in *I, George Nepia.* Never before has the story of the greatest of Rugby tours been so extensively and thrillingly told Never before have the players including the "dopy-looking coot" and tactical genius Mark Nicholls come alive as men and footballers. Never before has the power of Rugby to unite Maori and Pakeha in the forging of the New Zealand race been so well stressed.

Collaborator with Nepia in the writing of the book has been the prominent critic. Terry McLean, who on behalf of the *New Zealand Herald* and the *Weekly News* has become one of the most travelled of Rugby journalists. McLean has written eight other Rugby books, two of them in collaboration which have varied from biography to instruction to accounts of great tours made by All Black, Springbok, and Lions teams.

McLean and Nepia have known each other for a number of years - oddly enough, it was McLean's father who chose Nepia for his first representative match and their relationship has led to a book which may well become a classic.

Introduction

Boy among men

I was a boy living in Hastings when George Nepia was a man, as I thought, among the pupils at the Maori Agricultural College near the town. I saw him play a good deal, in those days as a five-eighth, and I applauded my father when he gave George his first promotion above club level into representative Rugby. In some sort of revue for some sort of local charity, Fred Hooker, Alan Bowers, Ken Hopkins and I of the Central School prattled through some piece which made the audience stir uneasily. Then came George Nepia strumming through "Beneath a Maori Moon" - which he can still sing like nobody's business - while the stage lights turned from brown to blue to yellow and he was revealed as an earnest, soulful gazer into infinity. I had never spoken to George at Rugby. Not even the fact that we were fellow-actors gave me the licence to speak to him now. There is always a barrier between the boy and his hero and not for anything would I have tried to penetrate the barrier between me and Nepia.

What I could not grasp at the time is now, of course, as plain as a pikestaff - that at the time when Nepia was my hero, he was also becoming a hero for the whole of the Rugby world. To thousands, millions, he was also, as he was to me, the personification of perfection in Rugby football - invincibly dauntless, preternaturally skilful, physically all-enduring.

Yet he was a boy, an unsophisticated production of the waybacks, with no particularly warm memories of childhood. It was as a boy, almost without any experience, that he went among the men who were the great players of his time on the most successful Rugby tour that has ever been made. Being inexperienced, he had no profound technique to call upon as required. Being a boy, more particularly a Maori boy, he was afflicted with the shyness which is the first great hurdle youths must jump. The mind flits back to the scene when, with his team-mates, he joined the S.S. *Remuera* at Wellington for the journey to England. This sturdy, strong-framed youth was of the company, he was an All Black - but he was to play in a position about which, practically speaking, he knew nothing. He was troubled, too, by the knowledge that his displays in the preliminary tour in Australia had been disappointing, if not deplorable. Moreover, he was of a team which had already been described as the worst ever to leave New Zealand.

Every circumstance suggested that the career of this boy would be as a candle, briefly to shine, soon to be extinguished.

If genius be described as the power of light striking through the gloom, then Nepia was that light. Within a few months, the boy who had been a hero only to a few barefooted kids playing around the fringes of the field had become a hero in every strata of society, from Royalty down. His name had become, as it has remained, a household word. He was a legend, mystic, wonderful. Even in those golden years of Rugby of the 1920s, when great players flourished - Nicholls, Cooke, Brownlie, Wakefield, Osler, Macpherson, Lawton; in every country, numbers stood out above their fellows - there was one to whom all turned, one whose greatness nobody ever denied.

Truly, George Nepia was more than a Golden Boy of the Golden Years of Rugby. He was the man who became, rightly or wrongly, the personification of his period.

Terry McLean

1. A Fullback - But Not by Choice

I did not want to be a fullback. When I was made one, I was sure I was going to fail. This was the end of my hopes. Even after I had played in the position for the first time, I knew in my heart that I would not be needed again. Later, a few weeks later, I had to give a talk on how to play fullback. My team-mates laughed.

Yet, such is life, it was as a fullback that I made my name and it is as a fullback that I am, I suppose, best remembered. To be more specific, it was as the fullback of the 1924 New Zealand All Blacks Rugby team, that which won all thirty of its games in the British Isles and France and so was christened "The Invincibles", that I made the name.

There was one other thing that has meant much in my Rugby life. I weighed thirteen stone three pounds when I was chosen for the tour and during it I got up to fourteen stone. I was strong and fit, I was only nineteen, Rugby was my life; and it was from the combination of these factors that I came to play in every game of the tour - thirty matches, playing twice a week almost every week for four months - at fullback. No other player, I have been told, has ever done this on a long tour.

Much else has happened to me in the rest of my life. I was fullback for the All Blacks who overwhelmed N.S.W. at Auckland in 1925 and who were, I have no doubt whatever, the finest Rugby team we have ever put on to the field in our own country. I toured Australia with the All Black team of 1929 and played in the four test matches against the British Isles in New Zealand in 1930. I captained the New Zealand Maori team which toured Australia happily and successfully in 1935. Then, right at the end of my career, I became a professional in Rugby League and for two seasons in England and a third in New Zealand I played this game. The decision to play League I afterwards regretted; it cost me friends; in retrospect, I would much rather have come to the evening of my playing days in the Rugby that was my first and only love. But necessity is the mother of many other things than invention and it was necessity which turned me to League. As a farmer on the East Coast, I had had a hard and heavy fight all through the great depression of the 1930s. Sometimes you got as much as sixpence for your pound of butterfat. You could be sure that for every gorsebush you grubbed out, two more bushes would immediately grow, and my farm was infested. I was heavily in debt. I was only able to go to Australia with the Maori team because that great leader of our people, Sir Apirana Ngata, insisted that I accept his present of three suits of clothing. In a word, I was just about broke. The £500 that I was paid to turn over to League, the money that I earned in it and from jobs in England, put me and my family back into circulation. I had not wanted to be a Rugby fullback. Yet it made me. I had not wanted to turn to League. Yet it saved me. If you wanted the story of my life, shortly, it could be told in those four foregoing sentences.

And now I am fifty-seven, happily married these thirty-six years to a beautiful and wonderful woman. My oldest son is dead, killed in Malaya in the service of his country - the severest blow I have ever known. My second son is in the New Zealand Army, stationed at the Papakura Military Camp, and he plays Rugby where I once did, at five-eighth. My daughter, married, has two children and sometimes takes up her old occupation of teaching in Gisborne. The youngest boy has taken over my farm at Rangitukia, on the East Coast. With two assistants, I run a 5,000-acre farm about twenty miles from Wairoa. It is Maori land which has been consolidated from many families. In addition I am a shareholder with many others in the income from the property. It is hard work, especially at mustering time when you must ride out at three in the morning to bring in the sheep from the high ridges and the deep valleys. When the sun gets up, the dogs sometimes run into the creeks and lie there to cool before climbing and working again. It is a lonely life, too, and the long hours between dawn and dusk are filled with tasks.

And yet as I ride and walk and work on this place high above Hawke's Bay, I think often with pride of the golden years of New Zealand Rugby of the 1920s and I remember with the fondest pleasure the men I played with and the games I took part in. The faces come vividly to my mind - Cliff Porter, bald even when he was our captain (and the best captain I ever knew) in 1924; Maurice Brownlie, hewed out of a trunk of kauri; "Bill the Bull" Irvine, who used to terrify opponents in the front of the scrum by butting them with his head of teak; Bert Cooke, who glided like a ghost into and away from his tackler; Jimmy Mill, the halfback who used to slip from behind the scrum like one of these modern sprinters getting away from the starting-blocks; and Marcus Frederick Nicholls, the one and only, saying in that husky, tobacco-stained sort of voice of his, "Let me have the ball, forwards, let me have the ball".

There are a great many other faces, too, from Bob Scott, the greatest fullback I ever saw, down to Don Clarke, who as a goal kicker has left us all for dead; I have a long memory, I have played and seen a great deal of Rugby and in all of my life I have never wanted for talk and thought about it.

So I am taking the liberty, in this book, of offering memories of games and players, especially of 1924, of talking a little about the trends of this great sport, and of indulging, now and again, in some discussion of the Maori people to whom I belong and of my life among them.

I had better clear the decks with one confession. If you see my name in the official Rugby books, it is as "H. G. M. Nepia". As the saying goes, there ain't no such animal. I was born and christened plain George Nepia and that's the way I will always be. In 1924, in England, we were impressed by the fact that many opponents had three or even four initials and that there were many, like Hamilton-Wickes, an outstanding threequarter, who had hyphenated surnames. "Plain 'George' is no good to you, Hori," said Irvine (all of the team called me "Hori" except that Irvine would sometimes call me "The Smoked Ham"). "You ought to get yourself a decent monicker."

I played around with a pen and a piece of paper. "How would 'H. G. M.' look" I said. "Champion. That'll do you." And so "H. G. M. Nepia" was born - and the spoof has become part of Rugby history. It just shows, I suppose, that you never know where your actions and deeds will take you.

At that, though, I suppose I could have made a guess that the joke would be treated seriously by some people. After all, I did not want to be made a fullback. So far as I was concerned, putting me there was the biggest joke of all my nineteen years. And yet, look where *that* joke took *me*.

2. The Pains of Growing Up

I do not look back with joy on my life as a child - yet it was as a child, and in the space of one game, too, that I learned to fight for myself as a Rugby player. I had always played with a sick fear. As a wing threequarter, I used to creep close to the scrum because there seemed to me to be safety in numbers. My father was ashamed of me and disgusted with me. He once came on to the field while I was playing and clouted me on the backside as hard as he could; it did no good that I was aware of.

And then in one game I was hurt in a charge and felt pretty seedy. When I came back on to the field, the strangest thing happened - I began to retaliate. Young Nepia was not a very good player - as it turned out, I was dropped from my team immediately after this match - but he was no longer a frightened one; and never again in my career, even in the test matches when the big forwards were running at me like the wind, did it ever occur to me to feel afraid.

Oddly enough, years and years later, it happened that Bob Scott, who was of course the fullback in the Kiwi Army team after World War II and who toured South Africa in 1949 and the British Isles in 1953-54 with All Black teams, was telling me of *his* childhood. His parents were estranged, Bob spent some time in an orphanage, the father died of cancer to end a period during which he and Bob had lived on their own in a one-roomed shack in Auckland. It was a sad story of hard times for a young chap; and suddenly I found myself saying, "Same with me, Bob. It was no fun for me, either." Someone who heard of this later put up the idea that we had both become internationals because of these difficulties. They must have made you determined to get on, this man said.

Perhaps so, perhaps not. I'll not argue one way or the other.

I was born at Wairoa on 2nd April 1905, and for the first few years of my life three of my cousins and I were reared by my widowed grandmother - a perfectly normal arrangement in Maori families. We lived where the Taihoa meeting-house is now and went to the Wairoa public school. The area behind the house was one big field and on this the Tapuae Rugby team used often to practise. The football field proper was behind the Ferry Hotel, on the north bank of the Wairoa River. When school was over, I was one of a group which used to make straight for one field or the other, either to play in a makeshift sort of way ourselves or to watch the Tapuae chaps at play. My hero was Kingi Winiata, who is still alive as a supervisor in Wairoa. He was, I am sure, a fine fullback. More, he was an artist as a kicker of dropped goals from the field. In one final for the championship, Tapuae against a team of Pakehas called City, Kingi within ten minutes scored 16 points with four dropped goals. He was a grand-uncle of mine on my mother's side and I wanted to be like him, a fine player, cool and assured. And a kicker, too, like Kingi!

At this stage, though I was so young, I could sense the pitifulness of my grandmother's situation. She walked over the bridge every day to the south shore to work in a boarding-house and she slaved to keep us four children in food and health. She used to come home late at night with things for us to eat and it was a good day when we had two square meals. I had a great love for her and as I grew older I wished that I could do something for her to ease her burden. One day it came to me that I should go to my father at Nuhaka, a largely Maori settlement a few miles east of Wairoa. My father had married a second time and my sister and I, the only two children of the first marriage, had gone to other places. I did not want to leave the frail old lady who was my grandmother, but I felt I had to go; and so one day, without a word to her, I climbed on board Wi Kaipuke's wagon carrying goods to Nuhaka. On the top of Te Uhi hill, I looked back to the home and I cried at the thought of leaving it. I wanted then and there to jump off the wagon. Wi Kaipuke saw the look on my face. He wrapped his long whip round my neck and kept it there until we reached Nuhaka. I had come home. I was eight years old. I was entered at the Nuhaka Maori School. I met my grandfather and my grandmother on my father's side, I met my aunts and uncles, my step-brothers and step-sisters. A new phase of my life now began.

It, too, had its grey side. My father was a dairy farmer who did not spare the rod. One of my jobs was to take the cream to the dairy factory every morning after milking. Sometimes the hands at the factory would sleep in and this meant that you sat in your cart and waited in the queue until they were ready to take delivery. School went in at nine o'clock, but when the hands were late you had no chance of being in class at that time. I soon found that it was no use pleading that I was not to blame for being late. If you were late, you got a belting. It was always a good one. In this phase of my career, my hands or my legs or my backside were often warm. Did this make me a better fullback, a better Rugby player, a better man? I wouldn't know. All I did know is that I would have liked to have been big enough to take a swing at those factory hands.

Not all of life was grey, though. Rugby called. Our horse paddock was the football field. Some way, every day, some of us got there. A cap served as the ball - your cap today, mine tomorrow, and with a bit of luck both would be more or less whole at the end of the game. You kicked off by throwing the cap to your opponents. Then on with the game! A try was scored by putting the cap down right against the fence. Horses were a hazard; you had to dodge them as well as your opponents. It was incredible that no one got hurt. This was our game for about two years until someone suggested that if we saved up we could perhaps buy a real football. What a day it was when that was bought. The King of England could have put his Crown Jewels by the touchline - we wouldn't have been interested.

It was during World War I that I was put into my first proper game, on the wing for Nuhaka school against Whakaki school, at Whakaki. I thought I was just it with a capital I - until we marched on to the field. What a feeling. I had the wind up. I was more of a hindrance than a help to our team. We won, but not by my efforts. That was the day my father whacked me. That was the day I crept close to the scrum so that I would not have to catch my man or even take the ball. I was a disgrace - but I did not give up the idea of playing football.

It was during kicking practices at school that I made one discovery. There were bigger boys than I there and some of them could kick the ball a long way - but I could outkick any of them. One of the biggest boys regarded this as an insult. He used to try and try, but always I could kick the ball the further. It made him mad. The practice would end with his threatening to kick me instead of the ball - and next day, I would still manage to kick further than he could.

In the winter of 1918, far removed from the terrible struggle for supremacy on the battlefields of France, several of us schoolboys were chosen to play for the Nuhaka club's junior team. I was still good old George Nepia, the boy with the wind up, until the second game. The crack that put me down stirred my temper. I got up and got stuck in. The selectors were not impressed. They threw me out of the team. They did me a good turn there. I now knew that I had the power to look after myself and not be frightened. Their decision only strengthened my determination to improve myself.

I was thirteen, husky but not tall, and no doubt a bit sick of tired factory hands. I returned to Wairoa to live and from there I went to the Waiatai Station, which was owned by Mr Frederick Steed, to work as a farmhand for thirty shillings a week. I had decided that 1 was going to Te Aute College, the famous Maori secondary school in Central Hawke's Bay at which had been educated many of our most famous men. This meant a long campaign of saving; and save I did, all through the year of the influenza epidemic in 1919 when no Rugby was played and our Maori Battalion came back from France to a welcome home on the old racecourse at Awatere in scenes I have never forgotten. A few months later, after the turn of the year, I went to Nuhaka to the Public Works gangs which were working on the building of the railway to Gisborne. All through that year, I worked on the formation. Slowly my savings mounted. The goal of Te Aute came nearer. Within the first weeks of 1921, I had saved enough. I was ready to go.

All Black Tour 1924

RECORD of MATCHES

MATCHES PLAYED	RESULT	TRIES For	TRIES Agst	Goals from Tries For	Goals from Tries Agst	Goals from Marks For	Goals from Marks Agst	Potted Goals For	Potted Goals Agst	Penalty Goals For	Penalty Goals Agst	POINTS For	POINTS Agst
AUSTRALIAN MATCHES													
July 5, v N.S.W	Lost											16	20
July 9, v Metropolitan	Won											38	5
July 12, v N.S.W.	Won											21	5
July 16, v N.S.W.	Won											38	8
NEW ZEALAND MATCHES													
July 23, v Auckland	Lost											5	14
July 26, v Manawatu - Horowhenua	Won											27	12
ENGLISH MATCHES													
September 13, v Devon	Won	3		1								11	0
September 18, v Cornwall	Won	7		4								29	0
September 20, v Somerset	Won	2										6	0
September 25, v Gloucester	Won	2										6	0
September 27 v Swansea	Won	9		4				1			3	39	3
October 2, v Newport	Won	2	2	2	2					1		13	10
October 4, v Leicester	Won	6		3								27	0
October 8, v North Midlands	Won	10	1	5								40	3
October 11, v Cheshire	Won	6	1		1							18	5
October 15, v Durham	Won											43	7
October 18, v Yorkshire	Won	8		6					1	2		42	4
October 22, v Lancashire	Won	7		1								23	0
October 25, v Cumberland	Won	11		4								41	0
November 1, v Ireland	Won	1								1		6	0
November 5, v Ulster	Won	6	2	5								28	6
November 8, v Northumberland	Won	7		3					1			27	4
November 12, v Cambridge 'Vty	Won	1		1								5	0
November 15, v London Cnties	Won	7		3								31	6
November 20, v Oxford 'Varsty	Won	5	3	5	3			2				33	15
November 22, v Cardiff	Won	3	1	2	1					1	1	16	8
November 29, v Wales	Won	4		2						1		19	0
December 2, v Llanelly	Won	2	1	1								8	3
December 6, v East Midlands	Won	7	1	5					1			31	7
December 11, v Warwickshire	Won	6		1								20	0
December 13, v Combd Services	Won	7		2							1	25	3
December 17, v Hampshire	Won	5		2						1		22	0
December 27, v London Cnties	Won	8	1	2								28	3
January 3, v England	Won	4	3	1	1					1	1	17	11
FRENCH MATCHES													
Jan. 11 v France	Won	11	3	2	1							37	8
Jan. 18 v France	Won											30	6

George Nepia's Record of the 1924-25 Tour, on the official tour card issued to the players (Courtesy Oma Nepia)

3. School by the Back Door

I have often wondered what Te Aute was like. Would have been like, I should say. I know the place well. It is set amid the rolling hills of Central Hawke's Bay and, as in my youth, it continues to turn out leaders of our race. It is a great thing, if you are a Maori, to be able to say that you went to Te Aute College. In my experience, the respect for the school is as great among Pakehas.

But the truth is, I never got there. A train whistle put me off. As the whistle blew, all the thoughts I had had about Te Aute flew out of my mind. I could only think of the friend who was leaving me. Of that, and the loneliness. I could not now define, if 1 ever could, what went through my mind when that whistle sounded. But it was because it did sound that I didn't go to Te Aute.

Let me put the story straight. A friend of mine in Wairoa was Eru Tengaio. Early in 1920, he was enrolled as a pupil at a school which was always called "M.A.C." and which was located at Bridge Pa, a largely Maori settlement a few miles from Hastings. The main school, a grey, concrete building, was heavily knocked about in the disastrous Hawke's Bay earthquake of 3 February 1931, and because that was also the thick of the great depression the college from that day ceased, in effect, to exist. Because its pupils were Maoris, it has always been known as the "Maori Agricultural College". It was built by the Church of the Latter Day Saints specially for the training of Maoris and it was staffed by Mormon elders under directions from the heart of the church in Salt Lake City.

As I have said, Eru had been a pupil and because his second year at M.A.C. and my intended first at Te Aute coincided, I arranged to travel from Wairoa with him, the journeys coinciding for all except the last fifteen miles or so from Hastings to Te Aute. We took ship in the Tangaroa, which seemed to me then to be very large but which was really very small, and next day we were at Napier. Then came the railway journey of about fifteen miles to Hastings and on arrival there I gave Eru a helping hand with his suitcases and other gear. I was feeling pretty blue. Here was my pal leaving me and I was going on alone to a place where I knew nobody and nobody knew me.

The engine sounded its whistle. In one wild panic, I grabbed up my suitcases and tore out of the carriage. "I am coming with you, Eru," I said. "Good," he answered. Outside the station, we found the M.A.C. bus, which for sufficient reasons was always called "The White Top". It was about dark when we got to the college and there were allotted our rooms - I am told that it is the American practice to have rooms at these schools rather than dormitories as they have at most New Zealand schools. Nobody seemed to me to be upset that I had come. They just accepted me and we talked a bit about things. I wondered what had hit me the next morning, which was a Sunday, because there was no breakfast and it was not until later that I learned that it is a common practice for Mormons not to breakfast on this day. But the point was, here I was at M.A.C. where no one knew me but where no one seemed upset that I was there.

And that was how and why, because of that whistle, I never got to Te Aute College...

On the Monday morning, I paraded before the principal in his office. I was scared about this, but he was very kind and, as they say in the joke books, he took down my particulars. Then he said: "What subjects are you interested in?" "Football and music," I answered. Then I had to tell him. "Sir," I said, "I really haven't enough money to pay for my schooling. What should I do?" "George," he said, "if you can play football - good football - I will see to it that you don't have to pay fees, this year and other years, too. How does that sound?" "That's marvellous," I said. "I just can't believe it. I..." And I went out of that room determined to become a good footballer. Fancy getting schooling for doing something you liked anyway! My word!

This was a school of no waiting, no delay. That very afternoon, I was at a training run of the First XV. I met a chap there, Lui Paewai, who was to be very important to me in later years. He came from Dannevirke, where his family held a high position among the Maori people. Lui was a slim, slippy sort of man, with sharp features coming down to a pointed chin. He looked the greyhound type. I was glad when they paired me with him. I was now even more determined to make a success of my Rugby. The very next day, with the club season still some weeks off, we were at it again. This time, the senior forwards and the third grade backs played against the third grade forwards and the senior backs. Lui was at first five-eighth and I at second and I am glad to say that I went pretty well. My being paired with Lui was perhaps the first significant step along the road for me in my playing career.

Being an agricultural college, M.A.C. required us pupils to do our whack on the college farm as well as work in the schoolroom. The Mormon elders kept us to our tasks. Their aim was, I think, to turn out well-rounded men of ideas and action rather than brainy men best suited for backroom jobs. We who came out of the school were supposed to be leaders of men, who from the religious background of the school could be influential among the Maori people in work, in domestic life, in behaviour - and the Mormons did not believe in idle hands. So we slogged in the fields and as the sharp frosts of Hawke's Bay began to occur it was sometimes hard to get out of bed in the morning. But for me it was life with a capital L. Among themselves, the Maoris have no trouble in living. If you have ever heard a group of Maoris nattering and giggling away to each other, you will understand that they see life with a great deal of humour. What is the use, we say to each other, of going around like the Pakeha, expecting the end of the world tomorrow? If you can have three meals a day and a bed at night, if you can live by the Golden Rule with each other, what need to fear the worst while hoping always for the best. We never have such a fear. We are ourselves, happy. And at M.A.C., even though I was a new boy, I was not a stranger. I was one of the Maori group - and that, if you understand me, is a complete statement. I could sing. Music, in fact, fascinated me, I had always been mad on it. And both in work and in play, this was a force in my life. It helped me, for we all sang. Have you ever heard a Maori who was a *bad* singer? There aren't many. Singing just comes out of us; it is, I suppose, an expression of our attitude to life.

And then there was the Rugby. By Jove, we worked at it. Most mornings we used to run for about three miles through the school farm to a back road and thence to the football field. On the field, we would gallop up and down for about half an hour, most of the time passing the ball if we were backs and dribbling it if we were forwards. My principal schoolmaster, Elder Moser, about whom I shall have more to say because it was he who taught me two tremendously important things about my Rugby, had, of course been brought up on American training principles and these we were now largely using. In theory, they sounded fine - just the job, you might say. In fact, they were merely tiring. By the end of the week, when we were supposed to be as fresh as daisies for the match on the Saturday, we could scarcely raise a gallop.

So our form as a school team varied a good deal and mine varied with the school. I went into the seniors and then I went out of them and once when I scored four tries on the wing for the third-grade team there was a protest against me at the next meeting of the Hastings sub-union because, so it was said, I was graded as a senior player and so could not play thirds. So back I went to the seniors. This time, I was put in as a siderow forward on the flank of the scrum in a match with the Hastings club team. What a joke! The flankers for the Hastings team were two brothers named Brownlie - Maurice and Cyril. I had never heard of them (and I am bound to say they had never heard of me, either), but one look was enough. Cyril weighed about fifteen stone, which was a tremendous weight for a forward in those days. He was a big, gaunt, fair-headed chap who had begun life as a centre threequarter and he could still run very fast. He was the immovable object and I, I regret to say, soon found that I was not the irresistible force. When I hit him, I bounced - backwards. Then there was Maurice Brownlie. He weighed only fourteen stone, but he gave the impression of being at least half as big again as that. He had a great, square face, a chest like a barrel and legs that reminded you, with their sinews, of the vines of a rata. He, too, was fast and he was strong - strong like a lion, quite unhurtable. They were both veterans of World War I, where they had served in the Mounted Rifles, and they had come back to farm on their father's place at Puketapu. They were hard men, like rocks. Against them, I felt like the fly crawling up the window - plenty to look at, but very difficult to get past. Hastings were so heavy, they heeled from every scrum and with every heel I darted from my place to get at their halfback. Every time, so I seem to remember, I ran slap into Cyril and rebounded flat on my back. He used to look around, bewildered, with a sort of What-on-earth-are-you-doing-there? look on his face. It took me a long time to see the joke.

At any rate, it was soon evident that I was not the forward everyone had been waiting for and after one more game in the scrum I reverted to the backs. I was chopped and changed in position and finally I said, Right-oh, if I am not given a permanent position I am quitting the game altogether. This had a splendid effect. Elder Moser placed me with Paewai at five-eighth. I knew nothing much about the requirements of second five-eighth play and very often I ran away from my centre threequarter or neglected other important fundamentals. But after a famous character of Hawke's Bay Rugby, Bill O'Neill, a leading referee, had come out to the college and lectured us with blackboard illustrations, I began to get the drift.

Then, too, we were all being stimulated by the presence in New Zealand of the first South African team to tour the country. As this team of great sprinters like van Heerden, who had run at the Olympic Games, and Zeller and of giant forwards like Royle Morkel and "Baby" Michau - they were tremendous giants of seventeen stone - went through the country, we followed every activity. We grew fearful for New Zealand's sake and we kept on talking about these "Springboks"-isn't it strange, I had never heard of the word. Then they came to Napier to play two matches, one against Hawke's Bay-Poverty Bay, a team which included the Brownlies and even Tom Heeney, the man who afterwards fought Gene Tunney for the world heavyweight boxing championship, and the other against the New Zealand Maoris, or, as they are always called among us, the "Maori All Blacks". (The names, "All Blacks" and "Maori All Blacks", were as new to me as the term "Springboks", but I soon grew to understand what they meant; I became haunted by what they meant and day and night the thought was never far from my mind that it *might* be possible, it *was* possible, for *anyone* to win selection in these teams.) We of the college were allowed to go to these two matches. I may seem to be making use of the long arm of coincidence by saying that the one who impressed me most of all in the first game was the fullback, Gerhard Morkel, a man who had toured the British Isles in 1912 with a Springbok team and who was then in his thirties, but it is quite true. I had never seen such kicking as he produced. I was fascinated by the length and accuracy and, of course, I was determined to become as skilled as he.

Meantime, there were the games to watch. The Hawke's Bay match was hard and vigorous, but the Springboks deserved to win. The Maori match was a sizzler. Maoris from all over the East Coast were there in hundreds and heaven knows what sort of struggles they had had to face, in the primitive conditions of coastal transport of those days, to get to the game. The tension was quite terrific. Spontaneously, someone would start up a haka and before you could say Taumatawhakatangihangakoauau others would be joining in. The game was fierce. Sometimes, our two Maori hookers would put their heads close together and come in at the forming scrum like a cannonball and you could see that the 'Boks did not like this. This was more than Rugby, it was a racial conflict and the excited crowd became super-heated when a mark which was claimed by Jackie Blake, the Maori centre, was disallowed and the Springboks scored at the other end after Zeller, so everyone maintained, had put his foot into touch. Never anywhere else have I known a crowd to become so passionate. The booing and snarling went out of the crowd into the game and the contest became a sort of primeval slaughter which the Springboks won by 9 points to 8.

Lord, what a day that was; and, as you can imagine, the impact upon us impressionable youths was electric. We were sore because we were sure the Maoris should have won. Within hours, twenty-four or so, we were even more sore. The *Daily Telegraph* in Napier got hold of the cable sent to his South African newspaper by a journalist, Blackett, who was travelling with the team. This was, said Blackett, "Most unfortunate match ever played.... Bad enough (Springboks) having play team officially designated New Zealand natives but spectacle thousands Europeans frantically cheering on band of coloured men to defeat members of own race was too much for Springboks who frankly disgusted."

From the Maori point of view, nothing could have been worse. The reference to the "band of coloured men" was, to all of us, grossly insulting. I propose to discuss all of this later. In the meantime, suffice to say that the hurt which was then done has never been forgotten and never quite forgiven.

Distractions apart, the game, as a game, had us in thrall. We practised what we had seen the Springboks do. We talked of the moves and thrusts that could fool the enemy. We hammered away at practices.

And I thought, and thought, and thought, about the glory that there must be in being an All Black or a Maori All Black.

The signatures of the 1924-25 team (Courtesy Museum of Rugby)

"All Blacks" Touring Team, 1924-25.

Manager

Captain.

Vice-Captain.

T E A M.

T E A M

4. Learning to Punt and Tackle

It meant much to my Rugby that Elder Moser, who was our coach at M.A.C., had been brought up in the American gridiron game. He did not, it is true, know a great deal about Rugby. We young men had to box along on our own a good deal, learning from opponents or matches we watched, and endlessly discussing among ourselves ideas for improving our team play. We had a great respect for him and I suppose it was a help that he was just as keen to learn all about the game as we were - but of tactics and strategy as such he had, quite obviously, not a great many clues.

But it was he who by example, inspiration or direction, taught me how to make a punted ball spiral through the air and, after this, it was he who taught me how to tackle and because at the height of my career, people used to remark about my skill in both, I must acknowledge what he did for me.

We had just started playing the kick-into-touch dispensation in New Zealand then, which meant that from anywhere between the 25-yard lines on the field you had to bounce the ball into touch on pain of forfeiting all ground back to the place opposite where you had kicked from. The effect of the spiral was to make the ball swing into the field and then surge outwards as the rate of spin decreased and this meant not only that you could afford to kick with a much greater confidence but also that you could be pretty certain of a much greater distance in finding touch. It is also a fact that a spiralling kick, especially when there is a bit of wind, is not too easy to judge on the catch and, of course, at a fumble the attacking side could dash in on the ball and go for its life.

It has been said that one of my special contributions to the 1924 tour was my tackling. Would you believe it, there was one particular reason for this. Elder Moser watched me one day a year or so before the tour. After the game, he tapped me on the shoulder. “When you tackle, open your eyes,” he said. If he had not said that, I would not have won that praise in 1924. I do not think I would have been with the team. “Open your eyes” ... it sounds funny, but that is the most important of all the bits that go into the good tackle.

I would like to spend a little time talking of these two aspects of my Rugby because it seems to me, the demands of the game still being much the same as they ever were, that some of the youngsters coming along might get a worthwhile hint or two out of my experiences. But first, I should like to sketch in the background to show how my Rugby was generally developing and to make it clear that experience is the most important of all teachers.

The first thing of importance about the season of 1922 was that Sam Gemmell arrived at M.A.C. Perhaps the name does not mean as much now as it did in my time. He was an All Black in 1923, a New Zealand Maori player from 1922 to 1929 and he was a first choice for Hawke’s Bay. He was a great forward. He was a strong, foursquare sort of build, especially powerful in the shoulders, and he hadn’t a friend in the world, on the other side at any rate, while he was playing. He really was a rugged hombre, but he never asked a favour on the field and his whole ambition was to get at the ball.

Sam took one look at our training, which was still around the farm and up and down the field, endlessly. We were mad, said Sam. Rugby was not a game of long-distance running, it was a game of violent sprints of ten and twenty yards. The only way to train for a violent game of sharp sprints was to do sharp sprints. So, in no time, he had us going at the sprints.

What a difference! Our whole team benefited. No longer were the forwards scrounging around, trying to get at the ball. They were there, with it, going forward. The back play took on zip. Willie Shortland was now our halfback, not a big man but quick and neat and good enough, later, to play for the Maori All Blacks. With Willie giving us the ball quickly, especially from the loose play, Lui and I were moving faster and more aggressively. Quite early in the season, the sole selector for the Hastings sub-union team, Jack McLean - father, by the way, of Hugh McLean, the All Black, and of Terry McLean, the writer - put Lui and me into a team and apparently the selector for Hawke's Bay, the famous Norman McKenzie, was impressed with us. He put me into the Hawke's Bay team which played Wairarapa at Napier on the King's Birthday, 3 June. This was one of the great thrills of my life. Unhappily, I was put on the wing, where I did no better than go through the motions. In the second half, I was at second five-eighth and here, I thought, I did much better; at any rate, the backline ran well and we won the game by 14 points to 12. However, that was the end of me for Hawke's Bay for the season. I played more games for Hastings and Lui and I, I like to think now, grew more dangerous as we developed more confidence, but each time a Hawke's Bay team was announced, I had to swallow a lump because I was not in it.

All of the time, unimpaired in enthusiasm, I worked at both the spiral kick and the tackling. As a former gridiron player, Elder Moser never ceased to astonish us with his skill in throwing the ball. He held it close to one end and threw it over his shoulder, not with the long unbroken sweep of arm we had been taught but with a chucking motion, exactly as if he were throwing a cricket ball. As the ball left his hand, he would flick his fingers down and off it would sail, for fifty or sixty yards, spinning like a top. Not many of us could kick the ball as far as he could throw it.

Having watched this, I started to think of the possibility of imitating this spiralling motion with a punted instead of with a thrown ball. Paewai, Tipi Kopua, our centre threequarter, and I used to remain after team practice kicking to each other and on one of these days I suddenly fired off a perfect spiral kick. (We used, incidentally, to call it "The Bullet".) I had by now made up my mind that such a kick was not feasible and when it came off I was shocked and so excited that I had difficulty in sleeping that night. I could scarcely wait to get to the field next day and I was, I can tell you, tensely excited when I had my first kick. Awful! I had another. Still awful. I slowed down my swing and gave the ball an easy thump. It wobbled horribly, a dreadful kick. Never had I known such disappointment. Not having told anyone what I was aiming at, I was too proud to ask for help or sympathy. I wasn't too proud to keep on trying, all the same, and night after night I thought about the way the foot should swing into the ball, the way the hands should hold and drop it and the height at which I should attempt to kick the ball for sake of length, power and accuracy. This was a double-sided operation. Naturally, I wanted to master "The Bullet" with both the left and the right feet and this meant adjusting, or transposing, each set of theories I was working on. Most interesting, most exasperating - but it had to be done. What Elder Moser could do with his hand, I was going to do with my foot - somehow. So on and on I practised. I found it a help, at times, to train at the manoeuvre of catching the ball while running back toward my own goal-line and of stopping, turning and getting my defensive kick away a split second before taking the tackle of the following-up forwards. My team-mates were always willing to help at this, even to the extent of getting a very fast man to follow up the kick. Without boasting, I would say that I got pretty good at this. It took timing and confidence and training was a great help to both. I found, too, that sometimes the spiral kick could be made accurately from a defensive position like this. It seemed that if you did not try too hard on a particular manoeuvre, it was easier to perform. But I was not satisfied with haphazard success. I wanted to have that kick at call, under any circumstances.

It came, eventually. As part of my stock-in-trade, it meant a great deal to my standing. But it did not come overnight. I worked and worked and, gradually, it was mine. And I would say now that the spiral, "The Bullet", is the cream on the coffee of good punting. A player aspiring to the first class must have it.

In the realm of kicking, the influence of Elder Moser was that I envied his hand-throw and set out to emulate it. He may never know that he was the inspiration. In the realm of tackling, however, he was the direct instructor. From him I learned all, to him I owed all.

It happened that, in my first two years at M.A.C., I had to do a good deal of tackling, the more so when I eventually was posted to the midfield backs. I have told how I lost my fear in football while playing at Nuhaka a year or two before. I therefore did not shirk the task of tackling. The difficulty was that I was always knocking myself about. Being game, I would go headlong into my man; being uninstructed, I would come out of crash with a clout over the ear or a belt on the eye or a thump on the jaw. Always something - and usually it was a good crack. Our normal practices, do you see, were the matches with senior backs and third-grade forwards against senior forwards and third-grade backs and these were conducted as if some of our ancestors had been meeting some of our other ancestors, with neither set of ancestors having much liking for the other. This was a he-man's game - and very often, so it seemed to me, I saw all the stars in creation after making head-on tackles of some of the characters on the other side. One of the senior forwards was especially tough. He came at me like one of those chariots out of Ben Hur.

Elder Moser could bear it no longer. He held me back after one practice in which I had, according to custom, seen most of the heavens, though it was still broad daylight. "George," he said, "you are doing everything wrong. You should not go down and wait for him. With his speed and weight, he will always knock you over. He might knock you out, too. The thing is, when he is a couple of yards from you, crash into his stomach with your shoulder. You won't then fall back, as you usually do. You will knock him backwards. The air will go out of his lungs and you might even knock him out, too.

We practised the Elder's theory. It was a good one. He was not, of course, elderly, though to our young eyes he did look a bit long in the tooth (I suppose he might have been in his late twenties). The point was that he was young enough and fit enough to put these ideas into active practice and it was on him that I did this early tackling.

It seemed to me I had got the whole idea right. "Now," I said, "what happens if the other chap comes at me a second time?"

"Don't go for his stomach," Elder Moser replied, "If you do, he will probably elbow you on your head. Go below his knees. Move into him from about the same distance as before, then hit him hard. You will knock his legs from under him and he will come down hard."

We practised, and it was so.

I said: "What about a third time? What do I do then?

"There will be no third time," said Elder Moser. "If you have made both your first and your second tackles the right way, the third time he will kick."

Two days later, we had our usual practice game and I was, I confess, nervous about how these methods of tackling would succeed. Just before halftime, the big forward who used to make a set at me got the ball and, breaking through, headed for me. He weighed fourteen stone, he was hard and he had a mean temper. I did not have time to think. I flew into him. My shoulder hit him fairly in the pit of the stomach. He flew backwards, I on top of him. He was knocked about a bit, though he wasn't concussed. He said: "You look out, the next time." I knew what he meant.

At halftime, Elder Moser came to me: "A perfect tackle, ehoa," he said. "Now don't forget the second time. You will be all right. Don't worry." Don't worry! If he only knew.

The game started up again. The big forward got the ball, well away from me, but he circled until he had me sighted. Then he came at me. He had murder in his eyes.

From a couple of yards away, I crashed into him below his knees, took his legs from under him and put him down with such a heavy thud on the broad of his back that he was knocked out. He came to, a sick man. The game went on. A third time, this chap got the ball. He happened to be right in front of me. I waited. I was ready. But I was not called. As Elder Moser had prophesied, the man kicked.

It happened a little time after in an important club game that I made one of these head-on tackles unsuccessfully. I was shaken up, quite hurt, in fact. After the game, Elder Moser came up to me. "You deserved that" he said. "You closed your eyes."

"What?" I said.

"You closed your eyes. Just before impact. The result was, you didn't know when you were going to hit him."

By Jove, I thought, he is right. I could recall that tackle vividly - my waiting for the man, charging into him, throwing myself forward and then, bang. By closing my eyes, I had ruined the timing of my tackle. It was as simple as that. Simple - and yet of tremendous importance.

I could not attempt to estimate now how many were the tackles of this sort which I made during my career. What I can say with perfect confidence is this: if you tackle the right way, they always kick - the third time.

5. Ranfurly Shield experiences

I am not boasting. By the time the season of I923, my third at M.A.C., came along, I could place my spiral punt fifty or sixty yards on to a handkerchief, seven times out of ten. I had by now spent a great many hours on perfecting the kick and it was pleasant to experience the rewards. It was helpful, too. For two or three years, largely at the direction of Norman McKenzie, Hawke's Bay had been fighting for a place in the sun. These were slump times, money was short and the tours and journeys were made on short commons. Once, indeed, the team, homeward-bound, reached Woodville Station, where there was a refreshment room, and there was not sufficient in the kitty to pay the price of the meal.

Communications in the province, especially north of Napier, were pretty primitive. The sub-unions did not see eye to eye with each other and between Napier and Hastings, the two principal ones, there was often argument. But Norman, a big, strong, compelling man, drove on: and the reward came on 9 August 1922, when Hawke's Bay won the Ranfurly Shield by defeating Wellington at Athletic Park. It was a Wednesday game. Hawke's Bay were making a tour embracing Wairarapa, Wellington, Otago, Southland, and Canterbury and they were a hard-luck, second-string province. Perhaps this influenced Wellington. More likely it was the fire of ambition which produced victory for the Bay, by 19 points to 9.

The shield, forty years ago, was *a* thing, but it was not *the* thing which it has since become. Nevertheless, the province was stirred and we, the players, felt the breeze. The excitement was great in the small crowd at Nelson Park, Hastings, when the team resisted the challenge from Bay of Plenty by 17 points to I6 - it would all have been over if Boucher, of Bay of Plenty had succeeded with a comparatively easy kick at goal near the end - and when King Country was heavily defeated at Napier at the end of the season it was pleasant to think that we were, so to speak, champions when the I923 season opened.

Pleasant, did I say? For me, the knowledge was a spur. I was eighteen, fully grown, and because Lui Paewai and I had had one match it seemed possible that we might be called upon again. I may have been too keen for I was inclined then, as I was later, to lose sleep before a match and I was not bad at worrying, either. But I had that spiral kick and I had, too, that tackle. And when I saw our two names in the paper in the team to play Wairarapa for the first challenge, at Napier on the King's Birthday, 3 June, I let out a cowboy yell. This, as they say these days, was the pay-off. And through all the years since, I have never forgotten the feeling of that moment.

We won the match, as I remember, by 6 points to nil. It was a hard game. Wairarapa's wing-forward, Jim Donald, was one of the fieriest men on the field I ever saw and his brother, Quentin, a hooker, was one of those outstanding sort of forwards New Zealand seemed to possess in abundance at the time - chaps who never seemed to have their noses far from the ball. In the backline, the big worry was Cundy, a tall, rather heavily-built man who was an exceptionally good kick, especially of dropped goals. Wairarapa a few seasons later became one of the strongest teams in the country. At this stage, though they did not have so high a reputation, they were hard-bitten, tough, country players. I saw a great many green jerseys that day and none of them ever seemed to be very far from me.

As for myself, I was now to make the acquaintance as a team-mate rather than as a club opponent of a number of men who were to exercise a great influence upon me and who at a later stage formed the backbone of the greatest provincial team I have ever seen. It has been said many a time since that the reputation of Hawke's Bay - and Norman McKenzie--was built upon "imports" - brilliant men who came to us for, putting it crudely, a consideration in the way of a better job than they had had. This is nonsense. On this day, I was in the company of Maurice and Cyril Brownlie, Jack McNab, Sam Gemmell, Lui Paewai, Bill Irvine, Alex Kirkpatrick and Jimmy Hill. They were *all* Bay men and *all*, either then or later, were All Blacks. We were not, of course, the combination that we afterwards became, but the natural ability was there. The Brownlie brothers need no discussion, except perhaps that Maurice was, I am sure, the greatest forward I have ever seen. Gemmell as a fire-eater could hold his own even with Jim Donald, which was saying something. Mill and W. P. Barclay were also Maoris, the one at halfback, the other at wing threequarter, and they were experts at the sort of football which was then characteristic of the Maoris - opportunistic, daring and brilliant - and which, to my own great discontent, seems to have been almost entirely replaced by stolid Pakeha methods. Irvine and Kirkpatrick were the Mutt and Jeff of the front row, the one round and tubby, the other lean and long. They were entirely dissimilar in personality, for Irvine, who had been a soldier in World War I, was a bluff and rugged character who helped his father run a hotel in Waipukurau while Kirkpatrick was a clerk in a giant meat-works company and at the beginning of a career which was to take him, among other things, to the deputy-mayoralty of Hastings, the presidency of the New Zealand Rugby Union and a high place in the Order of St. John.

So you can see, the local boys who made good in this particular match were first-rate, then or later, by any standards; and you can take it from me that when it became a case of Hawke's Bay beating the world, it *was* Hawke's Bay and, practically speaking, no one else.

This match, my first experience of the Ranfurly Shield, had one unexpected outcome for both Paewai and me. We were immediately chosen for the New Zealand Maori team which set off only a few days later for a four-match tour of Australia and an eight-match tour of New Zealand and which lost six of these twelve matches, including three in a row to New South Wales. Paewai did the right thing. He went home to Dannevirke and arranged to be picked up en route to Wellington. I went back to college to get my clothes. No sooner was I there than the principal called me in to his office. "George," he said, "I am not letting you go on this tour. You are too young." Of course, I reacted. I could look after myself. What about Paewai! What about the honour of the Maori team (if I were good enough to be chosen, they must need me) On and on I went. The principal shook his head. He was the boss. I didn't go. I suppose he knew - but I hope he didn't hear - the things I said about him.

Our next shield challenge was a narrow squeak. It was from Wellington and we won by 10 points to 6 - a dropped goal and two penalty goals to two tries. About this time, you never talked of Wellington without talking of Mark Nicholls.

He was the wonder boy, the chap who could do anything. I, of course, was still a young Maori, not far removed from the sticks and so I took everything at face value. We were on the field, waiting for Wellington, and I said to Paewai: "Which is Mark Nicholls?" Lui pointed. "That's him," he said. "What?" I said. "That dopy-looking coot?" His stockings came just about up to his knees. His shorts hung just about right down over his knees. He had sandy hair, his face was a bit pasty and he looked a bit skinny. "What?" I said again. "That coot?" "You wait," said Lui. "When he gets the ball, he is not so dopy. You will change your mind."

Lui was right. When Mark got hold of the ball, he knew exactly what he wanted to do with it. For me as a footballer, that was the first thing about him - his good hands. He fielded well, his pass was well-timed and his kick, either for touch or for the open field, was most accurate. For all that queer look of long stockings and long shorts, he could clap on the pace, too, very hard for ten yards or so. Oho, I said to myself, this is some player. And then I said to myself, George, I think he wears those things just to make people like you think he is a dopy coot. Mark *wasn't* dopy, then or ever. There was nothing much wrong with that team with him, either. At halfback was "Ginger" Nicholls, who had played for the All Blacks against the 1921 Springboks and who was very shifty and clever (Mark has always maintained that "Ginger" should have been first-choice halfback for 1924). Wing-forward was Cliff Porter, already nearly bald and as clever as a cartload of monkeys. "Nugget" Pringle was a great, tall, forward, as sinewy as a piece of rata. Fred Tilyard, a five-eighth, was one of a great Rugby family and "Snowy" Svenson was a wing who though neither very fast nor very tall somehow seemed to elude most tacklers. Collectively, this was a very tough team indeed. We were glad to get it on the slate.

The season contained more sensations for us and the greatest of all, when we played Canterbury at Hastings, was the tackle made by Irvine of "Jockey" Ford. We were leading by 9 points to 8 when Ford, who had been a sprint champion, was hell-bent for the goal-line with Jim Parker outside him, toward the end of the game. A try by Parker, another fast mover, would have settled our hash completely. It was a tremendous struggle.

The Canterbury backline included Bill Dalley (playing, believe it or not, on the wing) and "Curly" Page, who later became All Blacks. Page, in fact, captained New Zealand at cricket, which he continued to play at first-class level right up to the opening of World War II - an argument, I suppose, in favour of cricket over Rugby, for his career in it was twice or three times as long as it was in football. Canterbury had some great forwards, too, notably L.C. Petersen on the flank and Reid Masters at lock. Petersen was an All Black and tigerish and Masters, who by present-day standards was small for the lock position, did so much apart from merely locking the scrum that I have no hesitation in classing him as a great forward. There was a great to-do afterwards because it was asserted that the referee, Mr Charlie Atkinson, of Wanganui, should not have awarded us a try by Grenside because he had not touched down the ball properly. Maybe yes, maybe no. I came to know a good bit about the trials of refereeing many years later.

At the very end of the year, we twice played Auckland. We won the first by 20 to 5 and this was the important one because it was for the shield. We lost the second, which was played at the Auckland Domain to assist in the collection of funds for the Auckland War Memorial Museum which now stands, a handsome building, half a mile or so from where we played.

First, though, I would like to talk about the tour we made, as the Hawke's Bay team, of Bay of Plenty, King Country, Taranaki and Wanganui and in which we won all four games. This was my first experience of touring and I always remember it for special things like the hot baths at Rotorua, the hot baths at Rotorua and, finally, the hot baths at Rotorua. You would, too, if you were eighteen and a member of the Maori race staying for the first time in one of the great Maori centres. Ah, those baths! I have never lost my love for them. It was during the tour, too, that I became more deeply acquainted with one of the great gentlemen of Rugby, Mr Lou Harris, a Hawke's Bay farmer who acted as our trainer, masseur, host, and friend. All through the years, forty at least to my knowledge, Lou has been a stalwart of the game in the province. On this tour, he used to buy us cases of fruit and look after us in a thousand and one ways; and I am quite sure that all of the players of my time thought it only right when the Hawke's Bay Rugby Union, having built a great new grandstand not so very many years ago, called it "The Harris Stand"

And then, back home for the great match with Auckland. This was the fixture we *had* to win. Those cocky northerners said they had the greatest team in the country and we just had to prove them wrong. It took some doing, even though the final score in our favour was decisive. First, we went into camp for the week before the match. Then we trained and talked and thought about the match. Finally, at the kickoff, we were in the finest of condition; and I suppose it could be said that the team, for the first time, displayed the quality which afterward made it famous. I would not now justify the seriousness of our training for the match, for Rugby as an amateur sport must be incidental to the business of ordinary living, but those were the ways of the times and should be judged from that point of view.

Auckland's greatest player was Karl Ifwersen, a five-eighth who may even have been cleverer than Mark Nicholls, though that is hard to imagine. In a career spanning World War I, he had played Rugby, then turned to League, in which he became an international, and returned to Rugby when the League authorities disputed the payment of a doctor's bill he had received for an injury. By Rugby standards, he was getting to be an old man when I first saw him but, like Nicholls, he had just about everything. Most of all, so it seems to me now, he had the sense of the opening - 360 degree vision, it has sometimes been called. He had superb players with him among the backs - Freddie Lucas, the elegant sidestepper who never got his hair mussed in any game I ever saw him play (and I saw plenty); "Toby" Sheen who had been a wonderful schoolboy player at Christ's College; Don Wright, a skilful halfback whose omission from the 1924 team so enraged Aucklanders that they petitioned the Prime Minister, Mr W. F. Massey, to have him included in the team; then the incomparable Bert Cooke, a snowy-headed boy who stepped from third grade to senior to Auckland representative all within the year. What a player! In the forwards, Auckland had champions, too - Laurie Knight, of tremendous size and great ability; Len Righton, who stayed at the top class of provincial forwards for many a day, and Fred Arnold, a wing-forward who could run like a scalded cat.

When we had played that season, the people of Hawke's Bay gave us each a silver wrist watch and we all wore them proudly to Auckland to play the Domain match which was arranged on the spur of the moment. We were beaten in this by 17 to 9 and if you want to know the truth, I didn't play very well in it. But neither did the rest of us - or most of the rest of us, anyhow. Fortunately, no one asked us for the watches back when we returned to the Bay.

Comparisons, they say, are odious and because I am now among the old-timers I had better forbear from a discussion of the merits of the Rugby, especially the shield Rugby, of 1923 with that which has been played in these last few years. All the same, I do not think it can be doubted that the back play of that time was more vital than that of recent years. Ifwersen and Nicholls as tactical geniuses are not, let's face it, matched by anyone in New Zealand Rugby of the present day. Whether Cooke played at second five-eighth or centre made no difference; in each place, his blazing speed was the servant of highly-developed abilities in handling, kicking and running with the ball. There has not been a centre, these last few years, to compare with Blake, whose wings over the years scored a great number of tries. The backs were not given a pedestrian and ignoble part in the attack. They were, in fact, the spearheads. Say what you like, I'll always maintain that the standards then were extremely high for the simple reason that the competition for places was more severe than it has ever been.

Souvenir of the tour (Courtesy Museum of Rugby)

Action from the first 1924-25 tour match
Top: The crowd and play just before the first All Black try
Bottom: left: The Haka, right: action after a scrum
(Courtesy Oma Nepia)

6. First steps as Fullback

The year 1923 was important in my development. I could play my bad games, as against Auckland at the end of the season, and I would not pretend that I was the greatest five-eighth in the world. But I was strong, I was fanatically keen and in spite of my somewhat square, bulky build, I was rather quicker than I might have looked. I was gaining experience, too, and from each of these big matches was acquiring that feel, that know-how, which acquaints you with the shortcuts, the anticipation, which are so vital in Rugby of the first class. Really, I suppose, my mind was expanding to the needs of the game; or rather, I was becoming more aware of what could be done as well as of what should be done. There is a difference, you know. It sometimes seems to me today that players are so highly trained in what should be done that they tend to forget, if not entirely overlook, the things that *can* be done - if you are willing to try.

In becoming more aware of the mental aspects of the game, my mind was most active. I was eating, drinking, and most certainly dreaming Rugby. It was, I suppose, a state of enchantment, wonderful to experience - for who would not always want to be young and fit and possessed by an ideal? It was while I was in this state that I had two experiences, both so curious that they stayed in my mind and kept popping into my thoughts. Am I superstitious? Of course I am. I belong to a race which until a generation or two ago lived with and by Nature, reading in the sun and the moon and the stars and the growth of the fields and the forest all the portents of good years and bad, all the hopes of fine crops and the dread of bad ones. My people lived with their gods and set their lives by their moods. We modern Maoris could adjust our ideas about the mysteries of Creation but it was not within our power to expunge from our minds, from our bones, the instinctive reactions which had governed the race for so many hundreds of years.

So I was superstitious in my reaction to the first strange experience. It was at the Caledonian Hotel in Napier, after one of our Shield games, that Luxford Peeti, the father of Lui Paewai, spoke to me. "You should play fullback," he said. "You would be a better fullback than a five-eighth." "That is silly," I said. "Lui and I are doing pretty well at five-eighth, aren't we? We argued. I didn't want to listen to him. Luxford called Norman McKenzie over. They talked. "You should play Nepia as fullback in the Bay team," Luxford said. Norman was a very strong-minded man. He knew what he wanted. "Bosh," he said. He walked away.

That was not the last of discussions between Luxford and me. He started to give his reasons and they were, I must admit, pretty good. But Hawke's Bay already had two good fullbacks in Norman Kivell and "Frik" Yates. They had held their own against all the provincial fullbacks we had seen. There seemed no sense in cluttering up the field. I said so. But each time during the summer that I saw Luxford, he always came back to his points. You are a natural fullback, he said. You can tackle, you can catch, you can kick the ball equally well with either foot. Last of all, you are not frightened. On and on he went. And always, he used to finish up by saying: Some day, you will end up by playing there and I only hope I am alive to see it.

I was, of course, impressionable as well as superstitious. Luxford was the father of my greatest friend. I still thought he was wrong - and said so - but I could not ignore what he kept saying.

And then in the school holidays I went home to Nuhaka and one night got into a party which developed, after we had played games, into a session of fortune-telling from cards by a man called Ropitini. I was just looking on when he suddenly said to me "Let me tell your fortune, George."

He gave me the cards to shuffle. I did what I was told and handed them back to him. He began to lay the cards face upward on the table. As he did so, he began to speak (and I must tell you that he had a reputation among us Maoris as a seer).

"George," he said, "in the near future you are going overseas. You are going to be famous. You are going to be successful. Your name will become a household word, not only in New Zealand but all over the world. This is what the cards tell me - and they never lie."

Shall I go on with the story?

The Te Mori Rose Bowl is a trophy in Maori Rugby and quite early in 1924 it was at stake in a match between North and South teams of Maoris. The match was also a trial for the selection of the 1924 All Blacks. We went to a gymnasium in Auckland on a Sunday morning to train and on arrival there I was told by the Maori selector, Alex Takarangi, of Wanganui, that I was to play fullback. Luxford Peeti was there, too. He had been arguing with Takarangi, he told me, to play me at fullback. It had been a successful argument, though not because Takarangi had been visited with second sight. Alex wanted one of his Wanganui men, Peina Taituha, to play at second five-eighth instead of at wing because he considered him a certainty for the All Blacks. As far he was concerned, it was a help to him to have Nepia out of the road because, quite obviously, Nepia hadn't a chance of selection as a five-eighth and at fullback he would be out of sight and out of mind.

As for myself, I just stared when Alex told me the news. I knew nothing about fullback play. I had only once played there, against Wairoa sub-union for the Maoris in 1922, and I had made a sad mess of the job. So, at the training, I just went through the motions. When we got back to the hotel, however, I suddenly thought to myself: Blow it all, why should I worry. I will go flat out tomorrow. If I make mistakes, too bad.

Then I nipped around and found a cousin of mine, Walter McGregor, who played fullback for the Maoris in Australia in 1923 and who was to be my opposing wing three-quarter the next day. "What's the score, Walter" I said. "What should I do?"

He was a decent fellow and he knew his drill. This is what he said: "There are only three things you must do - *must* do. First, you *must* take the ball on the full, second you *must* find the line, and third you *must* tackle your man. That is all you need to do and if you do them, you will be all right.

That night, I hardly slept. I tossed around in bed until the early hours, trying always to think things out. The more I thought, the more jittery I got. Then I thought, Damn it all, I can only do my best. So I slept. In the afternoon, in the dressing shed, Luxford came in. Play your best, he said. I am sure you will make a name for yourself. He was the only one who had a good word for me.

Out we went and as the first scrum went down, I found myself more or less in my old position, having gone there unconsciously. The other side hooked the ball and one of their chaps kicked it. Our two five-eighths looked around to watch their fullback field it and I looked around, too, hoping that he wouldn't make a mess of it. Then it hit me. I was that fullback. Boy, did I run! Somehow, I got the ball on the bounce and, travelling flat out, kicked it back over my shoulder just as I took a hard tackle. When I got up, I was amazed to see the touch judge standing with his flag up about thirty or forty yards down the field. This seemed to happen all through the game. I would make a mistake, recover and manage to get a kick away, and almost always it was a good kick. How I did it, I haven't the faintest idea. It just seemed to happen.

Quite early on in the game, as I remember, Walter McGregor broke away and came down toward me. I drove him toward the sideline and in a crash tackle knocked him out. He came to well enough and played on, but after the game, he said to me "You are a beggar of a man. You ask me for some hints and then you knock me out." "Well," said I, "all in the game, eh, Walter?"

I have just as clear - clearer, actually - a memory of another incident. Jimmy Mill, the opposing halfback, broke from his own scrum on the blindside, beat our wing and came on toward me. I hung off and drove him, as I had Walter, toward the sideline. Then I took off in another crash-tackle. I expected to hit Jimmy. All I hit was the air - and the hard ground.

This was the only time in my whole fullback career that I drove a player where I wanted and then missed him completely. I had to ask Jimmy afterwards. "As soon as you waited and drove me on," said, "I knew a crash-tackle was coming. When you left the ground, I just stopped and back-pedalled a couple of yards. It was easy."

Easy! Well, well. The game finished. I had dinner. I went out into the long hallway and sat on a settee on my own. I was tired in the body and I was sad in the mind. This was the end for me. No more hopes of an All Black jersey for me, not this year, anyway. I was being as miserable as it is possible for a nineteen-year-old Maori to be, and that is very, very miserable indeed.

I felt a hand on my shoulder. It was Ted McKenzie, a huge big man from Wairarapa who was chairman of the All Black selection committee.

"Cheer up, laddie," he said. "And congratulations. You are in the next trial, at Wellington next Saturday. Go back home and train hard. You have a great future."

He went. Was he a ghost? Was I dreaming? Then came another selector, Ranji Wilson. "Congratulations, George," he said. "You are in the next trial. You played very well. Keep it going. You have a great future."

He went. It must be true! I must have another chance! Golly!

And then there came another one. It was Luxford Peeti. He didn't tell me to cheer up. He just threw his arms around my neck and kissed me on each cheek. "Boy," he said. "Boy, you are in the next trials. You will be an All Black. You wait and see." He may or may not have been crying. He was certainly as excited as I was.

And so it began. Later, you will hear how it ended.

And the fortune-teller? Dear old Ropitini is still alive. In the excitement of the trials and the journey, I forgot about him. Then, in England, I wrote him a letter to remind him of what he had said. Even to this day, he will tell you of what he once told George Nepia.

I still call him *my* fortune-teller. Do you wonder that I am superstitious?

7. Choosing "The Invincibles"

Even now, nearly forty years on, I can still hear the chant of the crowd: "We want Iffy. We want Iffy." Never was such a tribute paid to a Rugby hero. The man was not even an emergency. He had no part in the affair whatever. Yet the game could not proceed until he took the field.

This was early in 1924. From early in the season, trials were to be staged to choose the All Black team to tour the British Isles and France. The whole of the nation was involved. The football fever swept the countryside. I was as badly infected as the rest. More so, perhaps. As the weeks passed after the turn of the year, I grew more and more determined to win a place in the team. I trained harder and harder, kicking, running, tackling - and thinking, always thinking, about the game. In April, I left M.A.C. for Dannevirke, where Lui Paewai lived, and because he and others were just as keen as I, we all became slightly mad. Because Dannevirke lay under the mountains and was always wet, we had to do much of our training in a Maori meeting-house. When they are among themselves, Maoris, I should explain, are incapable of playing Rugby other than at their hardest. In this meeting-house, we crashed and bashed our way around, against each other, against the walls, against any obstruction, and the result was not at all good for the meeting-house. I am sure the elders were only too glad to see some of us called away for the Hawke's Bay-Poverty Bay-East Coast-Bay of Plenty combined team which was to play Auckland-North Auckland-Thames-Waikato combined at Auckland. The date was 10 May and if it is of any interest in these days, Auckland combined beat Hawke's Bay combined by 18 points to 9.

I have two intense memories of this match. The first is of the chant, "We want Iffy". During the play, an Auckland back, Victor Badeley, was injured. He was a brilliant player. I feel sure he would have been chosen in the All Blacks. Sad as it was, this injury was the end of his career.

As was customary, the reserve, a Waikato player, made ready to take the field. Then began the chant, "We want Iffy. We want Iffy." In no time, it was taken up all around the ground. The volume of sound was extraordinary. As we messed about on the field, so the noise went on. And presently, rather flushed, there appeared among us the cause of it all.

This was Karl Ifwersen who was by now, by New Zealand standards, an "old" footballer. He was almost certainly one of the most cunning tacticians in the history of New Zealand Rugby, but because he had been a League international it had already been decided that he would not be eligible for selection in the '24 All Blacks. Hence, he had not even been considered for the trial.

But at the disappearance of Badeley, the Auckland crowd, who idolised Ifwersen, took up the cry for his appearance. And so insistent was the cry that he had to be rushed into the dressing-room, put into togs and sent among us. Who knows, the reserve might have won a place in the team - but as things turned out he did not have a bolter's chance.

At any rate, the effect of Karl's appearance was magical. Up till this stage, the two teams had been about level in ability. With him there, Auckland became inspired. As I remember the play, they thrashed us.

And that brings me to the second keen memory that I have. I was cast against Bert Cooke. I was burlier than he was. I am sure I was stronger. Over a full hundred yards, I was, believe it or not, as fast. I do not think I was less brave in the face of the enemy.

And yet I couldn't compare. He was a ghost, a wraith. He had most wonderful acceleration and with it he spirited his way through an opening. He also had the surest of hands and his short punt over your head dropped exactly where he wanted it, your confusion being the greater because he could make the kick without putting his eyes to the ball.

When the game ended, I said to myself: That's that. I was a pretty sorry boy when I sat by myself in the hotel after dinner. The Te Mori Rose Bowl match for us Maoris was to be played on the Monday and I knew that I had a place in that. But I was quite sure that would be the end of me. It was over the next few hours, of course, that my whole Rugby life was changed by my being placed at fullback. If this had not occurred, I would not have been in the '24 team. Even a blind man could see that, as a five-eighth, I just didn't compare with Cooke.

I have already told how, on the strength of one game as fullback, I was told to report to Wellington for the next trial. This was North Island Possibles versus Probables and it was played on 21 May. My team, Probables, were beaten, 21 to 23 but the score was of much less consequence than the fact that the game was tremendously fast, gloriously exciting and inspiringly promising for the team to be chosen. Most of the cracks were there; one notable exception was Jackie Blake, our Maori centre from Hawke's Bay, who must have been a certainty for the All Blacks if he had not been taken ill. I was sad, too, that Peina Taituha had been passed over. I always regard him as one of the greatest players I ever saw; perhaps it was a mistake to try to match him against Cooke at five-eighth instead of leaving him to the wing but I would still say that he deserved further trials, at the very least.

The ball bounced my way. Whatever I tried seemed to come off. So my hopes soared higher when they told me I was in the North Island team to play South. It had not long been announced that the All Black fullback of the previous year, Dr R. G. B. Sinclair, of Otago, would not be available for the tour and the mere fact that there was, in effect, a vacancy, gave me cause for greater hope. That, and the bounce of the ball, made life worth living.

The interisland match was on 31 May and we were called to Wellington several days beforehand to practise. Some were even taken to Christchurch to see the South Island Possibles versus Probables match on 28 May. Someone told me to watch the way "Son" White, the great Southland forward, mastered a dribbling ball when he broke away on his own. I knew he would be awkward and difficult to handle but I thought there could be a way to dive at his feet and take the ball from him. Someone also told me to watch Jack Steel, a burly, thickset man of heavy thighs and strong hips, who was a champion sprinter and extremely powerful runner. I asked a lot of questions but still couldn't make up my mind how I would deal with him. Nothing for it, I thought, but to do the best I could on the day.

And so we went to Athletic Park on a dull and windless day and from the beginning we of the North were decisively in charge. Our backline was Mill,

Nicholls, Cooke, Svenson, Lucas, and Gus Hart and the combination was so sweet that Gus Hart scored three tries. Then in the forwards we had Porter, Irvine, Quentin Donald, Maurice and Cyril Brownlie, Harvey, "Nugget" Pringle, and Jack McNab and of the whole team only Pringle and McNab failed to win a place in the All Blacks. Seven of the South Island forwards - Munro, McCleary, Stewart, Masters, Richardson, White and Parker - were afterwards chosen, but only three of the backs - McGregor, Robilliard and Steel - made the grade and that accounted, I suppose, for the difference between us. We won by 39 to 8, six tries to one, and so rosily did the sun shine on me that I scored 17 points from a dropped goal, a penalty goal and five conversions. The bounce was kind to me, too. This was another experience of "one of those days" for me. They know their Rugby at Athletic Park, more so than at any other ground in New Zealand, and when they saw that spiral kick floating off for touches of fifty or sixty yards they said they thought I was a pretty good sort of player. If I'd been a real player, I suppose, I would have been so deeply concentrated that I wouldn't have heard a thing. But I heard this applause, all right; and as a keen student of music, I would say that this was the finest sound I ever heard.

Just in passing, I would say that I found that my tactics against White and his dribbling comrades were good. By pedalling backwards and sideways, I got these men to bunch together and then it was relatively simple to dive in, snatch the ball and get away a kick before I took the tackle. But I wasn't so successful - the first time - against Steel, who gave me the hip so aggressively that I bowled over backwards and saw all the stars all at once. Jack got away again later, bowling over two players with that massive bashing stride of his, and then it was me. I belted straight in, as hard as I could go. Down he went, with a split ear into the bargain; and so, once again, I had to thank Elder Moser for his detailed and patient training.

It is said these days that New Zealanders drop everything in the few days and hours before an All Black team is chosen for a big tour. In my experience, the excitement now does not compare with that of 1924. Wherever you went, in whatever company, the talk was Rugby. The newspapers splashed Rugby far more than they do now and people discussed players and games in far more detailed fashion. We had not long survived a great war in which 17,000 of our countrymen had been killed and thousands and thousands more wounded and I suppose sport was the best of all reliefs in those days of few cars and restricted social outlets. We chaps who were at the heart of the game were fools or heroes or plain no-hopers, but however good - or bad - we were completely involved in Rugby. Few people had any other thoughts but the players and the team and the prospects of the tour.

I am trying to convey something of the tension, the unbearable excitement, of the aftermath of the match when at dinner at Barrett's Hotel on Lambton Quay, the chairman of the New Zealand Rugby Union, Mr Stanley Dean, entered the room and in his inimitable voice commanded silence. He had, he told us, the names of sixteen "certainties" for the tour. They had just been chosen by the selectors and he proposed to read out the names to us. At the mere mention of the incident, I recapture the whole scene instantly. The noise, the drinking, the forced cheerfulness, the great players - the already All Blacks - the dark-skinned Maori boy (whose face, I am sure, was now the whitest it had ever been), the knives and the forks in their places on the tablecloth. And then, the silence... If our heads were all down, as in prayer, I am sure it was because each of us, in his own way, was praying. For this was the greatest moment in our sporting lives, perhaps in our whole lives.

And then it came, first out - George Nepia!

Stan Dean read on - Hart, Lucas, Cooke, Steel, Nicholls, Porter, Irvine, McCleary, the Brownlies. Parker, White, Richardson, Stewart, Harvey - great players, some of them incomparable.

And Nepia. If I'd been an Australian, I'd have said, "Stone the crows". If I'd been a Cockney, I'd have said, "Cor strike a light"

I was a Maori. I just couldn't say anything. Not for a time at any rate. Later, there was a reaction. Maoris when they are excited giggle better than anybody. I was a good Maori that night.

The last act had not been played. On 3 June, the King's Birthday, one more trial, Possibles versus Probables, was played, again at Wellington, and I was called upon once more. Why, I couldn't imagine, but perhaps the selectors in their wisdom appreciated that I needed every possible experience. It was a terrible day, a Wellington southerly at its worst, and my team, the Probables, struggled to a miserable victory by 16 points to 8. Paewai was hurt and that, I thought, might be the end of poor Lui. Bill Dalley, the Canterbury halfback was one who adjusted to the conditions and another was Ces Badeley, the older brother of the unlucky Vic, and himself a most experienced player. These two were magnificent. The rest of us battled grimly on.

My opposite number was Jack Harris, the Canterbury fullback, a first-class player who knew the position very much better than I did and who had won a great reputation in the previous year or two. It was about 11 o'clock at the Wellington Town Hall that night and I was sitting talking to Jack when the dance was interrupted. Mr Dean came forward. He had been given, he said, the names of the remaining thirteen players. He began to read them out. It was only a few minutes since I had been telling Harris that he was a certainty for the tour and as the names came out, one by one, I listened hard for his in particular. Stan Dean read off ten - Mills, Dalley, Cupples, Quentin Donald, Paewai (Hooray, hooray!), West, Ces Badeley, Svenson, Robilliard, Brown. Then there was a breakdown which lasted for what seemed to be a terribly long time. Then, finally - the cards had been mislaid - McGregor, Munro, Masters.

I turned to Harris. "I am very sorry, Jack," I said. He stood up. "The luck of the game, George," he said. "Good luck to you." He turned and went away and that was the last I saw of him for many and many a day. On the one hand, you had the jubilation and congratulations for those who had won a place. On the other, you had such as Jack Harris, passed over and, for the moment, brokenhearted. It is, as Jack said, the luck of the game. But it is cruelly hard to take when you are young and have put all your heart and soul into the service of the game and the winning of a place.

8. Sufferings in Australia

What a game life can play with you! As soon as I had been made an All Black and therefore proclaimed, in theory, as one of the best players, I proceeded to play some of the worst Rugby imaginable. Though I was only nineteen, I knew what was coming. Elder Moser had offered a warning. You must have relaxation, he said. You can't go on pouring out your best *all* the time.

In the trials, I had poured out my best. I suppose it was true to say that there had not been waking moments in weeks when Rugby had been out of my mind - and usually, it was right at the front of it. I was involved, as were many others, in the tension and excitement of playing and possible selection. It was like being in love, only worse. I was possessed.

And then, with reward, came reaction. When I returned to Dannevirke, I played in three club games, not too badly. But there were many farewells and congratulatory parties for Paewai and me, there was incessant talk about Rugby and what we were going to do; and gradually, I felt myself becoming listless. Mentally, I was dog-tired. This was mental staleness, which is a much more terrible thing than physical staleness. In fact, I doubt that you can get physically stale; but mentally - oh, brother!

And it was in this condition that I and twenty-two others of the twenty-nine in the team proper went off to Australia to play four matches. Ces Badeley was appointed captain and Mr E.A. Little, of Wellington, was our manager. We left Wellington in the *Ulimaroa* on 27 June and for two days its huge smoke-stack just about crashed into the Tasman with every one of our many rolls. Paewai was not with us and that did not help me, in seasickness or out. But mostly, as I soon found out, my form in the matches we played was attributable only to the staleness I was suffering.

We were beaten by New South Wales by 20 to 16 in the first match, played before 30,000 spectators at the Show Grounds four days after our arrival. Then we played Metropolitan, an entirely different team, and won by 38 to 5. In the second match with New South Wales, a week after the first, we won by 21 to 5 and there were only 8,000 spectators at the final test, a midweek fixture in which we really came right and won by 38 to 8.

Rugby was going through hard times in Australia just then. Queensland had given up the game and it was only in New South Wales - for practical purposes this meant Sydney - that it was played. The Rugby authorities had decided during World War I that the game should stop. A great number of their men had enlisted in the Australian Imperial Force and the organisation, so we were told, had dwindled into nothingness. Meanwhile, Rugby League, which had become strong before the war with players like Dally Messenger, continued to exist. Even in wartime, there must be recreation and relief from the dreadful business of casualty lists. What came to be known as "the cloth-capped brigade" took their pleasure in this type of football. By the end of the war, League was firmly in the saddle in both New South Wales and Queensland and it has remained the dominant winter sport in these two states ever since.

Rugby thus was in many difficulties when we played our four matches. But, by Jove, what talent Australians have in sport! New South Wales beat us on merit and even in the other matches, when we won decisively, they took some subduing. Crossman, one of their wings, was one of the greatest players I ever saw, or played against. He had football brains to go with extreme pace and this is the greatest combination you can get in the game. Nothling was a fine fullback and a good cricketer, too. Jock Blackwood in the last fifteen years or so has become very well known to New Zealanders as manager of a successful Wallabies team and as a personality at International Board level. "Bluey" Greatorex was a splendid winging-type forward and Wally Meagher, who played in the last test, was a halfback of distinction who in more recent years has been one of the most successful coaches in Australia. Several of these chaps had been in the Waratah teams which had beaten the 1922 All Blacks in two tests out of three - it's funny, but you meet very few New Zealanders who talk about our 1922 team - and several more continued to show such form that they were in the Waratah team of 1927-28 which made one of the most successful of all tours of the British Isles. They were the best of hosts, these Aussies, and they gave us a wonderful time; and I have always felt that it showed the kinship between the two countries when, just before the start of the last match, Ces Badeley got the two teams to give three cheers for the great swimmer, "Boy" Charlton, who had just won the 1,500 metres at the Olympic Games in Paris. This gesture, which we offered with the greatest pleasure, went down like a house on fire with the crowd.

The first match was a glorious game. New South Wales led 8-0 after twenty minutes. The pace was extremely fast and our combination was not good. I was not playing well and our backs were handicapped because Badeley at first five-eighth was not chiming in well with Jimmy Mill at half. A good many passes were dropped all around and the New South Welshmen weren't slow in making the most of the opportunities.

Getting beaten in an opening match is a wonderful tonic for any touring team. It brings you right down to earth with a bump. We did a deal of talking over the next few days and our practice sessions were serious and prolonged. The benefits were to be seen in the match with Metropolitan. Six of the ten tries we scored were dotted down by the threequarters. Nicholls was now at five-eighth and he and Porter towered above all for the rest of the short tour. Cliff was here, there and everywhere and wherever he was he was a ball of fire. So the combination of the backs and the power of the forwards gradually became too much for our Australian opponents. In the second test, we were well held for the second half after leading at half time by 18 to nil, but in the last one we just scampered around and the principal amusement of this was caused by the referee, one of the strangest I ever saw in action. Our hookers weren't allowed to heel, one of our forwards would have had to leave the field if the New South Wales team hadn't made a general protest - he had tackled an opponent high to stop him scoring and the referee didn't think this was right - and Nicholls was called for forward passing just about every time he threw the ball onward. Mark wasn't the sort of chap to take this lying down and at one stage he stopped dead, turned completely about and threw the ball toward our goal-line. "How about that one, Ref.?" he asked.

All through these matches, I strove as hard as I could. I worried a good deal, too. But I told nobody what was wrong with me. The kick I had had wasn't there. I don't think you could say I disgraced myself, but I wasn't playing as an All Black should and I was not showing the Australian spectators the form they had expected of me. That rankled with me, if with no one else, and it was during the tour that I vowed I would return to Sydney to show them that I really could play football.

We set sail for Auckland on 18 July in the *Manuka*, a ship which was old and small and not well equipped for the storm we encountered. It was a rotten trip. The wind blew hard, the seas were steep, and all of us were ill. At one stage, after some portholes had been stove in, we had to heave to. There may be worse experiences, but I doubt it. We were all afraid either that we were going to die or that we weren't; and when we received cabled news to the effect that we were to play Auckland on the day after our arrival, the general wish was to die. We did not in fact reach Auckland until just before midnight on Tuesday, 22 July, and some fourteen hours later we were at Eden Park to match what was almost certainly the next strongest team to Hawke's Bay in the country. Auckland had Ifwersen, Don Wright, Rupert McWilliams, Keary, Len Righton, Fred Lintott, Neil McLean, Dick Fogarty - a hard-bitten team, if ever there was one. Auckland also had 25,000 supporters, all of them convinced that gross injustices had been done to Auckland in the selection of the All Blacks. Auckland, moreover, didn't have the ground rising and falling in front of them, as we did. We played like a bunch of hoboes, who deserved to be beaten, as we were, by 14 to 3, and if the ground hadn't been heavy and tacky, we would have been hammered.

The hammering came the next day, in the newspapers. George Tyler, of the 1905 All Blacks, said in the *New Zealand Herald* that we were the worst team New Zealand had ever fielded and the *Auckland Star* was no more complimentary. It was freely alleged that we were the worst team ever to leave the country and that it was a disgrace we, and not Auckland, were being sent away. All this was a little hard to take, but take it we had to.

Nor was another match, with Manawatu-Horowhenua three days later, very much better, though we won it by 27 to 12. Our form was nothing like our best Australian standard. Mishandling led to scragginess and the combination and backing-up were deplorable. I have since come to believe that the whole team was suffering, as I was, from staleness. For the time being, the real will to play, let alone win, wasn't there. I myself was sick and tired of football and longing for the rest we were to get in the *Remuera* on the way to England.

Wellington was two and a half days of mad rushing about, farewells, speeches, and final drinks. In the good old New Zealand fashion, ear-bashing was practised on the grandest scale. There were seven speakers at the farewell dinner and at the State luncheon another seven, including Viscount Jellicoe, the Governor-General, said their pieces. By now, Stan Dean had become our manager and he was saying all the right things in our behalf. At the dinner, interestingly enough, one of the guests was George Williams, who had toured the world with the 1888 Native team, and other guests were George Dixon, "Mona" Thomson, Billy Glenn, "Massa" Johnston, Freddie Roberts, and Billy Wallace of the 1905 All Blacks.

And then it was four o'clock in the afternoon of Tuesday, 29 July, and the *Remuera* was pulling away from the Wellington wharf, outward bound for

Plymouth. There were thousands to shout and sing farewell to us. Never, no never again, will there be such a moment in our Rugby history as this. The great tour was about to begin. We were about to sail on an expedition whose yield could be equalled but never be beaten. Within a few short months, we were to become "The Invincibles".

Were we conscious of this high honour? Not really. Perhaps we were thinking more of a Wellington hatter. We had gone into his shop, several of us, to buy a hat. "I'll make a bargain," he said. "If you win every game, I shall give you each a felt hat when you return."

He laughed. We laughed. It was a good joke.

9. They Who Became Invincible

It is getting on for forty years now, but I can still see as if it were yesterday the stem of the *Remuera* cleaving the slow, silent swell, feel again the slight shudder passing through the ship at the plunge of the bow and watch the sharp, vivid little dart of the flying fish from the crest of the bow-wave. To north, to south, to east, to west, there is nothing, nothing but the limitless ocean stretching out to the haze of the horizon. You start by thinking of it as a region, a world, of utter boredom and before many hours have gone you are a slave to its enchantment. The long ocean voyage is the greatest boon man has ever had to set his mind at rest.

And I can see again, more vividly even than the flashing flying fish, the faces of my companions of the Invincibles. We have known each other, but up to this stage we have never really known each other. Now is beginning the friendship, the trust, the companionship which more than any other quality is to be the basis of our success. We are young - even Stan Dean is only thirty-seven - and that is a help. We are deeply, passionately interested in Rugby and that is a help, too. And, more than anything, I think we have a pride, and perhaps that is the greatest help of all; we have, after all, won our places after a series of hard trials and so there is a sense of the elite about us. It is said in after years, even by some of us, that there were players in the team who were not of the real international quality and sometimes the finger of scorn has been pointed because our forwards were smaller than they are today or because the backs were not Olympic sprinters or because the kickers were not Don Clarkes or Billy Wallaces. They may be right, these critics, even if some of them never saw us play, and it may be a strength of our Rugby that the All Blacks have never yet made a tour without someone afterwards making an agonising sort of appraisal of their defects rather than of their best qualities.

But for good or ill, all I can ever say about these dear companions of this most wonderful journey can be compressed into a sentence: Look at the record, look at the record.

So as we voyage, I look about me. Here is Mr Dean, an insurance officer of the South British company and chairman for the last couple of years of the New Zealand Rugby Union; a good player himself in prewar days, for Grafton in Auckland and for a club in Johannesburg. He has a decisive mind and a good turn of phrase and has wisely decided to leave the football of the tour to the players themselves. I have the greatest respect and affection for Stan; I do not think there could be a better manager.

Here is Cliff Porter, not yet thirteen stone in weight but so rolypoly in build as to look much more than that. He is a salesman who had played Rugby in Horowhenua before going to Wellington and though he is only twenty-four he is accepted by us as a natural leader. I become one of his special charges. He soon begins to call me "Hori", as do all of the rest of the team, and it is by this name that I am always known to them. I do not mind; it is a good name; and I soon learn that Cliff is always thinking of ways to improve my confidence and my technique. Later on this tour, I am going to find it very hard to keep on playing match after match. Cliff talks to me about the strain involved. "On match nights," he says, "drink what you like. You can drink yourself paralytic if you like." So I drink beer, enough to help me sleep like a child. He knows, this chap Porter, just exactly how to get the best out of a man.

Jock Richardson is to become famous because he will captain us in these internationals, a strange experience for one not appointed the leader of the team. Jock is a tall, Southland storeman of just under fourteen-and-a-half stone, and the mop of fair hair sticks up from his head. He is a silent chap, but a tremendous forward; and I would place him second only to Maurice Brownlie, who is soon appointed to the committee of management with Mr Dean, Porter, Richardson, and "Son" White. With his chiselled features, Maurice is the handsomest of men and I think perhaps that he may be the strongest man I have ever seen. He, too, is a leader in a "Come on" sort of way; but he may snarl to get the best out of you while Cliff persuades you to get the best out of yourself.

Maurice, of course, is a farmer, as is Cyril, his brother. At fifteen stone, Cyril is the biggest man among us at the start of the tour. He is rather less formidable as a personality than Maurice, perhaps because he does not take life quite so seriously. The unexpected thing about him is his speed of foot; he is, in fact, one of the fastest runners in the whole team. Like the Brownlies, Alfie West is an old soldier. He comes from Taranaki and lives under the slopes of Mt Egmont and there is a hard quality about his play which suggests the crags of the mountain. It is evident, at a later stage, that he is not now so good a player as when he returned from the war, but there are times when the old Alfie is once more at his best; and the try that he scores from a kickoff in the match with Durham is one of the great ones of the tour.

"Son" White, like West, is also thirty, but being a very light man of only twelve stone six pound he has worn better and his spring and vitality are combined with a profound technical knowledge of forward play. He is a storeman from Southland and they don't come any better, as footballers and, I should say, as Southlanders, too. Ron Stewart, a stock agent from Timaru, is the youngest of the forwards and in time he will become the biggest of them. He, too, has unusual pace and the value of his selection is to be proved in later years when experience disciplines his physical output so as to make the most of his strength as needed. "Abe" Munro, of Otago, is a front-row forward who weighs only eleven stone twelve pound and it is going to be his luck, because of a leg injury, to play in only four of the matches; but as an alert, merry sort of man he will be a great help all the way through, and as a drummer he is essential to our ship's orchestra. Brian McCleary, at twenty-seven, is one of the older forwards and is unusual because he has been a professional heavyweight boxer, champion of New Zealand no less. The marks of this sport show in his protuberant brow, but he is otherwise the gentlest of men. Read Masters is in the Post Office and if you could strike an average between the facial appearances of McCleary and Richardson you would very nearly arrive at him. He is to be our finest lock, with no fewer than twenty-two matches, and in every one of them is to play at a very high level of ability. There could not be a more conscientious man, in everything. Bill Irvine, though only twenty-five, is an old soldier and if ever there was a hard case it is he. Once, in Paris, he takes some of us youngsters on an expedition, the sort of expedition soldiers used to make while on leave. We return from it very shaken and Bill laughs at us for a bunch of softies. He is a character, a fabulous character; and if sometimes people say to me that it is wonderful that I have played in all matches, I say it is even more wonderful that "Bill the Bull" should play in twenty-seven of the thirty, for front-row is harder than fullback. Ian Harvey at twenty-one is only a year older than Stewart and at fourteen stone eight pound is the second biggest man in the team. Rugby is never going to be really kind to Ian. He goes to Australia and cannot play a match because of tonsilitis. He goes to Britain and suffers from, of all things, piles. In South Africa, illness afflicts him again. Fate never permits him to produce his true qualities in All Black Rugby. Quentin Donald, Irvine's principal partner at hooker, plays twenty-one matches and in every one of them manages to look the most worried man in the whole wide world. He is a farmer in the Wairarapa. He is also one of the most generous of men. A champion footballer, too.

And here among the forwards, only half an inch shorter than the tall Cyril Brownlie, is Les Cupples, a Bay of Plenty farmer who plays seventeen matches and who is fond of wearing butterfly-wing collars. We have not been journeying very long before Les arranges the best little hoax of the tour. Auckland are to challenge Hawke's Bay for the Ranfurly Shield and we are all desperately anxious to know the result. By sleight of hand, Les gets hold of a wireless form and writes out a message:

"L Cupples, *Remuera* via Panama.

"Call Bank London. Auckland 43, Hawke's Bay 5. - Parata."

Parata is, of course, Ned Parata, the Maori who is paramount chief of Rugby in Les's district. It is a very clever message because it is known to us that Parata and Cupples have some sort of financial arrangement. It is also clever because, as Cupples well knows, a closer score might have promoted argument, whereas he could always say, if taxed with the authorship, that he would never have thought of putting such an absurd score down. (In fact, the Bay won the match by 21 to 6.) All comes off most beautifully. The message is put on Stan Dean's table and when Cupples comes in late - purposely - the interest of all is aroused when Stan calls out to him. We are still interested when Les in the grand manner reads the message and then hands it silently to Mr Dean. And now comes the cream of the joke, for Stan, who is not in it - no one is, except a steward - reads it out as a news item.

And then - the Tower of Babylon. We Hawke's Bay men say that it's a stinker, no one could beat us by such a score. The Aucklanders say that it just goes to show, the mob who went to the match after the Australian tour were right when they said the whole Auckland team should have been chosen. The rest join in, on the side they care for. And "Cookie" says that if the score is right, he will donate £35,000 to charity.

A funny fellow, this Cupples. He takes us in, completely.

And then, finally among the forwards, is Jim Parker. Like Jack Steel, he has been a sprint champion and like the Brownlies and others, he is a returned soldier. Over a distance, he and Steel are the fastest men in the team. It has often been asked why Parker and not Porter played the internationals. The answer is simple. Porter could not persuade himself that the British referees were right in commanding that the wingforward should immediately retire to the rear of the scrum after putting the ball into it. He used to stay in the station these rovers as a matter of course adopted in New Zealand. Jim, on the other hand, worked on the theory that in Rome one does as the Romans do. He used to retire and not incur penalties and Cliff used to stay and be penalised. That, in a nutshell, is the story of the two men - but let it not be thought that Porter was a negligible factor on the tour. In fact, his was the principal voice, in all things. He was the greatest captain I ever played under.

And now for the backs. Steel is a great burly man of twelve-and-a-half stone and on his day he is indisputably the greatest of the threequarters. But Jack is an extremely moody man and as such his form varies from superlative to no more than plain good. Because of this, he is not, I would say, the most reliable of our threequarters. This man is "Snowy" Svenson, who wants nothing but a yard of pace to be incomparable. "Gus" Hart, a tiny chap, only nine stone twelve pound in weight, has this pace. He is a New Plymouth businessman and, a little unluckily, he gets only one international. He is extremely fast, with courage, and his twenty tries on the tour bespeak his quality. Also from Taranaki, and a member of a prominent New Plymouth firm of timber merchants, is Handley Brown, who is as young as Paewai and I. He has been a member, only a season before, of a brilliant schoolboys' team at New Plymouth Boys High and he is a player of great ability. Unfortunately for his record, he makes one very serious mistake against Newport and such is the competition in the team that this always handicaps him. Freddie Lucas is neatness personified in everything, not least in a sidestep a yard wide, and though he eats like a horse, he weighs only ten stone four pound. With a little more weight, and perhaps a little more speed, he would be the perfect wing; and he is very handy on the banjo and mandolin in the orchestra. Alan Robilliard, only twenty and a member of a well-known family of jewellers in Christchurch, suffers injury at an early stage and because of it plays only four games. He has the brilliant look, too, that is the sad part. Ces Badeley never does get a crocked knee right and so his games amount only to two. In any case, he would probably always have suffered from the competition of the Big Three, Nicholls, Cooke and McGregor; but it is an unhappy experience not to have the opportunity, because of physical impairment, to play a full part. Lui Paewai, too, suffers from the same competition and so he, too, plays few games. I do not think he cares for the cold of the English winter, either. He is not the Lui I have known at M.A.C., but he will come again.

Bill Dalley has made one of the halfback positions ahead of "Ginger" Nicholls and Don Wright because of his tremendous game in defence in the final trial when the conditions were so grim. He works in a stock-and-station firm in Christchurch and specialises in grass seeds. There is a four-square look of defiance and courage about the build of his shoulders, the set of his jaw and the colour of his eyes; and that is Bill - defiant and courageous, in all situations. And so to Jimmy Mill, quiet, delightful little Jimmy, so retiring of manner even in the way he goes on to the field. So far as opposing flank forwards and inside backs are concerned, he is too retiring altogether, for they find it very hard to get near him when he is running with the ball. He has been a crack cricketer and sprinter at Nelson College, running the 100 yards in little more than ten seconds.

And then there are the Big Three, though we haven't quite found them out to be so just yet. Neil McGregor, in the Customs Department, has an eye as blue as the deep sea and he is so much dedicated to Rugby that with team-mates in the Christchurch club he willingly trains on four or even five nights of the week. He has no spectacular burst of speed, but he has lovely hands and a good kick and he will stop an express train. Cooke is only nine stone twelve pound, too, and he is a genius, there is nothing else for it, he is a genius. His power of acceleration is phenomenal, he kicks with superb accuracy even on the dead run, he has the gift of being precisely in the right spot at precisely the right time for the really telling pass; and he will stop a mule train. I do not knows how it starts, but Cookie and Bull Irvine and I have a peculiar understanding; we cannot take the field unless we are next to each other in the team lining out. In the dressing room, you will hear Bill saying, "Where's that bloody Hori?" and "Cookie" might be saying something like that, too. Just a superstition, like the way you do up your boots, or brush your teeth, in an ordered pattern that you don't like breaking.

And then, finally, there is Marcus Frederick Nicholls, King of Petone, king of our backs, king of the tactics and strategy of Rugby. He is sandy even unto the tone of his voice and he is a genius in an utterly different way from Cooke. Mark plays his Rugby as other people play chess, by a series of openings which are aimed at an end result utterly confusing to the other side. He is my tutor and my friend. Very soon after the voyage has begun, we are involved in training sessions - PT at 7 in the morning, scrum and all sorts of other practice on half of the boat deck at 10.30, talks, lectures and discussions at 2.30. Each of us has to describe his conception of his position and when the talk is finished, everybody can say what he likes in criticism, helpful or destructive, it doesn't matter which. I talk on the art of fullback play. I am no speaker, anyhow, and what I say convulses some of the team. Mark honks louder than most and when he starts firing, I go down in flames. But Mark has far too much kindness to want to make me look a fool. He is deliberately getting a rise out of me so that I shall start thinking of fullback play, deeply and earnestly. That is Mark - thinking ahead, always thinking.

As the days roll along, we amuse ourselves on the one hand and train as diligently as we can on the other. Despite the netting put up by the ship's staff, two of the many balls which are kicked 'tween decks finish in the Pacific and they look very lonely as they bump up and down in our wake. They may even be there yet, souvenirs of our voyage. Maurice Brownlie, Masters, Richardson, and Dalley play the gazoos in the orchestra and Cooks gets himself elected to the side drum. Nicholls scores 40 retired in a North versus South cricket match which North wins. McCleary judges the boxing and tries to look like King Solomon after Cupples and "Ginger" Nicholls, who is a fellow-traveller, have fought the most hysterical bout in the history of the Pacific Ocean. Judge Acheson, of the Native Land Court, polishes up a haka provided in the first instance by Wiremu Rangi, of Gisborne, and we practise this with myself as leader. There are concerts at which I often have to sing and if I don't know as much about Rugby as Mark Nicholls I can sing better than he can. The orchestra turns out trumps for the Grand Athletic Fancy Dress Ball and Ron Stewart and Handley Brown win the prizes, Ron as "The Buccaneer" and Handley, believe it or not, as the "Panama Cabaret Girl".

We call at Pitcairn and after tasting the sweetest oranges I have ever known listen to some of the sweetest of singing as the islanders pull away from our ship.

The Panama Canal is all fascination as far as I am concerned. We look as if we are charging at a cliff, but it is only a lock gate and by and by we are sailing on a lake which seems to sit on top of a mountain. The ship takes in oil at Balboa and some of the team take in oil, too, though of a much different kind, and then we are out into the Caribbean and the Atlantic and the training stiffens, we are getting the feel of Britain into our bones.

And all of the time, in one way and another, we are deepening the comradeship which has opened out among us. In these later days, when teams hurtle the world in swift airplanes, the journey is one brief wonder which does nothing but get a group from one place to another. In our day, the voyage in the *Remuera* is the foundation of all our success. We have begun the journey as thirty individuals. We end it, at Plymouth, as thirty members of a team. This long voyage has created one quality above all others. This is trust. When you build this among men, you build such a wall that nothing will ever knock down.

10. Hard Days to Start With

Plymouth greeted us with the sun and the Lord Mayor and the President of the Rugby Football Union and a civic luncheon and we greeted Plymouth with a cheer and a song and a haka. This was a great day in our lives and there was no sadness - except for Steel, who in horseplay at the last of all our training on shipboard fell and broke his arm. To be sure, I did wonder what I had struck when I took a mouthful of champagne at the luncheon. I thought I must have drunk some sort of salty substance by mistake and I didn't like it. But I couldn't swallow it and I couldn't get rid of it because of the Englishmen sitting to my left and my right; so I had to pretend to drop my serviette and while I was under the table I spat out the stuff. I wondered even more what had hit me when we were in the train that afternoon to Newton Abbot, the place in Devon where the 1905 All Blacks had prepared for their tour and where we were going as a sentimental journey. I was sitting on the right side of the carriage, looking out at and admiring the beautiful English countryside and doing no harm to anyone. Suddenly, there was a hell of a row and a roar. A train on the nearby line was hurtling the opposite way to us. I'd never seen or heard of such a thing and it may be the biggest fright I have ever had. I jumped from my seat and rushed to the other side of the carriage. The others, of course, all thought this a tremendous joke and they kept chaffing me with the fact that "The Maori boy get the big fright, eh, ehoa?" They were damned right. I did.

Newton Abbot did us proud. The greetings were warm, everyone seemed glad to see us, they knew all about us. For myself, and, I think, for the rest of the team, these were wonderful hours. All through our schooling, we had been reading of England, its history, its geography, its place as the centre of our Empire. We had talked about it and wondered what it was like. Now to be in England was the culmination of our dreams. The effect upon us was like a heady wine - but not, so far as I was concerned, a champagne wine!

They were glorious hours when we got the feel of the turf under our feet and chased about the field with and after the ball. Many Devon people who came along to watch the first practices were disappointed because all we seemed to do was fool around with the ball; and it was not, in fact, for several days that we settled down to the sort of serious coordinated training they had evidently expected. Here I would like to make a point about the 1924 team, because it seems to me that what we did by way of preparation has not since been done by other teams and to my mind something has been lost as a consequence.

Our training was entirely supervised by Porter, Richardson and Nicholls and the tactics were principally dictated by them. During our voyage to England, Nicholls had been appointed captain of the backs and when Mr Dean stepped aside, all of the playing arrangements and preparations were left to the players or rather to these men who were in charge of us.

Porter approached the appointment of captaincy in some singular ways. He told us on the ship when broaching the idea of individual talks that he could not and would not pretend to he an expert on every position in the field. "You chaps who have played these positions know their requirements far better than I could ever hope to do," he said. "No one, therefore, is going to tell you how you should play the positions. But what I want is an adjustment between the positions, so that we all know what we are aiming for." Porter's skill was supplemented by the great ability of Nicholls in understanding the requirements of back play. Thus, our training runs differed materially from those that are common practice these days. We had no sideline coaches telling us what we should do and, more particularly, what we were not allowed to do. We did not endlessly rush around the training field from one ruck to another. The aim was to build up smoothness and quickness in passing, coordination between backs and forwards, and accuracy in the placing of kicks. Especially were we taught the importance of backing up, so that the man with the ball could be sure, a good percentage of the time, of support to one side or the other and, for preference, from both. As our tour developed and our team grew stronger and more confident, this backing-up became our hallmark and I would doubt that our ability in it has ever been surpassed. It is the great quality of New Zealand Rugby which has been lost and if, as I often think, one reason is the change-over from the 2-3-2 scrummage formation to the 3-4-1, another is the coaching policy which now governs all play in all positions - and from off the field, at that.

I am, of course, celebrated in the history of this tour because I was the one who played in every match of it. Strangely, as I discovered years later, I could have lost this record in the opening match, against Devon at Devonport. As I have related, I did not play well in Australia. Nicholls has even said that I was "bloody awful". The selection committee remembered this while discussing their team for the first match and it was proposed that I not be played until I had had the chance to work up confidence. Then it was recalled that our 1905 All Blacks had won this match by 55 points to 4, even though Devon in the previous season had won the county championship, and it was inferred that the county would still be weak. This opinion was strengthened after we had watched a game between two club teams which were so weak it did not seem to matter who played fullback.

In the event, we won this match by only 11 points to nil (although Porter should have added further points when he drop kicked a goal from a mark, but the referee did not see the ball pass over the bar). F. W. Sanders, the captain of Devon, had won three caps for England in the year before and J. C. R. Buchanan, another forward, had already played ten times for Scotland. They were the leaders of a fine, dogged pack which bustled about the field after the ball and which gave all of us no rest whatever. Another factor was that with the rain which set in in the second half our superiority in handling disappeared. Mostly, however, as we were all agreed, the real trouble was that we played badly below the form we had expected to develop.

We had some difficulty with the interpretations of Mr R. A. Roberts, the referee from Gloucester. Porter learned from the first that when he stayed at the mouth of the scrum while our men were heeling the ball he was offside. This jarred us all, for it was something we had not encountered in New Zealand or Australia; and we now began to learn of the hard times and the abuse which had been suffered by David Gallaher while he was leading the 1905 All Blacks in the same playing position as Porter. Cliff often argued the point with referees and sometimes, by the power of personality, he convinced them that he was right and they were wrong. At other times, the penalties were called against us.

This was our team for this, the opening match of a long, arduous and successful tour: fullback, Nepia; threequarters, Svenson, Brown, Lucas; five-eighth, Cooke, Nicholls; half-back, Dalley; wing-forward, Porter; hookers, Munro, Donald; middle row, M. Brownlie, Masters, Stewart; back row, West, Richardson.

It took us half an hour to score, "Snowy" Svenson having the honour of running in the first of the 175 tries we scored in our thirty games. About ten minutes before halftime, Svenson when blocked threw a pass infield and Cooke scuttled across the line for a try which I converted. In the second half, in the rain, the match slogged around in midfield. Brown got a try only five minutes after the re-start, and that was all we could get. The scrums were an eye-opener. The ball often had to be put in three and four times and the Devon hooker got his feet across the tunnel so that Munro and Donald could not chop at the ball. Not one word came from Mr Roberts and our forwards wondered what they were in for.

My own play was not too bad and the committee, so I gathered, had no hesitation in choosing me for the next match. I fielded and kicked pretty well and made one good tackle which, I was sorry to see, took the wind out of an opponent for a moment or two. But I suffered with the rest of the team in timing. It was already evident that we would have to work hard. The English Press praised Devon more than it praised us, but Colonel Philip Trevor, who had at times been a severe critic of the 1905 team, had a kind word for us in the *Daily Telegraph*. "I frankly think they are going to be very good indeed," he wrote; and in the same article, he said: "My opinion, for what it is worth, is that they are a very capable and dangerously attacking combination, who at the outset of their tour have rather failed to live up to their reputation."

So the tour was in being. Colonel Trevor had remarked that English teamwork had improved out of all recognition since the All Black tour of 1905. If he were right - and he was a most experienced critic - we faced a good deal of hard work over the next few months.

1924-25 Tour: Gloucestershire versus New Zealand
Top left: Gloucestershire team.
Top right: Mr W.S. Donne (President of the RFU in the centre)
Middle left: A new shirt for Gloucestershire's M.V. Shaw at half-time
Middle right: The New Zealand team.
Bottom left: Two local supporters.
Bottom middle: The crowd.
Bottom right: match action
(Courtesy Oma Nepia)

11. The Win We Should Not Have Had

For one reason or another, it took us at least a quarter of the tour, perhaps longer, to build up that confidence and combination which made us certain in our own minds that we were going to keep on winning. There were narrow squeaks in the early stages. Having beaten Cornwall in the second match by 29 to nil, Cooke playing with exceptional touch in a match of seven tries, we scraped by Somerset at Weston-Super-Mare by only 6 to nil and by Gloucestershire at Gloucester by the same small score. Then, having beaten Swansea by 39 to 3 - this was the team which the 1905 All Blacks beat by only 4 to 3 when Billy Wallace drop kicked a goal - we had the luck on our side when we beat Newport by 13 to 10 with a try by Svenson converted by Nicholls in the last minutes of the game. From this point, we began to improve very rapidly and it was not until we encountered Ireland in the first international, winning by only 6 to nil again, that we were seriously troubled.

I want to refer to some of those early matches because excuses other than our want of skill accounted for the low scores. As one example, rain fell for twenty-four hours before we played Somerset and casual water lay all over the field, to the inevitable detriment of accurate handling. We were nil-all here at halftime and the home forwards were having great fun sloshing around the field and making heroic tackles of our men. Cooke dribbled the ball over for one try and just before the end Mill nipped across for one of those famous tries of his from a close scrum close to the line. Svenson, "Son" White, and Robilliard were injured and a day or two later an X-ray examination revealed that the last-named had a broken bone in the foot.

If the weather was bad at Weston-super-Mare, it was simply frightful at Gloucester. The heaviest of rain began to fall in the early morning and it was still going strong at the kickoff. The ground was a Taranaki cow yard, old style, and everyone splished, splashed, and sploshed after the ball where-ever it was. Nicholls was a kingpin and Gloucestershire did not once reach our 25 in the first half. Donald scored a try early in the game and I placed a penalty goal which, of course, had to be disallowed when the ball was touched in flight by an opponent (you could move then during a penalty; now, you must stand still). Donald again scored in the second half which spell the Gloucestershire forwards played with great fire. Their captain, L. J. Corbett, a centre, afterwards played for England against us and he was obviously a good 'un; but the forwards were the boys. We were learning fast that the talk about effete Englishmen was so much talk. These boys could take it, and give it, too. Their standard was much higher than we had been led to expect and we were constantly told that it was much higher than the average quality put against the 1905 team. As a point of interest, incidentally, all our backs wore mittens. These seem to have gone out of fashion but for my money are ideal in such conditions as we encountered in this match.

We approached our first match in Wales - indeed, all our matches there - in a state of dedication. For nineteen years, all New Zealanders had believed that the only loss suffered by the 1905 team, to Wales at Cardiff by 3 to nil, had been a miscarriage of justice attributable to incompetent refereeing. We had been brought up to believe that Bob Deans, the centre who scored the try which was disallowed, had exclaimed on his death-bed, only three years later, "It was a try", and every New Zealand witness of the game was prepared to swear his life away to the same effect. All this had convinced us that whatever we did, we must beat the Welsh. There was another side to the same story. We had been told that the Welsh crowds used their powers as singers with the intention of putting opponents off their stroke. It was said that the effect of *Cwm Rhondda* or *Land of My Fathers* when sung by thirty or forty or fifty thousand people was terrifying. Well, we had been warned. No one was going to put us off our stroke. Hymns or no hymns, we hit Swansea like a tornado. The conditions were ideal and for the first time the real qualities of the side became apparent. Our forwards were wound up and after some unsteadiness which may or may not have been caused by the singing of the crowd of 45,000 they took control. The backs - Dalley, Nicholls, Cooke, Svenson, Brown, and Lucas - supplemented the efforts superbly and at times the scorer merely had to trot in his try, so completely had the defence been overcome. Dai Parker kicked a great goal against us from just on halfway, the ball bounding over after striking the crossbar, and we all recalled these, the first points of the tour against us, when he toured New Zealand in F. D. Prentice's British team six years later. It was said then that Dai and Irvine had had some disagreement in the Swansea match - a possibility, because they viewed the needs of front-row play more or less in the same light - and that Parker had waited for six years to settle the argument. It may have been purely a coincidence that Irvine's playing days ended after the first test with the British team at Dunedin - a match in which Parker packed down against him.

I had not been happy with myself in these early games. I was aware, better than anybody, how little I knew about fullback play. I used to lie awake at nights, fretting over my mistakes and worrying over how I was to correct them. We were a critical team who expected the best out of each other and I knew that bad mistakes could break me as, during the tour, they broke other people, in terms of test-match qualifications. I had determination, that was one thing, and I practised very hard. I also had Nicholls giving me a lift - along every now and again with a few words which made a tremendous difference to me. But it was in this Swansea match that, so it seemed to me, I began to play as I wanted. I was learning to combat the loneliness of the fullback position, my positional play was improving, and I was picking up some of the finer points. By some mysterious means, which I could never explain, I seemed to have natural anticipation and by the use of this I was able to cut off some of the corners and escape from some of the holes. It was all tremendously interesting, but it was also taxing on the nervous system. It was good to get a game like Swansea under the belt and to feel that I was knocking some of the rough edges off my play.

And then came Newport. Wow! We really did have the tremors in this one. We made some howlers. Svenson presented them with five points by stumbling when trying to kick the ball dead. Twice, early on, our threequarters failed to hold passes which almost certainly would have yielded tries. Brown just before halftime missed a great chance; believe it or not, this "broke" him as a test-match candidate for the rest of the tour. At other times, we were horribly bustled.

As we afterwards realised, Newport presented us with the sort of match that our leading provinces present to teams touring New Zealand. Their forwards played with sting and vigour, their backs tackled fearlessly, the whole team was animated by a do-or-die spirit. At times, the energy expended was excessive to the needs of the case and never in my life have I seen a more blatant late-charge than that with which a fiery forward named Tom Jones knocked Cooke cold in the second half. Bert had to leave the field on a stretcher and he was as groggy as a broken-down boxer when he came back nearly fifteen minutes later. To their credit, the crowd of 30,000 took the most violent exception to this and howled for Jones's blood. The referee did in fact order Jones from the field and but for the intervention of Porter and some of our other players, who pleaded for Jones, this would have been done. But the incident was one sidelight on the temper of the game. Newport were captained, incidentally, by Reg Edwards and the referee was Mr Albert E. Freethy, of Neath. We shall meet both of these characters on a more sombre occasion in the last match in the British Isles.

Newport scored in the first half from a memorable try in which eight men handled, Friend, a forward, scoring and Wetter, another forward and the captain of Wales, converting. We battled for twenty minutes in the second half before Mill scored from a scrum in front of the Newport posts and Nicholls converted. Porter, Nicholls, and I all had drop kicks at goal without luck, but Mark put us in front, 8 to 5, with a penalty from a difficult angle. Wetter tried a drop kick at goal and it was then that G. E. Andrews, a wing, scored when Svenson failed to kick the ball dead. F. Baker, the fullback, converted and with time running out and the crowd very nearly running wild with excitement, we were, putting it mildly, in the cart.

I noticed then that our mascot, a stuffed kiwi which was always kept by the sideline during our matches, had disappeared. (As I found out later, Newport officials who had "pinched" the springbok head of the South African team of 1912 for their clubrooms intended to do the same with the kiwi and had already taken steps.) It flashed into my mind that the disappearance of the kiwi could be an omen for the disappearance of our unbeaten record. Happily, Maurice Brownlie, Svenson, and Nicholls put an end to the thought. Brownlie fielded a kick which did not quite reach the touch and immediately passed to "Snowy". It was then that you saw what a great little wing Svenson was. He positively surged at the goal-line to score; and when Nicholls from a very difficult angle placed the goal, we were victors. Time was called only one minute later. Whew! What a game.

Tom Jones did not escape. The *South Wales Echo*, in as blunt an editorial as I have ever read, said: "The remarkably fine performance of Newport was sadly marred by an incident which excited the intense indignation of a considerable body of spectators. We refer to the action of Tom Jones in charging down and knocking out one of the visitors after he had parted with the ball. No one who witnessed the incident can recall it without a shudder. It was one of the ugliest things ever seen in local Rugby and we are at a loss to understand the lenient view taken by the referee. If it be pleaded that Jones erred by accident in the heat and stress of a memorable game, we can only say that a player who is liable to err so seriously ought not to be included in the team. Newport has no need of players of this type."

Straight-from-the-shoulder stuff, this. I have often thought our New Zealand Press could have been as merciless toward some of the players who over the years have fouled our game.

So we escaped. It was a lucky win. We made too many mistakes. But it was an important win, too. This was the turning of the tide. Moreover, there was one great lesson in it. Our forwards did not spend their time gunning for the Newport tigers. They concentrated upon playing Rugby. That, and that only, was the reason why we won.

12. Out of the team - Then In

We still had many hurdles to jump, but this was a great one to have behind us. For a purely selfish reason, I reacted even more joyfully than most. Somehow during the game, I put my thumb out of joint. It was painful and when Porter and Mr Dean had a look at it, they assured me that I would not be playing against Leicester in a couple of days' time. On the team board on the Thursday night, the selection was announced and when I saw that I wasn't included, I took a deep sigh. How nice, I thought, to watch other people play for a change. On Friday night, I frolicked instead of going to bed at ten o'clock, and I took my breakfast on Saturday morning with pleasant thoughts of how I would spend my time until the match. I was, in fact, on the point of going out somewhere or other when Mr Dean came to me. "George," he said, "you are playing this afternoon, after all." If I was wanted, that was that. The trouble was that I had the world's worst nervous system. In the last hours before a match, before every match, I used to go through agony. I couldn't sit still, I yawned my head off, I went endlessly to the lavatory. The stupid thing was that as soon as I took the field and heard the thump of the ball, all of my nervousness disappeared. Yet I still couldn't stop myself from developing pre-match tension.

I should say here that even though the Newport and earlier matches had shown that our opposition was strong and likely to become more so during the tour, the team rules as to behaviour, bedtime, diet and other matters which are now regarded as of such vital importance were very reasonable and restrictions were not imposed unduly. It was desired that we should go to bed at a reasonable hour on the night before the match, but nobody stood over us with a stick to see that we did. There were no rules as to smoking and beer drinking. In fact, I was the only non-smoker in the team - there used to be a wild scramble for my package in the free issue of cigarettes which we received from W. D. & H. O. Wills Ltd. - and as I have related, I was given licence to drink on match nights. As to diet, I had my own theories; on the day of a match, I made a good breakfast of bacon and eggs, tea and toast, but at lunch I only had one cup of tea and two small slices of toast, for this, I found, removed any sluggish feeling I might have developed on a full stomach. But other chaps could eat what they liked; and some of them, particularly the Hawke's Bay contingent, were among the world's best. The whole idea was that we should behave normally. Since our day, the faddists seem to have come into their own, not necessarily with New Zealand teams. I sometimes wonder whether Rugby has benefited from their zealous care of diet, hours of sleep, drying out for two or three days before a match and things like that. All theory and no play, you know, can make Jack a dull boy - and just look at some of the Rugby that these faddists have produced in their teams!

The Leicester newspapers on the night before the game said that "The Tigers" could only lose to the All Blacks by striking a day off. The same newspapers sidestepped the point when they reported our victory by 27 to nil. This was a vintage display for us, even though we had to play the last half-hour without "Abe" Munro, who wrenched a knee in the first half. Everything came off and despite my thumb I had one of my best games of the tour.

From here we went on to beat North Midlands 40 to 3, Cheshire, 18 to 5, Durham, 43 to 7, Yorkshire, 42 to 4, Lancashire, 23 to nil, and Cumberland, the county champions of the previous year, by 41 to nil. The scores speak for themselves. The All Blacks were now at peak. Badeley, temporarily restored to health, played brilliantly in our record score against Durham. Svenson against Durham ran in three tries in the second half and Hart in two matches scored no fewer than seven tries by dazzling pace. My own best scoring day came against Yorkshire when with six conversions and two penalty goals I scored 18 points.

Here and there, we ran into outstanding players among our opponents. At Leicester, one of the forwards was F. D. Prentice, who afterwards captained the British team to New Zealand in 1930 and who at his untimely death early in 1963 had been secretary of the Rugby Football Union for about fifteen years. The Cheshire team included leading players in J. V. Richardson and H. M. Locke, both of whom before or after played several times for England, and A. L. Gracie, a Scotsman who had won twelve caps by the time we met him. Gracie figures in one of the memorable events of all British Rugby. Playing as captain of Scotland against Wales at Cardiff in 1923, he suffered a broken nose and a kick on the thigh which left a permanent lump and the injuries emphasised the grim fact that with ten minutes to play Wales led by 8 to 6. Given a pass outside the Welsh 25 in the last minutes, he ran at tremendous speed through the defence and dotted down for a try which was converted to give Scotland their first victory at Cardiff in thirty-three years. The great point of his effort was that at the end of the game the crowd rushed on to the field and carried him off shoulder high.

Durham introduced us to two forwards, G. S. Conway and R. Hillard, who were to play for England against us, and the Yorkshire team included Harry Wilkinson, who toured New Zealand with the 1930 British team. Cumberland contained Jim Brough, a fullback who played for England against us and who afterwards became one of England's greatest players in Rugby League, which he played for a number of years. Lancashire's leading forward was A. A. Blakiston, who also played for England. It can be seen, therefore, that our opposition was far from second-class as to quality.

This phase of our tour was not without its difficulties. Newspapers were carping about our methods, some of which were said to be obstructive in intent. We ourselves were astonished when in the Lancashire match one of their forwards repeatedly obstructed and most recklessly used both his feet and his arms in the close-quarter stuff. No one said anything about this, least of all the referee, and at last, in self-protection, some of our forwards had to set about teaching him some manners. This was not a good game and at the dinner Mr Dean publicly regretted that the referee had not exercised firm control from the start. The referee, Mr D. Helliwell, a Yorkshireman, did not take this lying down. Said he: "The keenness that crept into the game was little or nothing. The All Blacks are following the famous 1905 team and are naturally out to beat their fine record. They will have harder games than the one today, but having refereed two of their matches and watched a third, I would say to them, 'You are doing a lot of good here, but don't spoil the game by attaching too much importance to the result'."

Mr Helliwell was entitled to his opinion, but the Cumberland match proved that the English could well cast out the motes from their own beams. The crowd of I6,500 was extraordinary one-eyed. We were given the bird. The Cumberland forwards got stuck in and their methods were so rugged that only by the greatest of good luck did Mill avoid a boot which would have knocked his head off. At the call of time, a Cumberland forward, not, evidently, a fine old English gentleman, belted Hart in the face, though whether it was because he did not like the face or because "Gus" had scored four scorching tries was not quite certain. This touching little farewell naturally provoked a reaction from our players and the best little dust-up since the Battle of Waterloo was in prospect until the police and some of our players moved in. The teams had to return to the dressing-rooms under police escort - and that, I swear, doesn't happen to teams which tour New Zealand. If it was true, as Mr Helliwell charged, that we attached importance to the result, at least we could say that we didn't strike opponents on the jaw after the final whistle had been blown.

Cartoon of the Leicester versus New Zealanders match on the 1924-25 tour
(Courtesy Museum of Rugby)

13. Ireland - And a Great Fullback

They warned us, some jokingly, some seriously, not to go to Dublin for the international. Too many Irishmen there, they said. Too many Irishmen with keen memories of the troubles, Black and Tans, Kevin Barry, Sinn Feiners, and all that. And indeed to goodness, as the Welsh might say, the city was a sight. The Post Office in O'Connell Street and the Law Courts were still hulks after the bombings of years before. Every building in the main street was scored with bullet-marks. As New Zealanders, we were remote from the quarrels but even we couldn't help feel the uneasiness. When we went north to Ulster after the test, the Loyalist police at the border searched our luggage for firearms and with their revolvers on their hips they looked grim and businesslike. Decidedly a strange place, this Ireland, at least in our time.

But I am glad I went. In spite of the rain and the wind, which in a real Irish way blew against us in both halves, we had the grandest of matches before we won the international by 6 to nil, and then at Belfast a few days later we played some of our finest football in beating Ulster by 28 to 6.

The experience, I am sure, was good for all of us. It was wonderful for me because, to my everlasting satisfaction, I saw Ernie Crawford.

Crawford was fullback for both Ireland and Ulster. He was twenty-eight when, in 1920, he was first chosen for his country and by the time we caught up with him he had won about half of the thirty caps he collected between 1920 and 1927. By our standards, then, he was an "old" man when we saw him; but I'll tell you this, until Bob Scott came along, Ernie was the greatest fullback I ever saw. Just to watch him did me more good than dozens of lessons on the theory of fullback play. He was an artist. He was not a big man - round about eleven stone, if that, I suppose. There was, in fact, nothing very remarkable about him physically, except that he used to take up a sort of guardsman pose, very stiff, while he waited to field a high ball. But he had everything. His kick was goodish long and extremely accurate. His hands were beautifully safe. On the tackle, he was deadly - and it was in this that I was specially impressed, for he had a way of hanging off until he had measured his man and his success at this seemed to confirm my instinctive approach to the tackling problem. Most of all, he seemed to have some power of personality which compelled your regard and which made him, I imagine, a most inspiring man to his comrades. W. W. Wakefield, the English captain of the time, somewhere or other wrote about Crawford's "brooding intelligence" and said that he "always seemed sinister during a game." We may not have been as impressionable as Wakefield, but I will say this, as soon as we saw Crawford we knew we'd come upon a man with class written all over him. I watched him do many things that I'd half suspected were possible to a fullback but which I had never tried because no one I had seen had attempted them, let alone brought them off. After the first game, I used often to lie in bed half of the night thinking of and memorising the things that Crawford had done. I said to myself, "If another fullback can do this, you can, too", and from these reflections there started in me the feeling that "If you make up your mind that you will do a thing and master it, you will bring it off. Nothing is impossible."

Ernie was a Northerner with a wit as dry as chip and he used this on the Southerners quite mercilessly. During a game he and Jamie Clinch, who was the toughest of the Irish forwards, used to abuse each other most dreadfully and at times, so I was told, inexperienced players tended to feel that they were about to witness the execution of one or the other by one or the other. When he wasn't abusing Clinch, Crawford was usually abusing the rest of the Irish team. I was sorry to learn in 1962 that he had died, for he was one of my heroes, but various people have told me that he will live forever in British Rugby. It was Ernie with his wit who concocted the name, "Alligadoo", to describe the administrator of Rugby or, in his words, "the b... who walks the touchline". This is now a favourite description in British football and I believe it will endure. So Ernie lives on, as he deserves, for ever.

There had been rain for a good many hours before the test and when it stopped in the morning it was replaced by a hard wind blowing down the ground. H. W. V. Stephenson, the Irish captain, took the wind as a matter of course and pretty soon a shrewdly-placed punt by Clinch put them on the attack close to our goal-line. From the start, the Irish pack tore in. Collopy, Crichton, and McClelland had been playing international Rugby practically since the war and Clinch and McVicker were at the start of long careers, so that the pack nicely combined maturity and youthful fire. It was real fire, too, no hankypanky stuff. I don't think our forwards ever enjoyed a match as much as this one. The Irish went at them exactly as New Zealanders go, or used to go, against each other, with nothing snide in the methods but with every man putting everything he had into the contest. There were some goods backs in the Irish team, too. G. V. Stephenson, one of the centres, played altogether forty-two times for Ireland and his record of most international caps stood for donkey's years until it was beaten by the Irishman, Jack Kyle, and the Welshman, Ken Jones, in the 1950s. His brother, W. W. V. Stephenson was a fine player, too, and the Hewitts, Frank at stand-off half and Tom on the left wing, were accomplished players who are remembered in New Zealand by their blood-relation, David Hewitt, who was so brilliant a centre with the 1959 British Lions.

The wind, as I remarked, was blowing hard and the Irish were soon tempted. They began to make use of it with kicks, some of them really long, and I had to do a good deal of hopping about to field the ball and return it to touch. All of this looked good from the Irish point of view, but really they were fooling themselves. They were denying themselves possession and you can't score tries without the ball. G. V. Stephenson fairly early on tried to nip through but for the most part the other backs probed at us with punts. Meantime, our forwards were steaming into scrums and mauls and lineouts. Richardson headed one grand foot-rush away from our goal-line and Parker, who had taken the place of Porter when the latter was injured against Cumberland, very nearly put Hart in for a try with a cross kick, "Gus" accidentally running into touch only a yard or so from the Irish goal-line. After the Irish had stormed back, we infringed out in front of the goalposts and Crawford only just missed his shot at goal. F. S. Hewitt was a lively sort of five-eighth, but Tom, his brother, made a mess of things with a cross kick when going at our line and we pulled away again. Our backs at last chimed in a dazzling run at the Irish goal, but F. S. Hewitt nailed Nicholls to stop the attack.

Following loose play about halfway New Zealand heeled from a ruck and Nicholls worked the blindside making ground to Crawford. He was closely pressed on the inside and could not draw Crawford properly and passed to Parker but Crawford with a magnificent tackle brought Parker down. Now came the rain, blinding sheets of it, and we all but scored when Crawford forgot himself and took a flykick at a ball. Nicholls short-punted from this and G. V. Stephenson had to carry the ball over the goal-line to save. Our forwards heeled from several scrums without reward and F. S. Hewitt with a clever dribble at last broke the attack. What they could do, we could do, too, and Dalley dribbled like "Son" White himself as he took the play down to the Irish line where Nicholls only just failed to hold the pass that would have meant a try. White almost immediately took a penalty shot at goal, without result and just on halftime T. Hewitt with side-stepping set up G. V. Stephenson, who gave to Gardiner who was pulled down only inches from our line. So it was nil-all at the break and if the Irish had made better use of the wind the scoring might have been in their favour.

The rain now stopped and the wind began to blow again - the other way. Collopy, McClelland and Brand soon led a rush at our line and we returned with a rush in which, most unfortunately, F. S. Hewitt was hurt in the leg. He had to go out to the wing, Gardiner going to flyhalf, and Tom Hewitt to centre. Cooke short-punted and G. V. Stephenson did the work of ten men in gathering the ball and kicking clear to save a try. In spite of the rain, our forwards now had their dander up. Parker fielded and passed to Nicholls to Maurice Brownlie. Maurice bashed down the field before passing to Svenson and "Snowy" dashed over for a try which I could not convert.

Three points were a great help in the conditions. Soon we had six. McDowell, the Irish half, was penalised in front of his posts for holding on to the ball and Nicholls turned his boot into a sort of spade to heft the ball over the bar.

For the rest of the time, if I may say so, we had the game in hand. When F. S. Hewitt had to leave the field for a time, Ireland lost Spain out of the pack to the wing. It was Spain's only match for his country, but the loss was severe, all the same. H. W. Stephenson made one fine run which looked dangerous until the wet ground cost him his footing. Crawford had another go at goal after Parker had been caught offside but his kick was charged down - I often wonder, incidentally, how some of our great kickers of modern times would succeed if this law about penalty kicks still obtained. Parker atoned for this mistake with a dribble of Soccer quality and Crawford gave yet another demonstration of his genius by trapping the ball with his feet before booting it to touch off the ground. Once, we looked really dangerous until Lucas sent Svenson a bad pass. Another time, G. V. Stephenson was away like a stag until he lost the ball in a half-tackle. He had another run almost as dangerous. Lucas and Svenson came back with a bout of inter-passing. Nicholls punted to within a yard of their corner-flag to set up a strong attack and as the minutes ticked away Hart almost went in at one corner before, on the call of time, Svenson was only beaten for a try when the ball bobbled into touch-in-goal only a second before he reached it.

Our team, for the record, was: Nepia; Svenson, Lucas, Hart; Cooke, Nicholls; Dalley, Parker; Irvine, Donald; M. J. Brownlie, Masters, Cupples; Richardson (captain), White.

Theirs was W. E. Crawford; H. W. V. Stephenson, G. V. Stephenson, J. B. Gardiner, T. Hewitt; F. S. Hewitt, J. C. McDowell; A Spain, J. D. Clinch, T. N. Brand; T. A. McClelland, J. H. McVicker; R. Collopy, R. Y. Crichton, W. R. F. Collis.

The referee was the Welshman, A. E. Freethy, whom we shall meet again.

So we had won our first international test. But for the conditions and two or three human errors, we would, I think, have won by a larger score. Even so, it was a hard game. The Irish forwards were magnificently virile. Clinch, who was as hard as a rock, roved about most effectively and a blanket would have covered the whole pack on many of the charges they made after the ball. This was the best forward pack we had so far encountered and it meant much to us in the future that our men were not only able to hold them but also, toward the end, came to dominate them. Brownlie, Richardson and White were magnificent and Parker with his pace must have scared seven bells out of the Irish insides. The conditions were made for Dalley, who was as tough as teak, and Nicholls and Cooke stood with fortitude to the battering of the Irish pack. The conditions were all against the threequarters, but ours made fine runs and would have done even better if their handling had been a little more accurate. As for myself, I would not quote Colonel Trevor were it not that this was my first big international. He wrote: "It was not a day for the making of personal reputation, but Nepia, if possible, enhanced his. I have spoken to men who have recently returned from witnessing some of the games played in South Africa by the British team and they tell me that in that country there is no fullback as good as Nepia. In England, Scotland, Ireland and Wales, I am sure he has no rival." This was hot stuff for me; but let me remind you again how I afterwards spent nights thinking about Crawford. I can safely say, for myself and all the other All Blacks, that Ernie was the best fullback we ever played against.

14. Charges of Obstructive Play

Having jumped our first test hurdle, we were now keen to take on the second, which was Wales. Meantime, there was work to be done, for matches had to be played against Ulster, Northumberland, Cambridge University, London Counties, Oxford University, and Cardiff and all of these were regarded as important and difficult opponents.

From the record, you will see that we beat Ulster by 28 to 6, Northumberland by 27 to 4, Cambridge by 5 to nil, London Counties by 31 to 6, Oxford by 33 to 15, and Cardiff by 16 to 8 and from the bare account you would almost certainly infer that Cambridge was the hardest match of the series, perhaps the hardest of the tour, with Cardiff next.

In actual fact, there has never been any disagreement among us that the hardest match of the entire tour was against Oxford. They were a team of greyhounds and they very nearly ran us ragged. Against Cambridge, by contrast, I was not called upon for one tackle and I can't remember that they were much in our 25. Cardiff, of course, was a tough encounter, for you can't take on any first-class club in Wales without becoming acquainted with the facts of footballing life, but I still award the palm to Oxford. This match illustrated that there is absolutely no defence against speed when it is properly developed and exploited. You can mass your defence here, you can place your secondaries there, you can think up all the signals you like, but if a man has the legs of you, and team-mates with the sense to give him a fair go against you, there's an end on it. Failure to understand this cost the British Lions of 1959 the chance to defeat us three to one in the test series and recent Australian teams in New Zealand have made the same fundamental error.

I always remember the match with Ulster because of the behaviour of Jimmy Mill in the dressing-room beforehand. Having failed to win selection against Ireland, he was, as I well knew, extremely keen to make his number good for the rest of the tour. When I saw him hopping around while getting dressed, I was reminded of his behaviour before some of the Ranfurly Shield games back home and I thought, "Ha ha, Jimmy's going to play what-oh today". With one exception, W. Hall for the injured F.S. Hewitt, at stand-off half, Ulster fielded the Irish backline and their forwards had the same bonny grit as the Irish pack, too. Hence the score of six tries to one flattered us not a little. But Jimmy was at the top of his form. Twice in the second half, he put men in for tries, the first being Steel and the second Parker, and in his adroit way he was the mainspring of many attacks. But the best effort of all came just before half time when five of the Ulster backs raced over the beautiful turf of the Ravenhill ground and seemed certain to score when Harry Stephenson was given the ball. Mill, however, appeared out of nowhere and with the kind of tackle Elder Moser would have praised brought the Irishman down with a bump. This was some feat, for late in the game, in a similar sort of movement, Stephenson again was given the ball and with no Mill present to stop him he simply ran away from us.

An incident of the second half which implicated me may bear the telling. To reach an Ulster kick, I had to work up top speed and when I had fielded the ball, I simply carried on upfield as hard as I could go, cut out a man, passed to Lucas and then watched Svenson go over after Lucas had given him the ball. This was Bob Scott stuff and it reminds me that time and again in the post-war era, when Scott was making a monkey out of all sorts of tacklers and teams, I was often asked why I had not made similar excursions - excursions of the Ulster match, as only one example. The answer was that I wasn't allowed to. Many a time during the tour, Cooke would turn to me and yell, "Come up, come on up". Nicholls would never have this. "Your job is to be the defender, the last line," he would say. "You leave the attack to us and concentrate on defence. That's how we want you." Whether I would have had the talent of Scott or some of these other moderns for the all-round sort of game that they play, I don't know, though the fact that I'd grown up as a five-eighth must have helped. In each of the important positions of Rugby, however, there are basic duties and defence, it cannot be questioned, is the fundamental requirement of the fullback, just as a good pass is the fundamental requirement of the good halfback. I don't regret the wastage of the opportunities I might have had, which in fact I would certainly have had in a team as brilliant as ours became. I did my job - and believe me, I did do a fair amount of running with the ball when the situation was favourable.

Mill continued to be an important man for the next couple of games. He ran in two tries and placed two conversions against Northumberland, a match in which Hart and Steel on the wings and Parker and Richardson in the forwards also showed particularly fine form, and then he scored the try which beat Cambridge. The ground for the latter match was deplorable, much worse than we encountered against Ireland. It was mud, sticky mud which seemed to reach up to your ankles. When the ball pitched down from a kick, it fell with a plop and stayed there; and even when it was lustily kicked by the forwards in a rush it would only travel a few inches and then stop. We were never afraid of being beaten, though we were afraid of a drawn game, more particularly after several rushes at the goal-line by our forwards had failed to yield tries because the ball always seemed to slip away from the man trying to score. So there were cheers from our side when, fifteen minutes after the start of the second half, Mill picked up a loose pass by A. T. Young, the Cambridge half, and with a skip and hop swerved in under the bar for a try. Nicholls kicked the goal and our chaps defended stoutly when Cambridge toward the end brought their fast wing threequarter, Rowe Harding, into a movement. Harding, who is now a judge in Wales, had toured South Africa with the British team in 1924 and he played many times for Wales. One of the Cambridge wings, Devitt, was, incidentally, a baronet and Young, the captain, who had also toured South Africa, afterwards became a noted player for England, for whom he won eighteen caps. W. E. Tucker, a forward, and who won three caps was, oddly enough, a son of a man who had won five.

London Counties introduced us to Twickenham, which is the finest ground I ever had the pleasure of playing on and the only one I have known where you hesitated to put your sprigged foot down because of possible damage to the turf. I have a singular memory of this place. The double-decker grandstands produced a curious sensation. You felt as if you were a dwarf, which was disconcerting; then the smoke from thousands of cigarettes, which you could see glowing as the afternoon wore on, gave the impression of a light, misty fog.

We had the devil of a struggle to get a grip on this match, for London had bags of pace and their pack included two champions in W. W. Wakefield, whom the English then and afterwards regarded as the greatest forward in Rugby, and R.Cove-Smith, who had captained the British team in South Africa and who played against us for England. The flyhalf or first five-eighth was an Australian, Tommy Lawton, who was so well regarded in Britain that he had became a member of the committee of the Barbarians club and who was so idolised in Australia that when, many years later, the Waratahs of 1927-28 could not persuade him from Queensland to Sydney to a reunion, they ended up by taking the reunion to him. One of the wings was R. H. Hamilton-Wickes, a man of tremendous pace. As you may see, therefore, we had problems on our plate. We led 5-3, then they led 6-5, then it was 10-6 to us - and by this time the crowd of 40,000 were screaming. This, in fact, was the score at halftime and it had been a gruelling forty minutes. No one had suffered more than Parker, who was set upon by the referee, Mr R. A. Lloyd, from the start. By halftime, it was quite obvious that Jim would have to shift and from the start of the second half he was an extra threequarter, with Mill putting the ball into the scrummage. The change was very much better than a rest. The whole team clicked and Cooke became superlative. I should mention that the match with Northumberland had important consequences, for one of the best players in it, if not the best, was McGregor at first five-eighth and he again played well at Cambridge. Against London Counties, the combination of Mill-McGregor-Nicholls-Cooke was fielded and from its success it was obvious that we had now discovered our most reliable and most dangerous midfield attacking combination.

The second half of the Counties' match was a trimmer. Within three minutes, Cooke ran and cross kicked to Parker who again set the backs going in a run from which Cooke whizzed in for a glorious try. Minutes later, Svenson, McGregor, Cooke, and Parker combined and the crowd cheered Parker's try from this effort. So the game went on - the loveliest of running, perfect backing-up, the champagne of Rugby in fact - to the climax when Parker by some miracle fielded a kick high above his head and for sixty yards or more ran away from the English greyhounds to score between the posts. Even if you paid men to do it, you could not get them to play better Rugby than was displayed in this spell.

I have mentioned before that we had been given the bird by some of the English writers. A gentleman named F. J. Sellicks, describing the Counties' match for the *Morning Post*, set not the bird but the whole blinking dovecote at us. "Their methods," he wrote in describing us, "were not exactly popular with the crowd and seldom has victory in a big match been received with less enthusiasm. Their besetting sins were offside play and obstruction, and though they were frequently penalised they escaped on too many occasions. I have no sympathy with some of the exaggerated nonsense which has been written about them - to say that five of them ought to have been sent off is sheer idiocy - but there is no getting away from the fact that some of them do habitually hang about offside and have apparently brought obstruction to a fine art.... The All Blacks are quite clever enough to win without resorting to unclean practices."

It would be foolish, forty years on, to reply to Mr Sellicks who by now may well be in the condition of the journal which printed his words, but I would swear this, that obstruction and offside play were neither practised nor encouraged in the team. We had too much trouble as it was with interpretations, especially against Porter and Parker, to court further penalties; as for obstruction, it's a funny thing that this is never done by your own team but always by the other side.

Oxford. Now there was a team. "Pup" Raymond and "Johnny" Wallace, fullback and wing respectively, were Australians. George Aitken, a centre, was a New Zealand Rhodes Scholar who captained New Zealand in the first two tests with the 1921 Springboks. G. P. S. Macpherson, the other centre, was a Scot with twenty-six caps, a magnificent player in every respect, and H. J. Kittermaster, the stand-off, was an English international. R. J. Hillard, of the forwards, played for England against us and in disgust at the fieriness of that match gave away international Rugby for all time.

H. P. Jacob on the wing very nearly scored in the first thirty seconds and it was he who opened the scoring a few minutes later. Though the game was only a few minutes old, I could hear the All Blacks panting from where I was and at times, I own, I did a bit of panting myself, for the pace was very fast. We all passed a hearty vote of thanks to Nicholls when he drop kicked a goal and Cooke deserved one, too, for a try between the posts. But even with a try by White, converted by Nicholls, we were still only 14-10 at halftime, for Macpherson scored just before halftime from one of Wallace's many cross kicks.

From the start of the second half, Oxford brought Raymond, one of the best threequarters I have ever seen, into the threequarter line and dropped G. V. Wesche, a forward, to fullback. Then they got stuck in again. First points came to us when McGregor put Maurice Brownlie between the posts for a try which Nicholls converted, but then Oxford struck back. Wallace wrenched the ball away from Robilliard practically on our goal-line and he and Raymond whizzed up to me where Raymond drew me into the tackle before giving Wallace the ball at about halfway. That was a sight to see, Wallace in front and the whole of our team, speedsters and all, flat out to catch him. But he got there and from wide out W. V. Berkeley converted his third goal. Despite all the stories you hear about Oxford as the home of ancient dignity, they can cheer there just as loudly as anywhere, and with every reason their heroes were getting plenty of cheers right now.

At this stage, in fact, the game was in crisis for with one more breakaway try like the last we could have been done for. It was now that Nicholls became the kingpin. First he helped in a try by Steel which he converted. Then, looking at him from behind, I had a unique opportunity to appreciate his tactical genius. He kept calling very loudly for the ball and slamming it down the field into touch. Soon after this try, he called again and when the ball came to him he hesitated exactly like a man picking the right place to aim for on the touchline. The dummy threw off his marker and Mark, as cool as could be, slowly turned around, sighted on to the goalposts, and let fly with the drop kick to end all drop kicks.

Instead of four points, we were now thirteen points ahead and the dropped goal, I think, finally and completely turned the match our way. Just before the end, Dalley cut away and Robilliard ended with a try which Nicholls converted to give him eighteen points for the match - he was in such form that he converted every goal he attempted. All the same, it was a near thing for us. Oxford's "wild

Colonial boys" infused a real Colonial spirit into the whole team. In pace and enterprise, they were our equals. I always regretted that I did not see Scotland use its great threequarter line of Aitken, Macpherson, Wallace, and Ian Smith, not to mention Herbert Waddell, the outside-half who in more recent times has become one of the leading administrators of world Rugby, for I gather that this was one of the greatest of British Rugby history. As is well known, however, the Scottish Rugby Union had decided not to play the All Blacks, and so we were denied what might have been one of the great exhibitions of modern Rugby.

Wales was different from England in at least one respect. It was soon evident that Cardiff had prepared a plan to upset our inside back combination, for W. Delahay, the stand-off half, and C. O'Leary, a loose forward, stood up offside to harass Mill and they pursued these illegal tactics so flagrantly that rough and hard play was provoked among the forwards. In England, the critics of the Sellicks' school would very likely have found us at fault. In Wales, where they really know their Rugby, perhaps better than anywhere else in the world, they were not deceived. Dr Teddy Morgan, the brilliant player who scored the try which beat the 1905 All Blacks, spoke as an expert when he said in the *Western Mail* that "in fairness to the All Blacks, I would suggest that the referee was far too lenient with both Delahay and O'Leary. In my opinion, this fact was the chief cause of the inability of the All Blacks to open up the game."

But we had Nicholls and if ever a match proved Mark's genius, this was it. Despite the close marking and the hard play, we led by 11 to nil at half time from tries by Lucas and White and a conversion and a penalty goal by Nicholls. Then in the second half, Porter, who was now playing in the scrum, got a try which Nicholls converted and this introduced a sour note because the crowd criticised the referee and, of course, the players took their lead from the crowd. I am not denying that Cardiff played out the rest of the match extremely well and the try which Delahay got, though scored from close to the line, was a beauty. But I think it fair to say that in spite of the hardness of the contest and the resurgence of the Welsh, we were decidedly the better team.

I was posted missing that night. I was supposed to go to the Cardiff Broadcasting Station with half a dozen others to perform the haka and to sing two songs in Maori. Somehow, I didn't get there - and I swear I wasn't paralytic drunk, either. Fortunately, another Maori, Major Dansey, who had played for Otago, was present and he masqueraded for me. To people who afterwards said that as a singer I was a very good footballer, I could only say I was sorry, I wished they had heard the *real* me. But then, of course, they might have said that as a footballer I was a very good singer!

London Counties versus New Zealand 1924-25 tour at Twickenham: The teams
(Courtesy Museum of Rugby)

NEW ZEALANDERS:

Back—**G. NEPIA (1)**

Threequarters—

A. H. HART (3) **A. E. COOKE (11)** **K. S. SVENSON (6)**

Five-Eighths—

M. NICHOLLS (12) **N. McGREGOR (9)**

Half-Back—**J. MILL (14)** *Wing Forward*—**J. H. PARKER (15)**

Forwards—

W. IRVINE (18) **Q. DONALD (20)** **M. BROWNLIE (21)** **R. MASTERS (26)**
J. RICHARDSON (23) **R. STEWART (24)** **A. WHITE (22)**

Referee—**Mr. R. A. LLOYD (Liverpool).**

London Counties versus New Zealand: The New Zealand team from the match programme
(Courtesy Museum of Rugby)

15. Sweetest of Victories

They are right who say that revenge is sweet. We beat Wales by 19 to nil, two goals, a penalty goal and two tries to nothing. The score was a point for every year that had passed since 1905, the year that a draw, perhaps a victory, certainly an unbeaten record, was filched from our All Black team. The victory was balm to our national pride. More, it was an inspiration; the ball was thrown about, our backs, our team, attacked and attacked again. We did not play for position for penalty kicks as has sometimes been done by All Black teams of the recent era. We played to cross that enemy goal-line, as often as possible. If, out of that performance, Welsh boys were persuaded of the right ways to play Rugby, were seized with the mystic spirit which pervades a great team in its hour of triumph, then we did more than win revenge, we uplifted the glory of Rugby.

I am sorry if I become a little emotional about this match. It was significant for New Zealand, it was significant for me. From the moment that we of the test squad went to Tenby, a tiny town in Pembrokeshire, to prepare for five days for the match, we were enveloped in a gathering mist of emotionalism. The Welsh at Tenby loved to have us, they praised the way of our daily training, they had us to their homes and in their slyly humorous way they told us that "Wales will beat you." Yet all of the time, they were preparing to commit themselves body and soul for their beloved Wales. When we removed to Swansea on the Friday, the atmosphere of super-patriotism could be cut with a knife. The Welsh came into our hotels, they offered us £10 a time for seats, they told us we were great players and a great team; and all of the time, amid all of the talking, we could feel them thinking: "Wales must beat them, Wales *must* beat them!"

All of this time, the excitement was growing in me, and in the team, too. We who were going to do what our fathers could not do could not restrain our growing jumpiness, no matter how much we tried to be offhand and casual. When I went to bed on the Friday night, it took me a long time, some hours, to get to sleep, though strangely I felt fresh when I woke. All through the Saturday morning, we would find ourselves starting but not finishing conversations, wandering about, sitting still, passing time, conscious always that out in the streets, away at the St. Helen's ground, thousands more were making themselves even more excited than we were. They could take relief in singing, we had to be silent; or, if we could not be silent, we had to try to talk when we had no wish to talk. At noon, they called us to lunch. I had my tea and two thin slices of toast, the others had their underdone steak. Then back to the sitting room, to lounge about until the call came: "Bus, chaps."

By now, I am riddled with nervousness. I want to be left alone, I don't want to talk to anyone. I hate anyone speaking to me or even attempting to speak to me. In the dressing-room, things are a little better. There is something to do while changing and making sure that I am properly togged. But when this is done, I am back with myself again. I can't even bear the masseur coming to ask if I want anything. By this stage of the tour, the team understand my moods, they leave me alone. Bill Irvine, always the jokester, calls out, "Look at the black panther, cooped up in a cage", but even Bill keeps away from me.

And above us, outside, in key with my nervousness, the emotionalism is gripping the 55,000 spectators. They are singing, singing to each other, singing above all for Dear Wales. It is a monstrous volume of sound and yet with my ear for music I know that it is sweet and harmonious an that there is a profound strain of pathos, of pleading, in it. This enormous crowd which could be saying to its team, "Kick them, kill them, murder them", instead is singing,
"Lead me on, Thou great Jehovah,
"Pilgrim through this barren land.
"I am weak and Thou art mighty,
"Hold me with Thy powerful Hand."
And then they turn from *Cwm Rhondda* to *Aberystwyth* and *Calon Lan* and even to *Men of Harlech*. And while this is going on, we twice have to go out to be photographed - Jove! what a business - "Steamship" Dean is reading out cablegrams of good wishes, I am walking about, sitting down, standing up, walking, going to the toilet, yawning. The singing mounts up and suddenly the muscles above my kneecaps are shivering and shaking. It is ridiculous, I cannot stop them. I am conscious, though, of the call to all of us. There is a flurry. I am looking for Cooke to be in front of me in the line and Irvine is looking for me to be in front of him. We must go out this way else, I think, we cannot go out on to the field at all.

Then we emerge on to the field and - is it not ridiculous? - I have no fear at all. My kneecaps have stopped their fluttering, I am completely calm. Why this change, why this silly nervousness for so long beforehand, I cannot explain. It is a part of me and I have to live with it.

But if the fierce emotion has gone from me, it is unrestrained in the crowd. There are bits and pieces before the match - our haka, led by Mill, and an amusing little parody of it, by the Welsh; the refusal of Wetter, the Welsh captain, to accept the ball Richardson has taken on to the field and the refusal of Richardson to accept an old-timer that Wetter offers instead; the intervention of Colonel Brunton, the referee, to make us all take the ball that he wants. And then everything is swamped when the crowd, this huge crowd of 55,000 and the hundreds more who are sitting on the roofs and chimney pots around the ground, rises and begins to sing:
"Mae hen wlâd fy nhadau yn annwyl i mi,
"Gwlâd beirdd a chantorion enwogion o fri;
"Ei gwol ryfelwyr, gwladgarwyr tra mâd,
"Tros ryddid collasant eu gwaed.
"Gwlâd! Gwlâd! Pleidiol wyf i'm Gwlâd.
"Tra môr, yn fur, i'r hoff bau,
"Obydded i'r hên iaith barhau."

This *Land of Our Fathers* is the final supplication, by thousands, by tens of thousands, to Wales to be victorious, to defeat us, to prove that the verdict of 1905 was just and proper. The sounds go into *our* heads and stay there, in my case forever. I can only imagine that their entry into the heads of the Welsh XV sets up such resolution and determination as shall conquer all pain, as shall drive the body long past the point of exhaustion. And now, with the kickoff, there is a vast scream to succeed the singing. All preliminaries are past. Nothing more can be done by anybody except the thirty players themselves. The game is on.

Wales put the ball into play and it was soon to be seen that the Welshmen, particularly the forwards, had in fact been inspired by the high emotionalism of the occasion. They were fast and fiery, their tackling was fierce and with their formation for the day of seven forwards, three halves and four threequarters they were evidently determined to knock us off our game. For the first twenty-five minutes, I thought, to be quite frank, that they had the better of us, though this period contained a penalty goal by Nicholls, a run by Steel which nearly yielded a try and an indication of the terrific strength of Maurice Brownlie when he scored with two men clinging to his back. Nicholls converted this try and with an eight-point lead we were, you might say, sitting pretty.

But the Welsh forwards were still full of fire and fury and it took a good many days for four of us, McGregor, Nicholls Cooke and myself, to recover from the hammering. But it was getting past the first quarter of the game when I, quite unintentionally, affected the whole of the rest of it by temporarily knocking out Wetter.

It happened this way. The Welsh forwards came down the field with the ball at toe. Wetter was in the van. I back-pedalled. It meant loss of ground, but I knew what I was after. I was seeking to drive them to one side and by compelling their attention as I moved I was diverting them from their task of watching the ball. As their eyes shifted from the ball to me, I pounced. I swept in, gathered the ball, shouldered my way through them and got my kick away. I was moving, you must understand, with every ounce of strength and energy that I had. Poor Wetter hit me, or I hit him, on the thigh, the shoulder, perhaps even the head; I don't know. But as I got my kick away, he went down. He had to leave the field for some minutes; when he came back again, by the luck of the gods he led another rush with exactly similar results except that this time, I drove in so hard that I somersaulted back to my feet before I got my kick away, more or less in a reflex action. This time, he was really groggy; for the rest of the game, he could only attach himself, more or less uselessly, to the back of the scrum; and, of course, Wales with fourteen men could have no real hope of defeating our fifteen, the more particularly because our fifteen were so very determined to win this one.

Rain was now falling and our players, having recovered from the initial shock, were gaining the mastery with dribbling rushes by the forwards and passing rushes by the backs. The Welshmen were wonderful in defence, stretching our men out in tackle after tackle. Both Cyril and Maurice Brownlie nearly scored and Parker actually did so, but the pass to him from Nicholls was forward. Then, on the call of halftime, Svenson kicked to touch near the corner-flag and from a hard scramble in the subsequent loose play Irvine scored.

So we were 11-nil at halftime, Wetter was a passenger, and by the feel of things we could not lose.

Nor did we. The Welsh, particularly at forward, made the most strenuous efforts and all Wales could be proud of her heroes, especially Johnson, the fullback, who was a splendid player. But we had the wood on them. Steel nearly got in, only to be finely tackled by Rowe Harding. On the other side of the field, Svenson slipped away on the blindside from a pass by Mill. We were now throwing everything into the attack. So were they, too. The forward struggles were no comradely gatherings by bands of brothers. They were he-men encounters with the devil taking the hindmost - if he could catch him. Colonel Brunton read the Riot Act once and at other times you saw more haymakers than in a dozen professional bouts or in all the golden fields of Hawke's Bay. But the boys were just being boys and all came right in the end. Before that happened, Cooke with his uncanny skill dribbled the ball down the field and on reaching Johnson kicked to his left where Irvine was running in support. Bill kicked on ahead to the goal-line and got there first for the final try which Nicholls converted.

We were great that day. Our forwards were heavy, mobile, and vigorous. Mill was magnificent and so were all of the backs, McGregor in defence particularly and Nicholls in cool direction of the attack. As for myself, I did not please Mr Sellicks, who in the *Morning Post* commented that I "kicked wildly more than once", while he added that Johnson's kicking was "certainly better than Nepia's", but I seemed to please some other people. "Observer" wrote in the *Western Mail*: "Nepia has won distinction wherever he has played in this country, but he has never given a better display than on Saturday. There were times when it appeared that nothing would stay the fierce rushes of the Welsh pack. By sheer strength, they barged their way through with the ball and there stood Nepia alone between them and the desired objective. Wing men dashing to the rescue appeared to have little chance of aiding the youth. Then suddenly, the rush, so typical of the forwards of country, has broken up in a remarkable manner. Nepia creeps forwards and unexpectedly dives at the ball. His judgment is uncanny and his pluck magnificent. He has snatched the ball from the toes of the men and his bullet-like rush has carried him through the mass. By a miracle he has kept his feet, and with the kick, which comes in his stride, he has cleared. There was a gasp from the crowd, which has been in a frenzy because a try had seemed certain, and then there is a cheer for the brave fullback."

Denzil Batchelor was kind enough to say: "How had the boy Nepia the finely-tempered nerves to stand the strain of appearing as target for the day in match after match, the beating off single-handed of the ravening packs and the threequarters line in full cry with his own single pair of whipcord arms?

"He was between short and tall and his thighs were like young tree-trunks. His head was fit for a prow of a Viking long ship with its passionless sculpted bronze features and plume of blue-black hair. Behind the game, he slunk from side to side like a black panther behind bars, like a lord of the jungle on the prowl for a kill.

"This was his concept of his function when the ball came to him: Rollicking first this way and then that, a few yards ahead of a bunched pack of bloodthirsty forwards, he rejoiced in the challenge. A lesser man might win applause by a fly kick to touch or even by going down like the boy on the burning deck, whelmed by destiny in disaster and immortality.

"Not so George Nepia. He leaped at the ball like an art critic snatching at a fault of technique by his best friend. He went to work backwards, a fury of shoulders, elbows and thighs storming through the massed ranks of the opposing pack. Eight to one were the odds which exactly suited him."

These were the players - New Zealand: Nepia; Svenson, Cooke, Steel;

Nicholls, McGregor; Mill; Parker; Irvine, Donald; M. J. Brownlie, Masters, Richardson; C. J. Brownlie, Cupples. Wales: T. Johnson; E. Finch, A. Stock, A. Jenkins, W. Rowe Harding; W. Delahay, J. Wetter (captain), E. Williams; S. Morris, D. Marden-Jones, D. Hiddlestone, D. Parker, C. Pugh, J. Gore, C. Williams.

The Wales versus New Zealand 1924-25 international.
Top: A cartoon from a Welsh newspaper
Below: Headlines about the match
(Courtesy Oma Nepia)

WONDERFUL SCENES AT SWANSEA

WILDLY EXCITED CROWD OF 50,000

16. Saucepans on the Goalposts

We were now on the last lap. Between us and England, the last match in the British Isles, lay Llanelly, 8 to 3, East Midlands, 31 to 7, Warwickshire, 20 to 0, Combined Services, 25 to 3, Hampshire, 22 to 0, and London, 28 to 3. Only in one of these, Llanelly, could we have been beaten; in fact, we might well have been. The great pace of Hart, who ran away from everybody at half-way, presented us with a try and for the other, by Svenson some twenty minutes after the start, we relied on our teamwork as much as on "Snowy's characteristic determination. The rest of the game was Llanelly's. This team with the curious name, which you can pronounce "Thlanethly" if you come from one school or "Clanethy" if you come from another, represents a town which is chiefly famous for saucepans and it is from here that the famous bit of doggerel sung by the Welsh as a song, *Sospan Fach* (Little Saucepan) originates. The goalposts at Stradey Park, though they were very tall, were tipped with saucepans - and how on earth they got them up there, I wouldn't for the life of me know. You are really into the heart of Wales here, for at least in our day there was more Welsh spoken than English. They were very one-eyed, which was forgivable because they had a good team, and they went wild with joy when E. Finch, one of their threequarters, scored. One newspaper said that I was completely hoodwinked by this try. Well, it's all a matter of which paper you read, I suppose. In actual fact, our forwards were waiting opposite the touch judge, about fifteen yards from our goal, for Finch to bring the ball back to throw in when one of the Llanelly forwards strolled ahead about four yards, called to Finch, who threw him the pill. The forward returned the ball and Finch strolled over. A try said the referee, Billie Llewellyn. A try? we said. A try? Come off it, mate. Believe it or not, it was a try; and the Scarlets really got their rag out for the rest of the match. They were inspired by that untranslatable Welsh quality which is called "hwyl" - you can make up your own mind about this pronunciation, but it's something like "wheel" with the "h" put in front of the "w" - and which is, I suppose, fervour augmented by super-determination At any rate, what with "hwyl" here and "hwyl" there, we were just about run over. McGregor and Nicholls couldn't play because of injuries from the test and Cooke played against doctor's orders and then only for one particular reason. "Cookie's" parents actually came from Llanelly, having migrated to New Zealand about three years before he was born, and the Welsh, of course, were wholly delighted that one of our great players was, so to speak, one of their own. They gave him a silver cigarette case, suitably inscribed, and Bert in his reply paid a particular tribute to the captain of the Scarlets, Albert Jenkins, who had played against us in the test. Thirty years later, Terry McLean was in Llanelly when Jenkins enthralled an audience with a description of how he had beaten George Nepia during the game. Frankly, I don't remember it, though Terry tells me Albert got a grand hand when he had finished his description. All I can say is, I am glad he didn't score a try as a result. If he had we'd have been shot. So would I.

I was myself pretty sore all over from the kicks and ha'pence that had come my way against Wales; but there was no question of my standing down. Here, as a personal matter, I would like to mention that my own unbeaten record was becoming, to me, an even greater problem than the team's unbeaten record. For much of the tour, I had roomed with Lui Paewai but when it happened that he wasn't playing in a particular match, he lived a normal sort of life, coming in at odd hours as you are bound to do when you are on tour. With one strain and another, I wasn't, I'll confess, sleeping as well as I would have liked and perhaps my extreme nervousness and irritation before the really big games was evidence of the nervous reaction of one match after another. About this time, Mr Dean and Porter twigged what was happening. For the rest of the tour, I had my own room. It made a difference. I had settled into a routine. I went to bed earlyish before matches, usually about ten if I couldn't find someone to talk to to keep me awake longer, and then I would very often toss and turn until one or two o'clock before I got to sleep. Always on match days I had breakfast in bed and then, later, I would get up and lounge around until my light lunch at midday. I don't mind admitting that I was under strain and doubt that I would have gone through the experience again. It was a relief, a major relief, when a match was done to sit with a beer and to talk and to fool about for a few hours, for then I had peace of mind and could forget the next assignment. I talk of these things only to disabuse those who may have thought, down the years, that I had made up my mind from the beginning to play every match of the tour. I was wanted. It was my duty. That was all.

What a relief it was to go from Wales, where they play such splendid football, where they know so much about the game, where they seem to conspire, as a nation, to beat you, back to Merrie England. East Midlands was good fun, especially for Steel, who got three tries, Cyril Brownlie, who got two, and me, who got five goals from tries. This was at Northampton, where the shoes were made, and we regarded Mr Bostock as one of the nicest of people when, having shown us over his factory, he took us to his sample room and told us to each take the pair of shoes of our choice. Warwickshire was good fun, too; Paewai, who had played well indeed against Llanelly, got two tries here and Steel scored three more. During this visit we booted a ball around on Big Side at Rugby School, the field on which William Webb Ellis originated the game by picking up the ball and running with it, and when we had completed this pleasurable visit we went on to take tea with Mr Gilbert, the man who makes the best Rugby ball that ever was made by the hand of man.

At this stage, we were stale, there was no doubt of that, and there was apprehension among us as we prepared for Combined Services at Twickenham. H. W. Stephenson we had already met as captain of Ireland, A. R. Aslett, who later won several caps for England, was a first-rate centre, and two of the forwards, W. G. E. Luddington and E. R. Gardner, were old hands in the England pack and very doughty ones, too. That great enthusiast for Rugby, King George V, had come along to see us and as an old Navy man he no doubt had his hopes that the Services would do what no other team had been able to.

In the event, our team reacted to the occasion with one of the grandest displays of the whole tour. Morrie Brownlie set sail down the field within a few minutes of the kickoff and four more men handled before Steel ran round behind the posts to dot down. Before halftime, Lucas went in at the corner and J. W. Forrest placed a penalty for them from a kick which hit the bar and bounced over. There was fire, vigour and beautiful tackling on both sides and I gave myself a little pat on the back when Stephenson, who could run like a hare, ended in my arms after a brilliant dash of about fifty yards.

We started the second half with a dream try when Masters caught our kick-out and put the ball to Porter, Maurice Brownlie, Mill, McGregor, Cooke, and Lucas for the latter to score without the ball touching ground. Masters was rewarded later with a try of his own, Steel capitalised one of the really great runs of the tour by our backs and before the end Lucas and Richardson each went over. Thus there were six tries, but between us White and I could only land one goal. It was, otherwise, to my mind, a glorious exhibition and bespoke the great qualities in our team, especially the speed of the backs. It is common talk that we New Zealanders cannot run as swiftly as footballers of other nations, especially Australians and the British. I'll simply say that I have never seen swifter backs than our '24 team fielded. At their best, as they were in this game, they were dazzling.

The fog of war settled over our match with Hampshire at Portsmouth - quite literally. During the second half, a ground mist descended so thickly that you couldn't see ten yards in front of you though by some optical illusion you could see the ball rise above the fog but then lose it as it descended. At one stage, when I was taking a kick at goal, I could see only the tops of the posts, but when I kicked the ball I lost sight of it completely until, again by some curious optical illusion, I saw it passing between the tops of the posts. It was extraordinary. Fortunately, it did not interfere with our play, a feature of which was that those great workhorses, McGregor and Donald, scored tries, McGregor getting two. Hampshire included none other than H. W. V. Stephenson again - by now, so we said, he was speaking with a New Zealand accent - and Hamilton-Wickes, not to mention C. A. Kershaw, the scrumhalf who in the four years before our arrival had formed one of the great partnerships of all time with W. J. A. Davies, whose international career, beginning in 1912, bridged the Great War and ended only in 1923.

They gave us four days' holiday after this match - a gesture that I commend to all organisers of all major tours. We spread all over the face of England, Scotland, and Wales and not to be confined to Rugby was joy indeed. Then, when we reassembled on 22 December, we still had five days of preparation for the match with London Counties. The effect was that we had a break of ten days, a wonderful boon. We went to Deal and because Deal is famous for its golf course we played golf. There were no left-handed clubs for me and I tried to hit the ball right-handed. I tried and I tried. I really did try. But I could not manage. I gave the ball a good kick instead. Cyril Brownlie placed a ball on a tee-peg, swiped, struck the ground at least a yard behind it and shattered his club in three places. He replaced the ball, got another club and had another go. Cyril was a big man, getting on for sixteen stone then, and he had power, bags of power. So he swiped again. The ball was having none of it. It fell off the tee. Sheer fright, we said. Cyril gave it a kick, too. We were no golfers, that was certain.

The Rectory Field, where we played London two days after Christmas, belongs to Blackheath, the oldest club in Rugby and which is called by its supporters simply "The Club". It was a terrible day. There had been rain for a long time beforehand, the wind was blowing, it was cold, by Jove it was cold. I wouldn't have taken a dog out in it myself - but there were 15,000 people present, few of them under cover. Decidedly, the English are mad. London on paper had first-rate players - Hamilton-Wickes, Jacob, the Oxford threequarter, J. C. Gibbs, who almost certainly was one of the fastest men ever to play Rugby, Gracie, the Scotsman, Hillard, the Oxford forward, and a number more of first-class players. We were not at all sure of our chances, but thanks in particular to Mill, McGregor, Nicholls, and Cooke, particularly the last-named, we soon got a grip. There were eight tries, all, oddly enough, by our forwards. Cyril Brownlie got the first after Cooke, high-punting, had caught the London fullback ball and all; Donald got another and Maurice Brownlie got a third, all before halftime. We saw the speed of Gibbs when he ran round our threequarters, booted over my head and won the race to the ball. He could fly, he really could fly.

Cyril Brownlie twice scored after halftime, and Parker, Richardson, and Irvine added the others. Even Mr Sellicks was impressed. "Considering all things," he wrote, "this must be written down as one of the most convincing displays given by the All Blacks since the beginning of their tour. Three months ago, before they had settled down, they were all at sea in conditions similar to those which obtained at the Rectory Field. Their forwards especially seemed unable to adapt themselves to rain and mud; they were always fairly fast but they were by no means clever and their footwork was strictly moderate. Now all this has been changed and on Saturday the forwards played first-class Rugby."

England was around the corner. Back we went to Deal to prepare. We were under no illusions. This was the crucial encounter.

17. Never Forgotten, Never Forgiven

Even after these many years, I find it painful to record the match with England. If there is bitterness in my account, you must forgive me. Between me and my memories of a tremendous struggle which we won by 17 points to 11 there obtrudes always the face of Cyril Brownlie, the man who was ordered from the field before the match was ten minutes old. I can see him setting off from the scene and walking with his head down for the dressing-room scores of yards away. I can see myself running up to protest, Wakefield grimly shaking his head and turning away when Richardson approaches him to intercede, the rest of us bewilderedly asking for an explanation. And still Brownlie is trudging from us. There are 60,000 people in the ground and not one of them can even whisper. In a silence so weird as to be almost frightening, Brownlie goes from us. We come upon him later, at halftime, in the dressing-room. He is sitting upon a bench, still in his togs. Brownlie has been a soldier and a farmer, as both he has become inured to the cycle of life and death that governs our lives. He is a big, powerful, mature man. Yet the tears are rolling down his cheeks.

You carry the lump in your throat for the rest of your life when you think of him sitting there in his loneliness. Poor Cyril! We did our best to comfort him, then, later and for the rest of the life that was cut off far short of his time. We made our first stand, many of us, by refusing to go to the dinner which was held in the evening. We made our second stand by disdaining all approaches from British officials or players over that weekend before we went to Paris. We had, as it turned out, a merry time, strictly among ourselves and we wanted no other company. The upshot was significant. Between the time of our going to Paris and returning to London to prepare for the homeward journey through Canada there was organised by the British Olympic Association at the Piccadilly Hotel a luncheon attended by so many personalities of British sport that out of it there grew the Sportsmen's Club which from time to time now entertains the great sporting teams or personalities who visit London. The Prince of Wales, who had been at the match and who had asked whether it would be possible for Brownlie to return to the field, proposed our health and presented a loving cup; and by the look of the guest list, there had never been a more distinguished gathering in the history of British sport. And Brownlie was there.

The referee was Mr Freethy, the Welshman who had controlled a number of our games. We liked him and I think he liked us. We asked for him for this match, and to that extent were the authors of our own misfortune. What he did was, however, inexplicable. He put Brownlie off the field and then reported Edwards, the captain of Newport, a man whose team had employed the worst of methods against Cooke, to the Rugby Football Union. It was small solace for us to learn in later years that Edwards, because of this report, had not afterwards been invited to play for England. If a man deserved a report, he deserved despatch from the field. We resented, we most bitterly resented, the despatch of Brownlie in any case; but what would cause an official to make flesh of one and fowl of another? This is the thing that sticks in my craw and always will.

In a statement at the end of the game, Mr Freethy said: "In some loose play, the ball had been sent away, and two or three English forwards were lying on the ground. C. Brownlie was a few feet away from them and as he came back he deliberately kicked on the leg an English forward lying face downward on the ground. I had taken my eye off the ball for a moment and, therefore, saw exactly what happened. Previous to this, I had warned each side generally three times and, therefore, I had no option but to send Brownlie off the field. I much regretted having to do this, but in the circumstances I had no alternative but to take this drastic action."

I would think I had as good a view as any of this incident. After a scrum had been formed about 30 yards from our goal-line, it screwed around and some of the English forwards collapsed. Brownlie was standing up when to my horror Mr Freethy patted him on the back and made a sign to order him off. I was horrified. I ran up to ask what was the matter and was told Brownlie had kicked Edwards while on the ground. I protested. It could not have happened. I had seen the whole incident. What Mr Freethy said had happened could not have happened. I am positive about this. When we spoke to Edwards, he denied that he had been kicked. I say no more.

The preparations for the match were thorough. I went through my usual pre-match torture which was varied on the morning of the game by a visit from Ernie Crawford, with whom I was photographed. Scalpers were asking for, and getting, £7 for a ticket. People waited from early morning, if not overnight, for gates to open. The attendance of 60,000 was the largest in British Rugby history. There had been four days of showery and stormy weather and the ground, though reasonably firm, was soft. The sky was overcast. There was no advantage in the quartering wind.

England had the outline of a great team. Hillard was the only newcomer in a most experienced pack of forwards. English people were convinced that Wakefield was the greatest forward in the world and while we could not agree that he was in Maurice Brownlie's class because he had not the power and sheer physical strength of our man he was without doubt a great forward. Blakiston, Edwards, Cove-Smith and Voyce were extremely hard players who did not give an inch of quarter for fear you might take an ell. Tucker's greatest days were to come. Even so, he was already a strong, fiery player. So was Conway. In afterthought, it was strange that Hillard had won a place, for he was wanting in that maturity of physique and know-how which distinguished the others and the several penalties he gave away through over-eagerness, one of them of great consequence to the result, were out of all character in their immature eagerness, with the dour and relentless men who were his comrades. Behind the vanguard, England were also well served. Young had recently been in South Africa with the British team and Kittermaster of the fabulous hands had played flyhalf against us for Cambridge. Corbett was a good West Countryman, a splendid centre, and Hamilton-Wickes and Gibbs on the wings were greased lightning. Only Brough at back and Davies in the centre seemed not to fit naturally into this group, much as Hillard seemed not to fit among the forwards. Davies, to be sure, was a Harlequin and he had won a cap before, but Brough, though later a famous player, especially in Rugby League, had not won a cap and it seemed to us a risk indeed to play an inexperienced and young man in so fatefully important a match.

Wakefield was credited then, as afterwards, with being the originator-in-chief of the attacking loose-forward play which in a generation or so since has been refined into an instrument of torture for the inside backs of modern Rugby. He had primed his men well, for the game had no sooner begun with their kick-out than they were at our throats. Other priming had been done. I will not charge that the English came on to the field to be deliberately dirty but I will charge that they had perhaps not drawn as nice a distinction as might have been done between rough and robust play. One must take notice of Read Masters, a man of innate gentlemanliness, and his remark: "I regret to have to record that the opening stages of this really great match were marred by excessive unpleasantness, but declare with all sincerity that we were the victims rather than the culprits." In the ferocity of the opening exchanges, Mr Freethy seemed to me to do no more than wring his hands in dismay and regret. He issued warnings, it is true - but what are these, when men are flying at each other's throats In this hour of desperate crisis, not so much for us or England but for the game, he wanted in the stature to take command, to compel a proper respect for the laws of the game.

The Brownlie incident came and went and for a time we were knocked completely off our perch. Parker had to join the scrum and we faced seven-eighths of the match with fourteen men, a heavy task indeed against such formidable opponents. Kittermaster and Young, if they wished, could frolic as they pleased, now that the vital chain in our defence was removed.

So it was in this state of disorganisation that we played the first quarter. The yield of it was a try for England, by Cove-Smith. It was a beauty, expressive of clever and experienced play. Voyce bore down on me with the ball at his feet and as I shaped to save he tapped it across my path and over the goal-line. Cove-Smith, who was at his shoulder, scrambled and dived for the try. It was our good fortune that Brough was too inexperienced to make the most of the place kick at goal.

The try passed through our team like an electric shock. The blunders we had been making were shed from our systems. Into the minds of all of us flooded the realisation that if we were to prove ourselves footballers of peculiar distinction, now was the hour. There was born then the New Zealand equivalent of the "hwyl" - a super-spirit, an ultimate desperation, a conviction that we would die rather than yield.

The English defence was superb. Our men went down like ninepins. With their great speed, too, their backs were poised for counter-attack. But nothing could stop us when Maurice Brownlie, picking up in the loose, made a break to put Nicholls, Cooke, and Svenson into a good position. The ball went from one to the other with precision. Cooke snapped into that glorious burst of his before passing to Nicholls and the latter passed to Svenson who scuttled in at the corner. Nicholls all but goaled, for his kick was a poster.

I had been getting a good deal of work and one of my kicks pitched out fairly close to the right-hand corner. Hereabouts, a scrum soon resulted and Mill sharply swept a pass to Steel on the blindside. Steel, a great, heavy, powerful man, barged at the goal-line quite unstoppably. There were outcries when Mr Freethy signalled a try. English players, and hundreds of English spectators, proclaimed that Steel had stepped into touch and Mr Freethy himself consulted the touch judge before making the award. But the touch judge, who was the English nominee, had no hesitation in saying that the run was fair. So we were 6-3. Just before halftime, the score became 9-3. Hillard impulsively rushed offside from a scrum close to the English goalposts and Nicholls thoughtfully went up to take the kick. He was powerfully adjured by Cooke not to miss the goal; but Mark was, as the saying goes, a great money-player and the chips were down for this kick. He did not miss.

If we had felt like flagging, the sight of Cyril Brownlie in the dressing-room restored our vigour. We were not going to let *him* down. By this stage, our situation was more serious. Steel had hurt his leg and against the pace of the flying Gibbs he was a dangerous risk. Parker therefore had to go to the wing leaving White to play as rover to a five-man scrum. There was steam still in our forwards, all the same, and in none more than Maurice Brownlie, who was transfigured. In the twelfth minute of the second half, some thirty yards from the English line, he picked up the loose ball. The spot was almost that from which Cyril had marched to the dressing-room The devil, or the angels, or both, were incarnate in Maurice. He did not so much run at the goal-line as surge at it. Gibbs was hanging on to him full stretch and two other Englishmen had a grasp, but nothing could stop him. It was, without doubt, one of the greatest tries a New Zealander has ever scored. I even like to think that only a New Zealander could have scored it. Nicholls was inspired, as the rest of us were; and from far out, almost at the touchline, Mark placed a beautiful goal.

We were not done yet. White snapped up the ball and after a run passed to Parker, who streaked in for our fourth try. We were 17 to 3, with twenty minutes to play. On we went. Mill went over the goal-line, McGregor did, too, but each was recalled. Nicholls was all but at the goal-line when Brough brought him down.

Now, with the match dying on its feet, our magnificent forwards were slaving off their last gasp. They were dauntless, they were unconquerable, but five or six could not hope to hold eight. The Englishmen began to run. Out went the pass to Gibbs and as he neared me he punted over my head. I raced with him, my elbow somehow crooked into his body - it was really he who was carrying me along - and when the ball bounced in the in-goal area it bounced fortunately for me. Gibbs passed a remark about my elbow, or me, or both. It was not Parliamentary language. Soon he broke away again - Heavens, how he could run! - and this time his kick left me stranded. I felt despair, knowing that I could not race him to the ball. It was then I saw Mill, dandy little Jimmy, sidling quietly up to make the force-down.

We were penalised and Corbett drop kicked a goal. At our last gasp, we penetrated once more into the English 25. We scrummed, and they won the heel. Cooke was out of position and with the overlap they ran the ball to Hamilton-Wickes on the left wing. As he came at me, Kittermaster called for the pass and with the ball in hand he raced far down to the goalposts, every step exciting a yet more thunderous cheer. Conway converted. It was a good try, a fitting try to end a tremendous game; but I will go so far as to say that if this had been a fifteen-a-side match from start to finish we would have won by at least twenty points. Secondly, I will say that it was our great luck that "Pup" Raymond was prevented by injury from playing. Had he turned out, our record would have been in peril. He was an accomplished footballer, more so than any of the English backs.

Poor Cyril is dead. I only wish he were alive so that he could hear from me, at this late hour, the conviction of all of us that he was not guilty.

These were the players - New Zealand: Nepia; Svenson, Cooke, Steel; Nicholls, McGregor; Mill; Parker; Irvine, Donald; C. J. Brownlie, Masters, M. J. Brownlie, Richardson, White. England: J. Brough; R. H. Hamilton-Wickes, V. G. Davies, L. J. Corbett, J. C. Gibbs; H. J. Kittermaster, A. T. Young; A. F. Blakiston, R. G. Edwards, G. S. Conway, R. J. Hillard, J. S. Tucker, R. Cove-Smith, T. Voyce, W. W. Wakefield (captain).

England versus New Zealand: Action from the international at Twickenham on the 1924-25 tour (Courtesy Museum of Rugby)

The Invincibles restaurant at Twickenham
(Photo: Peter Lush, Courtesy Museum of Rugby)

18. Paree and Points South

I was so hungry I could have eaten a horse. I did, too. And enjoyed it.

We were in the restaurant car between Calais and Paris, famished - and baffled because we could not understand the menu. I pointed my finger and put it in my mouth. The stewards understood. They brought us food. It was meat. Red in colour. Delicious to taste.

We scoffed away. Then someone idly remarked how peculiar was the colour, so different from the meat in England. Irvine, the old soldier, barked. "It's horse-meat, you blinking fools," he said. "That's why it's different."

Some of the team put down their knives and forks, got up, faces set stonily, and walked away. Not me. It was food, good food, as far as I was concerned. I announced that, horse or no horse, I was for it.

Next came an egg omelette, cooked in olive oil. Also delicious. I was enjoying mine immensely. Idly, I said to "Bill the Bull", "Funny thing about these Froggy hens, they lay eggs with black spots in them." "Be damned to that," said Bill. "Those are snails and frog legs." More of our team quietly put down their knives and forks and stole away. Not me. So far as I was concerned, there was more for the rest of us.

Paris. What a place. The mob was at the station. Screaming. "Portaire!" "Neekolls!" "Nehpeeah!" The lot. They knew us all.

This was encouraging. But they didn't play fair. They didn't warn me about the traffic regulations. When I got in the bus, I sat next to the driver. He pulled out from the station and hit the road. Give me strength, man, I said, you're on the wrong side. Non, non, he said. In France, the wrong side is the right side. At least, I suppose he said that. My French wasn't too good. All I could see was that we were on the right side and so far as I was concerned, that was the wrong side. So I put my feet on a projection, braced myself and closed my eyes. Mon Dieu, it was *terreebl!* Later, I got used to it - almost. But I never did quite get used to the French drivers. Stirling Moss was in the kindergarten class compared with those garçons.

We spent a week in Paris before our match with Selection Française (French XV to you). It is quite a place. With Irvine as a guide, you could see sights you would never see in Oamaru, Timaru, or even Waipukurau. In fact, I did see sights I have never seen in Oamaru, Timaru, or even Waipukurau.

Perhaps I had better stick to Rugby...

Selection Française scored first. They started passing in their 25 and at halfway Besson, one of their wings, got the ball. He went past me like one of those French drivers.

Mr Winston Churchill was in the audience. I have often wondered since whether he took home his own hat and umbrella. If so, I feel sure that he was the only cool-headed man among the 50,000 present. As Besson dotted the ball down, the sky was filled with hats and brollies, thousands of them, and the cheering rolled from the Pyrenees to the Rhine. It was incredible.

Except for another converted try at the start of the second spell, that was the end of the Frenchmen. Our chaps played magnificently, scoring eight tries in the first half and three more in the second. In order of appearance, the scorers were Porter, Hart, Cyril Brownlie, Hart, Cyril Brownlie, Svenson, Maurice Brownlie, Cooke (halftime), Maurice Brownlie, Cyril Brownlie and Svenson. I goaled two kicks out of six attempts and "Son" White got none out of five - perhaps the sights of Paris were in our eyes. Pelletey, their fullback, and Berrurier, a forward, both had to leave the field, Pelletey, as it turned out, with a broken leg, but the Frenchmen, even without full strength, played with great courage. The place, incidentally, was Colombes Stadium, where they had held "Paavo Nurmi's Olympic Games" only a few months before, and the turf was wonderful.

Did I say the French were excitable? Some time in the second half, one of their players came down the field and I gave him the old one-two crash-tackle. As I got up to turn away, I was kicked, fairly and squarely, on the bottom. I turned around, swearing away at him in English, or Maori, and he said some nasty things about me in French. Meanwhile, Irvine had observed the kicking - it was a good effort too - and as he arrived at speed he clocked the Frenchman with a right, a beauty, under the ear. The Froggy went down like a poleaxed ox. So far, so good, you might say. But we had forgotten those umbrellas. Within seconds, two or three hundred Frenchmen, all armed with brollies, were advancing on us and though my knowledge of French was strictly limited I knew that they were not speaking well of us. The play was on the far side of the field. It was no duty, it was a pleasure, for Bill and me to go back to it at speed.

Paris and Toulouse lie 480 miles apart and when you have travelled from one to the other in a train which for some peculiar French reason has square wheels you take a little time to recover. Hence it was fortunate that we were allowed another week of holiday before our match with France. The sights of Toulouse are not quite the same as the sights of Paris, though they bear some relation. More interesting - perhaps - was the visit to the Pyrenees, when amid wine and speeches we were taken in a train to a height of 6,000 feet to watch skiers and ice-hockey players, after which there was more wine. We all got a kick, too, out of watching Parker, McCleary, West and Robilliard play in a match between old-timers of the Pyrenees and Bayun-Biarritz counties.

Then came the biggest fight of the tour. On the field? Certainly not. The 1924 All Blacks had many strenuous encounters, but the toughest of all was getting into the ground at Toulouse so that we could play the French in the test match. Thousands of people jammed the entrance roadways. We literally had to fight our way into the dressing-rooms. A fence was pushed over and that made for some room - just enough, in fact, for us to scramble through a door in the grandstand. But it was a near thing. We very nearly lost the last of our thirty matches because we couldn't get on to the field to play it.

What a sight the place was! There were 35,000 spectators, far more than the capacity of the ground, and they were even sitting on the dead-ball line. Round about the field, too, there were dozens of French soldiers. Whether they were to protect us from the crowd or the French team from us, I wasn't sure. But I took jolly good care not to get mixed up with any crash-tackles. I could take a brolly on the beanoh, perhaps, but certainly not a bayonet through the vitals; and as far as I was concerned, once a Frenchman, always a Frenchman, even if he was a soldier.

It was a brilliant game. The All Blacks were not as hard and vigorous as they had been in the British Isles, but by now we had acquired such competence, such combination, such split-second switching of the attack, that it had become possible for us to gear our game according to the quality of the opposition. The French, as it turned out, were fine players. Their forwards drove in hard and well, their backs had pace and the whole team was inspiringly energetic. No matter how well we played, we couldn't be sure we didn't have a Frenchman breathing down our necks. But the one abiding difficulty of Rugby that they hadn't yet coped with was finish. They would make a move, build it up, have everything going to split or turn our defence - and then drop the ball, or pass forward, or do something really silly. It was unfortunate, and exasperating, for the players, especially as they had much more of the game than the score 30 to 6 in our favour would suggest; but we were most impressed, all the same. There was good stuff in the team. The basic idea was attack. We were all agreed that the French, one of these fine days, would become outstanding in Rugby.

We scored within the first ten minutes and appropriately it was Porter, in his first international of the tour, who got the try from a movement begun by Mill. Within another few minutes, Steel made a long and swift run to end off a movement involving Maurice Brownlie, Lucas and Cooke. Nicholls goaled from well out. By now, we were in gear and the attacks were strong and varied. It said much for the French quickness and determination that our scores were as restricted as they were. Cyril Brownlie began the third try with a run before he chimed in with Cooke, Lucas and Svenson, "Snowy" being the scorer. Cyril had a hand in the fourth try, too, making a break before sending White off on a long run. Just on halftime, Svenson broke clear and this time Richardson had to get the whip out to make the goal-line.

You could see the qualities in French Rugby by the way their forwards reacted from the start of the second half. For twenty minutes, they really did hammer into us. The reward was two tries, each of which led to hat-throwing. Cassayet, the captain, went over from a quick throw-in at a lineout and only a little later Ribere, another forward, scored from a scrum. This made the score 17 to 6 and the crowd was screaming.

It was then, I think, that you saw the real, the lasting greatness of the 1924 All Blacks. Despite the virtual loss of White, who went off and came back after an injury, the team set to work on victory. Nicholls set us marching down the field and the movement ended with Irvine bullocking over. Cyril Brownlie, Nicholls and Cooke next cooperated and "Cookie" whizzed through. Finally Svenson, after a run, cross kicked and there was Cooke for the catch and the last of the 175 tries. Not a bad total of tries, I would say, for 30 matches. Could they do better these days? Not ... likely.

Nicholls, incidentally, converted both of those last tries. And that was that. The long hard tour was over. And here, for the record, were the teams of the final match - France: R. Chilo; L. Halet, J. Baillette, J. Ballarin, A. Jaurreguy; Y. du Manoir, R. Piteu; A. Cassayet (captain), L. Bioussa, A. Boubee, F. Laurent, R. Montade, A Maury, L. Marcet, A. Ribere. All Blacks: Nepia; Svenson, Lucas, Steel; Cooke, Nicholls; Mill; Porter; Donald, Irvine; M. J. Brownlie, Masters, C. J. Brownlie; White, Richardson. The referee was Major H. E. B. Wilkins, of

England.

The dinner the Toulousians gave us was one of the wonders of all time. Even General Petain, the hero of Verdun and, later, the puppet of Vichy, was present. I rather fancy that by now I had conquered my dislike of champagne. The rest of the team certainly wasn't troubled. It wasn't long before we were all very, very happy.

Six of us decided to leave early to walk to the station. We grabbed our hats and sped away, laughing merrily. There, outside, was one of the sights of all time. Cooke was now *un general de l'Armee Française*. He was, in fact, Petain. At least, he had on the hat, cap, helmet or whatever it was General Petain was accustomed to wearing. As we moved along the street, one Frenchman after another exclaimed. Bert did not notice. It was a hot night. We were perspiring freely. Maybe it was the heat, maybe it was the thought that gendarmes would soon cook Cooke's goose. At any rate, we perspired.

McGregor staggered. He nearly fell. Alas, poor Neil, we said. He should not imagine that his stomach is cast-iron. He will get into trouble that way, the poor Scotsman, we said. But we must not leave him in trouble. Alas, poor McGregor. He must be taken to the station. He must be carried. Harvey, you are the biggest. You must carry him.

It was a hot night. We were perspiring freely. Our General was still out in front. We had a quarter of a mile to go. McGregor on Harvey's shoulder was like a bag of feathers. For a time. We came to the tunnel to the station. You must walk down it. Then up it. It was a hot night. In the tunnel, the air was stifling. McGregor was not now like a bag of feathers. He was like a bag of bricks. On, Ian, on, we cried. The grade in the tunnel, it is slighter than you think. The night air, it is cooler than you think. Remember, Ian, we cried, McGregor needs you. On, man, on!

Harvey puffed and panted on to the platform. As gently as a hen laying its first egg, he lowered McGregor to the platform.

As McGregor's feet touched the ground, he stood upright, bright, smiling, happy. "Thank you, Mr Harvey," he said. "Thank you." The Ride of the Valkyries was a quiet little trot compared with the chase of Harvey after McGregor. We talked of this, and many other things, as the square wheels clacked back to Paris and on to Calais in preparation for the last celebrations in London.

19. Why They Were Invincible

You can bet your sweet life that nothing's ever as good as it used to be, at least in Rugby. The All Blacks who tour the world these days step on a plane at Wellington and forty-eight or seventy-two hours later they are in London, having scarcely had time to learn each other's names. At the end of the tour, they step on a plane in London, whizz off to Vancouver, whizz from there to Honolulu and then whizz home, all inside the space of a week.

Compare these days with ours - with that long, leisurely voyage of six weeks in the *Remuera*, when we got to know each other so well, when we learned, at our team discussions, so much about the foundation of teamwork; with the long week before the internationals, when we could settle to the task undistracted by travel, new people, new experiences; with the wonderful fortnight in France (including the sights of Paree); and finally with the long, leisurely journey home, beginning from Liverpool on 24 January and ending at Wellington on 17 March - a journey over the wilds of the Atlantic, the vast breadth of Canada, into California, Tahiti, and Rarotonga before, at the very last, dear old Wellington opened its arms and its hearts to us. In sum, we were absent from New Zealand for the best part of eight months and I defy anyone to prove that the rush and bustle of today, the pursuit, so it seems to me, of profit out of players, can provide the enjoyment and the relaxation that we encountered.

If I become a little sentimental in this chapter, you must excuse me. I am thinking not so much of an exceptional record as of an exceptional team. That was the thing about 1924 - it was the team, not the player. I was very young and very busy, so that I was not perhaps aware that there was at times some strain. I know now that there were disappointed players and no doubt some of them felt keenly disappointed that they were not more often played. But within them, within all of us, was the feeling that the team mattered more than any of us. Don't for heaven's sake, imagine that we were a bunch of goody-goodies rushing around saying, "No, no, we mustn't do that, it wouldn't be good for the *team*". On the contrary, I think of such moments as the day Mr Dean came down the stairs in a bowler hat - we called it a "bun", or a "hard hitter" - because he was to be presented to King George V at the match in the afternoon with Combined Services. A bunch of the boys waited behind the door and as Stan passed it they swooped. Moments later, the hat had been kicked from one end of the room to the other. There was no course but for him to buy a new one - but for him, as for us, it was all part of the lark. I tell this little story only to emphasise that within the group there was a real, a tremendous affection. There was no outsider. You could say that, in the best possible sense, we grew as a group to love one another; and this was our strength, for out of the feeling came the trust and faith and willingness which made us, I maintain, the greatest Rugby team I have ever seen. Perhaps it is true that some of the modern forward packs are bigger than ours was - but ours had *fire*. Perhaps it is true that there have been great backs in modern teams - but ours was a great *backline*. And between those fiery forwards of ours and those brilliant, brainy backs, there was built such a coordination and combination as I have never elsewhere seen. After all, *I* do speak with an expert voice on these things. I saw every game, from the most advantageous position any critic could possibly have, and I was able to weigh, in relation to my own play, the qualities which were being developed in front of me. Could I pay a higher tribute than to say that in many of the games of the tour I had an armchair ride - because of the ability of the men up front?

The peculiar quality which the team developed and to which so many things contributed - the length of our touring together, the personality of Mr Dean, the restrictions which we applied to ourselves because we were considered to be too responsible and adult to need restrictions applied to us - stemmed from people like Richardson and Nicholls, the one so durable, the other so incredibly cool, calculating and clever. Most of all, speaking for myself at any rate, it stemmed from Porter. I do not need to tell you again that I was very young and unsophisticated and that, as such a player, I suffered as much as the next man from tensions and doubts and fears that I would not be good enough. Under a harsh, demanding captain, I could have been broken, my confidence could have been shattered. Porter never reprimanded, he only encouraged. I had, I remember, done some very silly thing indeed. "Never mind, 'Hori'," Cliff said. "We are only human beings. We all make mistakes." If he had only known, those words were as kind as any I have ever heard. They exemplified what I have said before about the '24 All Blacks. We were bound in all things at all times by all of those qualities which are implicit in that very simple little word: Trust.

London did us very proud indeed. The farewell luncheon organised by the British Olympic Association was the grandest occasion of this sort we had ever seen. These were still early days after the Great War and we all knew a good deal about General Sir Ian Hamilton, of Gallipoli, General Sir William Birdwood, of the Anzac Corps in France, General Sir Alexander Godley, of "Make them run, Alex" fame, who were at the top table. Then, elsewhere, there were men like Harold Abrahams, who had not long since won the 100 metres at the Olympic Games in Paris, J. H. Taylor, the famous English golf professional, Steve Donoghue, the jockey, P. G. H. Fender, the cricket captain, Ernest Barry, the world sculling champion, Jimmy Wilde, the boxer, Arthur Porritt, the New Zealand runner, Tom Newman, the champion billiards player, A. R. F. Kingscote, of lawn tennis - wherever you looked, you saw a champion of some sport or other. And to top off, there was the Prince of Wales to offer the toast to us and to say, among other things, that "combination, efficiency and fitness are the secrets of the wonderful success the All Blacks have had". In our eyes, he was quite a boy, was this "Prince Charming"- and it really was a moving moment for us when he presented Porter with a loving cup from English sportsmen.

Later that day, Sir James Allen, the High Commissioner for New Zealand, presented us with another loving cup, this one on behalf of the 400 New Zealanders living in Britain and of whom about 300 were present. This was a beautiful trophy which bore two inscriptions, the one a tribute to New Zealand and the other, in verse, a tribute to us. The one said:

"A loving cup from New Zealanders in the Old Country to the New Zealand Rugby Union, given in remembrance of the Tour of the New Zealand Rugby Football Team through England, Ireland and Wales in the winter of 1924-25. Record of Matches: Won 28, lost 0."

The other, which was written by the Hon. William Pember Reeves, politician, historian and a former High Commissioner in London, contained the following, which I think all of us of the team could still recite at the drop of a hat:
"To the shining leaf and the jersey black,
To the journey without defeat,
To the mighty heart of the striving pack,
And the runners with flying feet.
This loving cup, drink, drink in turn,
While memory stirs each breast,
And lift it high to the Silver Fern,
And the record which beat the best."

Each of us, to our great delight, received a replica of this cup. These were moving moments, these last hours in Britain, and they are crystallised for me in two or three particularly keen memories. Pember Reeves in his verse, *The Last of the Twenty Eight*, wrote:
"Kia Toa! New Zealand! See
Nepia guards the gate.
A rock and a house of defence is he,
A tino tangata great."

In later years, Denzil Batchelor was to write: "When I hear others debating whether pawky Drysdale, with his neatly-devastating tackle and crisp relieving kick, or Owen-Smith or Crawford, or H. B. Tristam himself will play in due course at fullback for the Kingdom of Heaven v. The Rest, I turn to stone. It is not for me a question of whether Nepia was the best fullback in history. It is a question as to which of the others is fit to loose the laces of his Cotton Oxford boots."

And perhaps the one I like best of all is told by Read Masters about the visit made by a few of the team, but not unfortunately, myself, to the King's College Hospital, where Porter inscribed a plate, "The New Zealand Bed", at the head of a cot in one of the wards. One little boy, born a cripple, said to Masters: "Is George Nepia in the party? I have read about his wonderful play, and I would like to see him, please." I wish I had been able to talk to that little boy. When you are fit and strong and, so they say, a great player, you come back to earth, you become very humble, when you talk to children who bear their afflictions very much more bravely than you when you perform your so-called great deeds. I wish I had been there to tell him what I thought of him, rather than to hear what he thought of me.

Action from the 1924-25 tour: The ball is passed away from the scrum
(Courtesy Oma Nepia)

Action from the 1924-25 tour: Porter dribbles the ball away from a scrum
(Courtesy Oma Nepia)

20. The Invincibles Come Home

There were times, I'll admit, when I would have been glad to exchange the S.S. *Montlaurier*, despite her 29,000 tons, for a fast modern aeroplane, for of her eight days on the 2,747 miles of the Atlantic with us on board no fewer than three were spent ploughing through heavy seas which crashed over the forecastle and bashed into the bridge before they fumed back to join the vast waters. It was during one of these three days that, at the dinner-table - and it was a good dinner, too - we suddenly heard a tremendous bang! bang! China and crockery on our table was smashed and there was pandemonium. We all, of course, stood up in alarm. All except one man, the ship's officer. "Everything is perfectly all right," he said. "There is nothing to worry about." Maybe not, for him. But that's no good to the Maori. Too far to swim.

Snow was falling heavily and the temperature was 15 below zero when we reached the port of St. John, in New Brunswick, on 2 February 1925. Eight days later, having completed 3,527 miles by train, we were in Vancouver. It was an enthrallingly interesting and comfortable journey. Often, at nights, we would be shunted off to a siding, so that we could be entertained in some town or city. Meantime, the accommodation was almost too good for a train and the meals were delicious. At an early meal, I asked for fish, as an entree. The waiter staggered in with a whole fish very nearly big enough to pull us, and the *Montlaurier*, through the eye of the storm. This was typical of the treatment we were given. During one of the breaks in the journey, at Calgary, we were royally entertained and at the ball in the evening, most of the 2,500 present were clothed, men and women, in cowboy style. We were led into the ballroom by Ike Ruttle, who was a rootin', tootin' son of a gun of the wild, wild west, and Ike, believe it or not, was mounted on a big black charger. As I remember it, the horse looked bored. Banff gave us two days of skiing and ice-skating and winter swimming sports in baths serviced by a warm sulphur spring and I wouldn't be surprised if they are still laughing, those people of Banff at the ice-hockey match we played against each other. We kept on going down before a hand had been laid on us - and did we go down!

Onward through the Rockies and the fabulous experience of two tunnels, one 3,255 feet long and the other 2,922 feet which describe complete circles. Onward to Vancouver where the Mayor greeted us and the band led us through the streets to our hotel. The tie here, as in all parts of Canada we encountered, was not Rugby, it was the kinship of Empire - a salutary memory, especially in these days, when it is not done to speak of the Empire at all.

We played two representative games in British Columbia defeating Vancouver by 49 to nil and Victoria, which is at the southern end of the huge Vancouver Island, by 68 to 4. Robilliard scored four tries in each match, in both of which our pace and switches completely bamboozled our opponents. A centre with the unlikely Rugby name of Brynjolfson drop kicked the only goal against us. For our Vancouver match, the attendance of 9,000 was the largest ever to witness an outdoor sports activity in the city and at Victoria there were another 8,000. By way of a farewell gesture, we picked up sides between the North and the South

Islands to play a farewell exhibition match, eight Vancouver men coming in to make up the numbers, and a pretty willing go yielded a win for North by 25 points to 14. Incidentally, I broke my duck against Vancouver by scoring a try. There were many other times during the tour when I could, I am sure, have scored. But I had my job to do - and why spoil the broth which someone else is so successfully cooking?

Apart from the last, these, as you may gather, were easy games. Yet it was at Vancouver that we played one of the hardest matches of the tour and for it suffered the loss of Richardson, with a broken leg, and Porter, with five stitches in a cut over the eye. The match, which was not a match, was played the day after our arrival in Vancouver. It was just on four weeks since we had last played, we had done a good deal of travelling and I suppose we just had to let off steam. Anyway, we picked up sides and in the presence of a few hundred spectators got cracking. What a game! You would have thought it was the grand final of the world championship. I seemed to have to crash-tackle one forward after another and as far as I could see everybody was crash-tackling everybody else. Talk about loving comradeship and trust and all the rest! I was reminded vividly of the encounters we Maoris played in the Maori meeting-hall at Dannevirke. Actually things got a little *too* serious and there were several casualties. But once the game ended, we were back to normal. The natives were shaken, all the same. I heard one chap say to another, "If they do that to *themselves*, what are they going to do to *us*!"

Now the tour was starting to run down. First, there was an 1,100-mile rail journey from Vancouver to San Francisco, made at a mean speed of twenty miles an hour in trains with elliptical wheels driven by sadists who hated their fellow-men, more especially in the darkest hours when the fellow-men were trying their best to sleep. But there were sidelights, particularly a visit to the top of a forty-two-storey building in Portland and a ferry trip over the Bay of San Francisco, before we took ship in the *Tahiti* and turned southwards for the Southern Cross and Aotearoa. There were diversions - the island of Tahiti, with a champagne lunch at four o'clock in the afternoon, and glass-bottomed boats in which you could see divers walking on the bottom, spearing fish; the island of Rarotonga, where we were marooned for two days because the *Tahiti* had to stand off until the gale blew out and where, during billeting, we all got drenched to the skin while waiting in the rain to see if it would be possible to pull back to the ship.

And then, on St Patrick's Day, at about ten o'clock in the morning, it was Wellington. I don't really know what we had expected. A bit of a crowd, perhaps, some speeches, a civic welcome, perhaps even a State welcome - but nothing, you understand, too much out of the ordinary. What an experience! The newspapers went crazy. So did the people. I rely on an old report to tell me that there were 40,000 in various parts of the city to see us. There were certainly 5,000 on the Pipitea Wharf. The welcome was quite unbelievable, then and all over. In the band that played *See the Conquering Hero Comes* the trombonist had stuck a red balloon at the end of the slide and every time he pumped the balloon danced wildly up and down. We had to give our haka, once, twice, a dozen times. Said Mr Mitchell, the chairman of the Harbour Board: "You have been the greatest asset, the greatest advertising medium that this country has ever had, excepting, perhaps, our Expeditionary Force at the Front." Our cars were decorated, "PORTER AND HIS GALLANT MEN VICTORIOUS EVERYWHERE", and at the Grand Hotel a large sign said, "WELCOME BACK TO THE HOME GOAL". The Mayor of Wellington, Mr R. A. Wright, told us we were heroes, more or less, and someone said, "Good on you, 'Monkey'." The Prime Minister, "Bill" Massey, said much the same thing at a State luncheon and at the farewell ball that night, when Badeley presented Mr Dean with a tantalus and White presented Porter with a silver rose bowl, the world and his wife also made it plain that for the time being the world was ours. A cartoonist, M. King, inscribed a cartoon "In Memory of the Pre-Tour Critics Who Croaked (once too often) 1924-25".

When Porter tried to reply to the presentation the emotion which so visibly gripped him was the heartfelt feeling of all of us. The same emotion gripped us again when on Wednesday 18 March, we began to part. There were tears, I don't mind telling you, and they were not the sort the crocodile sheds. By gum, what it would to be young again, to take on such a tour, to endure, to win, to know the best in the best of men! Perhaps it is true that, in some things, you live only once.

The Wellington reception was not the last for Paewai and me, nor, I suppose, for the rest of the team. Lui and I were carried shoulder-high from the railway station at Dannevirke. On the next day, the six Hawke's Bay players were given yet another welcome for heroes by the public of Napier. Nuhaka, where Lui and I went with my father and uncle-in-law, let its hair down for us; and then, for the moment, the situation became normal.

Or almost. The two of us went with my father and uncle to Gisborne on business of my father's and while there we were introduced to Apirana Ngata, the Maori leader, who asked the two of us to play in a Rugby match at Tiki Tiki on Anzac Day, my twentieth birthday. A big *hui*, Ngata said, was to be held at the church which had been built as a memorial for Maori soldiers killed in World War I.

When the time came, Paewai could not be present. I went to Tiki Tiki, the home of two Maori All Blacks, Pine Taiapa and Wallace Poi, and there I was given a reception by the Ngati-Porou people which would have been fit, I am quite sure, for a king. There were thousands of Maoris present, more than I had ever seen at any one place, and they were real Maoris, too. Someone began a haka at the reception. It was a real haka, bloodcurdling enough to make your hair stand on end. I am almost sure mine did.

I said to Pine Taiapa, "What sort of football ground have you got?" "As good as Athletic Park, Wellington," he said. "Ho, ho," I said, "that will do me." I think afterwards that Pine may be the big liar. The ground in fact is surrounded by manuka scrub. You have to fight your way through it. But as I plunge out of the scrub on to the ground, I see that people are coming from all parts all fighting their way to see the match; and all of them, willingly, are paying 10s. a head - a thing they didn't do at Athletic Park, willing or otherwise.

I played for Waiapu against Y.M.P., a Gisborne team which had been formed by the late Parekura Tureia, and in spite of lack of practice I seemed to do pretty well. At least, no group came to do a haka in front of me as a warning.

There was a ball in the evening. I went, of course, supposedly as a guest of honour. Many were present. During the evening, I was introduced to a young Maori girl, Huinga Raupani Kohere, whose father, Lieutenant Henare Kohere, had died of wounds in France.

She was the most beautiful girl I had ever seen.

I could say that this was another story. But it wasn't, and isn't. Within little more than a year, we were married. She is still the light of my life and the most beautiful woman I have ever seen. And she will figure, if only in the background, in most of the rest of my story.

The homecoming from the tour of the Invincibles was an experience ever to be treasured. But I know now, as I have for many years since in fact, 25 April, 1925, what the best part of it was.

21. Cured by Kowhai

For a few days between the winter and the spring, the kowhai blooms like gold in the New Zealand bush and to us Maoris it is a tree of peculiar importance because of its place in the changing of the seasons. It happened in 1925, while I was ambitiously trying to demonstrate to all that the reputation I had won in other countries was justified and while, too, my mind was much taken up with Huinga Kohere, that the kowhai became of particular personal importance to me. I would go so far as to say that it saved my career.

From Tiki Tiki and that momentous meeting at the ball, I returned to Dannevirke to engage in club Rugby and to try to play the kind of game I had managed with the All Blacks. As it turned out, my first big appearance was not at fullback but at second five-eighth. That was where I was put by the Hawke's Bay selector, Norman McKenzie, for the Ranfurly Shield challenge by Wairarapa at Napier on 3 June. I was very happy, I may say, to be in the backline with Mill and Paewai and it was a fact that Norman was a little embarrassed because two of his first-line backs, Jackie Blake and Tommy Corkill, had been selected for the All Black team which was chosen (exclusive of our "Invincibles") to tour in New South Wales. Nevertheless my choice in the position - which caused, as was to be expected, some discussion - was one example of Mr McKenzie's stubborn-mindedness in selecting teams. He remained sole selector for Hawke's Bay for many, many years and his team of the mid-20s was without question the greatest provincial side ever to be fielded in New Zealand, but like any other man he had his foibles and I rather think my field placing against Wairarapa was one of these. The fact was that just as Norman could never forgive me for later turning to League, so he could never quite forgive himself for having failed to recognise, though he knew my abilities better than anyone, that I had possibilities as a fullback. Add to this that in the days I am talking about he could be very sharp-tempered and that he was all pins and needles before and during a big game and you have some idea of his moods and their complexity. In this, he was a contrast with his brother, Ted, who was also a very able selector indeed but who was even-tempered and urbane of temperament.

At any rate, we won this challenge by 22 to 3 and my score was a goal from a try. In due course, a few weeks later, I was chosen for the North Island - as fullback - in the annual match with the South. The game was played at Invercargill on 25 July and I placed two goals from tries while we were winning by 16 to 5. It was perhaps a point of interest that only seven of us on each side came from the Invincibles and a further point was that a flank-forward of the South Island team, the Reverend G. V. Gerard, some years afterwards was made a Bishop and as such was taken prisoner during the fighting in the Western Desert.

But the point of greatest interest to me was the injury I suffered in tackling Neil McGregor too late in the game for any replacement to be necessary. His elbow struck my thigh and burst a blood vessel. The medical men told me it was a haematoma and said there was nothing to worry about. They might have been right - but I was conscious of the fact that the left leg had stiffened immediately after the collision and that I could not walk properly on it.

Norman McKenzie was as worried as I. He brought me back from Invercargill to Napier for treatment by a masseur, Hildebrandt, who had a reputation as one of the best physiotherapists in the country. While under this treatment, which went on for a fortnight, I played, as fullback, in a shield challenge made by Canterbury and which we won by 24 to 18, but I could not play against Southland three days later in a match forever famous because during it the referee, Mr Bill Meredith, of Auckland, told W. E. Hazlett, the nineteen-year-old forward from Southland, "Now then, Hazlett, you leave *Mr* Brownlie alone!"

It was not, in fact, for another fortnight that I could again play. Meanwhile, these were important days. Hildebrandt worked on me twice daily for a fortnight without real improvement. He even tried Turkish baths with the idea of heating my whole body so that the bruise would come out. Finally, he said: "George, I don't know what to do. I have tried everything. Nothing has happened. I'll have to call in a doctor."

In came the doctor. He examined the leg very carefully. "I will have to operate," he said. "The blood has congealed. If it is not taken away you could get blood-poisoning," "No knife for me," I said flatly. "I'm off."

I had already been told by Lui Paewai's mother that she would treat me. Kowhai, she said. The bark of the kowhai. That is what you need. She met me at the train at Dannevirke and we drove to the farm at Tahoraiti, a few miles out. There, in a stand of bush there were hundreds of kowhai trees. Mrs Paewai told me what I must do. Only the bark facing the rays of the sun was to be taken from the trees. Then we started. Not until we had filled two big sacks with bark did we stop. Later, I was told to cut the strips into short lengths of about a foot and to hammer each length until it was bruised. Next the strips were put into a copper full of water and for two or three hours I kept the water at the boil until it had turned to a dark tan in colour. This was ladled into a bath and as soon as the temperature was right I stripped off and lay full length. A full hour I stayed there before Mrs Paewai returned to inspect the leg. By now, it was discoloured in many places. When she went out of the room, I heard a bottle break. When she came back, she made me hold my leg out of the water. In two of her fingers, she held a smallish piece of glass and with this she started to dab my thigh, cutting little nicks all around the leg from the knee up.

More of the hot bark water was added. I must remain in the bath, Mrs Paewai said, for another hour.

I slept. When I woke, the water had turned a deep dark shade of brown. The colour seemed to be coming to the surface from my leg. I called out to Mrs Paewai. As she came in, I lifted my leg. From out of all the little nicks there was oozing dark blood. She was jubilant. She cried out in Maori, again and again, "Kua pai tou waewae" (your leg is better).

You will have no more worry, she said. In a week's time, you will be playing. There will be no more trouble. What a contrast, I thought. A Pakeha doctor had told me I would not play again during the season. The injury is too serious, he said. A Maori woman, using Maori treatment, had cured me. Play soon, she said.

Back in Napier, I showed the leg to Mr McKenzie and to Hildebrandt. Only here and there could you find trace of the nicks. The majority were healed. Mr McKenzie was pleased. Hildebrandt was ecstatic. "It is a miracle," he said. "I did not tell you, but I knew your leg was in a bad way. A very bad way. I doubt that an operation would have helped. I was almost certain your playing career was finished."

Not with Maori methods. On 22 August, only fourteen days after I had played against Southland, I played at Hastings against Taranaki - we won by 28 to 3 - and a fortnight later I took part in one of the most famous of shield matches. Hawke's Bay took the trophy to Wellington and justified the journey by winning a magnificent match by 20 points to 11, but in the minds of all who saw it the match was principally memorable for the try which Jimmy Mill and Albert Falwasser engineered between them. The game had not been going long when Hawke's Bay heeled from a scrum five yards from their goal-line. Mill whipped back over our goal-line and then curved out to the blindside, where he sidled past S. L. Bedell on the Wellington right wing. As Mark Nicholls came across for the tackle, Mill passed to Falwasser and the latter ran out of our 25 up to the Wellington fullback, N. A. Walters, just short of halfway. Albert now punted ahead, clapped on the pace and, gathering in the ball from the bounce, set off for the Wellington goal-line. There were 25,000 New Zealanders present and I'll swear they all screamed like Frenchmen as Falwasser reached for the goal-line and scored his sensational try. (Being Wellingtonians, the crowd, I will admit, did not throw hats or umbrellas - but if Falwasser had been a Wellingtonian, they might have.)

In spite of this beginning, we had the devil of a struggle for a long time, mostly because Nicholls was in such wonderful form in the Wellington backline and it was only in the last quarter that our forwards, or rather our whole team, took command. The score was 6-all at halftime and after ten or fifteen minutes of the second half Wellington led by 11 to 9. Strange as it may seem, we were saved by blue dungaree shorts - or rather, by the man in the blue dungaree shorts. This was Maurice Brownlie. Though they were not uniform, he had always worn these when playing for the Bay and being Maurice he was able to get away with it. For the match with Wellington, he had, however, given way and turned out in black shorts. At halftime, he rushed to Norman McKenzie. "Where are my blue shorts'" he said. Norman fished them out, Maurice put them on and with his dynamic leadership restored - because of the blue dungaree shorts - we progressed to victory.

One of my happy memories of this season of 1925 is that Jack Harris, the man who ought to have been in the 1924 All Blacks, at last won his cap. I had done well enough before and after the injury to justify so it seemed, selection for the All Blacks who were to play one test against a touring New South Wales team at Auckland on 19 September. This is one of the matches I vividly recall. All of the All Blacks but Arthur Lomas, a hooker originally from Thames, and Innes Finlayson, a tremendously tall flank forward from North Auckland, had been members of the 1924 team. The Australians had many fine players. Lawton we had met when he played for London. Meagher, his partner, was a fine scrumhalf, very quick and sturdy. Crossman, whom I still regard as one of the finest wings I have ever seen, was partnered by other speedsters in Bowers and Morissey. Judd, Ford and Blackwood were experienced forwards and Laycock was a good one, too, though he came from Walcha, away out in the sticks of New South Wales.

It has been said that this was the greatest All Black team ever fielded in New Zealand. Who could argue such a suggestion? While it is, I think, true that New Zealanders never really do see the best of All Black Rugby unless they journey abroad, there have been some wonderful displays down the years -the final test against the British team of 1930, the third tests at Christchurch with the 1956 Springboks and the 1959 Lions, the second test with the Australians at Dunedin in 1936 come immediately to the mind - and it would be presumptuous for me to extol my team above all others. But when you find a team, in an international, capable of carrying a kick-out to a try without the ball touching the ground, capable, too, of scoring no fewer than eight tries, it is evident that you are encountering a team of exceptional quality. That was what we did that day - and for good measure, Nicholls placed goals to six of the tries. We won by 36 points to 10 and I would count myself one of the most fortunate of All Black fullbacks, to have such brilliance in front of me.

Thus the season of 1925 came to an end. It was the end, too, of my association with Dannevirke, for I soon moved back to Nuhaka, to join the team that once would not have me, even as a junior.

But it was not the end of my affection and respect for the kowhai. Whenever I suffered injury, I always resorted to the treatment Mrs Paewai had given me, always with success. To this day none of my old injuries affect me. I tell the story, to illustrate the powers of the plant, of the player, a Maori who broke his leg in a club match at Tiki Tiki and who was told by his doctor, a Pakeha, that he would not play again that season. The player was given my treatment. Like me, his injury responded. The healing of the break was hurried by the kowhai treatment. He played again, well before the end of the season.

You may disbelieve, even laugh, if you like. All I say is, ask any elders among the Maori people. One and all will tell you that the kowhai is supreme for its curative powers.

22. A Year of Conflict

If Sherlock Holmes were still alive, I would willingly employ him to elucidate for me the mysteries of 1926. In many ways, it was a good year for me. On 6 May, I was married to Huinga Kohere in the Memorial Church at Tiki Tiki by her uncle, the Reverend Poihipi Kohere, and Canon Arthur Williams, and this, needless to say, marked this year out above all others. During this season, too, I played for Hawke's Bay in that series of matches in which we defeated Wairarapa by 77 to 14, Wanganui by 36 to 3, Wellington by 58 to 8 and Auckland by 41 to 11 - the greatest string of performances ever put up in the Ranfurly Shield competition - and for me, as for all others who took part, there was glory in these performances.

But this was a year with a cloud and I do not remember it too kindly. This was the year that New Zealand Maoris, for the first and only time, made a tour to Europe and when, for reasons which I shall explain, I was not of the number, though I had been chosen, some injurious criticisms were made of me. It was even said that I was so jealous of my reputation that I would not allow myself to tour abroad with an inferior team. Most remarkably, the team was at one of its final receptions when Mr S. S. Dean, as chairman of the New Zealand Rugby Union, read out a telegram to say that I was not available. It was signed, he said, "George Nepia". The point is, I never sent that telegram. I never wanted not to be with the team. The cause of Rugby, of Maori Rugby, lay much closer to my heart than my own reputation in the game.

That is why I say, if Sherlock Holmes were living at this hour, I would ask for his services. The trails are cold, but surely not too cold for such a man as he. Even now, nearly forty years on, I would like to have the mystery explained.

There is even another mystery Sherlock could unravel in this important year of my life. He could tell me what made the referee think I had acted so badly that I deserved to be ordered off.

For ordered off I was, quite early in the season. I was the captain of Nuhaka. It was a tough team. Rugby is always tough in Nuhaka and the team this year played the game much in the way we Maoris trained in the meeting-house at Dannevirke, much in the way the '24 All Blacks played each other when we had our first training run at Vancouver. We had our reward, for we won the Wairoa sub-union championship for the season and thoroughly deserved to, too. But it was still a great shock to me when against Athletic I was sent off. Two players from each side were having an argument and throwing punches at each other. I dashed forward to intervene, for I never got much fun out of seeing this sort of thing happen. To my astonishment, I had no sooner intervened than I was thrown out of the game and at the next meeting of the Wairoa sub-union I was stood down for two playing Saturdays. Well, well. That took a bit of explaining to the new Mrs Nepia. Huinga was teaching at the Rangitukia Maori School and I, too, lived in this district, returning each weekend to Nuhaka to play my Rugby. During the winter, I was busy with arrangements to buy a farm in Rangitukia and in the spring Huinga and I settled on the place. The farm carried ewes as well as dairy cows and on one of my last visits to Nuhaka before finally going north I took with me twenty-five or thirty cows I had bought from my father. This was not the sort of place where you sat on the verandah and watched the sheep making you a fortune. It was rough country and I could see some years of hard work in front of me before it was put into the shape I wanted. But I was young and strong. Huinga was with me and the world seemed a very good place to me.

By this time, most of the football of the season was over and my only real misfortune was to miss the Ranfurly Shield match in which Hawke's Bay, late in September, took the trophy to Canterbury and retained it against a very determined challenge by only 17 points to 15. Lui Paewai played in my place and from all I ever heard our chaps had a tremendous battle before they got home. Since that time, no shield holder has ever taken the trophy to another union. What a pity this is. The good that some of the great shield teams since World War II - Otago, Wellington, Canterbury and Auckland - could have done by the gesture would have far outweighed the risk of defeat.

Quite early in the season, we Maoris became involved in the trials for the selection of the Maori team which between 17 July 1926 and 9 February 1927, played forty games in New Zealand, Australia, Ceylon, France, England, Wales and Canada, winning thirty, drawing two, losing eight and scoring 741 points to 255. We of the East Coast areas went into camp for a week at Manutuke for expert coaching by Jack Hall, who had been a star of Maori Battalion Rugby in France, and afterwards we played in a trial at Gisborne. New men had come along of the likes of Rangi Harrison, a halfback, Naera Reihana, a great, big fierce-looking front-row forward, Api Crawford, a fifteen stone lock, Bill Lockwood, a fine wing, and Tom Dennis, another forward, and I thought all of these, but especially Harrison, were good enough for selection. After a further trial at Palmerston North, however, Crawford, Dennis and Lockwood were the only ones from the district who were chosen - not excluding me, that is.

I was not available for the first match of the tour, against Auckland, and which the Maoris won by 13 to 12, but it was while the players were at Auckland that I telegraphed Mr Ned Parata, the manager, to tell him that I would join the team in Wellington and to ask him to tell me the date of departure for Australia. I was at Rangitukia, which is or was remote, but not as remote as all that. At any rate, not having heard from Parata, I set off. I travelled all day by service car - and travelling on the Coast in those days really was rugged - and then I travelled again the next day to Napier to connect with the train to Wellington. Imagine my astonishment, and anger, when at Napier I learned from Norman McKenzie that the ship carrying the team had actually sailed that day.

Norman, I may say, was beaming with delight. He had not wanted me to go, he said. Hawke's Bay had a big season ahead and he wanted me. From his point of view, this was fair enough. Over the next few weeks, however, when I began to hear the whispers against me I myself was not so happy. Certain members of the selection committee, so it was said, and some or all of the touring team, had put it about that I had deliberately missed the ship because I did not want my reputation marred. Nepia, it was said, had a swollen head. He did not think the Maori team good enough for him.

What lies people will tell when they don't know the facts! Let me say straight out that I had every intention of touring with the team. This is surely the whole answer. Not until 1961, thirty-five years afterwards, did I hear, quite casually, of the most damaging piece of all of the evidence against me. In Gisborne on this day, Tom Dennis and I were chatting over the tour he had made and it was then that he recalled the last gathering at Wellington and the moment when Mr Dean had stood up and read out the telegram which said that I was unavailable and which purported to carry my signature. I am, I confess, baffled. I have no idea of the origin of this false message. My only regret is that I did not know of it in the days when Parata, Sir Apirana Ngata and other men of importance in Maori Rugby and Maori affairs were alive. With or without Sherlock Holmes's assistance, I would soon have got to work to find the enemy against me.

Peace! That team had a fine tour. Many of its players, W. P. Barclay, the captain, Falwasser, "Wampy" Bell, Willy Shortland, Sam Gemmell, Bill Rika, were outstanding. They played Maori Rugby, which is the only kind of Rugby Maoris ever ought to play, and they increased our *mana*. I wish that our people could have the experience of other grand tours like this.

So to the Ranfurly Shield. It was during the second spell of the match with Wairarapa, after we had led by 31 to 3 at halftime, that I prepared to field a high up-and-under kick. Suddenly a voice cried, "Let me have it", and as I took a look I was amazed to find that the voice belonged to Irvine. Having come from the front of the scrum to fullback, he made the catch, set up a passing movement and, presently, scored between the posts. I scratched my head. Well, well, I thought. Rugby really is turning into quite a game. Not so long afterwards, another Wairarapa kick sailed in my direction and I once more announced that "she" was mine. Not a bit of it. A loud, commanding voice broke my concentration. "She", it seemed, was his. As I looked, he made the catch, started up a passing rush and scored between the posts. It was Maurice Brownlie.

Now a fair thing's a fair thing but this, I thought, was carrying the fair thing too far. So all right, I said, you chaps can play on your own. I can see I am not wanted here. For heaven's sake, don't do that, Maurice Brownlie said. If you walk off, you'll be adding insult to injury. Things are bad enough now. All right, I said, but you chaps stay in your own positions. I rather think they were feeling that if they could come back and make catches and set up tries, I could go forward and make catches and score tries myself. There were seventeen tries altogether for us that day. Blake scored five and Maurice Brownlie and Cooke three each. There never was such a display as this. There never could be again.

It was only two days later that we put Wanganui, which was captained by the great "Moke" Belliss, through the cleaners. Then came the gradual build-up to the grand challenge from Wellington on 14 August. This was going to be our Nemesis. Nothing could withstand the might of Wellington. They had "Ginger" Nicholls at half and Mark Nicholls and Svenson at five-eighth. They had Porter as captain. They had Jim Moffitt, one of the great forwards of the 1919 New Zealand Army team, "Shag" Thomas, Ned Barry, Bert Wilson. This was to be the greatest Wellington team of all time. We had not a hope. The Bay was to bite the dust, more it was going to chew it, masticate it, be buried in it. There was no radio in those days, but the waves of propaganda blown in our direction were greater than radio. If one thing was certain, it was that we had no more chance of holding on to the shield than a snowball has of retaining its original shape on the hobs of Hades.

Der Tag. Four minutes: Nepia drop kicks a goal. Six minutes, eight minutes, or whatever it was: Grenside scores. In blocks of minutes, up went the blocks of points: Tries by Cyril Brownlie, E. Single, Grenside, Grenside again. Nepia was with us - dear Nepia! - for three conversions. It was 24 to us and nil to Wellington at halftime. At the interval, three Wellingtonians, Porter, L.J. South and Wilson, retire from the Wellington team and three more lambs came on. Barry scored for Wellington, Nicholls converted and Nicholls converted a penalty. Then the march began again - Alex Kirkpatrick, Kirkpatrick, Grenside, "Tuna" Swain, Grenside again. And Nepia - dear Nepia! - was on target with two and Grenside with one. They published pictures afterwards - Wellington papers did - to show "Ginger" Nicholls being cast about like a discus by the shocking Hawke's Bay forwards and they talked of murder at McLean Park, licensed murder. But there never, never was such a sick and sorry team in all of your born days as Wellington that night. We beat them by fifty-eight points to eight inside ninety minutes and no Wellingtonian could believe it. Dear old Nepia was worth his weight that day with 17 points, his best effort in a shield game. But, practically speaking, all that dear old Nepia had to do for ninety minutes was pick his teeth, scratch his head and stare in wonder. There never was such a display as this. There never could be again.

And then came Auckland, not so grandiloquently but with talent enough to suggest that they would be hard to hold. Their forwards, after all, included "Bubs" Knight, who was one of the toughest characters that ever trod the field, Rupe McWilliams, a brilliant player, Walter Batty, one of my favourite forwards, Angus Finlayson, a brother of Innes, and two champion hookers in Swin Hadley and Bert Palmer. Their backs had Don Wright, whose omission from the 1924 All Blacks almost caused Auckland to secede from the Empire, Charlie Cammick, a nippy five-eighth, Freddie Lucas, the captain, at centre, Lew Hook, who was a smart wing, and V. C. Butler, a fullback of considerable ability, and the team as a whole had that swift and elegant look which characterised the Auckland teams of the twenties. Lord love us, swiftness and elegance meant nothing that day. The Bay roused again. It was 19 to 11 at halftime - in these days of defence, dear, dear, it's usually about 3-0 at halftime - and afterwards the good old Hawke's Bay romp began again. Blake scored three tries for us and Cooke two and when these two chaps were running, either on their own or in partnership, the swiftness and elegance was on our side. We won, 41 to 11.

My time with the Bay was done. This was my cradle and with it I grew to manhood. No longer would I hear Norman McKenzie shrewdly analysing strengths and weaknesses or hear Maurice Brownlie gruffly calling to his forwards to catch up. No more would I see Mill sidling around the blindside for the tries that suggested he was an invisible man. No longer would I see Cooke bursting through the gap as suddenly as the burst of flame of spilled petrol or watch Blake, the most elegant runner of all, passing by a would-be tackler as neatly as a matador evading a rushing bull. Grenside, Paewai, "Frik" Yates, Lance Johnson, Cyril Brownlie, Kirkpatrick, Irvine, these and many other comrades I had grown up with in Rugby were to play on without me.

But never, never could I forget them. For this forever will be the greatest provincial team ever fielded and in its time it would have beaten every international team in the world with the possible exception of the 1924 All Blacks. Speed, combination, thrust, backing-up power - every quality that you like to think of in Rugby was here and here in abundance. There never was such a team as this. There never could be again.

A history of the 1924-25 tour written by tour manager Mr S. Dean
(Courtesy Museum of Rugby)

23. Rugby Out in the Sticks

From his prolonged and expert study of Rugby in New Zealand, Norman McKenzie was fond of saying that when country Rugby was strong, New Zealand Rugby was strong. I have talked much so far of great grounds - Twickenham, Cardiff Arms, Athletic Park, Eden Park, McLean Park - and of great games - Hawke's Bay in the shield matches, the All Blacks in tests, the flying threequarters of Australia and Oxford. Now I should like to show you the other side of the penny, the country Rugby, the *real* country Rugby, of New Zealand as it was in the days when Huinga and I first set up our farm and I, in deference to my experience, was made captain-coach of the Rangitukia senior team.

We were mostly Maoris. We were almost all inexperienced. Two or three had been to Te Aute College for a year or two and had acquired some basic skills. The rest knew Rugby only as they picked it up, by watching other players and by the natural gifts of eye, strength, in some cases pace and in all courage. That was the first thing - they all had bottomless courage. From the smallest to the biggest, they would take on anybody. The difficulty actually was to harness and discipline this courage. The Maori is born with a great competitive streak. He loves to get the better of his fellows and he is, I think, more naturally gifted than the Pakeha as an experimenter and thinker under fire. He has, however, great shyness and he hates most of all to make an exhibition of himself. No one ever got anywhere by saying to the Maori, "Righto, Hori, you do that." He just bridles and turns sour on you. But if you say, "Righto, Hori, let's *all* do this", and capture his enthusiasm, you've got the best student, and the most willing worker, in the world.

As I was to find. For this experience of coaching was unusual and demanding for me and, rather like the young schoolmaster, I had to make sure of keeping at least one lesson ahead of the class. From this collection of rather raw material, I am glad to say that we fashioned one of the best club teams that had been seen on the East Coast for some time. Our reward was the club championship of the Waiapu sub-union. Just as enjoyable to me was the proof that my experiment with a player had come off. This was a chap named Naera Reihana who had attempted to win a place in the 1926 Maori team as a forward.

After a couple of good long looks at Naera, I said to myself, "This man is wasted as a forward. He can handle like a back, he can kick, he can run like a son of a gun." So I put him at first five-eighth. Naera thought I might be cuckoo. So did most of the Coast. After all, he was fourteen stone, and this, at any rate in those days, was regarded as just a little big for five-eighth. But once he got the hang of things, Reihana was a five-eighth out of the box. He was as fierce as a lion and when he went for a cut-through you had to be pretty stouthearted, even by East Coast standards, to go in for a crash-tackle.

At any rate, Rangers of Rangitukia proved their worth so well that the Waiapu sub-union to which we belonged made me selector, coach and captain of their team. There were five sub-unions of the East Coast union. Though they were all more or less equal in numbers and material, Tolaga Bay had, I suppose, the strongest-looking side. The Reeves brothers, Stanley, Hedley and Gordon, were all fine forwards and Crawford and Lockwood, both Maori All Blacks, also played in the same team. I had with me at Waiapu the forwards, Pine Taiapa and Jim Garlick, both of whom had toured with the Maori All Blacks in New Zealand in 1922 and one of whom, Taiapa, had been with both the '22 and '23 Maori teams in Australia. I also had Wallace Poi, halfback of the 1923 Maori All Blacks and a lovely little player pretty nearly of the Jimmy Mill class.

For our first sub-union game, we were drawn against Matakaoa at Te Araroa. You may get some inkling of the tremendous enthusiasm of country Rugby from our experience, the more so because it was so entirely typical of what went on on the Coast in those days. We all assembled at Tiki Tiki and started off, about thirty of us, in a five-ton White truck. It had been raining for a day or two beforehand and the Coast, when it tried, could be as muddy as Taranaki. As we were to find out, within three miles of beginning the journey. Here, there was a long climb and the road was clay. So we all piled out, mud up to the ankles, and the poor old truck puffed away until, nearly a mile from the crest, it announced that it wasn't going any further without assistance. So that meant long ropes for the thirty of us. We pulled and heaved, laughed when someone blundered to his knees and with chugging from the truck reached at last the crest. But the road was still clay and still wet. So we needed the ropes again all the way down the hill to the bridge, on the other side of which, praise be, there was a metal road.

It was nearly two o'clock by the time we reached Te Araroa and we were not, you might say, in prime condition. But on to the field we gambolled and played and won the game. Te Araroa bore no grudge. The party at night was a good one. Off we went the next morning. Halfway, the truck stopped. We kicked it, swore at it, jumped on it, but the old White she would not go. The smart fellows rushed around the neighbourhood to borrow horses. The rest of us took to Shanks's pony for the eight or ten miles to Tiki Tiki. It was a long walk after a hard weekend but there was never a complaint, that was the thing, there was never a complaint.

A week later, we set out to play Ruatoria. I rode into Tiki Tiki and halfway had to put my horse to a flooded creek. It was an eerie experience, water up to your waist and only the head of the horse out of the water. It was cold, too, especially when you realised you had no change and would have to travel to Ruatoria in wet clothing. So what. We were all, or mostly all, in the same condition and Maoris get great amusement out of others' misfortunes.

By now, we were qualified for the final of the K. S. Williams Shield for sub-union competition. Our opponents were Tolaga Bay and we had to travel to Tokomaru Bay. We were all pretty sure that we were in for a he-man game. He-man was scarcely the word. Without doubt, this was one of the hardest games I ever played in. Up and down the field we rushed. The running was dynamic, the tackling heroic. The crowd on the touchline grew frenzied. This was not the final for a sub-union shield, this was the world championship. We were ahead, Tolaga Bay were level, they were ahead, we were level. We were still level as the game drew to its end and the cheering, the urging, the *shrieking*, made the display of the French crowd at Paris sound weak and puny.

At fulltime, the match was a draw. By the rules, we had to play on until one side scored to win or conceded a force-down to lose. Once more into the breach. Now we weren't playing for the shield. We were playing in that much older competition, for keeps. We crept down to their goal-line. Some part of the field was taken up by the players. The rest was taken up by the spectators. Even a deaf-mute would have found himself talking in that company. We scrummed close to their line. The ball came out to our side. Poi, our half, was told to run, kick, pass, jump on it. The advice came from several hundreds all shouting at the top of their voices. If poor Wallace had suddenly started to run madly round and round the field, he would only have been obeying the bits of advice that came to him. But he knew his own mind. He sidled round the side of that scrum like Jimmy Mill himself. Before Tolaga Bay knew what had happened, he was over the goal-line, touching down and the referee had his hand up to signal the try. What a scene! Waiapu supporters - and players - went mad with joy. Tolaga Bay supporters - and players - went mad with rage - only thank Heaven, not completely mad. Did anyone take the kick at goal? I haven't the faintest idea. We'd won.

Believe it or not, I nearly got my head knocked off - and by a Waiapu man at that. During the game, Reihana, my five-eighth, sold a beautiful dummy, slipped through a gap and drop kicked a goal. At once a roar went around the ground, "Nepia! Nepia!"

Back at the hotel, enjoying the beer, feeling like heroes - for Waiapu the year before hadn't won a trophy and now we had made a clean sweep of seven or eight - we all became aware of Reihana. He was yelling for me. "Come here, Nepia," he was bellowing. "I'm going to fight you. I'm going to knock your head off." "Well," I said, "that's a damn silly thing to want to do. What for?" "I drop kicked that goal," he said. "Certainly you did," I said, "and it was a beauty, too." "The crowd said you kicked it," he said. "What?" I said. "The crowd said you kicked it. They all yelled, 'Nepia! Nepia!' I want to fight you, boy. I want to show you I can kick goals better than you can."

He was a big, tough, he-man even in a big, tough, he-man district. Nothing came of the argument which, as far as I was concerned, wasn't an argument at all. But here, in essence, you had country football - its passionate enthusiasm, its cheerfulness, its ruggedness.

Yes, the country football of New Zealand of that time was strong. And New Zealand Rugby of that time, so I will always maintain, was the strongest it has ever been.

Changing codes: Nepia with Jim Sullivan (Wigan, Wales & Great Britain) after his debut for Streatham & Mitcham RLFC. The clash of the two great full-backs had made headlines in all the newspapers. Wigan won 11-3. (Photo: Courtesy Les Hoole)

24. Apartheid in Sport

It is not perhaps generally known that until a late hour of 1927, at the end of which the All Blacks who were to tour South Africa in the following year were chosen, Jimmy Mill and I were strong candidates for the team. Not until the eleventh hour was it decided by the New Zealand Rugby Union that it would be impolitic for us, as non-Caucasians, to attempt to travel in a country whose policies toward non-Whites were even then severely restrictive.

Mill and I, you may be sure, did not cry ourselves to sleep over this decision. Unhappily, this is an issue which has grown in importance and from pride of race, if for no other reason, I am compelled to discuss it.

I have already made mention of how the country was scandalised by the publication, the day after its despatch, of the message which the correspondent, Blackett, sent to his newspaper in South Africa about the match between the Springboks and the New Zealand Maoris at Napier in 1921. Putting aside all of the moral issues involved in the actual fact of publication in New Zealand, I feel bound to say that the sentence, "Bad enough having to play team officially designated New Zealand natives but spectacle thousands Europeans frantically cheering on band of coloured men to defeat members of own race was too much for Springboks who frankly disgusted", provoked a reaction and bitterness which within the heart of the Maori race have neither been forgotten nor forgiven.

The omission of Mill and myself from the 1928 team was a deliberate and conciliatory act by the New Zealand Rugby Union. So was the decision not to commit the New Zealand Maori XV against the Springboks who toured New Zealand in 1937. By 1949, when we were again to send a team to South Africa, the New Zealand union had reaffirmed its policy and the Maori people, much influenced by their greatest player of the time, the superb midfield back, J. B. Smith, who agreed with the decision, said nothing. By 1956, when the Third Springboks visited New Zealand, it was judged safe to play the Maoris against them but so apprehensive were some officials of a racial conflict that the Maori team took the field brainwashed of any normally aggressive Rugby attitudes and were very thoroughly beaten. So it was not until 1959, and under a Pakeha leader at that, that the Maoris really made known their dislike of the New Zealand union's intention not to consider Maori players in the selection of the team which was to visit South Africa in the following year.

It is true that the protests which were made then, and again in the early months of 1960, tended to become tinged with radical politics. It is also true that among those who protested were Pakehas who were using us as a race for the purpose of pushing the kind of politics we as a race would not touch with a barge pole. Nevertheless, on many a marae throughout the country, there was a responsible opposition to the decision. In the years since 1921, the world had seen the deplorable effects of apartheid applied by successive South African Governments and culminating in the deplorably restrictive attitudes of the Afrikaner Nationalist Governments of Dr Malan, Mr Strydom, and Dr Verwoerd. As non-Caucasians, coloured folk if you like, we Maoris disliked this treatment of the millions whose skins were the same colour as ours. Most of all, perhaps, we were saddened, disappointed and humiliated by the attitude of the body, namely the New Zealand Rugby Union, which purported to be our guide, philosopher and friend. If you look down the years of organised rugby in New Zealand, you will be struck by the importance the Maori segment assumes in affairs, not only in quality of leading players but also in actual numbers of participants. It is, as only one example, an indisputable fact that on a comparative basis, far, far more Maoris play Rugby up to a senior club level than do white men. Willingly, consistently, with the enthusiasm which I have tried to demonstrate in the previous chapter, the Maoris have given their loyalty to the game and to the controlling authority of the game.

Loyalty begets loyalty, so they say. I wonder. My charge is that the New Zealand union, at this vital hour of challenge, sidestepped its obligations to us, the Maori people, for reasons that do not stand examination. There was a feeling of courtesy - which I would say was misplaced - towards the wishes of our South African hosts; there was the honouring of an obligation to the South African Rugby Board, which overlooked a much older, closer obligation to Maori Rugby and to the Maori race as a whole; and there was a fear of the consequences - international, sporting and financial - of a cessation of tours between South Africa and New Zealand. The New Zealand union's profit from the tour of the '56 Springboks was about £98,000 and the provincial unions which staged matches benefited to a comparable degree. In the final analysis, we Maoris, or very many of us Maoris, considered that the union had put aside the reciprocal loyalty which they owed to us for the sake of the profits they could see forthcoming from the 1960 tour and all subsequent tours between the two countries.

I think we have won, all the same. Fortified by some inspiring political leadership, Pakeha and Maori of the New Zealand race have in the years since 1960 moved more steadily toward that state which was described by Governor Hobson at the signing of the Treaty in Waitangi in 1840 in the memorable phrase, "Now we are one people". In that state, I do not think we, as New Zealanders, will permit our New Zealand Rugby Union to maintain Rugby relationships with South Africa until and unless the South Africans accept us, Maori and Pakeha, as indeed one people. I marched for that concept at a protest in Wellington before the 1960 tour. So did many Maoris; and many Pakehas. We were one people. In the main business of living, as in Rugby, we must always be so.

Notwithstanding that I was prevented from suffering, with Maurice Brownlie and his team, some of the great difficulties that the All Blacks encountered in South Africa in 1928, life in these early years on the East Coast was not without its rewards for me. In 1928, as an example, I was made captain of the New Zealand Maori team which defeated New South Wales by 9 points to 8 at Auckland. A Canterbury player, G. H. Mehrtens, was preferred to me in two of the three tests against New South Wales and V. C. Butler, the Aucklander, had the post in the other. The All Blacks, who, of course, were selected in the absence of the main contingent in South Africa, won the first test by only 15 to 12 and the second by 16 to 14 before losing the third, 8 to 11, so that I gained some satisfaction from our Maori team's performance, even though we had to place three penalty goals to get home.

We had good players - Falwasser and Dick Pelham in the threequarters, Paewai at five-eighth, Shortland at halfback, Sam Gemmell, Bill Reside of

Wairarapa, W. Rika of North Auckland and Whai Pine of Wanganui in the forwards, but they had some outstanding ones, too.

Sid Malcolm, the New South Wales captain, was one of the great halves of the world in his time and Cyril Towers at centre had every quality of the first-class back, not forgetting the best quality of all, a Cooke-like ability to build up speed into and away through an opening. I remember very well, too, Bob Loudon, a fine forward, and most of all, one of the greatest characters in all Rugby, W. H. Cerutti, a front-row forward who has been known as "Wild Bill" in the thirty-five years he has been coming to New Zealand. Like Bill Irvine, Cerutti always believed that while on the job you played hard, the harder the better.

At this time, though only seventeen, he figures in one of my favourite Rugby stories. During the first match of the tour, against Auckland, he got into holts with "Bubs" Knight, a massive man who was one of the toughest players I ever saw. Bill apparently had the best of the argument because "Bubs" vowed, after being chosen for the test, that he would turn this young whippersnapper into sausage meat. In the test, when "Bubs" wasn't concentrating as sharply as he ought to have done, "Bill" apparently got in the first punch. This put "Bubs" into a rage and for several lineouts he chased Cerutti up and down while the referee, Frank Sutherland of Auckland, plaintively asked for a bit of football from both. Finally, Knight caught up. "What are we going to do, Cerutti?" he bellowed. "Play football?" For a moment, the bashing forward became the bashful boy. "Yes, Mr Knight," said Cerutti - and from that moment there was sealed a lifelong friendship between the two.

In 1929, I again captained the Maoris, this time in an-end-of-season match we lost to Cliff Porter's Pakehas by 18 to 37. More importantly, I again became a touring All Black, for I was named the only fullback of the All Black team to tour New South Wales and Queensland and to play three tests with Australia. From a personal point of view, I was delighted at the selection. My failings in Sydney in 1924 had never ceased to rankle. Now was my chance, five years later, to prove to Australians that I was as good as I was supposed to be. There were three of us from 1924 in the team - Porter as captain and Dalley as halfback - and the other two fully understood how I felt. There were some other good players, too, among the threequarters - Sid Carleton, of Canterbury, and Grenside, both of whom had toured South Africa; in the five-eighths, Herby Lilburne, also a '28 tourist, and Charlie Oliver, the latter being one of the four or five men in New Zealand sporting history to be capped at both Rugby and cricket; in the forwards, Rupert McWilliams and Eric Snow, of 1928, "Beau" Cottrell, a first-class hooker from Canterbury who these days wears a wooden leg as a souvenir of war service in World War II, Bert Palmer, another fine hooker who about four years later died from the effects of an injury in a club game, Athol Mahoney, a great man-mountain from Bush Districts, and Dick Steere, a fine, strong lock. We all set out on this tour with high hopes and it was a very great shock for us to be beaten in each of the three tests, by 8 to 9, 9 to 17, and 13 to 15. In fact, we only won six of our ten games, for we drew, nil-all, with New South Wales at the opening of the tour. This is by far the worst record of any All Black team in Australia and I am afraid you never hear us mentioned in any discussions of the finest teams to leave New Zealand.

It would be pointless after all these years to try to square off for a miserable record, but there were circumstances severely limiting to our hopes. Dalley was injured in only the second game and a replacement, W. C. T. Leys, had to be brought from New Zealand. Porter soon suffered a poisoned arm which put him out of action. As for myself, I also soon qualified for the entertainment committee. I severely strained my back - I made for the kowhai baths (successfully) as soon as I returned home - and played only three games and half a test match.

For me, the tour had only one real highlight. In the opening match with New South Wales, I was faced with three men, Towers, Sid King, and Eric Ford, all of whom had been threequarters in the successful Waratahs' team which toured the British Isles and France. Said the *Arrow*, a sporting weekly of those days: "Nepia rose to his best, eliminating those risky fireworks by which he was misjudged when he was here before the last team went to England. If one incident is talked about in years to come more than any other, it will be the try that did not come to New South Wales when Nepia shot off from Towers and tackled King as soon as he had the ball in his fingers. It was bad luck for the home backs to lose that try after so smartly engineering it, but they would have scored it against an ordinary fullback. Next time, Towers will know a little more about the ability of Nepia. All the players concerned in this little episode will be able to smile as they think it over. Nepia was a veritable Horatius with his mates down the field watching his remarkable effort after they had been beaten."

Actually, I did this twice during the game. It was a matter of driving them together by back-pedalling and compelling them to take their eyes off the ball to switch on to me. Once they did this, I was able to choose my moment.

But this lone incident was small compensation for the sufferings, personal and general, of a most unsuccessful tour.

25. Mr Baxter Cries "Wolf"

Cheats, wolf-hounds, obstructionists - Oh, there was gay old name-calling in 1930, the year that James Baxter brought his British team to New Zealand. Rugby diplomacy consisted sometimes of getting in the hard word first. The game, too, sometimes consisted of getting in the hard blow first. Except, of course, at Timaru, where Henry Rew, one of the English forwards in the team, got bitten....There was a great scandal about this, as you may be sure; but really, far worse things happened. For from this tour was accelerated the move to outlaw the New Zealand 2-3-2 scrummage formation and when in due course this was done a year or so later, the great era of New Zealand Rugby in international engagements, dating from 1904 when D. R. Bedell-Sivright's team was beaten in New Zealand, and carrying on to 1930, when we beat the British, three to one, came to an end. Of recent years, we have taken justifiable pride in great All Black forward packs (though I would have no hesitation in pitting the '24 or the Hawke's Bay packs against any of them), and in fabulous goal kickers like Don Clarke, with, occasionally, a superlative back of the quality of R. A. Jarden or J. B. Smith distinguishing himself. But in fact we have been denied the quality of the *team-play* which characterised the Rugby of this great era and unless and until something practical and permanent is done about the scrummaging I am quite sure we shall never again see this kind of play. In international competition, as we sometimes saw in 1924, as we saw, too, in 1930 when the British fielded their biggest and best pack, the New Zealand formation could be at a disadvantage. It is not logical for seven men to have the better of eight, especially in a prolonged forward encounter. But no other formation that I have seen or that has been evolved has so much encouraged speed as did the 2-3-2 and it is for the want of this that the Rugby of the post-1930 era has so often been so wretchedly bad. With the 2-3-2, the ball came like a flash to the stationary halfback and from him, if he were any good, it was transferred to five-eighths, who were really flying. It was then that you would see, as I so very often did, the lovely sight of a backline in formation moving at irresistible speed into the attack. Cursed as the game is today by scrounging loose forwards and defensively-minded backs, cursed above all as it is by the slow heel, this is not the sort of sight you see in Rugby these days - and the game is the poorer for it.

What about the roving wing-forward of the 2-3-2, you might say? Was his function not obstructive in implication, if not in intent? Yes, I agree, it often was. But the point was that the speed of the heel defeated, in time, even the most blatant of obstructionists. In the most important of all of the contests of 1930, the warfare which was constantly waged between Cliff Porter on the New Zealand side and Roger Spong, the flyhalf or first five-eighth, on the British, you saw very clearly the advantages of our scrummaging formation and the disadvantages of the 3-2-3 formation which was then customary.

Spong was a great player, very nearly a genius. He was quick, lively, courageous, a fine handler, a nippy runner and a brilliant improviser. I would unhesitatingly rank him among the three or four greatest players I have seen in this vital position. He was so good that he was always a nuisance to us and if he had had the luck always to be served by good scrumhalves - it was the major tragedy of the tour, of course, that he lost his club-mate, Wilfred Sobey, in the very first match - he might have dictated our defeat.

In the event, Porter came to dominate Spong by driving him into attempts at the inside break, that is, the attempt to thrust through the defensive screen between the side-row forwards and Porter himself. This was disastrous, as was best to be seen when the All Blacks won the final test by 22 points to 8, a tremendous victory in an international.

There was one valid explanation for the dominance eventually exercised by Porter. This was the slow heel. As the ball maundered from front to middle to back row of the British scrum and finally emerged into the hands of the scrumhalf, Porter could poise himself to put Spong off-balance. When Spong did receive the ball, the dice, as it were, were loaded against him. He was hurried out of stride, he was unbalanced. By contrast, the New Zealand five-eighth was very often able to dictate the play, this notwithstanding that Ivor Jones, the principal British loose-forward, was an extremely agile and clever player on both attack and defence. I say this now, advisedly, that had Spong received as swift a service as the New Zealand five-eighth did, we would have lost the series. It is surely the last word - it is, at any rate, mine - that he could only have received that kind of service from the 2-3-2 formation.

Douglas Prentice, the captain of the British team, was appointed in the place of W. W. Wakefield when the latter, because of injury, withdrew a few weeks before the team took ship. Prentice, who had played against us at Leicester, in '24, was, like Wakefield, past his best, but in any case he would have had to be a notable player and personality to dominate Mr Baxter, the manager who was so soon to sit New Zealand Rugby back on its heels. Mr Baxter was a cultivated English gentleman of the old school, and from the first he was a personality whom New Zealanders found it easier to dislike than to like. There seemed to be a measure of disdain in his attitude toward the wild colonial boys of New Zealand and Australia, as was instanced in his celebrated remark about the presence and strength of Rugby League in Auckland - "Every town must have its sewer".

It was at the dinner after the opening match at Wanganui that Mr Baxter made the first of his pronouncements about the wing-forward. "The ordinary man who tries to play wing-forward is nothing more or less than a cheat," he said. "He is deliberately trying to beat the referee by unfair tactics."

Mr Baxter at that same dinner and in the same speech made some very wise observations indeed. The New Zealand Rugby Union, he said, had pronounced against wing-forward play but had thrown the onus of correcting his malpractices on the referee. This had thrown a tremendous responsibility on the referee, who had too much to do at the pace the game was played. The actual onus of correcting wing-forward play was on the clubs and especially on the committees which chose the players. If a committee saw a man who was guilty of malpractice, it should be perfectly frank and not play him.

These are very wise words which still hold good today but which, I regret to say, are still not taken notice of by too many club committees. As always happens in controversies, however, only the main element of Mr Baxter's statement was remembered by the public and the Press. Wing-forwards cheats? New Zealand wing-forwards? What a terrible, damaging, shocking, uncalled-for, impertinent, appalling accusation! Mr Baxter should be hanged, drawn and quartered, or publicly horsewhipped. We were a simple people in those days. The whole country was stirred. The indignation was violent. For a time, the tour was under a cloud.

Meantime the British were employing their great speed in the backline to defeat Wanganui, 19 to 3, Taranaki, 23 to 7, Manawhenua, 34 to 8, and Wairarapa, 19 to 6, and it was not until they were outmanoeuvred by Wellington by 12 to 8 - the first of the contests between Porter and Spong - and then committed high school blunders against Canterbury, who won by 14 to 8, that some of the defects became noticeable. Meanwhile, the New Zealand selectors had been at work on trial matches and they called me to the final one at Wellington. Having been around for a few years, I was being spoken of as a veteran, but at the ripe old age of twenty-five I was still able to bring off a few catches and tackles and make some good kicks into the howling wind and so, *old* and all as I was, I was given another cap. There were seven of us from 1924 in the team - Lucas, Cooke, Mill, Porter, Irvine, Stewart and myself, and Nicholls was an emergency. Lilburne, Hazlett, McWilliams and Finlayson were members of the 1928 team in South Africa and the newcomers were George Hart, of Canterbury, a brilliant running wing, Don Olliver, of Wellington, another clever threequarter, Cottrell, the Canterbury hooker, Dick Steere at lock (both of whom had toured Australia in 1929), and one of my greatest friends, Walter Batty, of Auckland, in the back of the scrum.

We were favoured to win the first test, which was played at Carisbrook in Dunedin. We lost it by 6 to 3 when Jack Morley, the Welsh wing, took a pass from Ivor Jones just before I made my tackle and ran on to score in the corner in the last half-minute of the game. I had had success in my career in bundling two or three runners together or in persuading the ball-carrier to hang on too long and I was to perform this feat again; but against Jones and Morley, I had no chance whatever. These were Welshmen, trained in the hard school of Welsh club Rugby; and when you encounter such men, you know that you are confronted by skilled practitioners who are footballers to the fingertips.

This was a memorable match in many, many ways. There was snow on the field and the hills behind Carisbrook were white when we took the field, the British blue-jerseyed and white-panted and ourselves in white jerseys and black pants. It was deathly cold and within minutes the ball was a greasy pig. Not, you might say, the most propitious of circumstances for a test match. This perhaps is one of the great glories of Rugby, that when it is played under extreme difficulties, as it was this day, it brings out the heroic streak in men. From the kickoff, it was a hard, tense struggle in which the British forwards held the All Blacks until toward the finish, and in which their backs were decidedly better than ours. Where Mill and Lilburne were unhappy in passing and fielding, Paul Murray, the Irish half, and Spong were secure and adventurous. The same contrast applied with the outside backs, for Harry Bowcott and Carl Aarvold were brilliant in the centre and Morley on one wing and Jimmy Reeve on the other were quick and sure-footed, whereas only Cooke and Hart of our line looked really thrustful and dangerous. Their fullback, Jack Bassett, was a good 'un, too.

He was, of course, a Welshman in good standing and he had a ton of pluck and quality about him.

The British scored after only seven minutes when Murray flicked a pass to Spong who instantly cross kicked to Reeve on the other wing. After making the catch, Reeve streaked past Hart to go in at the corner. This was the only scoring of the half. "Bunny" Finlayson was magnificent in the All Black pack and Cooke was uncanny, a true genius, in the backline, but the big British forwards kept thwarting our pack and their backs had too much toe to be caught by our backs. I was too often under pressure to be in danger of death of cold and it was a pleasure to find that my touch-kicking had not suffered for want of representative play or that I had entirely lost the art of dealing with oncoming forwards. Porter, oddly enough, got the bird from the crowd, who took to him for, as they called it, offside play, and poor Jimmy Mill's struggles with his hands were not well regarded by these critical Otagoans, either.

So they led us 3 to nil at halftime. Within three minutes of the start of the second half, we were level. From a scrum after a dropout at their 25, Mill sent the All Black backs away in one of their few clean runs and when Hart received the ball from Lucas he had sufficient leeway to speed past both Reeve and Bassett and to score near the corner. My kick hit the post and bounced away.

For a good deal of the rest of the game, we were on the attack. Olliver dropped one ball with a try at hand and I went pretty close with a penalty kick after Bassett had deliberately thrown the ball into touch. Cooke snapped through and all but got there and Lucas might have got there from a fine cut by Hart.

And then it was just on time and a draw appeared certain when, at a scrum almost on their goal-line, Ivor Jones cut off a pass from Mill to Lilburne and set off. In a bound, he had sliced our line. He came racing up toward me with Morley alongside him and Lucas and Cooke madly speeding in my support. It was a grim moment. I back-pedalled a bit and tried to shift Jones into second gear. But he was as clever as I, or cleverer, for he gave a bit of a dummy to put me off; and I am sure we both knew, as I went in for the tackle, that if Morley held the pass they'd be dancing in the streets of Newport that night. That was the perfection of it - the inspiration of the interception instantly followed by swift, straight running and well-ordered support from Morley. It was the ABC of Rugby - but how often, even in test matches, do you get past the AB stage? Out of admiration, as footballers, what these two Welshmen did, I think we All Blacks willingly conceded them the match. I know the crowd did. The yelling and cheering as Morley and Cooke ran stride for stride for the corner, with Cooke perhaps gaining an inch at a time, could be heard all the way to Port Chalmers and when Morley dived to score to win the match the whole ground went cuckoo. You live only once, but it was worth living to see such a finish to such a match that day. And I must say I turned pink, or whatever it is Maoris do turn, when Mr Baxter at the dinner that evening paid a tribute to the most magnificent fullback it had ever been his privilege to see. Imagine it? Me.

The British were carefree boys who liked their parties and their attitude to the in-between matches was gay, if not careless. In the tests, especially the first three, all was different and I will say now that we, the All Blacks, were downright lucky to win the second by 13 points to 10. In fact, I am sure we would not have won had not Murray dislocated his left shoulder in a hard tackle a few minutes before halftime. Ivor Jones, who came out of the scrum to substitute, did well, exceedingly well when you consider the closeness of the score, but of all of the technically demanding places on the field the halfback's is the most difficult and for want of the quality that Murray had been displaying the British backs were unable to get that yard of advantage that can make all the difference.

Even with Murray's departure, however, the British could still have won if Aarvold, in almost precisely the same situation as at Dunedin, had acted with the Rugby wisdom of Ivor Jones. He slipped Lucas and came rushing up to me with Tony Novis in support. The score was 8 to 5 in our favour, as it had been at halftime, but Novis was so very quick and skilful that this was five points for the asking - and, of course, we won only by 13 to 10.

As Aarvold came toward me, I back-pedalled to make him misjudge the distance between us. He turned his head to find Novis and at that instant I back-pedalled again. As soon as he turned his head to me, I stopped dead. Then, in that fraction of a second as he turned his head towards Novis again, I made my crash-tackle. I caught him, as I intended, ball and all. "You bastard," he said. "Who the hell taught you that trick?" "It's always seemed to me the right thing to do," I said - and we went on with the game. But I am as sure now as I was then that if Aarvold had passed the ball to Novis the first time, neither I nor anyone else would have had the ghost of a chance of catching the latter. I relate this incident only to prove my theory that you can catch even the great players like Aarvold by making them momentarily confused in the mind.

Before halftime, Nicholls had goaled from a mark, the British backs, Murray, Morley and Aarvold had replied with a brilliant movement which yielded a try to Aarvold and a conversion to Prentice, and Hart used his great speed for a try which Nicholls goaled.

Afterwards, we went to 13 when Nicholls ran the blind-side so cleverly that after he had passed to Olliver and Bassett, the latter just had to trot over for a try which Nicholls converted with a great kick from the sideline. Then, from beyond halfway, Ivor Jones set Aarvold going into a gap and none of us had the ghost of a chance of stopping him. It was a try between the posts for Prentice to goal - and I wondered afterwards, as I often have since, whether Aarvold should have been horsewhipped for not giving Novis that try before he was praised for his effort in scoring the other two brilliant efforts.

So to Auckland for the third test and one of the best-planned and greatest tries I ever saw. But perhaps I might pause for a moment at Wellington, for the match between the British and the New Zealand Maori team which I had the honour of captaining. We lost this, by 13 points to 19, but it was the sort of game which is recalled with satisfaction by all who took part in it. Using their great speed, the British swept through for three tries, one by Morley and two by Novis, and not too long after half time they led by 14 to 3. It was then that our chaps began to play real Maori Rugby. The ball whizzed from man to man, the switches of direction and the variety of passes were disconcerting and our forwards - great, burly men like "Baby" Kahu and Reg Wanoa (the latter, incidentally, an ordained minister) and clever chaps like "Wampy" Bell, of Southland, and Toby Robinson of Canterbury - really piled in. Constructiveness was the theme. It was great to watch and good to play; it was rewarding, too, which is more than can be said of the modern Maori tendency to play safety-first, Pakeha tactics. Our backs, who were very well served by Rangi Harrison, made a break in midfield and when Dick Pelham, the centre, scored between the posts, one report said that his "finishing dash was like a streak of light". I placed the goal for the try and then our backs began to run again, getting the ball smartly to Jack Ruru on the left wing. Ruru a year or two before had played for Hawke's Bay while still a pupil at Te Aute College. He was a footballer of most unusual talent and we were all greatly shaken when, only a year or two later, he died after an illness while still in his mid-twenties. At this time, he was at his best and when he received the pass, he went for the goal-line like a rocket. First, he bumped Morley and then, going in at the corner, he not only resisted one of Bassett's heavy tackles but actually knocked him sprawling before grounding the ball. I placed the goal from the sideline and there was only a point between the two teams, with the crowd now wild with excitement.

We gave the British another fright when Ruru immediately made another hard run, but this time Bassett enfolded him in a terrific tackle. They retaliated with a superb movement begun by Spong and ended by Novis slipping our other wing, Ropa Watson, also a young and promising player, for a try which Brian Black converted. Just to show you how great the excitement had become, in the last minute, in taking a kick at goal from a long way out I had to wait while the referee cleared the crowd away from the goalposts. By the time the ball was on its way - and missing - the field was teeming with spectators. Some of them even carried me shoulder-high from the field. If I may say so, I had had a good game, one of the best I ever played in New Zealand, and it was pleasant to be rewarded for this as well as for leadership of a fine team which had played the game the way Rugby ought always to be played - by Pakeha, I may say, as well as Maori.

So to Auckland, nearly a week of practice and the unfolding of the Nicholls master plan for a try by Lucas on the left wing. As those of the '24 team well knew, when Mark had an idea in his head, it stayed there until there was a good chance of executing it. He knew Eden Park pretty well, well enough to know all about the prevailing sou'-wester which blows from the left-hand corner of the field, looking westwards, more or less diagonally down the field. It is a steady and sometimes a hard wind and in Nicholls's view it tended to be stronger and steadier above the height of the goalposts. His aim was to kick the ball from the right-hand side of the field towards the posts, but more or less across the wind and his theory, carefully expounded, was that as the velocity of the ball lessened it would balloon away from the posts out to the left. If everything worked right, so Mark said, Lucas would catch the ball at sufficient speed to outflank all defenders and with any sort of luck at all there ought to be a try between the posts as a reward.

From time to time during the week, we all took part in this manoeuvre - which was to begin, incidentally, with Nicholls switching places with Archie Strang in the five-eighth line. Not too often did it either come off or look like coming off; and I am afraid that Mark heard some hard words about the futility of the scheme.

The British had been beaten the week before by Auckland by 19 points to 6, but with the return of Spong to flyhalf in place of T. C. Knowles the appearance of the team was wholly changed. This notwithstanding that N. Poole, the Cardiff halfback who played in trousers so long that they hung very nearly below his knees, was not really of the first class. The British had a decided advantage in weight in the forwards, George Beamish, their greatest player, being sixteen stone four pound, a tremendous weight for those days. For one reason and another, we had lost our two biggest men, Stewart and Finlayson, the replacements being Walter Batty, of Auckland, and Hugh McLean, of Wellington - an older brother, as a point of interest, of my collaborator. Bill Hazlett at fifteen stone was easily our heaviest forward, McLean, Rupert McWilliams and Steere were between fourteen and fourteen-and-a-half stone and the rest ranged down to Cottrell, who was a couple of pounds under thirteen stone. It was so comparatively light a pack that apprehension about our chances was voiced, especially after the closeness of the match at Christchurch. In the event, the new men had an enlivening effect. The spirit was strong, the average pace was high, the fitness was admirable. McLean, who had to wear Jersey No. 13 because Hazlett "threw his rank" in the dressing-room and refused to wear the number, scored two tries, Batty and McWilliams were equally as energetic and Porter had the best of an intense personal battle with Spong, who was as lively as a jumping jack.

And the great plan came off with perfection in every particular. The British were first to score. Spong took a pass from Poole and sliced past Porter and Strang up towards me before giving Bowcott a hard one to handle. The Welsh centre took it like a charm and Ivor Jones completed a brilliant movement by placing the goal. From this stage, our forwards were countering the British superiority in the tight with swift raids in the loose and our backs, particularly Cooke, were making decisive tackles to stop the many attempts at penetration by Aarvold, who was neglectful of Reeve and Morley on the wings. All through the first half, there were raids and counter-raids. And then a scrum was called, round about the British 25, out by the right-hand touchline. Nicholls signalled as he went into first five-eighth. Lucas edged wide and Morley unconsciously abetted the plan by moving closer to his centres.

At the heel, Mervyn Corner snapped the ball to Nicholls. Mark scarcely paused. His kick was a long, raking one which travelled toward the far post and then began to bore away to the left in the wind. Meantime, Lucas was streaking forward. He made a perfect catch fifteen, perhaps twenty yards from the British goal-line. And to this day it seems to me as if twenty-nine players stopped dead to watch this thirtieth man complete the final movement of a tableau. I doubt that Morley had time even to wave goodbye as Freddie sped past. As for Bassett, he had no earthly chance. It was *the* perfect try. Justly enough, Strang made no mistake with the goal and we were 5 points each at halftime.

There was no doubt we were the better team in the second half. Our forwards were beginning to dominate in the line-outs and their energy in the loose was admirable. From one of these catches and heels, Nicholls kicked back toward the blindside wing and McLean, the first of the pack as Bassett tried to clear from the goal-line, charged the ball down and followed in for his first try - a great way, of course, to start an international career. A little time later, we heeled again. Nicholls started to scuttle as if intending to give Cooke and Lucas a bit of an overlap. Suddenly, he stopped dead, wheeled and with all the time in the world drop kicked a goal.

The British retaliated and there were particularly bad moments for us until Porter shrewdly intercepted a scissors pass when Bowcott and Aarvold were steaming at full speed. Corner and I seemed to have the whole of the population of the British Isles charging at us when between us we stopped one rush only a yard or so from the New Zealand line. Helped by Batty, we escaped. And not too long afterwards, Corner, a tiny man, ran around the blindside, brought the loose forwards into the movement and put in a pass which McLean turned into a try.

15 to 5. We were sitting pretty. But the last minutes were still important, not merely because Aarvold scored a try from which Black placed a goal, but also because the glaring piece of obstruction involved later provoked Mr Ted McKenzie into an attack on the British team at the test-match dinner in the evening. "There have been points in the British play to which strong exception can be taken," he said. "I have noticed frequently cases of obstruction and what we in New Zealand know as shepherding. Some of the instances of obstruction appear to have been deliberately studied. I will not pretend that our owners are perfect, but I will say that the British team is a fine enough side to win matches without resorting to obstruction and similar tactics which may or may not be intentional." Ted, as I think I have mentioned earlier, was a great, big, bald-headed man of quiet demeanour who listened much more often than he spoke, but now he was very determined and, I think, coldly angry. Aarvold at one stage tried to interrupt and Ted blistered him with a "I am speaking at present, Mr Aarvold, not you." It was a sensational occasion, unparalleled in my experience, and I am bound to say that the British neither liked it nor took any care to hide their feelings about it. It is a long time ago, too, and there have been many sensations since those far-off days. But I feel compelled to say this, that the substance of McKenzie's criticism was wholly justified. The British, designedly or otherwise, *did* obstruct. And it was right that McKenzie should tell them this to their faces rather than seek out the newspapermen for an exclusive story or complain officially to the New Zealand Rugby Union. It took moral courage and I am sure all of us players greatly admired this aspect.

Paul Murray returned to the British team for the final test at Athletic Park in Wellington. Nicholls was put to the touchline with injuries and Lilburne was recalled to our team. We could not be beaten in the rubber, but they could still square it and the excitement in the days beforehand was considerable. As a team, we had our own little excitement, too. The New Zealand Rugby Union of those days did not act toward the players in the generous attitude so common today. It was, in fact, believed among players that the only hope of appointment to it was incontrovertible proof that the candidate was descended from, and had all the worst characteristics of, Ebenezer Scrooge in mid-season form. We felt this blast of miserliness in the issue of tickets - I think we were to get one a man - and there was indignation among us. Porter called a team meeting. "This is the story, chaps," he said. After he had expounded the case, he said, "Are you with me?" "To a man," we all answered. Cliff then told the bigwigs, bluntly, that unless the allocation of tickets was improved, the team would not take the field. (We wouldn't have, either. We were solid.) The Rugby Union "alligadoos" were pretty shaken. They gave us what we had asked for. The story was never told and not even the Pressmen who knew us very well had an inkling of it.

We won the match by 22 points to 8. The British scored the best try of the game when Novis, playing at centre, swished past Cooke and myself, but by and large they weren't in the hunt and even without Nicholls our backline was, I think, superior in combination and soundness.

And then it was no-side. A great series of matches was over. More important, New Zealand, questing for a place on the International Rugby Board, was preparing to accept those portions of the international rules relating to the scrummage - and, afterwards, to the kick into touch between the 25-yard lines - which were to have such a catastrophic effect upon our Rugby of the next decade.

And most important of all from a personal point of view, this was the end in international Rugby of all of us who had made the great tour of the Invincibles. Irvine had had to bear, at his own cost, the consequences of his injury in the first test. Cyril Brownlie presented Norman McKenzie with his last pair of football boots. Maurice Brownlie retired to his farm and never again attempted to take a leading part in Rugby affairs. Quiet little Jimmy Mill faded away to his farm. Cooke and I, some time later, turned to Rugby League. Nicholls played a season or two more and then it was time even for his quenchless genius to cry hold, enough. I suppose, one way and another, I played longer than anybody.

And so, down through the years, Time, the unconquerable adversary, won one battle after another. The incomparable Invincibles were no more. I speak with very deep feeling. I speak with sorrow.

And yet - and yet there is a satisfaction beyond the comprehension of those who have not been of the company. The colour may fade, the braid may lose its lustre, the cap may shrink to a travesty. But the honours remain to record the prowess of the New Zealand footballer.

Top: Streatham & Mitcham RLFC 1935-36. Nepia is third from the left in the front row.
(Photo: Courtesy Les Hoole)

Below: Streatham & Mitcham's Kiwis
(Photo: Courtesy Les Hoole)

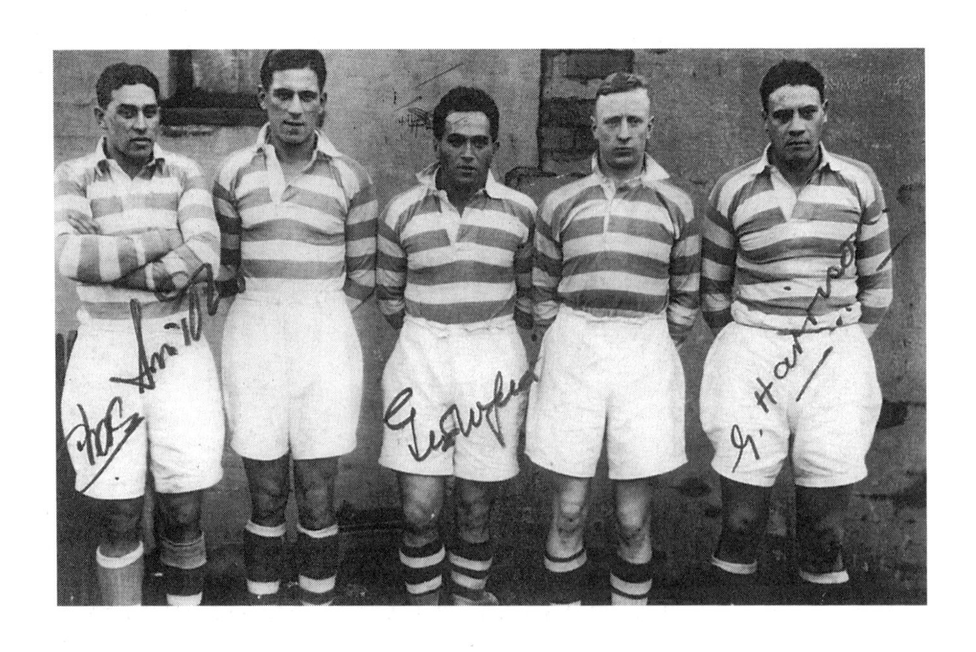

26. Triumph in Australia

So far as I was concerned, the Great Depression of the early 1930s was as good as a knockout blow on the point of the chin. I switched my farm over to dairying before the winter of 1931. The price for butterfat promptly tumbled. Not that it made much difference. Those were the days when you could buy wool for threepence and fourpence a pound - and believe me, at that price, you're not so much scared that the wolf will be at your door as that, any time, you'll have to start barking at his. By this time, we were in the midst of raising a family which finally numbered three boys and a girl - George ("Dedum"), Kiwi, Winstone, and Oma. With them, my wife and the farm to look after, topline Rugby, so far as I was concerned, was out. For the next three or four years, I played club football on the East Coast and sometimes I went with a representative team to Wairoa to play for the Barry Cup, a sub-union competition which aroused great interest and rivalry. During these years, the All Blacks twice went off to Australia, in 1932 and 1934, and an Australian team toured New Zealand in 1931, but I was not interested for one reason above all others: I could not afford to be.

The year 1935 was different. Though I was still extremely hard up, the Rugby programme whetted my interest. First, an All Black team was to travel to the British Isles, the first since our great expedition of 1924. Second, a New Zealand Maori team was to visit Australia. I was greatly interested in these tours for two entirely different reasons. While I knew that I did not stand a bolter's chance of selection for the All Blacks - and, frankly, I was not greatly interested, my economic circumstances being what they were - I was determined to do all I could to get a Maori wing threequarter from Wairoa named Charlie Smith into the team.

For the second part, I was greatly interested in the expedition to Australia. As I have mentioned once or twice before, I vowed in 1924 that some day I would show the Australian audiences that I really could play Rugby. The visit with the All Blacks in 1929 helped a little, but not so much as I would have liked. Now, with the Maoris, there would be a chance to show that Nepia was not such a bad sort of player after all.

It has been said many a time, by responsible people, too, that I switched to Rugby League because I was disgusted at my omission from the 1935 All Blacks. Here and now, I give the lie to this. I was thirty. I had been out of representative Rugby for five years. It would have been unreasonable to expect that I could fly into the team. Besides, those three little words, pounds, shillings and pence, danced in and out of my mind a good deal in those days. I had the bank manager much more on my mind than I had the All Black selection committee.

With Smith, it was different. He was a big man of nearly fourteen stone, extremely powerful of shoulder and thigh and with a surging, unstoppable run at the goal-line. He had played for Hawke's Bay for a year or two and a majority of players seemed to share my feeling that he was the finest wing in the country next to George Hart. He was so powerful, that was the thing. Like Jack Steel of old, he had the strength to shatter your tackle. He had good provincial performances behind him and in his appearances in various of the ten trials which preceded the selection of the All Blacks his form was good until he unluckily injured his shoulder in the final North Island trial at Palmerston North. That tore it, so far as he was concerned. Though selected for the final trial at Wellington and a general favourite for the team, he was yet another of the many victims of that blindness which besets selectors when they come to consider the qualifications of men who have not appeared in the last trial of all. So he was passed over and players like Nelson Ball, of Wellington, and Henry Brown, of Auckland, who were simply not in his class, were preferred. I would be much inclined to say that this was the worst piece of selecting I have ever known in New Zealand Rugby - and Lord knows, our committees have done their share of crass acts.

The All Blacks' loss was to prove the Maori team's gain. After taking part myself in the series of All Black trials all the way up to the final one, I returned to Gisborne to play in the Maori trial for the team to tour Australia. I had been asked if I would be available by, among others, Kingi Tahiwi, who was the representative of the Maori Advisory Board to the New Zealand Rugby Union and who was to be the manager of the touring team. My answer was that I could not afford to go. If I remember, I had one suit of clothes to my name. My football boots would have shocked you. I am not trying to tug the heartstrings. Those were the average conditions of small farmers in those bitterly hard days.

Sir Apirana Ngata, the great Maori leader of the East Coast, spoke to me. It was essential that I go, he said. I had the mana and the experience to make a success of the tour. I need have no worry about clothes. Everything would be provided for me, as a loan if I liked. Sir Apirana was a most persuasive man. He talked and I listened. On the night of the trial, I learned that I had been chosen and made captain. I could not conceal that the appointment gave me great satisfaction. Now would be the chance to show the Australians what I was made of. Yet I was not entirely satisfied. Before the team was announced, I was called into the room and given the names to read. From the expression on my face, Sir Apirana twigged that I was not happy. "Kaore ite pai kia koe?" he asked ("You don't agree with it"). Why, I said, did you leave out Everard Jackson? He has a bad ankle, Sir Apirana replied. A weak excuse, I said. A sprain would heal long before we were to arrive in Australia. You have left out one of the best forwards in New Zealand. He should be in the All Blacks going to England. My arguments and pleas made no impression. I left the room disgusted. Maori selectors as well as Pakehas, so it seemed, could make their mistakes.

We had a programme of eleven matches in Australia, including four matches in Queensland, one at Melbourne against Victoria, two in the interior of New South Wales, one at Newcastle and the equivalent of three tests with New South Wales, all at Sydney. We were beaten in our second game, by Queensland by 39 to 22 - skittery Rugby, with our chaps not yet settled into combination - and by New South Wales 13 to 20 in the second of the tests. For the rest, we were victorious and our scoring total of 256 points to 132 was, I felt, highly satisfactory.

On the journey to Sydney in the *Wanganella*, I deepened an acquaintance with one of the most wonderful men of all Rugby. This was our co-manager, Billy Wallace, the 1905 All Black, whose standing as the greatest back ever fielded in New Zealand has never been seriously challenged. He could and did play equally well at fullback, wing threequarter, centre threequarter and even five-eighth and until the arrival of that goal kicking wizard, D. B. Clarke, no one had ever approached his record of 367 points for New Zealand in 51 games. In addition to his greatness as a player, however, Billy was, in my experience, unrivalled as a dissector of tactics and strategies. Only Mark Nicholls ever approached his class in this respect - and significantly enough, for more than a year before the trip to Britain in 1924 Mark had lunched every day of the week with Billy while they discussed the problems of the game. As Nicholls had done, I too, found his conversation and ideas wonderfully stimulating. There are many tales told in Rugby of that South African genius at Stellensbosch University, A. F. Markotter, who could discern a great forward in an inside back, or vice versa, and who harangued the selection committee until, perhaps in despair, they decided to send the unknown Danie Craven to Britain as halfback with the Springboks of 1931. Wallace had that same gift of penetrating, or X-ray, vision. Between us, we proved the All Black selectors more than doubly wrong by making Charlie Smith a champion five-eighth during the Maori tour - and in his subsequent career in English League he spent a good many of his 500 matches in the flyhalf position.

Wallace and I, I regret to say, had to do a good deal of shuffling of players during the tour in Australia. On the way over, I gave a series of lectures on conditions in Australia - hard grounds, tough football, the need of fitness, things like that. I specially stressed that the climate was dangerous because it made you eat and eat and if you did not watch out, your weight could suffer. The Maori boys listened to me solemnly and nodded their heads wisely. Good old George, you could see them thinking, he really does talk sense. From the moment we hit Sydney, however, some of them succumbed to the climate. They began to eat and eat. Maoris are among the world's best at putting on weight and our chaps were among the best of Maoris. No wonder Billy and I had to do so much shuffling.

Nevertheless, it was a memorable tour. The Sydney newspapers soon latched on to "Dynamite" Smith, of whom it was said: "He demonstrated his favourite battering-ram tactics and crashed three opponents out of his course to score the only try for the Maoris. If the All Blacks have a better man than Smith, then they must have a great threequarter line." Several forwards became outstanding - men like George Harrison, of Taranaki, who afterwards had a long career in League in England; Peter Smith and Hawea Mataira, of Hawke's Bay; Len Kawe, of King Country; Jim Brodrick, of Bay of Plenty; Walter Cooper, of North Auckland; and George Reedy, of East Coast. The backs, too, furnished some outstanding men, among them Jack Hemi, a great goal kick who became a star in League, Smith, and our East Coast halfback, Rangi Harrison, who of all the halves I have ever seen most closely resembled Jimmy Mill in style and brains.

Not making excuses, I would say that our defeat by Queensland was attributable more to an influenza epidemic which had hit our team than to the three dropped goals which played so important a part in the game. Nevertheless, F. Vincent, the Queensland fullback, played brilliantly and his retirement before half time with a leg injury in the return match had a decisive effect upon our win by 15 to 13. Of this match, one newspaper - and they all gave us great space - ran its report under the headlines, "Maoris Turn Tables in Sizzling Union Game - Real Delight to Spectators", and that seems not to be the kind of Press All Black teams have had in Australia in recent years. This sort of Press continued throughout the tour. In Sydney, for instance, we encountered the heading, "The Most Colourful Team in Rugby Football", and out in the sticks there was another one, "Unexpected Brilliance in Backs and Forwards". Perhaps the world was starry-eyed in those days - the Rugby reporters anyway. They looked for the good things and praised them. Today, it sometimes seems to me, the aim is to find the bad things and talk only of them.

I imagine that the tour must have been made by the first match with New South Wales, which we won at the Sydney Cricket Ground before 28,811 spectators. W. S. Hamilton in the *Sydney Sun* said that the crowd was "roused to wild enthusiasm right through the second half. They saw movement without a halt and a wonderful exhibition of robust football." It was certainly great stuff for the troops. So the tour went on, with good football the paramount ambition of every team in every match and with the ball bouncing well enough for me to rate supporting headlines, "The Greatness of Nepia", "Bluffed His Side Out of Danger Like Poker Adventurer", in *Sydney Truth*.

There were, as a fact, several aspects of this tour which gave me permanent pleasure. It was at Dubbo that some speaker made reference to the fact that our party included two great fullbacks in Billy Wallace and myself. "Well," said Billy in that characteristically quavery voice of his, "I did not see myself play but I have seen George Nepia at his best and if it is true that I am in the same street as him, then I am a proud man." Then the *Sydney Mail*, a weekly which used to be published by the *Sydney Morning Herald*, had this to say: "In one of his books, Matthew Arnold has written, 'Genius is mainly an affair of energy', but Nepia showed how genius was the conserver, not the consumer, of energy. It was the easy, graceful, unflurried polished manner in which he performed all his tasks which impressed and which indicated how his long football education and experience have developed the instinctive sense which compels correct action for each separate circumstance. His positional play and handling were faultless, his kicking, left or right foot, was prodigious and his tackling and fielding of the ball on the ground remarkably sure. We know how difficult of attainment is perfection but we know also that Nepia has mastered all the difficulties of a fullback's job to such an extent that his technique and execution have reached perfection. Never before has this thirty-year-old, shy, unassuming master played so ably in Australia."

And with those words, with our record as a team, I think I can say that in the fullness of time I was able to discharge my debt to Australia.

We returned to Wellington in the old *Manuka* and in a howling southerly two days after arrival were beaten by Wellington by 11 to 9. Many of our men had been bedridden all the way across the Tasman and after one look at that wind-torn field of Athletic Park they felt inclined to go back to bed again. It was a change to play in good weather in Auckland. This was a mighty tough battle which we won by 14 points to 10 and from which I had to retire halfway through the second spell with a leg injury. But it was a pleasure to prove to a New Zealand audience that our good performance in Australia was skill and not luck. This was one of the happiest of my experiences in Rugby and to the members of the team who are still alive I would say, sincerely, "Ehoa, ma tena koutou."

27. Why I Turned Over

We Maoris had all known that Charlie Smith was bitterly disappointed at his omission from the 1935 All Blacks. His success in Australia, particularly at second five-eighth in the final test with New South Wales, deepened the feeling that he had been unjustly treated. It had been held against him that he snatched at the ball. The criticism was trivial. It had also been said, in New Zealand as well as in Australia, that the omission was more than a mistake, it was a tragedy. All of these things were working away in Charlie's mind and when, soon after the Maori tour had finished, we went to Wairoa for a Barry Cup match I was not surprised to learn that he was favouring an idea of turning to professional Rugby League in England. The approach had been made from an Aucklander, Eric Bennetts, who for years had written about League for the *Auckland Star* and who acted as an agent for an English club.

Though the offer was only for £100, a trifling sum these days, I urged Charlie to accept it. I was still as sore as he was about his omission from the team. Jokingly, I said to him: "When you get to Auckland and see that agent, you can tell him I'll play Rugby League, too."

Smith departed. I went back to the farm. My joke passed out of my mind. There was fencing and weeding and milking, the unceasing round of jobs of farm life, and this was the last bad year of the depression, though it still looked as if it might last forever. One day, out of the blue, a telegraph boy arrived with a reply-paid telegram from Bennetts offering me a job with League in England. I said to myself, I'll fix this bloke. My reply was, "Offer accepted. £500 or nothing." I said to my wife, Huinga, "I do not think we will hear another word." Two days later, Bennetts telegraphed that the price was accepted. Now this was a pretty pickle. For two days, my wife and I discussed all angles. At the end, she said that I ought to go, I could not now back out.

I encountered then, and even to this day I sometimes still encounter, a positive and adverse reaction from Rugby people to my going over to League. At the time, it was alleged that I was furiously angry at my omission from the All Blacks. It was also said that I was disloyal to the game which had done so much for me (no one, of course, ever inquired about the hours I had spent making myself a good player). Some people became very bitter indeed. Their attitude suggested that I was little better than a criminal.

I have already, I hope, disposed of the crazy idea that I acted like a spoiled boy over the All Black selection. Now let me take you to Rangitukia in 1935, to a small farm which was still yielding, as it had done for the past several years, a dismally low income in relation to the work that was put in. A young family occupied that farm, all in need of the clothing, the care, the attention for which money must be earned. The master of the house had three suits, one of them, believe it or not, a dinner-jacket. The other two had been presented to me for the Maori tour. The mistress's wardrobe was not filled with gowns. It was a grey world. There seemed not much prospect of improvement. Only a year or so before, thousands had rioted through the streets of New Zealand's main cities in the demand for work and food and social justice. No one who ever lived through that depression as an adult or adolescent could ever forget the cruel experience.

To us on that farm, £500 was like a million pounds. Immediate debts could be paid, some definite plans could be laid for the future, most of our anxieties about the welfare of the children would be dispelled, at least for a time.

So I went. I say now that I did not willingly go. My heart was then, as it will be forever, in Rugby. I say, too, that if the Labour Government had come into power, with the guaranteed price scheme for butterfat, in 1934 instead of 1935, I would not have gone. I could have seen that farmers would be offered a margin of security which up till then they never had.

So I went. And not for anybody will I now rat and say that it was a mortifying experience, that League warrants the description Mr Baxter gave it, that I suffered purgatory for every moment I spent in the game. On the contrary, I found it, to play, fast and exhilarating. It stood to reason that with twenty-six instead of thirty men on a field, there was more room to manoeuvre. Moreover, it was a professional sport and as such it was rigidly governed. The demands were constant and they were high. If a trainer, the boss man, called for a practice at seven o'clock, you did not arrive at seven, or ten past, and start changing and nattering. You marched on to the field, fully prepared, at seven o'clock. If you were slack and uninterested during a training session, you could be made to train an extra half hour on your own - and like it or lump it. Cash ruled all considerations.

My club, Streatham and Mitcham, was supported by another club called Acton and Willesden and the two were ruled by the one sponsor, S. E. Parkes, an enthusiast, and a businessman, who was trying to persuade Londoners to support Rugby League. During my second season in London, Acton and Willesden was disbanded and as manager of Streatham and Mitcham, I had free call on their best players. This made Streatham and Mitcham a powerful team, good enough to win the first six games of the new season.

It was then that I found that Parkes proposed to offset his losses on Acton and Willesden by the transfer fees he would secure for his best players in the new combined club. Charlie Smith was first to go, for £1,250 Then followed George Harrison, of the Maori team, Eddie Holder, a 1934 All Black from the West Coast, and myself. I do not think Parkes liked to see us go and for my part I had got on well with him. But he was primarily a businessman and as such his heart was ruled by his head. Cash, as I say, was the consideration. It must always be, in any professional sport. For instance, in my first season I found that there was an animus against me in other clubs. I wondered why until I found that Parkes was charging these other clubs twenty-five per cent of their gates for my appearance. It was business, do you see. I was a commodity and had a price and he was determined to get the best he could.

It is not for me to argue whether pounds, shillings and pence should so dominate the considerations of a sport or pastime. Let me say, simply, that out of his abilities at Rugby League many a young man has established a livelihood, if not a fortune, which he would never have got in any other way. If a man had the instincts of a great writer, it would surely be wrong to put him to pick and shovel all his days. So in this hard, unsentimental place which is what the world really is, it is surely right for a young man - if he so wishes - to make the most of his talent.

After all, when anyone still accuses me of desertion, I must remind him that the £500 saved me and my family. Would my accusers have stood to me if I had not taken the step?

I trained hard on shipboard on the way to England. By the time I arrived I was, I thought, fit. I was down to play two days after arrival against, of all teams, Wigan, the famous side of which the fullback and captain was Jim Sullivan. This was a legendary character, a famous Welshman who had, as they say, "gone North" to make his fortune in League and who for a long period in the twenties and thirties was first choice in English international League teams. It was a hard assignment to match him, the more particularly because my knowledge of League rules was so sketchy. Compared with Rugby Union, too, I found this new game fast and open. I soon realised that for the time being I was two or three yards too slow and would need to train to make up the leeway. Nevertheless, the special correspondent of the *Daily Despatch* was admiring. "The Rugby League game," he wrote, "owes a great debt of gratitude to its two greatest fullbacks, Jim Sullivan and George Nepia, not only for an epic display of football but also for a fine exhibition of sportsmanship. For eighty minutes, they hammered away at each other with almost cut-throat rivalry. At the end, they left the field arm in arm. What did it matter if 20,000 people almost completely forgot the rest of the players. Perhaps they, too, sensed that this historic battle, although only the first, may well be the last. If only these two great warriors were ten years younger! What a contrast in styles. Jim Sullivan, big, slow-looking, almost awkward - but oh, how safe. And George Nepia, on tiptoe with his spectacular ballet-dance clearance - but just as safe. Right from the start, they went to it with grim determination. Long-range kicking bouts only proved what great players they both were. But honours went to the Maori. Four times during the game, he bamboozled the Wigan captain with that famous spinning shot. Each time the ball dropped to shoot off at an amazing angle."

My first appearances did not set the Thames on fire. My fielding and tackling were up to standard, but I was not kicking the goals and these are vital in League. Nevertheless, we as a team were doing reasonably well in every particular except that we found it difficult, if not impossible, to wean Londoners away from their beloved Soccer. I was at this time manager as well as captain of the side and by way of variation I placed myself, with some success, at centre threequarter. Here I could be a help to Smith and Holder and here, too, my own play improved so much that I scored more than a century of points, including 82 points from 41 goals.

For want of public support, however, the fortunes of Acton and Willesden and of Streatham and Mitcham began to decline. Early in the season of 1936-37 - 1 had contracted, incidentally, for the two seasons, '35-'36 and -'36-'37 - Trevor Wignall reported in the *Daily Express* that Mr Parkes had lost about £30,000 in his attempt to start Rugby League in London. He also said, accurately as it happened, that some of us New Zealanders in the club had not received our wages of £7 10s. a week for about a month. Smith had now gone to Halifax and Holder to Wigan. On 29 December 1936, having in the meantime scored more than fifty goals for Streatham and Mitcham, I, too, went to Halifax, making my first appearance on New Year's Day at centre. Later, I displaced Lockwood, the

Halifax regular fullback for the two previous years, and apart from time off for injury I spent the next two or three months in Halifax colours. It was then time for me to come home and having, as a formality, been placed on the transfer list, I upped sticks and left.

Professional club League was, and I am sure still is, a hard game. It has its objectionable features, as when a team is promised a bonus if it wins a key match. Anything then goes and the tackling can become brutally tough. But the standard of play, there is no question, is very high. The passing and catching are outstandingly good, the tackling is severe and sleight-of-hand has to be practised to penetrate the defensive screen. Lancashire and Yorkshire are cold places in the winter, but in my time the warmth of the hospitality offset much of the natural longing for Maoriland and to the people of the various towns the leading players in the local teams were tin gods. I was even commissioned to write the story of my life in the *Halifax Sporting Green*, though what the effort was like I now haven't the faintest idea. As I have remarked, it was a hard, tough sport. There was no favouritism. It did not matter who you were, if you were not good enough out you went - and no humbug. It was enlightening to encounter this attitude. It did me no harm - and if, at any time, I did wonder what was going on, I needed only to think of that £500 to remind myself of some of the virtues of the sport.

All that needs be said about my career in English League has been, I think, said by George Harrison, whose career was longer than mine and who was a most successful forward. "George Nepia's ability as an amateur is well known," Harrison wrote, "but I was one of the few New Zealanders fortunate enough to see his first professional game. It was also the first time he had played on the same field as Jim Sullivan, who is considered England's Nepia in the professional code.

"Though George had only been in England for two days and was badly handicapped by being unfamiliar with the League game, his form was of a very high standard. Apart from that first day, I have played in many games with and against both Nepia and Sullivan and have had the opportunity of judging each on his average standard of play.

"There have been great controversies about these two famous fullbacks. In my opinion, Nepia showed more initiative and was more versatile than Sullivan. Moreover, Sullivan seemed unconsciously to dominate his team-mates, often to the detriment of their play, whereas Nepia invariably had a stimulating effect on his side.

"There is no doubt that George was a great drawcard. Of his many brilliant performances, one incident in particular stands as something only he could have achieved. Streatham and Mitcham were playing Salford on the latter's home ground at Manchester. Allan Edwards, the Salford international threequarter, had broken through and was coming at top speed down the line with only one man to beat - George Nepia. George, hurrying across, offered Edwards the old, but nevertheless tempting bait, the touchline gap.

"Edwards appeared to have swallowed the bait and Nepia clapped on the pace for the kill. Then like a flash, without slackening speed, Edwards turned inside. Going at his speed, he would have been past any other man in the world - including Jim Sullivan. But the next moment, Edwards shot straight up into the air and crashed down flat as Nepia half-somersaulted backwards and gently stroked him under the chin in passing."

I was happy to come back to New Zealand, to Huinga and the children. Rangitukia was good to see, too. But there was half a season of League left to play and Grey Campbell, the chairman, Jim Rukutai, Emie Asher and others of, or connected with, the council of the New Zealand Rugby League were anxious for my services. I arranged to play for the Manukau club in Auckland and by urgent request soon went off to Christchurch to make a couple of appearances there.

Meantime, the Australian Kangaroos were in Auckland on their way to England and they played their first test with the Kiwis on the day of my last appearance in Christchurch. On the Wednesday, having returned from the south two days before, I turned out for New Zealand Maoris against the tourists. We won the match. It was an excellent game, too. Right away, I prepared to leave for Wellington to see the Springbok Rugby team play the All Blacks in the first test and to take part in a reunion of the Invincibles which had been arranged for that weekend.

Then the Maori League councillors came at me again. Would I play, they wanted to know, in the final test with the Kangaroos on the same day as the Rugby test? I did not hesitate. Certainly, I said. It was a fine, a thrilling match. They led us by 15 to 8 at halftime. We had a couple of new caps who were not quite in their best form and the team was just a little disjointed. At halftime, our manager spoke very sharply to these chaps. They were letting the side down, they were doing this, they weren't doing that. I couldn't stand the tirade any longer. Leave them alone, I said. They're doing their best. They've got over their nerves by now. Everything will be all right in the next half. Leave them alone.

I wasn't the captain, but I had to say these things. I well knew that nothing so quickly upsets a new player as abuse. I was proved right, too. In the second half, these chaps came right on to their game. The Kiwis really tucked into the Australians. We stopped them from scoring, but they couldn't stop us. Slowly, we caught up. In a sensational finish, we got home by 16 to 15.

So I said farewell to big football. It was in a sensational manner, too. In the second half, the Australians took a penalty at halfway and used it to direct a long kick over my head. As I was running back, I took a quick look at the forwards who were bearing down on me and after gauging the flight of the ball knew instinctively that they would reach me simultaneously with the catch. I knew, too, that there would be no beg pardons. This was a test match and it was being played for keeps.

Instead of waiting for the ball to come down to waist level before catching it, I reached up my arms above my head, caught the ball in my outstretched hands and instantly drew my arms down, sitting violently backwards as I did so. (This may have saved my life. It certainly saved me from serious injury.)

As I sat down, I thudded, as it were, on to the thigh of Pearce, the big Kangaroo forward who weighed nearly sixteen stone and who was travelling at maximum speed. Instantly, I heard a loud crack. I rose up, got away my kick and turned to him. There, to my horror, I found him lying in agony. His thigh was broken. I did what I could. That evening, when the Australians were leaving for England - and I am glad to say that they took him with them - I went on board the ship to wish him and the team well. They bore no grudge. It was an accident. But it was, all the same, a terrible moment.

And so the last page was ready to be turned. Perhaps I may finally quote the reporter who remarked that "There were some League critics rather sceptical of the high praise handed out to Nepia and some who confessed that they had been unfortunate in that, over a long period of years, they had not seen the great Nepia play an outstanding game.

"But in the 1938 season, Nepia by an extraordinary display of fullback skill silenced all Carlaw Park critics. He gave a display which left them wondering just how good the same Nepia was in the palmy days of his football career."

I wouldn't know. As Billy Wallace remarked of himself, I never saw George Nepia play.

28. My Four Children

I live now, as I have done these last few years, on a high, hill-country station about twenty miles from Wairoa. Over recent years, there has been consolidation of the fragmented Maori lands and the farm I am on, in which I have a family interest, comprises 5,000 acres of sheep and beef-cattle country. For a good many months of the year, the two men and I who work the place are kept pretty busy in the open air. It is a good life. My friends tell me that I look fit. My weight is little more than it used to be in 1924. I go into Wairoa once a week to pick up my mail, to discuss the property, to have a beer or two and a talk with old friends like Charlie Smith, who is now a successful contractor in the town. When I can, I get to the Rugby matches in Wairoa, Gisborne, or Napier. There is no greater joy than discussing with your cronies why the game now is not nearly so good as it used to be.

My own place has gone to my second son, Winstone. My daughter, Kiwi, was a schoolteacher before she was married and settled in Gisborne and though she has children of her own she sometimes goes back to teach. Our grandchildren are the finest in the world and I cannot blame Huinga when, now and again, she decides that she simply must go to see them at Rangitukia or Gisborne. For their part, they dote on her and you can see how refreshed she is when she comes back to our lonely place.

For lonely it is. Wairoa is just around the corner, but somehow it is a long corner; and so, for me in particular, there are long spaces of time when in the midst of mechanical tasks I find myself thinking back over my life, especially my career in football. As surely as I start to think of this, I find myself remembering thirty grains of maize and a kitchen table-top, two brown faces, one lined with middle age, the other blooming with youth. I start, too, to think of that phrase of Denzil Batchelor's as to which of a number of fullbacks he mentioned "was fit to loose the laces of my Cotton Oxford boots"

I think, naturally, of many other things. Huinga was - and is - a fine musician and to my delight each of our children had a good ear and could sing. As we all grew up together, we as a family obtained the greatest pleasure, in church and at home, in song and in music; and I can remember, as clearly as if it had happened five minutes ago, how when we had learned a song or a hymn everyone took his part naturally and accurately, so that in the harmony there was a rare contentment. This faculty, which by God's grace we all possessed, played no small part in our upbringing and in the creation of that family spirit which means so much in life.

I think, too, of how our difficult life was improved by the guaranteed price system which offered even the farmers of our small standing real security and, comparatively, an amazing prosperity. With the coming of the war, of course, life offered other difficulties. Many of the Maori and Pakeha boys of our district rushed to join up and with their going those of us who remained realised that we, too, must play our part with harder work on our places and in the community effort. Under the wartime amnesty, all of us who served were granted reinstatement to Rugby and as a contribution to my old game I began to coach and to referee. Down through the years, I had much fun as a referee. It was strange, but pleasant, to look at the game from another angle and to appreciate at first hand how difficult and taxing a referee's life can be. After the war, I became a representative referee and even rose to the heights of controlling matches for the Olympians, the club in Gisborne which puts on festival-type matches. On one grand day in Auckland, I refereed for the Barbarians, that fine club which has done so much good for the game in the north, and toward the end, when someone had scored a try, they would not let the game go on until I had taken the kick at goal - and converted it, too! Happy days these: and happy memories they give me.

I took to coaching with the best pupils of all - the youngsters. The headmaster of Rangitukia school, George Cormack, asked for a hand and when we had been going for a bit we took to thinking to ourselves that one of these days we would beat the daylights out of the Te Araroa school where the team, coached and well-trained by the headmaster, Harry Black, had had an unbeaten record for a number of years. In the first year, Te Araroa beat my boys twice, but by the second game my lads had improved markedly. In the second year, which was 1942, the difference between the two teams was closer and by 1943 I knew that we had the makings of a team which would defeat all comers on the Coast. Halfway through the year, a new boy, John Wilson, came to us from Wairoa and at the first sight I knew that he was a born footballer who only needed training and experience. This I gave to him, as hard as he could take it, and though he returned to Wairoa before I could complete my lessons I had satisfaction when, in after years, he had consistent success in professional League in England.

Associated with Wilson in our success against Te Araroa was another boy. Which brings me to the grains of maize, the table-top and the earnest faces. This boy was my eldest son, George, whom we nicknamed "Dedum".

I coached George at Rangitukia school and, at night, I coached him in the kitchen. The top of the table was marked out as a football field and the grains of corn represented the thirty players. Night after night, month after month, the two of us talked Rugby. I taught him all that I had learned, all that I knew. As he grew, and saw more of the game, his questions sharpened. He wanted to know the answers to this and to that, the way to do unusual things, the means of strengthening attack or defence. Often and often, the two of us would go out on to the field, kicking, catching, running, passing. At Rangitukia, I played him in every position from hooker to fullback. I wanted him to develop ball sense and my idea was that as he acquired this he would some day take naturally to the position he liked best. By the time he went off to Gisborne High School, "Dedum" knew as much about Rugby as I did. He only wanted plenty of football to bring it out of him.

At Gisborne, as I knew he would, he progressed to the First XV. He played then as a halfback and on the day that I saw the team defeat Sacred Heart College, of Auckland he formed a really splendid combination with Brian Fitzpatrick, who was afterwards an All Black in Australia in 1951 and in the British Isles in 1953-54 and with August Tureia, who came from a great footballing family on the Coast. During one term holiday, Rangers of Rangitukia asked George to play against City of Ruatoria in the Whakari Cup competition for club premiership. He turned out at half and I, the other George Nepia, was at first five-eighth. I am sure I was the proudest parent in all the land, the more particularly because he played a lovely game which greatly helped us to retain the cup.

Though I did not try to influence him, secretly I hoped that he would covet the fullback position. On and on he went at Gisborne, five years in all, and during all of this time his footballing technique was markedly improving. As I had foreseen, he needed only the experience to bring out of him all that he had learned with the maize and the table-top.

Coincidentally, his ambition to become a soldier strengthened into a passion. From his first year at high school he talked always of the Army. As a senior student, he was nominated for a cadetship at Duntroon, the Royal Military College in Australia, and for his sake we were as disappointed as he when he failed to qualify, by only a few marks, at the course at the Trentham Military Camp in Wellington. Still, he would not be satisfied. On every holiday, he talked ever-lastingly to Huinga and me about the Army.

At the end of his school days, "Dedum" joined the Ministry of Works in Gisborne and when the Poverty Bay representative team went on tour to Bush Districts, Wairarapa, Horowhenua and Hawke's Bay, he was one of the party. To my delight, he was at fullback. He came home complaining. "Pop," he said, "why on earth did you name me 'George' Every time I step on the field, everyone expects me to do things just like you used to do. And I can't. Why didn't you give me some other name!" I felt sorry for him. I knew how he felt. But when I answered, I told him what I sincerely believed. "Boy," I said. "You have everything. I have taught you all I know about fullback play. All you want is a lot of football - and the big stuff - to bring it out." It was true, too. They played a game in Gisborne, Olympians versus Poverty Bay, and once more I was the proudest father there ever had been in Rugby football. The Olympians made me captain and fullback - I was about forty-eight then - and Poverty Bay made young George captain and fullback. It was age versus youth and I was proud to acknowledge that the son outkicked the father. It was my spiral against his, the one I had taught him - but he had the youth and the power and I could not match him.

And then, inevitably, he joined the Army. They posted him to Linton Military Camp, near Palmerston North. He took to the life as a duck takes to water. He continued in Rugby, too, with greater skill than before. Manawatu made him their fullback for a South Island tour; and I was amused later to hear that a number of my old friends of the Invincibles had been to see him and to make a fuss of him. One of them said to him, "You aren't bad, son. You have everything your father had. But you have a long way to go." Young George took all this in good part. He was in the Army and it was the life he had always wanted.

And then, in 1954, he was posted to the Fijian Battalion for service against the Chinese bandits in the heart of Malaya. They are great natural Rugby players, the Fijians, and it said much for George, who was now a sergeant, that he was ranked as the finest fullback in the battalion. Major Genge, his commanding officer, told me that when the Fijians played a British Regimental team young George played a great game. "I have seen you play many of your great games," Major Genge wrote to me, "and I am proud to say that young George excelled himself. It was as if I was watching the father all over again."

As I pause for the moment on the bare hillside of that Hawke's Bay farm, I can see scores of miles north to the table-top in the kitchen and the grains of maize and the two heads solving yet another of the innumerable problems of Rugby. And I can see, too, far across the seas to Malaya, to the dark forests and the swarming vegetation.

For that is where young George lies, killed in action in the service of his country.

When he went, I lost a son. I lost, too, a friend. And perhaps Rugby, who knows, lost the one who would have unloosed the laces of those Cotton Oxford football boots....

Appendix I

GEORGE NEPIA'S FIRST-CLASS RECORD

Of Nepia's forty-six matches for New Zealand, thirty-eight were played in succession -a record.

During his first-class Rugby career, he played 129 matches, as under:

New Zealand	46 matches
New Zealand Maoris	15
Hawke's Bay	28
East Coast	I5
New Zealand Trials	9
Tai Rawhiti	7
North Island	3
Maori Trial	1
North XV (Canada)	1
Hawke's Bay-Poverty Bay-East Coast	1
Poverty Bay-Bay of Plenty-East Coast	1
Olympians Club	1
Southern Maori XV	1

Nepia's 100th first-class game was for Tai Rawhiti against Te Waiounamu at Christchurch on 22 August 1931.

Appendix 2

THE 1924 ALL BLACKS

	Age	Height ft in	Weight st lb
Fullback			
G. Nepia (Hawke's Bay)	19	5 9	13 5
Threequarters			
H. W. Brown (Taranaki)	19	5 9¾	11 7
A. H. Hart (Taranaki)	26	5 6½	9 12
F. W. Lucas (Auckland)	22	5 10	10 4
A. C. C. Robilliard (Canterbury)	20	5 10	11 8
J. Steel (West Coast)	24	5 10	12 7
K. S. Svenson (Wellington)	25	5 7	10 12
Five-Eighth			
C. E. O. Badeley (Auckland)	27	5 7	10 9
A. E. Cooke (Auckland)	22	5 9	9 12
N. P. McGregor (Canterbury)	22	5 7	10 6
M. F. Nicholls (Wellington)	22	5 9¾	11 0

L. Paewai (Hawke's Bay)	19	5 8½	11 8
Halfbacks			
J. J. Mill (Hawke's Bay)	24	5 7	10 12
W. C. Dalley (Canterbury)	22	5 4½	10 2
Wing-forwards			
C. G. Porter (Wellington) captain	24	5 8	12 8
J. H. Parker (Canterbury)	27	6 0	12 7
Hookers			
Q. Donald (Wairarapa)	24	5 10	12 6
W. R. Irvine (Hawke's Bay)	25	5 7½	12 12
B. V. McCleary (Canterbury)	27	5 9	13 1
H. G. Munro (Otago)	27	5 9	11 12
Locks			
R. R. Masters (Canterbury)	23	5 11½	14 0
I. H. Harvey (Wairarapa)	21	6 1½	14 8
Side-row			
M. J. Brownlie (Hawke's Bay)	26	6 0	13 13
C. J. Brownlie (Hawke's Bay)	27	6 3	15 0
J. Richardson (Southland)	25	6 1	14 5
L. F. Cupples (Bay of Plenty)	26	6 2½	13 12
Back Row			
R. T. Stewart (South Canterbury)	20	6 1	14 0
A. H. West (Taranaki)	30	6 1	13 12
A. White (Southland)	30	5 10½	12 6

Manager - Mr S. S. Dean (Wellington).
Weights given are at the time of selection.
Eleven members of the team served in World War I.

Appendix 3

MATCH RESULTS OF 1924-5 ALL BLACK TOUR

1924	
13 September v. Devon	won 11 - 0
18 September v. Cornwall	won 29 - 0
20 September v. Somerset	won 6 - 0
25 September v. Gloucestershire	won 6 - 0
27 September v. Swansea	won 39 - 3
2 October v. Newport	won 13 - 10
4 October v. Leicester	won 27 - 0
8 October v. North Midlands	won 40 - 3

11 October v. Cheshire	won 18 - 5
15 October v. Durham	won 43 - 7
18 October v. Yorkshire	won 42 - 4
22 October v. Lancashire	won 23 - 0
25 October v. Cumberland	won 41 - 0
1 November v. Ireland (1st International)	won 6 - 0
5 November v. Ulster	won 28 - 6
8 November v. Northumberland	won 27 - 4
12 November v. Cambridge University	won 5 - 0
15 November v. London Counties	won 31 - 6
20 November v. Oxford University	won 33 - 15
22 November v. Cardiff	won 16 - 8
29 November v. Wales (2nd International)	won 19 - 0
2 December v. Llanelly	won 8 - 3
6 December v. East Midlands	won 31 - 7
11 December v. Warwickshire	won 20 - 0
13 December v. Combined Services	won 25 - 3
17 December v. Hampshire	won 22 - 0
20 December v. London Counties	won 28 - 3

1925

3 January v. England (3rd International)	won 17 - 11
11 January v. Selection Française	won 37 - 8
18 January v. France	won 30 - 6
14 February v. Vancouver	won 49 - 0
18 February v. Victoria	won 68 - 4

Appendix 4

1924 INVINCIBLES PAY TRIBUTES TO NEPIA

MR S. S. DEAN: George Nepia achieved great success as the complete fullback and imbued the team with the utmost confidence. He will forever in the world of Rugby football be ranked among the great fullbacks.

CLIFF PORTER: How often have I been asked, who was the greatest fullback I have ever seen? Unhesitatingly I state - George Nepia. Remembering all of those magnificent fullbacks I have seen play in New Zealand and overseas, and fully realising how much the game has changed, George Nepia is the champion of them all. George earned this great distinction from the remarkable manner in which he played thirty games out of thirty with the 1924 New Zealand team and he continued to play up to his reputation on his return to New Zealand. How did he earn his great name? Because, in the thirty games played, never once can I or any member of our touring team recall a solitary mistake in George's play. He was magnificent. His positional play, consistently accurate and long line kicking, and deadly tackling, had to be seen to be appreciated. George could extricate himself from the almost impossible. Many times I have seen him confronted with three players storming down on him and with only George to beat for a certain try but no try was scored, and mind you one occasion was while playing the Welsh International and once against the British team. Perhaps the greatest tribute I can pay George is the fact that all of us had so much confidence in his ability as the last line of defence we rarely backed him up but just left it to Nepia. Weighing about thirteen stone three pounds, and standing five feet nine inches high, George had his twentieth birthday during that tour of England, was the idol of football supporters almost everywhere, and the most modest fellow one could wish to meet.

MARK NICHOLLS: George Nepia is the only Rugby player I know of who became the greatest player in his position, in the world, at the age of nineteen years. This reputation he maintained throughout his career. In the fundamentals of the game he was as near perfect as humanly possible. He was, in addition, a very good place kicker and drop kicker, and he stood alone as a punt kicker. In the first test match against the British Team of 1930, played on a mud patch at Dunedin, he covered the full length of the ground in two punts from successive penalty kicks, with a ball that other players had difficulty in kicking thirty yards. I played with him often and he was the perfect team player. He was named as one of the five players of the year in *Wisden's Rugby Football Almanack* of 1924-25, was acclaimed by Rugby writers wherever he played, and we of the 1924 team were of the same opinion. We were a happy band of footballers. After the tour of New South Wales we knew that we had the makings of a great team. The outstanding brilliance of some of the players made it possible to build a team whose defence and attack were so co-ordinated that every team we met was defeated. Our team spirit was extraordinary and the trust we had in each others' capabilities resulted in fine *esprit de corps*. We had, too, a great trust in our manager. Stanley Dean was a strong-minded, dominating personality and a brilliant speaker. He was chairman of our selection committee and of all our team talks, to which he contributed as much as any of the players. He co-ordinated the ideas expounded at the team talks into a set pattern of play (mainly defensive) and we were fortunate to have him at the head of the team. He thoroughly understood the value of team combination and the placing of certain players in certain positions to achieve the best combination. As captain of the backs it was my job to confer with him in the preliminary selection of the backs prior to the final selection by the committee and it was as the result of these talks that the test team of backs evolved. I wish the authors of this book complete success. It should appeal to all players of the 1920 - 1935 era, their descendants and all followers of the game of Rugby football.

W. C. DALLEY: One of the outstanding features of the tour was the wonderful display of Nepia. His rocklike defence gave the whole team confidence. We will never forget that occasion during the Welsh test when the Welsh forwards were sweeping toward our line in a dangerous movement. George dived at their feet at full speed, picked up the ball, sent the Welshmen sprawling in all directions and then found the line with a magnificent kick which landed in touch in the Welsh 25. In passing, I would say that the 1924 team were the happiest of any I have been associated with.

R. T. STEWART: As a team-mate, I saw Nepia develop from a youngster of high promise into a fullback of uncanny skill and tremendous pluck. I know I am not alone in saying that New Zealand never saw Nepia at his best, magnificent though he may have been on occasions. That was the good fortune of the Rugby enthusiasts of England, Ireland, Wales and France that winter thirty-nine years ago when he became their idol. To have this sturdy, cheerful and utterly reliable Maori youngster as rearguard was a great boost for the tourists, particularly when hard matches were taking their toll in weariness and tension. Having seen most of the big-name fullbacks of South Africa, the British Isles and Australia in action from 1921 to the present day, I have no hesitation in saying that Nepia was the master of them all.

J. H. PARKER: After all these years, it takes a grand sportsman as well as a great player to be a household name in international Rugby. Such a sportsman, such a player, was and is George Nepia. In the last forty years, I have been fortunate to do a lot of travelling, but wherever I have been I invariably have found someone interested in Rugby and, not surprisingly, the name of Nepia has always cropped up. September 13, 1924, against Devon at Devonport, marked the birth of the Nepia legend. His first "take" was unbelievable - right off the feet of the forwards, a shake of his hips, forwards flying in all directions and then, bang! Away went the ball to gain more than half the field of play. High balls, balls on the ground, they made no difference to Nepia that day and he never lost that confidence right through the tour. It was eleven years before I saw him lose confidence in himself. It was in the final trial for the 1935 All Black team to go to Britain. Everything seemed to go wrong and in desperation he tried every trick he knew, but without success. It was left to Gilbert to hold the fort for New Zealand, but great player though he was, he suffered by comparison with Nepia. As to the merits of Nepia and R. W. H. Scott, let me say that both were magnificent players. On a wet ground, with the ball kept low and forwards pressing home dribbling rushes, Nepia could halt the attack and turn defence into attack. On a dry ground, with the ball played high and a fullback called on to take high balls, weave and evade, Scott was a master. I would have Nepia with the ball close to the ground and Scott with the ball in the air and evasive play called for.

A. C. C. ROBILLIARD: Although almost forty years have slipped by since the great tour, time will never dim the memories of those exciting times. Great days and great players. The success of the team, I would say, could be attributed to the bond of friendship which strengthened as the tour progressed. Speed, initiative and teamwork were certainly there, but for a team to get through with an unbeaten record there must have been an incentive. Could it have been a determination to call the lie to those critics who dubbed the team the weakest ever to represent New Zealand?

H. G. MUNRO: I recall with pride the outstanding achievements of (in my opinion) the greatest fullback of my time - George Nepia or, as we called him, "Hori". This Maori boy won the highest admiration of all who were honoured to play in front of him. Courage, personality and inspiration all went to make him the grand footballer that he was.

A. WHITE: I have played in front of a few fullbacks in my time, but I have never seen Nepia's equal. On the boat deck going to England, he said to me, "I'll show the so-and-sos I can play fullback" - and by hell, he did. He is still the greatest fullback we have seen in our time.

NEIL MCGREGOR: If any man should know the story of the 1924 tour, it should be George Nepia, for he saw it all from behind while playing in every game - the dropped passes, the missed tackles, the breaks through, the sidesteps and dummies. All the details were there before him. Ah yes, and how many times we left it to one of the finest fullbacks in the world to tidy up our errors - and more often than not, we did not drop back to cover him, such was our supreme confidence in his ability. As a footballer, he was superb. "Hori" seemed to mesmerise the opponent with the ball and it was a rare thing indeed for him to fail to put his man on the ground, hard. In the arts of fullback play, he excelled, catching from the most awkward positions, running hard and, above all, being in the right place at the right time. This was the genius of "Hori" on the field. And off it, he was a most pleasant personality and a staunch friend. Which brings me to the most important thing of all about the tour, the great and lasting friendships which endure to this day, nearly "forty years on".

And there was one other thing: As players, we were not over-confident of maintaining our unbeaten record. It came to the stage that before each game someone would remark, "I suppose this is the day we will be beaten". But it was a grand tour with a grand lot of friends and "Hori" was the idol of the crowds. And now let us see what he is like as a story-teller.

Appendix 5

HINTS FROM NEPIA ON ARTS OF RUGBY

Tackling head on: If you go down on half-bended knees and wait for the runner to come to you, his knees will knock your head. On the other hand, if you crash into him from a couple of yards away, his body is slack. He will be unprepared and the impact will be so heavy that he will be chary of repeating the attempt. It is important that your charge and dive are made at velocity to counter the speed of his movement.

Side tackle: You must drive your opponent into a position where he cannot jazz backwards. When he is in this position, you must crash into him. Your head must be in front of his body and your arms around him. If your head is behind his body, he has every chance of breaking through your arms.

Running-away tackle: This is the simplest of the lot. When you are at striking distance, crash into the opponent. Aim for the middle of his shoulders, for you will then hit him about the waist and shoulders. If you aim for his legs, nine times out of ten you will miss him completely or at best only just touch his legs. You must allow a margin for the fact that he is running away from you.

As to tackling generally, the great need is not so much fortified by robustness as a grasp of the fundamentals, fortified by practice, practice and more practice. With practice is born confidence and that makes everything easy. When players are frightened or scared on the tackle, it is because they have not been properly taught and so have not developed the requisite confidence. When you can tackle well, you revel in the challenge. It is a wonderful feeling to know that whatever may come along, you have the answer.

Defensive kicking: It is a good thing for a back, especially a fullback, to be able to kick defensively for touch over his head. The first requirement is to be able to catch the ball at full arm's length while running towards your own goal and with the ball coming over your shoulder. This is easily done after sufficient practice. It is then desirable, as you make the catch, that your kicking leg should already be lifting so as to be at waist height when you bring the ball down. On no account, in these defensive situations, should the ball be brought to the body after the catch. This means a waste of precious time in getting the ball into position. The catch should always be made in the finger tips at arms' length.

Where you have a little more time for defensive kicking, it is a good trick, immediately you have made the catch, to bolt for the open side of the field for about ten yards. Invariably, the onrushing opponents will stream across the field to cut you off. If, after you have run those ten or fifteen yards, you stop still and turn in your tracks, you will find that you have all the time in the world to make your kick.

Defence against a dribbling rush: When as usually happens, three forwards come at you with the ball at their feet, it is essential that you move backwards and to one side of them. Start then to angle on to the man nearest to you so as to drive him on to the centre man, who is generally making the dribble. The closer they are, the better your chances of getting the ball away. As you move backwards, you must keep your eye on the ball but you must also vary this by looking at the players. This will allow you to see when they lift their eyes from the ball to look at you - as they always do. At this moment, you go in for the ball from a sideways position. You must be balanced on your feet to take the shock of the bumps you will get from the man nearest to you and the centre man, but by going in from the side you will have the chance to gather the ball and to get the kick away. The kick, of course, must be made in stride. It does not matter which side you drive the players from. The point is that there is a critical moment when they are uncertain as to what you are going to do. It is then that you must strike.

When three players come at you with the ball in hand, you must also set up uncertainty in their minds and compel them to drive toward each other as in the dribble. This is done by back-pedalling and angling on to the outside player who in turn tends to move toward the middle man. In self-defence, the middle man moves outwards - and that it how the fatal grouping begins. On no account let the players come abreast of you on the right angle. You are, in fact, a little forward of them. The art then is to persuade the first man to pass by feinting a crash tackle at him. Automatically, he turns his head to make his pass. This is the split second you wanted. Instead of throwing yourself at him, you go for the middle man at such velocity that he is knocked on to the outside man - and very likely, your legs will get in the way of the man nearest to you. You will find yourself, if you make this tackle properly, landing on your hands and stomach and from this position you will be able instantly to regain your feet and to take command of the situation.

The operative word in all these defensive situations is courage. If you have courage and a knowledge of the fundamental requirements, you will succeed. You cannot, in fact, fail.

Part 2: Continuing the Story

1. Guardian of the gate

Ropitini, who was said to be a seer, handed over a pack of cards. "Shuffle them," he said to the youth. "I will tell your fortune." It had been a school holiday party, many laughs, much fun. The youngster riffled the pack. Ropitini began to put down the cards, face up. He turned serious. "Soon," he said, "you will be going overseas. You are going to become famous. Your name will become a household word. You will become known, not only in New Zealand but also all over the world." He glanced keenly at the boy. "This is what the cards are telling me about you," he said. "The cards never lie."

Within months, the youth, who was George Nepia and who was only 19, had been chosen, though he knew nothing of the demands of the position, as the sole fullback for the 1924 All Blacks who were to play more than 30 matches all round the world. It is unlikely that so much of a gamble has ever been taken for so important a position in a major international touring team. In a preliminary, four-match tour by a truncated team in New South Wales, the play of Nepia excited some anxiety in his teammates. On the voyage of several weeks to Britain, senior members of the team earnestly discussed the possibility that the national selectors had been too optimistic. The tour committee talked of helping the boy's confidence by playing an experienced hand, Mark Nicholls, who was already an outstanding All Black, at fullback for the first game.

The committee talked itself into, and out of, the proposition. Nepia was played in the opening match, against Devonshire. He placed one goal after a try and failed to convert two others. The All Blacks scratched a little in winning the match by 11 points to nil. Within 24 hours, it seemed as if the gamble had paid off. Said London's *Sporting Life*: "Nepia is a great back in the making. He has safe hands and a long, low, raking kick." The paper's critic thought it wise to add that "Nepia, along with the whole of the outsides of the All Black team, has not as yet assimilated the British style of finding touch." The *Morning Post*, only a notch below the celebrated 'Thunderer', of *The Times*, said: "In Nepia, the All Blacks have an excellent fullback, strong, fearless and with plenty of resource."

The die was cast. Nepia had played well enough to be chosen again. He remained, in fact, the only fullback choice of the entire tour; 28 matches in England, Ireland and Wales, two in France, two in British Columbia. The team won every match, sometimes skitteringly, as against Newport, Cambridge University, Ireland, Llanelli, even England, more often it won decisively; and since no international touring side had ever before won every match, this one was christened, 'The Invincibles'. Writing about the remarkable tour, four years after the event, in a book co-authored with Howard Marshall, England's captain and greatest forward, Wavell Wakefield said: "There is one member of the team who deserves special mention. Nepia took part in every match; and though I saw him only three times, he seemed to be the best fullback I have watched or played against since the war. His exceptional physique gave him first place. His perfect catching of the ball, his kicking and his amazing power of breaking up a forward rush by whipping the ball off the ground and charging backwards into and through the oncoming forwards marked him out as player of a generation."

Fair words; supplemented, as to generosity of tribute, by the decision of *Wisden's Rugby Almanack* to name the young man as one of its Five Players of the Year.

Nepia came home to adulation. At a *hui*, a meeting of thousands of the Ngati Porou tribe at Tiki Tiki, nearby to Ruatoria, Nepia, about to play for a local team, Waiapu was glimpsed on his own by some specially enthusiastic young braves. In his honour, they began a haka, a war-dance of welcome. The gathering was convulsed. Perhaps, not even in Wales, has there been such a tribute to a rugby player.

Ropitini, it was clear, was some seer. His schoolboy, as he had foretold, had become known all about the world. On the evening of the match, a ball was held. Nepia was introduced to Huinga Raupani Kohere. She seemed to him the most beautiful woman in the world. She was, too, a person of distinction. Her father, a clergyman of the Anglican faith, had died of wounds while serving with the Pioneer Maori Battalion on the Western Front, in France. She was high born in the Ngati Porou, which believes itself to be the highest born of all Maori tribes. Nepia was Ngati Kahungungu, of Hawkes Bay. It was made sternly clear to him, as he pursued this beautiful young woman, that his wish to marry her was opposed by Ngati-Porou elders and kinsmen of Huinga. The two were made to wait almost for two years before, at last, they were married in the utterly beautiful Tiki Tiki church which had been built as a memorial to the Maoris fallen in France.

It was a marriage made in heaven. The four children, George, Kiwi, Oma and Winstone, learned from the excellent singing voice of their mother and the fine voice of their father the joys of family sing-songs. They were growing up happily on a small farm at Rangitukia, no great distance from Tiki Tiki and Ruatoria, when the Great Depression smote. Nepia, who had played on and off for the All Blacks and other teams of distinction, captained the New Zealand Maori on a tour of Australia in 1935. By then, he was, practically speaking, broke. For the sum of £500, he signed to play rugby league in England, first for Streatham-Mitcham, later for Halifax. He returned to play for New Zealand and to uplift the hearts of league supporters who saw him inspire their Kiwi team to recover from 8 to 15 at the half to beat the Australians by 16 to 15.

Then WWII, which restored him to rugby, and a decision, spurred by the death of George junior in action against the Chinese bandits in Malay in 1954, to manage a Maori farm near Wairoa. Succeeding years contained some hard times - it seemed ignominious that one who had exactly fulfilled Ropitini's fortune-telling should spend some years making whiteware in a Masterton factory. In the mid 1970s, Huinga and a friend left the home she and George had made with Kiwi and her husband, Ted Rowlands, and set off for Masterton town centre for some shopping. On the way, the two women came upon a Health Department caravan, sent around the town to offer, gratis, chest x-ray examinations. Huinga gaily laughed at her friend. "Why don't we two old ducks try this thing out?" Within days, she had a note from Masterton Hospital: "Please call. We would like to take further tests." Within weeks, she was dead.

George Nepia died then. He lived on, for about ten years; and from time to time the fame which had always accompanied him spurted. Touring with the New

Zealand Maori team in Wales in 1982, he went out to midfield, alone, on the St Helens ground in Swansea on which, with brilliant individual play, he had helped the '24 All Blacks to avenge the defeat of their men of 1905. The Welsh crowd stood to him. This was the mighty Maori, the nonpareil at fullback; there had never been a superior and few indeed worthy to rank as an equal - it being always understood, in any discussion, that Nepia forever was *primus inter pares*, first among equals. In early 1986, he received a notification which stirred him as few things, other than his marriage, young George's death, and his selection as an All Black, had ever done. The South African Rugby Board advised that, by unanimous vote of its members, it had elected him to the post of honorary life vice-president.

A week or so later, he was the central figure in a Television New Zealand programme, *This Is Your Life*, which offered reminiscence from such as Alan Robilliard, who had toured with him in 1924, Harry Bowcott, a Welsh centre threequarter who had starred in the 1930 British Lions' tour of New Zealand and who played against Nepia in all four internationals, and Bob Scott, a fullback, post WWII, of such skill that Nepia could sometimes be heard whispering, "This man was greater than I ever was." The programme, which was scheduled to run for 30 minutes, extended to 42. It was watched by 1.2 million New Zealanders, or more than a third of the population. It was the ultimate leaf of his crown from the oak.

Within weeks, George Nepia, aged 81, died in his sleep at Winstone's home in Ruatoria. Television New Zealand again ran the programme, to an audience even larger than the first. Through the press and from radio, critics, friends and admirers poured out tributes to this singular man. All too seldom, as is well known, does sporting fame extend beyond the playing days of the man concerned. Todav's hero is tomorrow's nonentity. For example, in rugby none but a zealot - who might be thought crackpot - could name you, offhand, the members of the 1908, 1924, 1967, even the 1983 All Blacks. To look back upon the career of Nepia, dating almost from the night of Ropitini's inspired glimpse into the future, was to surmise that the man who had been projected to fame as violently as if he had been fired from a cannon's mouth had seldom, if ever, lost his hold upon the public, he had always been, for them, a famous figure.

To what end? Sometime in 1985, Terry McLean, a writer who had collaborated with Nepia in the writing of a book, *I George Nepia* (McLean's title), remarked to the secretary of the East Coast Rugby Union, Mrs Kath McLean - no relation - who lives in Ruatoria, that he was contemplating further writing about Nepia and would like to visit him in Ruatoria. "I do not think you should delay too long," said Kath. She knew George well - he collected milk and papers from her store every second day. Terry McLean did not call. He asked Kath, later, after the death, why she had urged speed for a meeting. She feared, Kath answered, that George had for some time been beginning to "go". "George did nothing, because he had nothing to do," Mrs McLean said. "He used to get in his car and drive to the football park and just sit there, on his own, staring."

It was a poignant utterance. So to the man who had become famous, and great, almost from the time of Ropitini's facing of the cards, had come, at the end, nothing? Nothing caused by the irreparable losses, first of young George, who had been coached to become a finer footballer than his father, and second of Huinga, she of the regal walk and bearing and the wonderful qualities of a truly beautiful woman?

It may be permissible to surmise that Ropitini, the Nuhaka fortune-teller, sought to encourage the young Nepia because of his knowledge of the family background. Nepia's parents divorced. He lived, according to Maori custom, with a widowed grandmother before returning to his father. Peta Nepia was a hard stern man who used the rod. The boy was happy to be sent, at last, to Te Aute College, the great Maori school south of Hastings. At the train's stopover in Hastings, Nepia was consternated by the departure of friends who were heading for the Mormon college Maori Agricultural College (MAC), south-west of the town. On an impulse, he jumped from the train and journeyed with his friends to MAC. As the only non-Mormon, and penniless into the bargain - his fees had already been paid to Te Aute - his situation was delicate. From Nuhaka came angry word that Peta would disown him if he did not proceed to Te Aute.

A Mormon teacher at MAC, Elder Moser, turned out to be more significant to the young Nepia than any other person of his rugby life. On espying the boy's playing possibilities, he undertook to fund Nepia's education. He taught him, precisely, the way to punt the ball off the side of the foot - left or right, it didn't matter - so that it spun through the air like a bullet, and in the last yards of flight, curved left or right according to the foot used. He taught him, even more precisely, the tackle as standardised in American gridiron football. This requires the tackler to be off his feet, diving at terminal velocity, as his shoulders make contact with the ball-carrier. Only a few New Zealand rugby men have been renowned for skill in tackling. Wanting the head-and shoulder-guards of gridiron, tackling in rugby, especially head-on, can be painful, not to say dangerous. Of all modern All Black fullbacks, only Fergie McCormick, could be classed in Nepia's company, and even he was never so consistently and overwhelmingly strong as Nepia.

Moser, a keen psychologist, sensed the passion which enwrapped Nepia as he approached the game. It was he who arranged that the school, which numbered fewer than 100 pupils - Nepia, incidentally, did not embrace the Mormon faith though he had good cause to respect its magnificent work among his people, especially in reducing the incidence of drunkenness - should travel to Napier in September of 1921 to watch the Springboks play a combined team from Hawkes Bay and Poverty Bay. A forward of the home team was none other than Tom Heeney, who six years later unsuccessfully challenged Gene Tunney for the world heavyweight boxing championship. Nepia was fascinated especially by the powerful Afrikaner, Gerhard Morkel, still esteemed as perhaps the greatest of South African fullbacks, and who had toured the British Isles in 1912-13 before qualifying for the tour Down Under. One of five brothers of the team in New Zealand, Morkel had all the qualities of greatness - size, balance, power, courage and a superb understanding of positional play. Nepia was impressed. Himself a five-eighth, without even a notion of wanting to play fullback, his technical judgments were so sharpened by Moser that he looked upon Morkel with a clinical interest and was greatly taken with the breadth of the man's skills.

Nepia remarked in his book that he played his boyhood rugby with fear. By sharpening his techniques, especially in tackling, Moser cast that from him. Teammates did, too. One was Sam Gemmell, a magnificent forward whose left hook might have been quicker than Heeney's. Another was Albert Falwasser, a superb wing who ran with his head slanted slightly back so that, on a cold day, his breath looked like puffs from a steam-engine. Willie Shortland's misfortune was that, fine as he was as a halfback, Jimmy Mill, another Maori, was finer - and faster. Some of these men were scarcely schoolboys - Gemmell, born in 1896, actually served in France - and it was little wonder that they played senior club in the senior club competition of what are now the twin cities of Napier and Hastings. Played well, too. Gemmell played for Hawkes Bay from 1921. Nepia in the same year and just a month past 16, played for East Coast Districts. A year later he was settled in the Hawkes Bay team.

As Nepia progressed in his rugby, Luxford Peeti, father of George's great friend and fellow five-eighth, Lui Paewai, began to urge that his natural place was at fullback. Peeti put this to Norman McKenzie, the legendary selector-coach of the Hawkes Bay Ranfurly Shield teams from 1922 to 1926 still considered to have been the strongest provincial sides ever fielded in New Zealand. McKenzie said "Bosh!" and passed on. In early 1924, an All Black trial preceded by a couple of days the important trophy match of Maori rugby, the Te Mori Rose Bowl, North against South, played at Eden Park in Auckland. It had additional standing as a trial for the All Blacks. The Maori is a political animal, not least in sport. Alex Takarangi, a high priest of the Southern team, wanted Peina Taituha, who was also from Wanganui, played at five-eighth because he was sure that, given reasonable luck, he would qualify for the All Black tour. Since Nepia had been chosen for five-eighth, Takarangi moved deviously. The outcome of the manoeuvrings was an instruction that Nepia, who had played at five-eighth in the trial, was to play the match at fullback.

Nepia was shaken, appalled. "But I know nothing of fullback play," he said. The selectors declined to explain. He rushed to his cousin, Waiter McGregor, who had toured Australia the year before as fullback of the New Zealand Maori team. "What do I do?" the youngster pleaded. McGregor offered the fullback's creed: "Catch the ball on the full. Every time you punt, find touch. Tackle your man. That is all you need to know. That is all you need to do."

Nepia could have been singing "Glory, glory, hallelujah" after the game. He caught the ball. He kicked it out. He tackled his man - all except Jimmy Mill, who with a deft double-shuffle evaded the flying body and skipped on for a try. But there was no "Hallelujah" in the Nepia heart. He cowered. It was the end of him in the big time. A hand touched him on the shoulder. "Well done," said Ted McKenzie, chairman of the All Black selectors. "We have put you in the next trial. You have a great future. Congratulations."

Nigh on 40 years had passed before Nepia and Terry McLean published *I, George Nepia*. As if it had happened yesterday, Nepia could recite to McLean the precise circumstances of the days following the Rose Bowl match - the choice of North Island versus South, his selection in the team, his discovery that, with faith in their hearts, the seven selectors had chosen him as the *sole* fullback of the tour. He was entranced, he was exhilarated. If his play in Australia cut him down to size slightly, he learned much rugby lore as the All Blacks steamed in the

Remuera to London. Soon enough, he made an idol out of Cliff Porter, the captain, who though but 25 years old exuded authority and confidence. In no time, he was so much the mate of 'Bill the Bull' lrvine, a hardy warrior returned from the Great War, and Bert Cooke, a genius in the making, that they always had to line up together as the team marched onto the field. Another returned soldier, Maurice Brownlie, was already an idol because he had been Nepia's captain in Hawkes Bay's matches. So through the list. It was a companionable team, with some ineffectives in the forwards. A talented back, Handley Brown, was scorned because his father had given him too much money and Handley, with the team disapproving, chased the bright lights. An arresting feature was that so many of the team were thinkers about the game. Nepia, as the railway crossing notices of his homeland insisted, pursued a policy of "Stop. Look. Listen."

Nepia was chosen for the first game. The die was cast. Nepia it was to be. So the world saw the wonder of a teenager, still wet behind the ears, who in no time was displaying such skill that the All Blacks, to a man, never turned about when the ball was kicked behind - 'Hori', their 'Hori', would surely place it before them. If the team had its squeaks, he himself displayed an extraordinary consistency. Twenty-eight years after a skittery victory over Llanelli, Bob Stuart's All Blacks of 1953-54 were entertained to an evening in the town of the "Little Saucepan" and discovered that the star turn was to be, as it had been on many such nights over the years, Ernie Finch's recital of how, having doubled around his marker, he had then swerved past Nepia to score 15 yards in from the touchline. You could hear a pin drop as Ernie Finch warbled. Had he faltered, the audience, to a man, could have offered the right prompt -- they, too, knew the story by heart. As and when Ernie described how he had beaten Nepia, - Nepia, Nepia, the unbeatable -- the audience grew rapturous. Ah, Ernie was their man, their hero, forever.

Nepia played, in all, 46 times as an All Black. Nine of these were internationals. Never much of a goalkicker, though his punting, left barrel or right, had been emulated only by Bob Scott, he scored for his country 99 points from tries, 39 conversions of tries and six penalty goals. Because of a blazing controversy which had attended the 1921 Springbok team's defeat of New Zealand by 9 to 8, no Maoris, not even Mill and Nepia, were to be considered for the 1928 All Black tour of South Africa. Nepia claimed later to be more dispirited by his omission from the New Zealand Maori team of 1926-27 which won 30 of its 40 matches in France, England, Wales, Australia, Ceylon, British Columbia and New Zealand. Both he and Mill were said to have been misinformed by telegraph and Nepia disclaimed any authority for the announcement by the chairman of the New Zealand Rugby Union, S.S. Dean, that said he was not available. One witness, Wally Ingram, a newspaperman and radio personality who at the time was living in Gisborne, disputed Nepia's statements. He claimed there was never a moment when Nepia wanted to tour. The two men are dead. So is their controversy.

By the end of WWII, Nepia was most heartily back into rugby, not least refereeing, an aspect of the game which all too seldom has appealed to retired All Blacks. At 42 he made his last playing appearance in a first-class match. His hope now that young George would become greater than he; and under the kitchen lamp, on many a night on the farm, the father would instruct the son in the skills of tactics. Father Nepia wanted his son trained in medicine. Son Nepia preferred the Army - as, indeed, did Oma, who retired as a senior warrant officer with 27 years of service in the New Zealand Army; young George - 'Dedum' as he was known to the family - in time was posted, in the rank of sergeant, to serve with the magnificent battalion Fiji had sent to the troubles in Malaya. He was killed by the Chinese in the heart of the jungle. It was a poignant moment when father George, reading the last chapter of the book which had just been published, came to the account of his son's death. He wept.

Fame was never far distant from George Nepia. He was esteemed beyond any reckoning he might himself have attempted. Though by now an octogenarian, he displayed, in *This Is Your Life*, the special qualities which had placed him apart -- the modesty, the bearing, the smile, the charm of the greeting between himself and his beloved Kiwi and Oma, the deeply lined face which was the book of his life. He had delivered, to a Pakeha's game, the outstanding qualities of Maori warriorhood - strength, pride, determination, craft, skill.

At the end of the Invincibles' tour, the British Sportsmen's Club persuaded none other than the Prince of Wales to offer the toast to the team; and there was charm in his statement that "combination, efficiency and fitness are the secrets of the wonderful success the All Blacks have had".

Coincidentally, a former New Zealand High Commissioner in London, the Honourable William Pember Beeves, penned verses proclaiming the quality of the team.

Kia Toa! New Zealand. See
Nepia guards the gate!
A rock and a house of defence is he,
A tino tangata great.

Of George Nepia it could be said that he was unforgettable because, like the Pilgrim, he was Valiant in Heart.

Did such a man deserve to spend not a few of his last days, sitting in a car, staring at a rugby field?

George NEPIA, born Wairoa, 25 April 1905; died Ruatoria, 27 August 1986.
New Zealand 46 matches, 1924-30, MAC, Dannevirke Aotea, Nuhaka, Rangitukia Rangers, Hawkes Bay, East Coast, New Zealand Maoris 1931-35. Streatham-Mitcham, Halifax, Manukau Rovers, New Zealand (rugby league) 1935-38.
Farmer, whiteware factory hand.

Originally published in *New Zealand Rugby Legends: 15 reflections* by Terry McLean Moa, Beckett 1987

Nepia's First Game

Wigan's "Star" Man Outclassed

Streatham & Mitcham Rugby League:
Headlines from Nepia's first game, and an advert for the Streatham & Mitcham club

WORLD'S FINEST RUGBY FULL-BACKS CLASH AT STREATHAM

2. Famous fullbacks

In this chapter, written for this book, Terry McLean looks at the careers of the other three great All Black fullbacks - Billy Wallace, Bob Scott and Don Clarke.

The happy circumstances of the attendance at an international match at Wellington's Athletic Park some 30 or 40 years ago of, in order of playing years, William Wallace, George Nepia, Bob Scott and Don Clarke brought great joy to, in particular, press photographers. The four were identified as the greatest fullbacks in New Zealand's rugby history. Having regard to the excellence of later exponents, in particular Fergus McCormick and Christian Cullen, this might be argued.

Yet who could doubt the quality of William Wallace, the leading points-scorer of the 1905 All Blacks in their tour of the British Isles, France, New York and British Columbia, of George Nepia, an untried youth of 19 who played every match at back in the tour of the Invincibles of 1924, of Bob Scott whose difficult boyhood after the Great War - an orphanage, a hut alone with his father - vested in him the mind of a Grand Master of chess (he was stating fact, not conceit, when he remarked, "I can see three moves ahead") - and lastly, but most decidedly not leastly, Donald Clarke, who in 221 matches at first class level scored no fewer than 1,851 points.

Billy (William) Wallace

Let us survey the careers of Wallace, Scott and Clarke - all gifted men. Wallace, who in no more than 112 matches rated as first class depended for his ranking as an immortal largely on the tour of the 1905 All Blacks. For this gifted team, unbeaten in all but the international with Wales and that because of an exceedingly doubtful decision by the Scottish referee John Dallas, scored in his matches 246 points from 27 tries, 74 conversions, three penalty goals and two dropped goals. By modern standards the few goals from penalties is astonishing and unbelievable; in the professional era of today, a high proportion of victories depends on accurate goalkicking from penalties.

In the 34 matches of the tour, Wallace played no more than nine times at fullback. He played wing threequarter 14 times, centre-threequarter twice and once at second five-eighths (inside centre). George Gillett, rather too heavily built for the fullback position of today, played 14 times at fullback on the tour and ten times at wing-forward, the rover position forever identified with David Gallaher, the captain of the team and a sportsman who with grace and gallantry said of the Welsh that they were the better team on that unforgettable day at the Arms Park in Cardiff when his team lost 0-3.

Wallace, a man of piety, averred that he himself could have scored the try from which, because of its place and his precision he would have goaled; but, hearing a cry of "Bill, Bill," from the young centre, Robert Deans, he made a pass which turned out to be fatal.

Deans, it seems clear, did place the ball over the Welsh goalline but then let it lie to await the approval of the referee, the unhappy Scot, John Dallas. Nine or ten nominees as referee by either the Welsh Rugby Union or the All Blacks had all been rejected.

Mr Dallas was handicapped by the Norfolk jacket he wore. He was even further handicapped that his boots had bars, rather than sprigs. Thus he was some distance short of the goalline at the moment of Deans' putting the ball down and letting it lie. A Welsh player meantime thoughtfully placed the ball a foot or two inside the field of play; and Mr Dallas, according to his appreciation of the relevant Law, ordered a five-yard scrummage. (New Zealanders have preferred to overlook the fact that the Welsh won the ball at this scrummage and cleared it downfield).

It became a conviction in the mind of every man, woman and child in New Zealand that the Welsh had cheated to win.

In 1935-36, an All Black team known as the Third All Blacks again made the Grand Tour. At the formal dinner following its international with Scotland, John Dallas was placed with a New Zealand centre, Harcourt or "Pat" Caughey, perhaps the most handsome man who had ever worn the All Black jersey. The two men almost instantly became warm friends.

At the stage of the Piping of the Haggis, Dallas said: "You know, Caughey, I was at fault in that match in 1905. Because of my clothing, especially the boots, I was well behind the play and I could only rule on what I saw. But, on reflection - an exercise I have carried out many times in later life - I am persuaded that Deans did score." Later in life, Caughey was knighted for his services in the public arena (he was a brilliant chairman of the Auckland Hospital Board and attended to many other matters). In business he became managing director of Auckland's largest and finest department store, Smith & Caughey.

Wallace's career at first-class level began in 1897 and carried through to his last appearance for the All Blacks in 1908 -112 games at first-class level. In his club, Poneke, he was much influenced by an older man, Syd Nicholls, three of whose four sons, Mark, "Ginger" and "Doc" were to become All Blacks. A man of acute vision and high analytical skill in all matters bearing upon the playing of rugby, he soon discerned the immense talent in Wallace. Hour by hour, he coached the youngster.

Years passed until young Mark, by far the finest player of the three brothers, placed himself in the hands of the man who had been the wonder of the age. Summing up the tour of the Invincibles of 1924, a great Cambridge University and Welsh wing threequarter, Rowe Harding - for most of his working life a judge of the High Court in Wales - remarked that one truly great player was essential to the standing of any superior touring team. Porter's side, he said, had been specially fortunate - it had fielded both Nicholls and A. E. Cooke. The latter was turned into a wonderful centre threequarter when he himself favoured second five-eighths. Nicholls, said Harding, was specially gifted in the scheming of attacks. The one enduring misfortune in Nicholls' career and life was his manner of speech - it was extraordinarily foul.

Wallace's standing with his teammates was graphically illustrated a couple of generations later by "Bunny" Abbott, a champion professional sprinter. Abbott was no great shakes in rugby but his speed could be valuable. He had become the outstanding farrier of the many racing clubs of the Wellington area of the North Island and he was hewing assiduously when a questioner put to him the words: "How good was Billy Wallace?" Abbott paused, lifted a large hand far above his head. "Up there," he said. In its simplicity, it was a supreme tribute.

Wallace stood 5 feet 8 inches tall and weighed 12 stone - not a memorable physique in these days but notable as a man of strength and intellectual quickness in his time. Any thoughts that he was exceptionally speedy were removed by a leading English critic, E. H. D. Sewell, who remarked that he did not have unusual speed but compensated by the quickness of his reflexes and his appreciation of attacking skills.

Gallaher's team had reached Wales, then enveloped in the first of its several Golden Ages, at the end of a long and demanding tour. The New Zealanders were tired - they had had enough. But national pride compelled them to pursue the unbelievable - an unbeaten record. Playing Swansea, a great club, the All Blacks lagged 0-3. No-side was nearing when Wallace illustrated his genius. "The ball," he wrote, "came to me right on the halfway line and close to the right-hand touchline. I had to chase before it was blown into touch; and then, turning around, I ran infield and up toward the 25-yard line. Then I let fly with my left foot. The wind carried the ball fair and true between the posts. All of the Welsh scribes described the kick (which won the match 4 to 3) as a great fluke. In fact, it was one of the best I ever kicked."

A supreme tribute was paid to Wallace at his retirement. The Wellington rugby public - all of Wellington in those days - subscribed to a fund of 400 sovereigns; which presented to "Carbine" allowed him to set up in the Mount Cook district of the city where as a child he had often played matches with a blown-up pig's bladder, to establish an iron foundry which he kept going until the end of his working days. Wallace was "Carbine" most of his playing days. He was named for the New Zealand stallion which carried 10st 5lb in a field of 38 runners and still swept the field by two / three lengths in the Melbourne Cup, the great two-mile handicap race run every November and on the day of which all work ceases in Australia at 15.00 hours Eastern Standard Time and in New Zealand at 17.00 hours New Zealand time.

The New Zealand Union was chary with its offer of life-memberships; but though Wallace served for some years on the governing committee and managed - and coached - a most successful team in Australia in 1932, he was never offered the distinction. But the true nature of a perfect sportsman was to be seen when, in 1908, he attended the funeral of Bob Deans who sadly, had played an international against the 1908 touring Anglo-Welsh team while suffering from appendicitis. This rapidly worsened after the game. Billy Wallace, the man who had passed the ball for what ought to have been an unbeaten record, knelt at the side of the open grave. It said much of the man that he wept bitter tears before the diggers began to fill the grave.

Bob Scott

It is unlikely that any All Black has known so difficult a childhood as Robert William Henry Scott. His father was so gravely during the assaults on Gallipoli in

1915 that he spent six months in a hospital in Malta before being sent to England for further treatment. Invalided home to New Zealand, he met and somehow married a lass 19 years his junior. Scott, born on 6 February 1921, was followed by two sisters. The family circumstances were so severe that all three children were placed in a Masterton orphanage run by the Salvation Army. Scott then renewed family life at Tangarakau, a settlement in the King Country established principally for the men who were building a railway line from Stratford in Taranaki to a junction with Taumarunui in the King Country. The land was mountainous. Home comforts were sparse.

At primary school, Scott took eagerly to the playing of rugby. Oddly, he could not win a place in the school team, which was principally organised by the captain, Jack Sullivan, who in pre-war days was on the road to monumental greatness as a player.

Post-war, Sullivan became chairman of the All Black selection committee and coach of the All Black team which toured South Africa in 1960. By this time Scott had become one of the immortals. He chided Sullivan: "You never chose me for the Tangarakau school team." "For one good reason," Sullivan riposted. " You were no good then and you still aren't any good."

Scott's parents again parted. Bob and his father headed to Auckland, Here, they lived mostly in the area known as Freeman's Bay. Its reputation was unsavoury, its housing inadequate. Scott recalls an old shed in which the two lived. They found another place heated by an ancient pot-bellied stove. Income was meagre with a capital M.

Father Scott expired in 1934, never quite well after the horrors of Anzac. He had done one thing right by his son - he had sent him to primary school and in Standard V1, at Ponsonby school, Scott was first choice for fullback.

The times of the of the Great Depression were tough. Scott worked where he could and when he could. His mates played rugby league for the Richmond club. Scott could not desert them. He played league, too, and in late adolescence, often showed the qualities of his later greatness.

In 1942 he was called into the Army and was very much a handyman as the unit's team won the Auckland Rugby Union's championship of the club season. Despatched with his unit to Egypt, he was placed In the 1st Divisional Ammunition Company. As Army jobs go, it was safe enough; but a nervous man might have wondered at his fate if an enemy bomb had struck his truck with its full load of ammunition for the front-line troops.

As winter 1944 enveloped the battlefields, Scott qualified for the Div Amn team which won its way to the final of the competition for the Freyberg Cup, the trophy donated by the General Officer Commanding, Major-General Bernard Freyberg VC. On 8 December 1944, the team played the 22nd Infantry Battalion, the motorised unit of the 4th Armoured Brigade. The place was Forli, the field impossible; except for the tiny grassy area a few feet wide and a little bit longer. The rest was mud, mud, glorious mud, up to the eyeballs and beyond of the 30 players, the referee and the touch judges. Remarkably, the 22nd had been withdrawn from its placings in the FDLS, the foremost defended localities of the front at Faenza, a few miles to the west; and at one extremely tense moment (for the 22nd), the tackler of the Div. Amn man was not a certified opponent but a sergeant in greatcoat, battle bowler and rifle on his side.

Two Two, as it was usually known - except by an Adjutant was answered all calls with a boisterous "22nd to None!" - fielded at fullback a Maori, "Mick" Kenny. For excellent reasons, he was deemed to be an All Black in the making. In fielding, tackling, kicking, he was exceptionally skilled. It was Kenny who had played at back in the great match with South Africa which proceeded the battles of November 1941 which were concerned with the Port of Tobruk - and as to which, the Division's finest officer, Major General Howard Kippenberger remarked that this was the finest hour of the New Zealand Division.

The match fielded 2 NZ Div against S South African Div. Heroically, New Zealand, captained by Jack Sullivan, had won by 13 to 8 after an encounter fit for Valhalla. (In all of the Western Desert, there was one bottle of Stella beer; and gracefully, Freyberg VC shared this at his bivvy tent with Sullivan.)

Kenny was there, heroic. By the time of Forli, rather more than three years later, he held the rank of sergeant and the reputation of being the sort of soldier headed for a commission on merit - a tough demand in the 22nd.

All the way around and about the Western Desert, all the way up the Italian peninsular, Kenny, as and when wanted, had displayed, in one match after another, on sand and grass (and mud), qualities of greatness, all being well , he could not fail to win the All Black jersey once the world became normal.

"As we took the field at Forli," Scott has always recalled, "I knew that, no matter how well I played, I could never beat Kenny. My feeling was that I was privileged to play against the man."

From that one patch of grass, Lieutenant Lin Thomas (who pre-war had played for Wellington Province) drop-kicked the goal which meant victory for 22 by 4 to nil. Post-war, Scott had great fun talking at reunions of various units. "After the match," he said, "General Freyberg made a strong attempt to present Div. Amn with the cup. He knew which was the better side." General Freyberg was also at fault in a remark to a burly lock of 22, Terry Miles - the unit's principal cook - "This is a beautiful medal, is it not." "I dunno," said Miles, "I haven't seen it yet." After which, the GOC remarked: "This is a beautiful medal, as you will see when I hand it to you"

Both Scott and Kenny played magnificently - but Scott was aware he would not stand a chance of selection in the post-war Army team which was being talked about.

On 15 December, one week later, the 22nd was front-line in the attack of Faenza, some miles west of Forli. Kenny foremost in his platoon, was raked across the chest by a burst of Spandau. His wounds were grave. A hardy man, he survived to RAP. CCS, No.1 General Hospital and, finally, his native Wellington. Old hands who were sure his playing career was ended did not know him. Within a year or two. he was playing at club and representative level, even captaining New Zealand Maoris. He held onto life until 2001. His funeral was enormous.

Even then, Scott faced problems. Foremost was a tiny fullback wearing, believe it or not, size 4½ boots, Trooper Herbert Cook. In the years before joining the Div., he had played a good deal at first class level in four seasons in New Zealand. It was impossible not to be charmed by the man. Arriving at the scene at high speed, he would gather the ball off the top of his toes. Scott would sourly observe: "No one gave me credit for being there, waiting for the ball." Senior members of the Kiwis took long to acknowledge that the player who knew where the ball was to pitch and who made sure of getting there first was superior to the player who got there by the skin of his teeth.

Scott had one other problem at the Kiwis - the division between rugby and league. Like his great Kiwi and All Black team-mate John Simpson, the prop, he had played league in adolescence because that was the game of his friends.

Divisional authorities were not happy. Steps had been to be taken for each man to be cleared of his past.
If it came to be known that these fellows might have been paid - when more than likely, they would have had to cadge their tram-fare - there might be the devil to pay. At last after it had been established that the two played because their friends played, all problems departed.

The records of Trooper Cook and Driver Scott bear comparison. In 20 games of the official tour, Cook scored one try, 37 conversions, 19 penalty goals and one drop goal - 138 points. Scott played 13 games, scored one try, 42 conversions and 14 penalty goals. Cook played internationals against England and Scotland, Scott against Wales and in each of' the two French tests. The next highest scorer was Lieutenant Jim Sherritt with 24 tries. In all of their tour, including the five games in New Zealand long after the tour proper was finished, the team scored 145 tries, 79 conversions, 33 penalty goals and five drop goals 712 points; some going for a bunch of soldiers.

In a curious way, a gesture at the end of the match against Scotland, in which they had been beaten by 11 to 6, had extraordinary significance. Ever since, in 1904, the Scot, D R Bedell-Sivright, had been ungracious about New Zealand following the defeat of his Anglo-Welsh side, Scots and New Zealanders had tended to be at odds. Hence, the gallant touch by the Kiwis' captain, Charles Saxton, in walking a distance to congratulate the Scottish skipper on the victory of his team, Saxton warmed a good many cockles. Hereafter, the rugby relationships of the two countries have seldom been other than ideal.

Hereafter, Scott, in many a match, whatever the level, personified glory. After Australia in 1947, his skipper, Fred Allen, said he was the greatest of all fullbacks. After the All Blacks' uncomfortable tour of South Africa in 1949, where the hosts in all matches scored no more than eight tries, Hennie Muller, a genius in his own right, proclaimed Scott to be the greatest footballer the game had produced.

He retired in 1952, yielded to the All Black selectors who urged that he make the long tour of the All Blacks in 1953 - six and one half months, all long journeys by air - the Arms Park at Cardiff volleyed and thundered appreciation for his farewell match versus the Barbarians. He left Auckland to take up a partnership in a small men's clothing store in Petone, a Wellington suburb which had bred Mark Nicholls. During 1954, he played one club season for Petone; and Monday morning by Monday, would receive brickbats and plaudits in about equal measure from the greatest people of sport, true fans.

And he himself stored in his mind, forever, the game he played against Canterbury in Christchurch and almost at the very end of 38 matches in the United Kingdom, France, Germany and New Zealand. He sometimes mused aloud: "I failed with one kick at goal. Elsewhere, wherever I was the ball came to me. I did not fail a tackle, or funk a rush. It was so perfect, it was unreal."

Let one incident demonstrate the skill of Scott, the unparalleled skill of Scott. North Island played South Island at Athletic Park in Wellington. Scott fielded the ball on the touchline, grandstand side. A Southerner, Gillon, a wing threequarter, and not a bad one, either, rushed hard at him. Now Gillon was experienced and sensible, he must have known of the law that an enemy fullback in such a circumstance is at your mercy. For a long moment, the world of rugby football was the world of these two men. It was a tableau. Now must the mighty Scott meet his man.

Scott moved his shoulders, and made the motion of a step toward the wide open space to his left. Like a puppet on a string, Gillon headed infield, into nothingness. Scott cleared.

Not often is it possible, whatever the sport, to see technical perfection perfectly displayed.

Golf hit him. A left-hander, he reduced to scratch. In retirement, at Tairua, sited on the Coromandel peninsula of North Island - eastward bound, first stop South America. He took to lawn bowls. In no time, he was club champion, then centre champion. His son and daughter were not astonished. Nor was Irene, his petite, London-born wife. For five of the war years, including the Blitz, she served in the London Fire Brigade. Bob Scott in sport took on many perils. None surpassed those his wife had so often faced.

Scott sums up his career in sport with a remarkable statement: "The toughest, most demanding of all sports," he says, "is lawn bowls."

Donald Barry Clarke

As to the scoring of goals in rugby, whether place, drop or, once in a blue moon, from a mark or fair catch, Donald Barry Clarke broke all records which had been set by such illustrious predecessors W. J. Wallace, George Nepia, Bob Scott and a singular character, Fred Fuller, who though Maori was auburn or ginger, in complexion.

Clarke had physical advantages over all of these men. He was 1.88 metres (6ft 2in) tall and weighed, at career-peak, 17½ stone. Such massive weight and strength did not much hamper his mobility; and, on occasion, agility. During an international at Athletic Park in Wellington, an English wing threequarter, J. R. C. Young - among the fastest of English track sprinters -stepped to evade Clarke. One more wisp of room and he would have been uncatchable. A dart by a massive hand checked the flight and, dramatically, Young went to ground.

Even more arrestingly, in the third test of the tour by the 1959 Lions, David Hewitt, an astonishingly swift centre-three-quarter, breached the All Black defence and, with Tony O'Reilly in support on the wing, raced toward Clarke. Evidence at lengthy inquests did tend to suggest that O'Reilly, himself extremely fast, tended to edge ahead of his support. Yes or no, Hewitt. like Young, bore infield. Once more, the defensive arm flicked. Yet again, a certain try flicked out.

There were touches of an innate skill with Scott's beating of a man when no more than two were involved in the play - that immediate, natural reaction which might be called genius. Clarke's career at first-class level was long - 1950 until 1964. Though already large, he was no more than 17 when a selector of exceptional perception, R. A. Everest, placed him in the Waikato team to challenge North Auckland for the Ranfurly Shield, the supreme emblem of inter-provincial rivalry.

The match was played on Rugby Park, a remarkable ornament of the town of Wangarei - which in turn was the headquarters of the North Auckland provincial union. In winter - and rain fell often in the winterless north - spectators did not so much watch games as listen to them. The mud offered sounds ranging from the slur of a trombone to a gooey plop.

At 17, Clarke in experience was a boy. Yet, when offered - twice - chances to convert the penalty goals which would turn the shield over to Waikato, he showed no trace of nerves. The immortal Gilbert Mark II of those days gathered mud as it absorbed water. And foothold, naturally was chancy. With sublime ease, Clarke hefted the goals.

Vastly different were the conditions at Bloemfontein in 1960. No-side was no great distance when Wilson Whineray's All Blacks, lagging 3-11, were awarded a penalty in midfield at about halfway. Whineray demurred as to the possibility of converting the penalty into a goal. By now a man of exceptional experience and skill, Clarke was not troubled as Whineray rather fiddled with the ball. "She'll be right, 'Skip'," " he proclaimed presently, a puppet appeared on a string slung between the uprights. As at Wangarei, in the heart of Vrystaat, skill and confidence had blended.

But the match was yet to be saved. (Before kick-off, in accordance with custom, members of the international Press had had their little gamble as to the outcome of the match. The variations were remarkable; but none compared with the belief of Reg Sweet. He had flown with the Desert Air Force "up north", as South Africans said of the war in the Western Desert. It could be surmised that the experience of flying and fighting in clear air turbulence had steadied the Sweet nerve. Calmly, he noted that the match would end in a draw, 11-11. As words of this passed among the corps, the verdict was unanimous. Poor Reg, it was agreed, was barmy.)

Well, the play was now into the last 60 seconds when two All Blacks' midfield backs. Kevin Laidlaw and Frank McMullen, one with a kick and the other with a dive, scored a try. The spot was wide out by the left touchline, the distance 35, perhaps 40 yards. Had Whineray been of the Faith, he would have been uttering Hail Marys by the tongue-load as he handed Clarke the ball.

Clarke's brother, Ian, a prop-forward in the team, as flag-bearer for his team during play, was guarding the left-hand upright as his kid brother let fly. Soon, it was to be seen, he was capering, capering in delight - and the Gilbert was still way out there. Sure enough, all Kiwis among those present - were either capering or cringing. The ball passed well above the bar and, more importantly, between the uprights. 'Donny Boy" had done it again. Sweet. a gentleman, refused to crow. And, for once in the heart of Afrikanerdom, the cry was not VERYSTAAT! " Rather, it was "All Blacks!'·

Thus was Whineray's team the first from New Zealand to be offered the chance of a victory in a series in South Africa by a regrettable refereeing misjudgement in the early minutes of play in the fourth and final test at Port Elizabeth, the All Blacks were denied - many of the used the term "robbed" - of a glorious achievement.

Clarke had early known international fame. The Springboks of 1956, through their manager, Dr Danie Craven, had but one objective in their mission to Australia and New Zealand. In his first public utterance at the Town Hall in Sydney, Craven proclaimed: "We have come here to win!"

They did so in the approach run through Australia. So to the opener in New Zealand, against Waikato, the champion province. The rugby correspondent of the New Zealand Herald, which had a wide circulation in the Waikato district, offered the opinion that Waikato would win. An opening goal by Clarke enthused, if that were possible, the 27,000+ spectators in a ground which could not possibly accommodate more than 25,000. A device of Everest's, to have his wing threequarters hurl the ball at line outs, soon had the 'Boks ducking to avoid death by Gilbert. Waikato won - and Clarke goaled as and when wanted.

Some time later came the third of the four test of the tour. This was played at Christchurch, a hotbed of provincialism and one-eyedness. There had been physical doubt Clarke, not forgetting the nervousness of a first international. The selectors kept everyone guessing - the Wonder Boy might not be fit. Well, 10 r a dozen minutes into play, 40 yards distant, a penalty was called against South Africa. True, and a little further than necessary, the ball travelled to its destined three points. The All Blacks won,. Danie Craven said it was the roughest, dirtiest test match ever played. Dear Danie - he was such a good loser.

Three years later Clarke was to be hailed and reviled in a series against the '59 Lions. In the first test, at Carisbrook in Dunedin, a local referee, Alan Fleury, in all blew 40 penalties. Clarke was untroubled to goal no fewer than six of these. Meanwhile, the Lions had capered all about the field while scoring five tries and just one conversion. So New Zealand won, 18 to 17; and the local sports edition hit the streets an hour or two later with the verdict that this was "the saddest day in New Zealand rugby history."

The Lions continued to prance, hither and thither, with rugby of glorious, passionate quality. Canterbury offered remarkable resistance. One Lion, Ray McLoughlin, broke a hand on the skull of "Grizz" Wyllie. Another, Scotland's "Sandy" Carmichael, was bombed at every scrummage by Alistair Hopkinson. No rainbow ever wore as many colours as on the Carmichael conk.

Don Clarke, it had to be said, bore no blame for grievous occurrence. Yet a good many, surely a majority of the 60,000 who watched the final test at Eden Park declared themselves, at no-side, no Clarkeans. The half was reached at 3-3. Four minutes later came the movement which proved the Lions to be superior in thought, action and achievement. At a scrummage by the left touch, 40 yards from the All Blacks' goal, the Lions heeled. To Mulligan, scrum-half. Thence to Risman, fly-half, O'Reilly boring in, to Scotland - ah! Scotland - to P. B. Jackson, Warwickshire and England, on the right wing.

"Jacko", admittedly, was no Jesse Owens. On the other hand, while Owens ran very fast in one direction, Jackson seemed to run at respectable speed in all directions at once. Valiant was Clarke's attempt to stop the try, what hope had he with 60,000 urging "Jacko" to run, for once, precisely the right direction for the try. Simply, it was wonderful.

The end was nigh. Lions 9, All Blacks 6. Over to you, "Donny Boy" - a penalty attempt from perhaps 35 yards, wide to the right. As Clarke hacked his place, and began his approach run, he was enveloped - in his native land! - by a monstrous roar of disapproval. Eden Park, to a man, wanted the Lions to win, partly in tribute to the flair and imagination in their play, partly in reparation for those six monstrous goals of Carisbrook.

Had he been Mr Punch, Clarke might have said: "Well, you can't win 'em all."

He carried on until 1964 before, physically, his joints told him he had had enough. He later left New Zealand to settle in South Africa. Late in 2001, Clarke, with his glorious Patsy, returned to Auckland to speak of his cancer. No fewer than 61 All Blacks of his years greeted him.

"It will not be long" said an All Black who was qualified in medicine, "before Don departs". The months passed into the heart of 2002. He seemed almost as large as ever. Perhaps he remained a living miracle.

3. *This is Your Life*

In 1986, three months before he died, Television New Zealand featured George Nepia in their This is Your Life *series. Below, Bob Parker recalls his experience of making and presenting the programme, and Peter Lush reviews what was a memorable occasion and tribute.*

Making the George Nepia *This is Your Life* programme was one of my career highlights. George was a man of great humility, with a twinkling sense of humour.

Researching the show also brought me into contact with George's family. The characteristics of humility and generosity had clearly been passed on through the family genes.

A beautiful moment that the TV show I presented did not quite capture occurred when going into a commercial break I played for George his hit record *Neath the Maori Moon. This is Your Life* at that time went out live from the Avalon television studios.

As the record began to play it was clear it had a major emotional impact on George. He listened intently to the music and his voice from many years earlier. On screen the Network went into a commercial break, but in the studio all eyes in the audience stayed on George as he stood, at first mouthing, and then his voice growing in strength, fully singing along with the old 78rpm recording. There were tears in all of our eyes as this great old man sang his heart out.

I told the director to run the tape and capture this moment that, although the television audience at home could not actually see or hear, was clearly something magic.

As the record played out and finished, George stood motionless for a few seconds, tears running down his cheeks. Then he looked at me, gave a wonderful warm smile and sat down again.

In a couple of minutes we were back on air and carried on with the show.

When it was all over, George thanked me for bringing back so many memories. He then told me what had been going through his mind as the old song had played. That song was always for my late wife he said, and when I began to play it he had though with great emotion of her and his love for her. He said if he had not stood up and sung the song he could not have gone on with the show.

We had most of the moment on videotape, and so later that week it was shown in context on the Saturday sports programme. Once again people were moved by the sincere and humble nature of one of our greatest sportsmen, and surely one of the great all time New Zealanders.

I always felt privileged to have been part of bring George and his story to another generation of New Zealanders.

Bob Parker, (former host and researcher *This is Your Life*)

George Nepia: This is Your Life

This is Your Life is a long-established, well-tried and tested programme. The "victim" is suddenly confronted by the host, holding an impressive looking book and, suitably shocked, goes into the studio to great applause, to meet family members, friends and colleagues from their past.

The impact in New Zealand of the programme about George Nepia has been described elsewhere in this book. An audience reckoned to be a third of the country, over-running by 12 minutes, and repeated soon afterwards. In fact, the programme served as a wonderful tribute to Nepia. The presenters were not to know that he was to die within three months of it being shown.

Nepia was "confronted" by presenter Bob Parker while signing his name on a wall of signatures of famous people who had stayed in the James Cook Hotel in Wellington. His initial response was "Good God". Parker looked shocked when Nepia claimed not to have heard of the programme, and after they entered the studio asked for reassurance that the great man had heard of the programme, which he admitted with a wry smile that he had.

The programme started with the introduction of some famous All Blacks in the audience. But soon we were into the great early days of Nepia's rugby career, the 1924-25 tour. Wonderful old film was followed by pictures of Nepia's reception in 1982 on the Maori tour in South Wales. He was then joined by fellow tourist Alan Robilliard, who said about Nepia's play on the tour: "It was tremendous having him behind us - he gave us confidence - we didn't have any worries."

Then he was joined by Terry McLean, who recalled how his father had been a selector for the Hastings sub-union team and had spotted Nepia's potential at a young age. He also explained how Nepia had added the initials H and M to his name – H. G. M. Nepia – so as not to feel out of place with all the multi-initialled English players. Terry McLean said that Nepia had everything for a rugby player "balance, fabulous hands, a prodigious kick - all the qualities for a great rugby player" and was "a dedicated servant of the game for his whole life".

Later, another surprise guest from that tour was the Kiwi – the tour mascot – shown in photos on the tour, and loaned by the New Zealand Rugby Museum. It was another first – the programme's first non-speaking guest!

A tradition of these programmes is that guests come from far and wide. Herbert Bowcott came from Wales to pay his tribute, having watched Nepia on the 24-5 tour, and later played against him in 1930 in New Zealand. He spoke of how Nepia was still regarded as a legend in Wales, and that young kiddies in Wales still regarded Nepia as the best full-back ever, having been told this by their fathers and grandfathers. He also added that five South Wales clubs all claimed to have the jersey that George Nepia wore in the 1924 match against Wales on display in their museums!

Just before the commercial break, Bob Parker revealed that Nepia had made a hit record in the early 1930s, *Beneath the Maori Moon* and played it on an ancient 78 record. What the viewers at home did not see was Nepia signing the song during the commercial break, to the delight of the studio audience. This was included in the repeat of the programme. Reports from his playing days often mention his singing at receptions and dinners, and clearly he had a fine voice.

Nepia's son and daughter, Oma and Kiwi, spoke movingly about their father. Kiwi said he was a "wonderful father" and Oma descried him as a "fine, very hard working, generous man" and recalled how he had seen him play rugby on four occasions. There was also film of the church where he was married, with the stained glass windows in the church of his late wife Huinga's father and cousin who had been killed in World War One and film of the farm where Nepia had raised his family, and the rugby pitch he had played on at that time. There was also a wonderful interview with fellow farmer Victor Rickard who famously said that "George, you were a good farmer" – from a farmer's view a greater compliment than anything that could be said about his rugby.

Another guest was former All Black full-back Bob Scott – one of the great All Blacks in that position. He recalled playing rugby as a child, when the argument was always who among the children would "be" George Nepia in their games. He added: "George, you were the one who set the standard we all hoped to achieve." He jokingly questioned George's change in rugby life to become a referee - "inhuman", and then recalled how he had finished one game by converting the last try! He finished by saying that his life-long friend George Nepia was "A great All Black fullback and also a great New Zealander"

The parade of All Black talent continued with Don Clarke – "The Boot" – who had travelled from South Africa for the programme, and had not seen Nepia since 1966, when they had been in Wellington with Billy Wallace and Bob Scott. He saluted Nepia's "fabulous achievements - you record will always be marvellous".

And through all this, Nepia smiled, greeted old friends, and seemed slightly overwhelmed by the whole event. During the break he had said he "got the shock of his life" when presented with the programme, but was very pleased: "thank you so very much". He came across as a modest man, looking back in old age on a lifetime's achievements on and off the rugby field, with friends and family.

Rarely can so much All Black rugby talent been assembled in one place. In these days of professionalism, what would a team selected from the stars present that night be worth? What we can be confident of is that Nepia would have been selected to play full-back, despite some illustrious competition. As Bob Parker said, quoting British writer Denzil Batchelor in *I, George Nepia*, "When I hear others debating who will play fullback for the Kingdom of Heaven versus The Rest I turn to stone. It is not for me a question of whether Nepia was the best fullback in history. It is a question as to which of the others is fit to help him on with his Cotton Oxford boots."

From a personal point of view, I found the programme very moving. I never believed I would see Nepia, one of my heroes, on television, answering questions abut his life and clearly held in great esteem and affection by so many. Apparently the party after the show was a great occasion, going on very late.

The obituaries and tributes to Nepia on his death three months later were fine and fulsome. But maybe this programme was the best tribute, showing his achievements, surrounded by friends and former teammates, truly one of the great New Zealanders.

Peter Lush

Charlie Smith greeting George Nepia at Halifax station when Nepia had joined Halifax. Also in the photo are Arthur Archbell (Halifax Secretary) on right, A. Wade (left) and H. Webster (centre) - Halifax directors (Photo: Courtesy Robert Gate)

Nepia and Arthur Archbell before Nepia's debut for Halifax against Leeds on 1 January 1937. (Photo: Courtesy Robert Gate)

Part 3: A great rugby career

4. Hawke's Bay and the Ranfurly Shield 1923 to 1926

Hawke's Bay came to dominate the Ranfurly Shield in the early 1920s. From being a minor New Zealand provincial side to become the major side was an incredible achievement and at times they fielded nine or 10 All Blacks.

The Ranfurly Shield was, before the advent of the Super 12, the major New Zealand competition in provincial rugby. When one considers the opposition that Hawke's Bay had to face, sides such as Auckland, Canterbury and Wellington having far greater resources and populations to call upon, their achievement is even more remarkable.

Hawke's Bay 6 Wairarapa 0 4 June 1923

Despite heavy rain 5,000 spectators attended and saw the home side win a close forward-dominated game with a penalty by Nepia, "a beautiful goal from near the sideline" according to the *Hawke's Bay Herald*, and a late try by Smith.

Hawke's Bay: Yates; Barclay, Kirwan, Mapu; Paewai, Nepia; Mill; Martin-Smith; Gemmell, Walker, M. Brownlie, McNab, C. Brownlie, Kirkpatrick and Irvine.

Hawke's Bay 10 Wellington 6 28 July 1923

Another close encounter saw Hawke's Bay sneak home at McLean Park through a drop goal by Yates, a penalty goal by George Nepia and a goal from a mark by Fitzpatrick. Despite Wellington scoring two tries the goals were sufficient to see the home side home. The *Hawke's Bay Herald* reported that "The home backs were disappointing and lacked the essential combination and nipiness", and 'Touchline's' notes said that: "The inside backs (Kirwan, Nepia and Paewai) combined well enough up to a point but lacked snap in their attack".

Hawke's Bay: Yates; Grenside, Kirwan, Mapu; Paewai, Nepia; Mill; Martin-Smith; Gemmell, Walker, M. Brownlie, McNab, C. Brownlie, Kirkpatrick and Irvine.

Hawke's Bay 15 Poverty Bay 0 11 August 1923

Despite the rain and a sea of mud, Hawke's Bay fought the next challengers at Nelson Park Hastings and secured an easy win with tries by Kivell, Nepia, Mapu, Mill and Brownlie, none of the tries being converted. The local paper reported: "Worse conditions than those under which the match was played could scarcely be conceived. Paewai was facile at picking up the greasy ball and as usual combined nicely with Nepia".

Hawke's Bay: Yates; Grenside, Kivell, Mapu; Paewai, Nepia; Mill; Batchelor; Gemmell, Walker, M. Brownlie, McNab, Daley, Irvine and Kirkpatrick.

Hawke's Bay 9 Canterbury 6 15 August 1923

Four days later, again at Hastings, Hawke's Bay held off Canterbury by a point in front in front of 5,000 spectators. Grenside scored a try for Hawke's Bay and it was two Maori Agricultural College students who scored second-half tries: Nepia and Paewai, none of the tries being converted. The *Hawke's Bay Herald* said: "No other game has created more interest among rugby enthusiasts than the Ranfurly Shield match." It concluded: "At the conclusion of the game the crowd mobbed the field and carried the winners off shoulder high."

Hawke's Bay: Yates; Grenside, Kirwan, Mapu; Paewai, Nepia; Mill; Walker; Gemmell, Ormond, C. Brownlie, McNab, M. Brownlie, Irvine and Kirkpatrick.

1924

Hawke's Bay 30 Wairarapa 14 — 3 June 1924

Nepia did not play in the early part of the season due to an All Black trial game, which also included Paewai and McNab. Despite this, Hawke's Bay won easily, with their forwards dominating the game.

Hawke's Bay 46 Poverty Bay 10 — 21 June 1924

Five of Hawke's Bay's six All Blacks returned for this game, at McLean Park with an attendance of 4-5,000. Nepia, playing at full back for the first time, converted two of the 11 tries and added a penalty goal. Early kicking by Nepia drove Poverty Bay back and he tackled Whaitiri well. He also converted a try by Ormond after 20 minutes. A Nepia penalty goal increased the score to 8-0. A further try by Grenside was converted by Nepia to bring the score to 13-0. The *Hawke's Bay Herald* reported that "Poverty Bay's forwards worked their way to the Hawke's Bay line only to find Nepia a stumbling block." Hawke's Bay ran away with the game in the second half for an easy victory.

Hawke's Bay: Nepia; Grenside, Barclay, Falwesser; Kivell, Mardon, Mill; Walker, Gemmell, Ormond, C. Brownlie, McNab, M. Brownlie, Kirkpatrick and Irvine.

Hawke's Bay 35 Nelson 3 — 16 August 1924

Hawke's Bay won easily against Nelson who were competing in the Shield for the first time. Nepia did not play in this game.

Hawke's Bay 23 Auckland 6 — 23 August 1924

Hawke's Bay faced an unbeaten Auckland. Despite being behind early on, Hawke's Bay scored a sound victory. Nepia did not play in this game.

Hawke's Bay 31 Manawatu 5 — 30 August 1924

The champions played their final shield game at Hastings and won comfortably with tries by Corkhill (3), Falwesser (3), Mardon (2) and Hingston scoring tries. Nepia did not play in this game.

1925

Hawke's Bay 22 Wairarapa 3 — 3 June 1925

The local paper reported that "Hawke's Bay backs possessed much more driving force than the wearers of the green jersey, much of which was due to the complete understanding between Mill, Paewai and Nepia, all three 1924 All Blacks. A free kick to Hawke's Bay saw George Nepia find the line at the visitors' 25. A scrum followed the line out from which Mill secured and dummied two opponents, Nepia passing out to the wing and Mill ran into score." Nepia converted to make the score 8-3.

The report continued : "The fortunes of war were against Wairarapa. They had a fine rally and reached Hawke's Bay's line where Nepia just beat Clark in a race for the ball to touch down" On a fine day with 8,000 spectators, the Bay backs

dominated and scored tries by Grenside (2), Mill, Brownlie and Mahoney; Nepia and Miller converted one each and Wylie scored from the mark.
Hawke's Bay: Yates; Grenside, Kivell, Falwesser; Nepia, Paewai; Mill, Walker, Gemmell, Miller, C. Brownlie, Mahoney, Craven, Wylie and Swain.

Hawke's Bay 24 Canterbury 18 5 August 1925
Eleven of the Hawke's Bay side had represented New Zealand. Morrie Brownlie scored first for Hawke's Bay and they led 14-8 at half-time, Falwesser wrapped up the scoring with a try in the corner. Irvine converted.
Hawke's Bay: Nepia, Grenside, Blake, Falwesser; Corkhill, Paewai; Mill, Walker; Ormond, Gemmell, C. Brownlie, Mahoney, M. Brownlie, Irvine and Fitzpatrick.

Hawke's Bay 31 Southland 12 8 August 1925
On a cold day, Hawke's Bay had to contend with a strong wind in the first half but in the second had their usual good finish with tries from Blake, Walker, Gemmell (2), Kirkpatrick, Brownlie and Falwesser. Nepia did not play in this game.

Hawke's Bay 28 Taranaki 3 22 August 1925
Hawke's Bay were in fine form with Nepia leading the way. At half-time Hawke's Bay led 17-3, Barclay (2), Blake (2), Grenside, M. Brownlie and Wylie scored the tries with Mill kicking a penalty and converting a try, Irvine also put over a conversion. 'Notes on the Players' in the *Hawke's Bay Herald* was for once critical of Nepia, saying: "Nepia did not cause much of a sensation. Most of his work could be done at leisure as the play went, and on the 3 or 4 occasions when he was hustled he was found badly wanting and was pulled out of the more twice by good luck. His play in the open showed a far greater regard for the entertainment of a doting public than the occasion warranted".
Hawke's Bay: Nepia, Falwesser, Blake; Grenside, Barclay; Paewai; Mill, Walker; Gemmell, Swain, C. Brownlie, Mahoney, M. Brownlie, Irvine and Fitzpatrick.

Hawke's Bay 20 Wellington 11 5 September 1925
A huge crowd of 22,000 turned up at Athletic Park, Wellington, Hawke's Bay having taken the match to Wellington, as they were allowed to by the rules. The scores were level at half-time with tries for the Bay by Falwesser and Grenside. Swain scored two tries in the second period, Blake and Morrie Brownlie finishing off the home side. Among the 22,000 spectators there were two special trainloads from Hawke's Bay. Nineteen All Blacks were on the pitch, including nine of the 'Invincibles'.
Hawke's Bay: Nepia, Falwesser, Blake; Grenside, Corkhill; Paewai; Mill, Walker; Gemmell, Ormond, C. Brownlie, Mahoney, M. Brownlie, Irvine and Fitzpatrick.

Hawke's Bay 34 Otago 14 9 September 1925
At Nelson Park, Hastings the 19th attempt to deprive Hawke's Bay of the Shield came from Otago. Otago led 14-3 at half-time but were overwhelmed in the second period with tries from Blake (2), Mill, Walker, Falwesser, C. Brownlie and Ormond. Nepia was unable to play.

1926

Hawke's Bay 77 Wairarapa 14   3 June 1926

Over 8,000 fans saw the Bay run up a record score. Blake (5), Cooke (3), Corkhill (2), M. J. Brownlie (3), Craven, Tait, Grenside and C. J, Brownlie. Grenside converted eight of the tries and M. Brownlie five. The scale of the victory was great, but the side did include nine All Blacks. However, Nepia failed to score.

Hawke's Bay: Nepia, Grenside, Blake; Tait, Cooke; Corkhill, Mill, Walker; Craven, Swain, M. Brownlie, Mahoney, C. Brownlie, Irvine and Fitzpatrick.

Hawke's Bay 36 Wanganui 3   5 June 1926

Hawke's Bay scored another heavy win at Hastings with Cooke (3), Grenside (2) Swain (2), Kirkpatrick, Tait and Irvine scoring tries, with Grenside converting two tries and Mill one.

Hawke's Bay: Nepia, Grenside, Neal; Tait, Cooke; Corkhill, Mill, Walker; Craven, Swain, M. Brownlie, Mahoney, C. Brownlie, Irvine and Fitzpatrick.

Hawke's Bay 58 Wellington 8   14 August 1926

A record crowd of 14,000 at McLean Park saw another challenge from Wellington. Nepia "drop-kicked a magnificent goal giving Hawke's Bay the lead after 4 minutes" according to the *Hawke's Bay Herald*. At half-time Hawke's Bay led by 24 points with tries by Grenside (3), C Brownlie, and Single, Nepia converting three. In the second half Grenside scored two more, with other tries by Johnson, Blake, Cooke, Kirkpatrick, and Swain.

From a scrum H. E. Nichols and then Tait made a great run only to be stopped at the 25 flag by a splendid tackle by Nepia. The local paper reported: "The stolid faultless defence of Nepia added to the effect"

Hawke's Bay: Nepia, Grenside, Blake; Paewai, Cooke; Johnson, Mill, Walker; Single, Swain, M. Brownlie, Mahoney, C. Brownlie, Irvine and Fitzpatrick.

Hawke's Bay 41 Auckland 11   21 August 1926

Another large crowd of 8,000 at McLean Park saw a strong challenge from Auckland.

Auckland took an early lead, but it was short-lived for almost from the kick off Batty was penalised for offside and Nepia from 10 yards on the Auckland side of halfway placed a "fine goal". Nepia repeated his Wellington effort and drop-kicked a wonderful goal to put Hawke's Bay 6-3 ahead

The *Hawke's Bay Herald* reported that "A bad kick by Johnson enabled Lucas to find a hole in the Hawke's Bay defence but Nepia retrieved the position and sent away a beautiful line kick. Webber, Batty and Cammack were associated in a clever play that tested the Bay defence but Nepia was again the stumbling block."

Nepia landed two penalties, then Cooke scored a try and Nepia converted. A Cyril Brownlie try made it 14-3. Just before half time Blake scored under the posts with Nepia again converting: 19-11. In the second half M. Brownlie, Blake (2), Cooke, Mahoney and Swain scored additional tries with Grenside converting two of them.

The *Hawke's Bay Herald* added: "If anything apart from their own lack of condition beat Auckland it was the unruffled coolness of Nepia's play. He was like an evil fate hanging over the heads of the Aucklanders and the desperation he caused them by his accuracy and persistence in driving their attacks back, and in upsetting their splendid and powerful attacks was in small degree their undoing. One Auckland player expressed to the writer his opinion that Nepia should be disqualified for not being human, another that he shouldn't be allowed to play in boots, they found him a terrible nuisance."

Hawke's Bay: Nepia, Grenside, Blake; Jensen, Cooke; Johnson, Mill, Walker; Single, Swain, M. Brownlie, Mahoney, C. Brownlie, Irvine and Fitzpatrick.

Hawke's Bay 17 Canterbury 15 18 September 1926

In front of a crowd of over 23,000 at Lancaster Park, Christchurch the Bay had a stern test. Cooke opened the score with a try, with Corkhill adding a further try: 8-0. Irvine added a further try to make it 11-0. Canterbury came back into it and two tries from Cooke and Grenside made it 17-15 and the Bay had to hold out for a famous victory. Nepia did not play in this fixture.

At the end of the season the Hawke's Bay side was dismantled with players such as Cooke, Irvine, Nepia, Johnson, Paewai and Mill moving to other parts of the country and thus were unavailable for selection. Hawke's Bay lost the Shield in 1927.

George and Huinga Nepia on his return to New Zealand after finishing playing Rugby League in England for Halifax. He was met by Mr E. Asher of the New Zealand Maori League Control Board and Mr G. Grey Campbell, chairman of the Auckland Rugby League.
(Photo: Courtesy *New Zealand Herald*)

5. The Invincibles' place in history

Rugby Union is wont to be careless with its history, on occasion conflating myth with reality as in the naming of the World Cup after William Webb Ellis. There are extenuating circumstances for this.

The game lacks the extensive statistical underpinning which enables followers of cricket and baseball to compare past with present. It has only a limited tradition of high-quality descriptive writing, while its complexity means that it has changed immensely over time. The spectator who watched cricket or football in the 1920s would doubtless recognise the modern games, even if elements within them would come as a surprise. It is far from certain that a rugby fan of comparable vintage would be able to say the same. There is little film extant from before the 1950s, meaning that players further back than Cliff Morgan or Colin Meads exist largely in the memory of the dwindling numbers who saw them play in the flesh.

All of this makes comparison difficult, yet there is little doubt of the quality and enduring impact of the Second All Blacks of 1924-5. This is made particularly obvious at Twickenham, the headquarters ground of the Rugby Football Union. This stadium too would befuddle the returning inter-war - or for that matter 1970s - spectator. It still occupies the same land that it has since 1910, but not a single structure remains from a quarter, let alone three-quarters, of a century ago. Yet the naming of its numerous bars, meeting rooms and conference suites reflects the game's earlier history. Most, quite rightly, pay tribute to the great heroes of the English game - names like Obolensky and Wakefield. Yet one of the largest is named for the 1924-25 All Blacks, the 'Invincibles'. George Nepia and his team-mates led by Cliff Porter stare out from photographs onto the milling masses of the early 21st century.

It is a fitting tribute to a team who, in an era when long-distance travel of any sort was a rarity, spent eight months away from home, travelled to the other side of the earth and back and handled everything it could throw at them, winning every single match. Any number of things can derail the best team in the world on any given day. Tiredness, boredom, complacency, bad luck with the bounce of the ball or a marginal refereeing decision, injuries (particularly in an era before replacements), a simple off day or inspired opponents. If an unbeaten run lasts long enough it becomes in itself a psychological burden, particularly as landmarks loom. To go through 30 matches 12,000 miles from home and never once succumb to any of these possibilities (not to mention the little matter of having a player sent off only eight minutes into your toughest match) is little short of miraculous.

The sheer scale of that undertaking meant that tours of Britain were a once-in-a-lifetime experience for most players. In the first half of the century All Black teams came to Britain once per decade - and not at all in the decades (1910s, 1940s) which were interrupted by war. Not until 1963, when prop Ian Clark made a second All Black tour with Wilson Whineray's tourists, was it possible for a New Zealander to make two trips, while the Invincibles were the first touring team from anywhere to visit Britain since the second Springboks in 1912. Mark Nicholls, an all-time great whose test career lasted almost a decade, was capped only 10 times. A modern All Black may win that many within a few months of his first appearance. The Invincibles' wing 'Snowy' Svenson scored in all four internationals on the tour, yet these were the only caps he was to win

The New Zealand they represented was also very different to that of today. It was a new country - only detached from the rest of Britain's Australasian possessions when it chose not to join the Australian Federation in 1901, and a Dominion only since 1907. The Maori Wars which had threatened British control in the second half of the previous century were still well within living memory.

Formal colonial status had been replaced with what the historian James Belich has called 'Recolonialism' - economic dependence upon Britain through exports of dairy products and meat and an official ideology emphasising British origins and allegiances. In 1921 340,000 tons of produce left Britain for New Zealand on the freezer ships that, from 1882, had made this massive trade possible. The farmers and meat packers enriched by this trade dominated politically – New Zealand's first Labour government would not be elected until 1935. The Prime Minister William Massey was a 'British Israelite' who believed the British were the chosen people, had in the words of his biographer "a mystical faith in the divine mission and permanency of the British Empire" and had opposed Dominion status, preferring to remain a colony. Recolonialism was reinforced by New Zealand's contribution to the First World War. From a nation of little more than a million people, 100,000 served in the British forces and 58,000 were killed or wounded. Young New Zealanders were brought up on the text book *Our Nation's Story* - the nation in question being Britain.

New Zealand proclaimed itself '98.5 per cent British' - as Belich points out, a figure which not even Britain attained. Within the Invincibles the names of Robilliard and Svenson testify to a slightly wider range of origins than the slogan admitted.

So too do those of Mill, Nepia and Paewai. While the Maoris had proved themselves tough and resourceful warriors during the wars of the late 19th century, many had predicted that they would eventually die out or be assimilated in an Anglo-Polynesian hybrid race. Such views were apparently borne out by the 1896 census showing the Maori population down to 42,000, or about five per cent of the population. But in spite of cruel setbacks like the Spanish Flu epidemic of 1918-19, which hit Maoris disproportionately, they recovered rather than dwindling further, with numbers doubling by 1936. This was accompanied by the greater political and cultural confidence expressed in movements like 'Young Maori'.

There is a sense in which Nepia, Mill and Paewai were the sporting expression of this revival, picking up the tradition established by the Maori team of 1888 which was the first to travel from New Zealand to Britain, undertaking an extraordinary 14-month, 107-match marathon. A member of that team, Tom Ellison, who captained New Zealand, proposed the resolution which made black the colour of the national team's shirts and in 1902 published *The Art of Rugby Football*, the first New Zealand coaching book.

By 1924 Rugby Union's status as New Zealand's national game, summed up in John Mulgan's description of it as "the best of all our pleasures... religion and desire and fulfilment all in one" was unquestionable. The All Blacks were sufficiently important that Massey and his deputy Prime Minister Gordon Coates, who would become Premier in 1925, were prepared to intervene in a dispute over selection immediately before their departure. Chairman of selectors Norman MacKenzie, under pressure to take an extra player at the last minute, responded that he was happy with the team as it was and that while Massey and Coates might be good at politics they had something to learn about rugby. One in five males between 10 and 29 played in school or club teams and Rugby Union had, Belich notes: "twice as many club members as the next most important sport (tennis) and four times as many as soccer and league combined".

The 1905 Originals, had given the new nation a focus for its identity. The match against Wales, the only defeat of that tour, was to Sir Keith Sinclair "New Zealand sport's Gallipoli," and of equal significance, the Welsh historian Gareth Williams suggests, to the new Wales which had emerged from the heavy industralisation, immigration and Anglicisation of the late 19th century - a rare collision of two moments of national foundation. The continuing fascination of the 1905 team for New Zealanders has been confirmed within the last twô years by the popularity of Lloyd Jones's remarkable novel *The Book of Fame*, based on the tourists' experiences.

A strong element in that enduring fame has been the 'did he, didn't he?' debate over Bob Deans' 'try' for the All Blacks. New Zealanders have emphasised Wales winger Teddy Morgan's written 'confession' to Invincibles' captain Cliff Porter that, as the man who tackled Deans, he knew that he had scored. Welshman have remained more impressed with centre Rhys Gabe's rejoinder that he, and not Morgan, was the man who had made the tackle. Gabe remembered that Deans had attempted to struggle forward rather than simply grounding the ball and asked why he needed to do this if, as he asserted, he had already reached the tryline. As the long-lived Gabe was to write in 1954: "The more this incident recedes into antiquity, the more nebulous becomes the truth about it."

What is not in question was that the first All Blacks introduced Britain to rugby of a sophistication it had not previously encountered. They were happy to share their wisdom following the tour. In 1906 Dave Gallaher and Willie Stead, captain and vice-captain, published *The Complete Footballer on the New Zealand System*, a 322 page volume of which Gareth Williams has written: "Their penetrating discussion of the game - lines of running, angles of packing, miss moves, compiling statistics on different phases of play - brought a startlingly new technical discussion to rugby literature, raising it to a level of sophistication previously unheard of and rarely exceeded since".

This magnum opus had its context in an already well-established tradition of tactical analysis and innovation. Graeme Barrow dates specialisation by New Zealand forwards to the mid-1870s "at least 40 years before any other rugby-playing country." This accompanied the introduction of a two-man front row, as opposed to the three-man back row used in other countries. Following the Maori tour of 1888 the eighth forward was detached from the scrum to become a 'rover' - neither back nor forward.

This was not the disadvantage it might have seemed at scrummages. As specialists the New Zealanders were much more adept at scrummaging than opponents who packed down in the order in which they arrived at the scrum. In addition their 2-3-2 formation formed a wedge, driving inwards to create pressure on the opposing hooker, while British teams using the 3-2-3 merely drove straight ahead.

The 'rover' put the ball into the scrum, while the scrum-half waited behind to collect it, enabling the much quicker launching of attacks. The problem, so far as British observers saw it, was the positioning of the rover. Gabe explained: "When the opposition heeled he performed the function of a scrum-half, but when New Zealand obtained possession, he remained still and was legally offside, being in front of the ball and not in a scrummage. Moreover he was guilty of passive obstruction, for the opposing scrum-half was obliged to run round him." Barrow is scarcely exaggerating when he describes the rover as "the most controversial position in rugby history".

Furthermore the New Zealanders expected their forwards to be attackers, prepared to handle and pass, as well as merely ball-winners. This was accompanied by the attitude of mind which has distinguished New Zealand teams throughout their history, and which Mulgan argued made them adept in other fields as well: "I found in wartime that there was a considerable virtue in men who had played games like professionals to win, and not, like public-school boys and amateurs, for exercise."

Unsurprisingly British teams, starting with county champions Devon who were massacred 55-4 in the opening match, were overwhelmed. This result shares with England's 1950 Football World Cup defeat by USA the distinction of, in legend at least, having been widely disbelieved by the sports desks of the London newspapers when it was received down the wire.

Wales

It was not until they reached Wales at the end of the tour that they encountered opposition of comparable strength and low cunning. Wales was in the midst of its 'First Golden Age', which would bring six Triple Crowns (France did not play its first match until 1906 and would not be serious competition until the late 1920s) between 1900 and 1911. Its clubs were immensely powerful - both Cardiff and Swansea came close to beating the All Blacks. And its leading players were quite prepared to seize New Zealand's weapon in the quest to slay it. In the international Wales employed Cliff Pritchard of Newport as its own 'rover', then scrum-half Dickie Owen ignored him for the first quarter before passing to him in the reverse pass move which created space for Teddy Morgan's try - the only score of the game. The Welsh backs had also, almost unprecedentedly, met to rehearse the decisive move. It must also be remembered that the All Blacks were by this time tired, and weighed down by the pressure of their unbeaten run. Gabe recalled visiting them at their hotel and finding them: "Keyed-up and ill at ease with the thought of a possible defeat".

Most importantly the triumphs of the Originals were accomplished in the arena that mattered most to New Zealanders: Britain. The rivalry that was in time to be most significant, with South Africa, had yet to be launched in 1905 and would only be in its infancy in 1924, following the first meeting between the All Blacks and the Springboks in 1921.

The Invincibles arrived in Britain - and played - in the shadow cast by the Originals. The British game they found was differently balanced to that encountered by the pioneers of 1905, or for that matter their successors of 1935 and 1953. Those teams all found Wales in periods of prosperity, and would lose to them. The Invincibles arrived when Wales was in its worst period before the 1980s and 1990s. Between 1923 and 1928 Wales would win only seven matches out of 26 - with five of the wins against the still negligible French. They failed to beat England between 1922 and 1932.

This had implications beyond the international games. For most of the last century, the toughest games experienced by All Black teams outside the internationals were almost invariably against the Welsh clubs. Cardiff and Swansea were both unlucky not to win in 1905. Swansea would beat the 1935 team, and Cardiff their successors of 1953 (who also drew with Swansea), followed by Newport in 1963 and Llanelli in 1972. Until Ian Kirkpatrick's Seventh All Blacks came unstuck against North West Counties at Workington in November 1972, their only defeat outside Wales in six tours and nearly 70 years had been by England in Obolensky's match in 1935, although Ulster drew with both the 1935 and the 1953 teams.

Even in 1924 one of their closest calls came against Newport, who were inspired by the 35 year-old Jack Wetter, a survivor of the Welsh game's more prosperous days who had first been capped in 1914. Llanelli held them to 8-3. Otherwise they were hardly troubled - Swansea saw the first warning that this team might be truly exceptional as a club record 40,000 crowd watched the All Blacks win 39-3, leading one Welsh correspondent to plead that "panic must be avoided at all costs". Swansea also hosted the international, where New Zealand's 19-0 win was hailed for its avenging margin of one point for every year since the defeat of 1905. Unlike Twickenham, the St Helen's ground has changed so little that Nepia found it immediately familiar when he returned with a Maori touring team in 1982. The Swansea crowd recognised him in return, rising as one spectator to cheer him as he walked across the front of the main grandstand.

Welsh weakness helped, but should not be taken to imply that the Invincibles had it easy. The 1920s may have been a time of famine for Wales - always recognised by New Zealanders as the one part of Britain that rivalled their own fervour for the game - but they were one of feast for the other three home nations. In 1936 the rugby writer and commentator H. B. T. 'Teddy' Wakelam asked writers from each of the four nations to nominate a year in which his country had particularly excelled and write a chapter on it for his book *The Game Goes On.* His chosen Welshman, W. J. Hoare - better known to readers of the *Western Mail* and *South Wales Echo* as 'Old Stager' - chose 1905. His other three writers went for years in the mid 1920s - H. J. Henley choosing 1924 for England, Jock Wemyss 1925 for Scotland and R. W. Harland 1926 for Ireland.

Harland said the 1924 to 1929 period was one of Irish rugby's "two periods of maximum brilliance". The best of that period would come a little after the visit of the Invincibles with the 1926 team, nominated by Harland as the best of the lot, losing a first-ever Grand Slam to one of the best Welsh displays of the decade at

Swansea. Between 1926 and 1928 they were to win nine of their 12 Five Nations matches, sharing the title with Scotland, also at a historic high, in the first two years.

Elements of that fine team were already present when the Invincibles visited Lansdowne Road. Nepia was warmly complimentary about his opposite number Ernie Crawford. The brothers Hewitt - founders of an extraordinary dynasty - brought both power and intellect to a three-quarter line also featuring George Stephenson, whose 42 internationals were to make him the world's most capped player until well after the Second World War. Among the forwards was the inimitable, irrepressible 'Jammie' Clinch, fondly remembered for his genially combative response to like-minded Welsh forward Arthur Lemon "I'll make an orange of him."

England were still more powerful - stronger, arguably, than they were to be for nearly 70 years. They had just won consecutive Grand Slams, and three in four seasons since 1921 in a period whose only defeat was a stupefying 28-6 defeat by Wales at Cardiff in 1922. This was the era of Wavell Wakefield, when some of the lessons taught by the 1905 All Blacks at last started to be applied by British players. Forwards performed allotted, specialised roles at scrum and line-out. Wakefield recalled: "We did start the essence of jumping and support play and, even more to the point, we worked out precisely what the functions of the back row forwards were in both attack and defence".

A back rower himself, Wakefield was exceptional in both modes, developing the concepts of cover defence and 'cornerflagging' and harassing opposing defenders when chasing the cross-kicks in which his teams specialised. In this period England were both durable and more consistent in selection than has often been the case. Four of the pack who faced the Invincibles - Wakefield (31 caps), Ronald Cove-Smith (29), Tom Voyce (27) and Sam Tucker (27) would head England's most-capped list until Eric Evans (30 caps) broke their monopoly in the late 1950s and Budge Rogers (34) finally overtook Wakefield in the late 1960s.

England provided, as Nepia recalled, a fitting climax to the tour and a challenge that brought the best out of the Invincibles. In most years, they or Ireland would have been good enough to win the Six Nations. 1924-25 was not, however most years. Ireland were building towards a historic high, and England just coming down from one. Scotland were at what - the triumphs of Mark Morrison's teams in the 1900s and the Grand Slams of 1984 and 1990 notwithstanding - would still be recognised by most historians as their all-time peak.

This was the season in which everything went right for them, with the Grand Slam resoundingly clinched on the back of the extraordinary attacking skills of their threequarter line - Ian Smith, George Aitken, Phil MacPherson and Johnny Wallace. Aitken had been an All Black in 1924, Wallace would captain Australia in the late 1920s and Smith too had been born in Australia, so proving that the 'kilted Kiwi' phenomenon of recent years was not the complete novelty it has sometimes been painted. If asked about their qualification all might have replied, as a testy Obolensky was to do when quizzed by the Prince of Wales a decade later: "I attend Oxford University, sir." Scotland scored 17 tries in their four matches, a truly remarkable number by the standards of the time, with the prodigious Smith claiming eight of them. Smith's career total of 24 international tries would survive as a world record until 1987, when it was overtaken during the inaugural World Cup by David Campese, and is still the highest in the Five/Six Nations.

Yet they did not play New Zealand.

It was not the Invincibles' fault. The Scottish Rugby Union, against stiff competition the most bloody-mindedly reactionary body in the game, was still furious about the financial arrangements for its 1905 game against the All Blacks. Doubting that the New Zealanders would attract a decent crowd to Inverleith, they had insisted on a £200 guarantee rather taking a share of the gate money, and had been furious when the tourists had walked off with a four-figure profit. It further rankled that the invitation to the 1924 team had been issued by the (English) Rugby Football Union rather than the International Board and the Scots used this breach of protocol as an excuse for declining the fixture.

In so doing they robbed themselves for a second time. It was potentially one of the all-time great rugby occasions, a climacteric to match the 1905 clash with Wales. And great though the Invincibles were, it would have given Scotland perhaps its best ever chance of beating New Zealand, something it has still to achieve in 23 meetings over 97 years. Like Brian Lochore's 1967 All Blacks, denied a trip to Ireland for the much better reason of Irish fears of the foot and mouth epidemic raging that year in Britain, the Invincibles were denied their chance of becoming the first All Blacks to beat all four home nations on a single tour, a distinction which finally fell to Graham Mourie's team in 1978. This is the single asterisk against the Invincibles greatness, that they did not, unlike the 1905 team, meet the best opposition Britain had to offer. But you cannot ask any team to do more than beat every opponent it is allowed to play.

The truly remarkable thing about their feat is that it was achieved with only limited possession. The seven-man scrum may have prevailed in 1905, but by 1924 opponents were coming to terms with it, and exploiting their three to two advantage in the front row. Teddy Morgan, Wales's try-scorer in 1905, was the first British writer to recognise the 1924 team's extraordinary talent. At the beginning of the tour he proclaimed them "A great side and worthy successors to the 1905 side. They have youth, brawn and wonderful playing capabilities. No club side will beat them and it will be a very fine international side that will hold them". This showed him as a considerable more adept assessor of talent than Originals hooker George Tyler, who as Nepia remembered condemned them as 'the worst team New Zealand has fielded' on the strength of patchy performances on the preparatory tour of Australia.

At the same time Morgan said the seven-man scrum plus rover was "purely defensive and cramped up in attack" and that they would be better to play eight "all shoving". If Morgan's fears about their attacking potential were not fulfilled, the seven-man formation left the Invincibles permanently short of possession, with most accounts of the tour estimating that they won only around 30 per cent of the scrums.

This was a foretaste of the eventual demise of the seven-man scrum. In 1928 the All Blacks, hailed on departure as the strongest ever to leave New Zealand, took a fearful mauling in the scrums in South Africa, from provincial teams as much as the Springboks. The South African 3-4-1 scrummage formation, eventually adopted world-wide, achieved the same drive inwards as the 2-3-2, creating intolerable pressures on the two-man front row. In 1930, British Lions manager James Baxter condemned the rover straightforwardly as a 'cheat'. Mr Baxter was not a man chosen for his diplomatic skills. Asked about the popularity of Rugby League in Auckland he commented that "every town must have its sewer". He was, though, a significant figure in the Rugby Football Union at a time when the RFU was vastly the most influential voice on the International Board. In 1932 the International Board ruled that all front rows should have three men, ending the seven-man option and converting the rover into a number eight forward. New Zealand took some time to recover - the 1935 team was so out-scrummaged in its defeat by Swansea that the home team regularly took the option of the scrum instead of a line-out. In 1949 the All Blacks were in such desperate trouble in South Africa that a special scrummaging session had to be arranged with Springbok coach Danie Craven. The 4-0 defeat on that tour drove New Zealand rugby into a long spell of ultra-physical, forward-fixated introspection.

John Reason and Carwyn James suggest that the 1924 team's loyalty to a formation which was clearly failing was rooted in tribal reverence for the memory of the 1905 team. Gallaher, rover as well as captain and chronicler in 1905, may have strengthened this ancestor worship by falling on the Western Front. Yet still they won, 30 times in a row.

One reason for this was that they had remarkable players. Maurice Brownlie was a lock of Meads-like presence and quality - while there are outside-halves of 6ft 3in and 15st today, someone of those dimensions in 1924 was a true giant. Add in athleticism, combativity and ball skills and you had an authentic holy terror.

Among the backs were the first and second five-eighths, Bert Cooke and Mark Nicholls. Rowe Harding, who played against them for Swansea, wrote of them: "One great player single-handed can effectively be stopped; but two, playing together in a side where the other players are sound, honest footballers can accomplish miracles. Nicholls and Cooke were an extraordinary combination. Each was the antithesis of the other, and yet each completed the other. Nicholls was an unassuming, unobtrusive player, Cooke was spectacular in everything he did; but Nicholls was the man who opened up the narrow gap through which Cooke flashed at lightning speed."

Yet Harding was also convinced that "their greatness was collective rather than individual... The All Black pack was good, but its individuals were no better than a dozen forwards of the home countries... One could name off-hand half a dozen better natural players in Britain than the other men who formed the other parts of the All Blacks back division, but they would not have done as well. Most of our teams in this country consist of 15 players. The All Blacks' team was a machine comprising 15 mechanical units, and had all the efficiency of smooth-running machinery."

Leonard Corbett, who played against them at centre for England, reached similar conclusions, writing 30 years later of "Teamwork of the highest order allied to a high standard of physical fitness, determination, speed and backing up.

A feature of the tour was the piling up of points in the closing stages of many of their engagements. The forwards were tall and heavy, yet their size seemed in no way to impair their mobility. Close hand to hand passing amongst members of the pack was a form of attack to which most of their opponents had no effective answer. Always there were one or more colleagues within a yard or so of the tackled or half-tackled All Black when they were launching an attack. Even in the act of passing they continued to pass, and pass accurately, so that the movement was carried."

Their forwards, he said "could handle the ball like threequarters...they knew exactly what to do with the ball when they found themselves in possession," while the backs based themselves on "short, quick passing in close formation and straight running". While individually no more talented or resourceful than many opponents their "additional thrust and determination" and complete mutual understanding made them "a formidable striking force". They were also exceptional opportunists: "It is doubtful whether before or since any side has developed to so great an extent the art of taking advantage of errors by their opponents".

This remarkable teamwork was achieved in the face of considerable dissension off the field. Skipper Cliff Porter was at odds with his management, who persisted in preferring Jim Parker as rover for the tests even after Porter had recovered from the ankle injury that kept him out of the first international against Ireland. Nicholls, a far from 'unassuming, unobtrusive' man off the field was never an easy colleague and his falling-out with Maurice Brownlie was to have repercussions when he was chosen as vice-captain to the great lock forward for the 1928 tour of South Africa.

The Invincibles and the Originals laid the foundation for the enduring charisma of the All Blacks. They help explain why New Zealand, in spite of not having won any of the last three World Cups, has in rugby the glamour that Brazil has in football. Australia have, after all, won two of the last three World Cups. Springbok teams had Grand Slammed the home quartet on a number of occasions before Mourie's men finally did it for the All Blacks. Yet the All Blacks are the team who can fill any stadium in the world.

There are good historic reasons for this. Australia's standing as a world power is still recent, dating back only to the remarkable team who dazzled the home nations in 1984. The Springboks went into exile for most of the two decades before the abolition of apartheid - and when they did appear, excited as much fear and loathing as admiration. The All Blacks have been with us continuously for almost a century. For few other countries is the outside world's perception quite so heavily reliant on rugby. Australia plays many other sports exceptionally well. Perceptions of South Africa were for most of the past century overlain by distaste for its politics - rugby more than any other game was entangled with apartheid. Formidable though South Africa's record, its victories at home to New Zealand before 1960 should perhaps be marked with an asterisk for their refusal - shamefully accepted by the New Zealand Rugby Union - to admit players defined as non-white. Rugby makes much of its capacity for generating fellowship and camaraderie. It is hard to generate much fellow-feeling for people who would refuse to accept George Nepia as an equal.

There is something beyond this. South Africa has sent some magnificent teams to Britain. Those of 1906, 1931 and in particular 1951 bear comparison with any All Black team. Yet how truly memorable were they? A whole series of All Black moments have etched themselves upon the mental landscape of the British game, granting men like Obolensky a kind of immortality. Springbok teams have generated nothing quite so memorable - the nearest approach being the story of the Scottish fan emerging from their 44-0 beating in 1951 with the words 'and we were damned lucky to get nil'. True, it could be argued that the main Springbok failing has been their disinclination to grant British opponents memorable victories such as those claimed by Wales in 1905, Swansea and England in 1935 and Cardiff in 1953. But the two great All Black sides of 1905 and 1924 lost a single match out of more than 60, and left an impression which echoes resoundingly the best part of a century later.

So were they the best ever? Greatness, insofar as that much-abused concept means anything at all, is subjective. It lies in the eye of the beholder - one reason why such questions provide such a rich source of debate. The conditions and structures of international rugby have changed enormously over nearly 80 years since. The comparison between the contemporary and the historic is affected by more than perspective. The modern team plays much more frequent and continuous international rugby - Christian Cullen played as many tests in a few months after becoming an All Black as Nepia did in his whole career. Since 1987 judgments have been heavily, and rightly, influenced by the greatest test available to a team - its performance in the World Cup. Thus the All Black team who from 1995 to 1997 played perhaps the best rugby seen in recent times are likely ultimately to be seen as rugby's answer to the Hungarian football team of the early 1950s - a team whose greatness is qualified only by a single failure, but that in the most important match in which it played.

Earlier teams stand in greater isolation - combinations brought together for a single tour which, because international rugby was so intermittent, would hardly be seen again subsequently. Thirteen of the 31 Invincibles were new All Blacks, and nine would never play for them again after the tour. For nine, including such an unquestionable success as Svenson, never played for them again. Only the British Lions play under such conditions nowadays.

So who were the true greats? A preliminary list might include such combinations as the 1931, 1949 and 1951 Springboks - but with an asterisk against the first two for the grimness of their rugby and the second for the absence of Maoris in the All Black team they beat 4-0. Australia offers its teams of 1984 and 1991. In the northern hemisphere the claims of the Welsh teams of the 1970s are clouded by their failure ever to beat the All Blacks while the English of the 1990s underachieved in World Cups and the French, in spite of a fine record against the southern hemisphere, have yet to put together a spell of dominance to match either. The British and Irish Lions of 1971 and 1974, as a federation of national teams, rather defy fair comparison.

Great All Black teams? Those of 1905,1924,1967,1978,1987,1995 and after have perhaps been the most memorable. No sporting entity has generated a more consistent level of success over a longer period. In weighing the claims of the Invincibles, one should remember the vital respect in which they differed from the other teams in that list - that they struggled for possession. One could argue equally that great teams should be strong in all aspects of the game, or that true greatness lies in overcoming adversity - in this case a handicap that almost every other team would have found terminally disabling. It does seem reasonable to suggest that no team in history has made so much of so little possession.

In the end, though, all is subjectivity, and the impression made on hearts and minds. To see that packed grandstand at Swansea rise to George Nepia, nearly 60 years after his great triumphs on the ground, was to be left in no doubt about his and his team's impact on the hearts and minds not only of those who played against or saw them, but on the generations that have followed. It is impossible to say whether he or they were the greatest ever. But that they were truly, lastingly great is without question.

Rugby League in New Zealand: Nepia playing for Hornby against Addington on 31 July 1937 at Monica Park. Below: The team sheet from the match (Photo and team sheet: Courtesy Bernard Wood)

CANTERBURY RUGBY FOOTBALL LEAGUE

ADDINGTON—Black and White

Fullback		R. Barbarell 1	
Three-quarters	H. Sykes 2	A. Brown 3	L. Bench 4
Five-eights	L. Young 5	D. Wilson 6	
Half-back		G. Farmer 7	
Forwards	G. Briggs 13	Reg Ward 12	B. Fraser 9
	R Price 11	J. Manson 10	
		E Barbarell 8	
Reserves	Ray Ward 14	A. Geddes 16	

HORNBY—Black

Fullback		George Nepia 16	
Threequarters	M. Standeven 1	R. Timms 2	K. Bannan 3
Five-eights	W. Fagan 5	C. Taylor 6	
Half-back		F McGarry 7	
Forwards	W. Woodgate 13	J. Airey 12	W. Vivian 8
	J. Forster 9	W. Dunn 11	
		N. Vivian 10	
Reserves	F. McKenzie 14	W. Sinclair 15	

Referee—Mr. H. A. King Touch Judges Messrs E. Geary and L. Drury

Saturday next. August 7th, 1937

Inangahua (West Coast)

Versus **Canterbury**

At Monica Park, at 3 p.m.

G. Nepia will make his final appearance

6. The 1924-25 tour match reports

The full match reports in this chapter have been reproduced from Athletic News, *a weekly newspaper that provided comprehensive sports coverage in Britain at this time. The matches included are the three internationals and the match against London Counties, Nepia's first match at Twickenham. All the reports were by 'Mercian'. There are also some other brief extracts from other reports of the tour, from Nepia's personal collection of reports of the tour, supplied by Oma Nepia .*

1 November 1924: Ireland 0 New Zealand 6

- **The first rugby test**
- **New Zealanders Scramble Home in Rain-spoilt game at Dublin**
- **New Zealanders 1-1-6 Ireland 0-0-0**

Except, perhaps, to those who took a deep personal interest in the game, the first international match of the season was not particularly thrilling. The weather spoilt it.

But, although the second half, played in a steady, soaking downpour, had its full share of mistakes,

The game did teach us one thing. It revealed the adaptability of the 'All Blacks'.

From hence on, some of us will hesitate before we assume that a heavy ground and a wet ball is equivalent to a serious handicap to our visitors from overseas. It affects them: it leads their

players to use some of their wonderful aptitude for quick running and passing, but it only reduces

their efficiency in the same ratio that it affects their opponents.

They are by no means fair weather players, and although, like all teams that go in for the open game, they prefer a dry ball and a sure footing, they are by no means novices at playing that other type of game which is bred by rain.

It is just as well to make that clear because, as I say, other teams who may be called upon to play them on a wet ground, getting wetter as the game goes on, will find that chuckling over the prospect may be merely a waste of breath.

I am not suggesting that the Irishmen indulged in any kind of vain hope that the fates were being kind to them, but, at the same time, the one expression which was heard above all others before the game started at Lansdowne Road was "well, this ought to suit Ireland".

Any idea that some of us who had only seen them play on firm grounds may have had that the New Zealand forwards' one weakness would be found in inability to dribble themselves, or in stopping their opponents dribbling, was quickly shattered. Their rushes were every bit as good as the Irish,

And a 15 stone forward going down on the ball was frequently a pretty effective answer to the Problem as to whether they could check an "irresistible" Irish rush.

The opportunists

Wet or fine, the opportunism of the New Zealanders is always something to marvel at. It is as marked in defence as it is in attack. There is hardly a man on the side who is not, to use a familiar expression, "as quick as lightning" in turning an opponent's mistake to advantage.

In the first half, waged at great pace, with the ball first at one end of the field and then the other, the Irishmen must have thought they were a score of New Zealanders on the field. It was not altogether difficult to set up an attacking position, but it was an impossible job to drive it home.

Ireland, I thought, had two weaknesses. One - it was more noticeable at the start of the game than later on - was when the scrummage half-back, with all the forwards up and packed, waiting until the New Zealanders were ready with special formation to get down.

The other was at centre, where there were too many attempts to cut through the New Zealand defence which is too sound to have any hope of this manoeuvre succeeding, and surely it would have paid Ireland to have sped the ball out to Harry Stephenson, or, at any rate, to have tried to punt aas a variation of the attach to break through.

The fact that chances were not taken is not a matter for blame, and, in any case the Irishmen were not alone in this, for which most of the fault can be blamed on the weather.

There was less excuse for Crawford's failure to kick a goal from a penalty kick in the first half. The angle and the distance were favourable and success might have made all the difference to the match.

At the same time, every credit must be given to the Irish full-back for his play generally good, his fielding of fly-kicks were hardly the stamp of a great full-back, but most of his catches were well judged and his kicking was both long and well directed

Until T. Hewitt was injured - he was off the field for an appreciable spell in the second half – and came back limping, he was good as any man on the Irish side, while his brother was also very sound.

The Irish forwards played gamely enough, and men like Crichton, M. Vicker, Brand and Clinch never tried, but when the wearing down process carried out by the heavy New Zealanders told its tale in the end. Any side that hopes to do well against the New Zealanders must lay the foundation upon big, strong forwards. The small man has little chance against these speedy giants.

Singularly enough, the Irish forwards did better in healing in the second half than they did in the first, for whereas in the opening period they were beaten for possession twice for every once, in the second half they were actually able to claim a majority of one.

Crawford's tackle

The New Zealanders may not have been as impressive in attack as they have been - compared with the Welsh team that so hopelessly overran the English side in the mud in Cardiff in 1922, they lacked the ability to turn circumstances to their account - but their defence was superb. Some of the Irish attacks must have ended in scores against most teams: against the "All Blacks" they were like the dashing of waves against the cliffs of Dover.

Teams that tackle the New Zealanders except, perhaps Nepia, whose spectacular saves aroused many an outburst of enthusiasm, added to their reputations.

All the play that was worth watching was seen in the first half, and Ireland came as near scoring in that period as did the New Zealanders. To the surprise of those who had the earlier opportunities of seeing how quick the tourists are to seize upon openings to score it was strange to see at last half a dozen favourable prospects let pass, for at the last moment the ball would either be knocked on or the holder would go under a desperate tackle.

The finest tackle in the whole match - a flying dive at Parker by Crawford - saved Ireland in the first half, and enabled them to cross over with a blank scoresheet.

Then came the rain which washed out all the brightness there had been in the first half and turned the game into a scramble. It was mostly the New Zealanders' half , but the whole of the scoring was confined to a period in of a minute or so some ten minutes after the interval.

The "All Blacks" had heeled and Cooke kicked. One of the Irish backs - I think it was George Stephenson - gathered, an instead of kicking to safety, ran. He was brought down, and the ball went out to the tight Svenson who just scrambled over.

The penalty followed close upon it heals: it was for offside and White had an easy task.

That ended the scoring and were the only two tangible points in a game that might have well been worth a long journey to see. As it was, it developed into too much of a scramble.

It was not rough, for Mr Freethy always had the players under admirable control. Free kicks were rather numerous – twelve to Ireland – and eight to the winners.

New Zealand: - G. Nepia, A. Hart, D. W. Lucas, K. S. Svenson, A. E. Cooke, M. Nicholls, W. C. Dalley, J. H. Parker, Q. Donald, W. R. Irvine, R. R Masters, M. Brownlie, J. Richardson (capt.), L. F. Cupples and A. White.
Ireland: - W. E. Crawford, H. W. Stephenson, G. V. Stephenson (capt.), J. B. Gardiner, T. Hewitt, J. C. McDowell, F. S. Hewitt, T. N. Brand, W. R. Collis, T. A McLelland, J. McVicker, R. Y. Crichton, R. J. Collopy, J. D. Clinch and A. Spain
Referee: A. E Freethy, Welsh RU.

15 November 1924: London Counties 6 New Zealand 31

- **Brilliant Play Gives the Tourists a Sweeping Victory Over London**
- **New Zealanders 5-2-31 London 0-2-6**

Any doubt, born of comparatively modest performances against teams that have tackled them resolutely, that the New Zealanders lack real greatness was completely shattered at Twickenham on Saturday.

In some quarters the match with a picked London team was regarded in the light of a mainstream test, but if such a view was flattering to London, there was, nevertheless, some justification for the opinion that if our touring visitors could account, with any completeness, for an opposition that included English internationals like Wakefield, Cove-Smith and Hamilton-Wickes, Lawton at half-back, and the balance made up of men particularly all well-known in rugby circles, then the victory over England itself was increased.

If all that can be regarded as the test then the All Blacks passed through it with amazing success. They proved, without any question, that the better the strain, the better they pull. On paper they were set a hard task, and they won with all the ease that is reflected in a twenty-five point margin.

Theirs was a great performance. All that can be said to minimise its value is that the London team were playing together as a team for the first time, while there was one palpable weakness. Lawton at half-back was anything but the commanding figure he can be and the centres, good as their defence was in the first half, failed to play anything but obvious and orthodox football.

Then there was the question of speed. That was one of the dominating factors in the game and its possession was all on the other side. The London backs are fast enough to hold their own in ordinary company, but compared with Cooke and Nicholls and Parker, they were simply not in the same parish.

Cooke and Nicholls

Held in the first half, even led at one time by a point and crossing over with a four-point advantage, the New Zealanders altered their formation. Cooke, who had been playing in the centre, went to three-eighths, Svenson took the vacant place in the centre, Parker was put on the right wing and his position as the wing forward fell to McGregor.

Then we saw the New Zealanders at their best. Cooke and Nicholls were superb – those two men are two danger spots to any opposition.

It may seem exaggerated language, but I doubt if more brilliant football has been seen in this country than was given us by the New Zealanders in the second half.

The London men, with good reason, seemed at a complete loss to know how to cope with such a variety of methods as their opponents adopted, and above all, they appeared to be completely baffled by the wonderful skill and pace of Cooke and Nicholls.

Since I saw them last, they have gone in more for kicking, and, in the first half especially, whenever Nicholls got the ball, he almost invariably kicked it angle-wise over the heads of the London backs. Fortunately, Franklin was usually safe enough to reach it and get in his kick.

This tactic, followed up as it was by fast backs, put a continual strain upon the defence. The forwards, too, were just as tireless in their energy, indomitable in their method and relentless in their tackling but although Wakefield (playing better than he has so far this season) headed one or two magnificent dribbles in the second half, and Browne was one of the outstanding figures of the first half, there is hardly much question that grim way the All Blacks' pack stuck to their task told its tale and paved the way for the glorious work of the men behind.

For there are too many palpable weaknesses behind to justify a hope that triumphant tour of an invincible side was to come to an end. The obvious, carried out none too promptly, will never beat our visitors.

Except to those who actually saw it, it is difficult to believe that sound backs like Hamilton-Wickes, Aslett, Richardson, Millar and Lawton, could be so outclassed as they were in the second half. At times they were left standing by the quickness of Cooke and Nicholls who ran broke through like lightning, ran like deer and when their own share of the job was done, always found someone up to carry on the good work.

Wonderful second half

London have the consolation of feeling that no defence could have survived the thrusts of brilliant players who rose to new heights as Cooke and Nicholls did. Cooke, especially, on this form, bids fair to qualify among the greatest backs the game has produced.

Enough, perhaps has been written to show that this match at Twickenham was extraordinarily attractive. It was the level pegging first half with plenty of incidents in that forty minutes, but the memory of a number of features which would, in the ordinary way, make up a match, were completely obliterated by the second half performance.

It will be a very long time, indeed, before any single member of that great crowd forgets the deadly, darting runs of Cooke and Nicholls, the amazing quickness with which they saw an opening and went through it, the pace at which Parker went down the ring wing and around the defence, the way forwards and backs handled the ball and ran with it, the ease with which any London attacks were dealt with and the almost uncanny knack these All Blacks have of covering one another.

A mark near the touchline in the London twenty-five, a kick across the field, a forward dash and Brownlie opened the scoring ten minutes from the start with Nicholls converting. Ten minutes later, Browne and Wakefield headed a raid into the New Zealand quarters. The ball was slung rapidly out to Millar and he just got it down in the corner – too far out for Richardson to convert.

Another ten minutes and Millar, after a run, kicked into the centre. Stewart gathered and tried to run. He was tackled, and Wakefield opened the way for Millar to get over again.

London's one point lead lasted for five minutes, and was ended wheñ poor marking at the line-out gave Brownlie his chance to cross. At half-time, the score stood at ten points six in the All Blacks' favour.

The scorers in that ever-to-be-remembered second half were Cooke and Parker with two each and Richardson one, Nicholls kicking three more goals.

London: H. W. F Franklin (Old Blues and Eastern Counties), R. H. Hamilton-Wickes (Harlequins and Middlesex), A. R. Aslett (Richmond), J. V. Richardson (Richmond and Middlesex), R. K. Millar (London Scottish and Kent), A. T Lawton (Blackheath), A. P. Guthrie (Blackheath), W. W. Wakefield (captain, Harlequins and Middlesex), W. F Browne (Harlequins and Surrey), J. H. S. Drysdale (Blackheath and Kent), A. W. L. Row (St. Bartholomew's Hospital and Middlesex), R. Cove-Smith (Old Merchant Hospital and Kent), R. R. Stokes (Harlequins and Middlesex).
New Zealand: G. Nepia, A. Hart, A. E. Cooke, K. S. Svenson, N. P. McGregor, M. Nicholls, J. Mill, J. H. Parker, W. R. Irvine, Q. Donald, J. Richardson, R. R. Masters, N. Brownlie, R. F. Stewart, A. White.
Referee: R. A. Lloyd (Lancashire RFC)

29 November 1924: Wales 0 New Zealand 19
Avenging Of All Blacks

- **Wales Beaten for Pace, Strength, and Science In Hurly-burly at Swansea**
- **New Zealanders 3 2 19 Wales 0 0 0**

For twenty minutes or so of the game at Swansea, it was a question of whether this was a Rugby match or whether the lightweight, middle and heavyweight boxing championships (all-in) of the British Empire were being decided.

This tendency to make a 'rough-house' affair of it was the most unsatisfying feature of a game that in a good many respects was unsatisfactory generally. We saw New Zealand forwards and Welsh forwards mixing it badly – and one was just as bad as the other, saw one of the Welsh backs up to tricks that are only legislated for under the powers possessed by the referee.

Colonel Brunton would have been justified in sending more than one man off the field; but perhaps he took the less provocative course of issuing cautions. The Newcastle official handled this, his first international, in an excellent manner, and it was anything but the easiest of tasks that he was set.

The temptation to substitute boots and fists for clean handling and headwork, coupled with a set of backs miles below the standard of that wonderful lot whose victory in 1905 the New Zealanders have now avenged, were responsible for another unsatisfactory aspect, namely the failure of the Welshmen to produce a good standard of football, so generally associated with their play.

They were not good enough to make an open game of it themselves, but they were good enough to stop the New Zealanders producing bright and entertaining play.

Probably because we did not see the All Blacks scoring wonder tries, we shall be told that they are not a great side; my own view is that their strength lies in their adaptability, that they can win just as well when the other team make an open game of it as when there is a sort of 'muzzling' order given.

And it is rather idle arguing that because one side can attack for long periods, they do not deserve to lose. The fact remains – we saw it at Swansea for 20 minutes at the opening of the second half - the New Zealanders do not let their opponents score. It really seemed as though Wales might have gone on attacking all night and half-way into Sunday and still they would not have crossed the line.

Weakness of Wales

Obviously, Wales have not it in them to beat a powerful team like these All Blacks. Their forwards are the best part of the side. They can heel well, they can dribble the ball along, and they can stand (and give) any amount of hard handling. In Johnson too, they have found a sound full-back. He was a bit slow at times, and he was not always sure with his touch-finding but he did a lot of clever fielding, kicking and stopping to atone for these other failings.

Then Rowe Harding made the best of the few chances that came his way. Once he nearly rounded Nepia when there were only a couple of years between the full-back and the touch-line, and on another occasion, after an attempt to kick over Steel's head had sent the ball into the latter's hands for the New Zealander to sprint for the line. Harding turned in his track and was fast enough to overhaul the All Black winger after he had beaten Johnson.

Finch, on the other wing, was disappointing. He was given a good chance to score early in the game, and had his speed been equal to its repute, he must have gone over but McGregor came across and got him almost with ease.

The Welsh centres too were not good. Jenkins was not worth the resuscitation and, like Stock, was variable. Delahay may have been plucky but did not show much discretion in the choice of men to 'square up' to. Eddie Williams was fairly good.

As for Wetter, one has the deepest sympathy with him. Some malign fate seems to dodge him in these big games. Just as he was crippled against England in the early part of the match at Twickenham, so he was damaged now at Swansea. His knee went and so did Wetter. He came back at half-time and fine as was the spirit that prompted his return. I think it would have been of greater service to Wales had he stayed away.

For the captain was so useless, that, he went into the pack, or rather he put his head down in the last row and tried to push off his one sound leg, leaving Hiddlestone to carry on behind.

Quite the most picturesque figure on the New Zealand side was Nepia. It was not so much his kicking, nor the better sense of position he has developed since the earlier part of the tour, which attracted attention, but it was his daring dives and the amazing accuracy of his kicking that beat his opponent which aroused wholehearted enthusiasm.

Nepia, who might well be known as the human catapult, is just as audacious and successful as Maraburg, the never-to-be-forgotten South African full-back.

After Nepia, Cooke – faultless in defence, dashing in attack. This Auckland boy stands out as the supreme artist in a talented side. Throughout the whole game, he made but one mistake, an unusual one for him, for in the movement which proceeded Svenson's try, he tried to get through himself when he had an unmarked man on his left and the line hardly ten yards away.

Nicholls was not quite so much in the picture as usual, but at the same time, he played a full part in goal-kicking, and in addition to landing a penalty, converted two of the four tries.

Parker, chosen to play in preference to Porter, was something of a wanderer on the face of the ground. I don't know whether it was any views that Colonel Brunton had of his duties as a wing forward, or whether Wetter's movements had anything to do with it, but Parker was sometimes seen as a wing
forward, sometimes as a wing three-quarter back and sometimes as a centre. He has all of the attributes and none of the failings of the handy man.

Many Missed Chances

There were just over fifty scrummages in the 80 minutes and cutting out the free kicks - six to Wales and five to New Zealand - which mainly came from scrummaging offences, the New Zealanders were beaten in getting possession on 27 occasions. Singularly enough, they were as good as Wales in hooking in the first half and it was in the second, when Wales had only six workers down, that the All Blacks lost most ground.

There was one period in the second half when Wales seemed to have taken up quarter permanently in the New Zealand half, when the Welshmen heeled the ball out from seven successive scrummages. With anything like scoring backs, such opportunities ought to have served Wales well but the chances were spoilt once by Stock trying to drop a goal, twice by Williams being held when trying to break through and twice by passes being knocked on.

Still, if the New Zealand forwards had no pull in hooking, they could claim a distinct advantage in the line-out where the height of such men as C. Brownlie (6ft 3in), Cupples (6ft 2in), Richardson (6ft 1in) and N. Brownlie (6ft) were utilised to the full. Compared with these men, Donald, with his 5ft 10in is merely a pigmy but, for all that, he played wonderfully well.

The game was nine minutes old when the first score came. One of the Welsh backs – I think it was Stock – was offside and Nicholls had a fairly easy penalty goal. Then Wales ought to have scored had Finch been faster and McGregor not so fast but at the end of twenty minutes, N. Brownlie found gap a in the defence and, with Nicholls kicking another goal, the Tourists were eight points up.

Another chance came Wales' way when Johnson might have kicked a penalty goal, but, instead of this asset, there came a liability in the way of Wetter's retirement. And he was away, Richardson, taking the ball from a Welsh throw-in scored from a line-out so that at half-time the New Zealanders had the useful lead of eleven points.

There was no score at all for half an hour after the restart. Then the All Blacks got busy and in the last ten minutes, Svenson got a try and Irvine and Mill shared one between them, Nicholls converting the last.

Wales: T. Johnson (Cardiff); E. Finch (Llanelly), A. Stock (Newport), Albert Jenkins (Llanelly), Rowe Harding (Swansea), R. Delahay (Cardiff), J. Wetter (Newport - capt.), E. Williams (Neath), S. Morris (Cross Keys) , D. Marden-Jones (London Welsh), D. D. Hiddlestone (Neath), D. Parker (Swansea), C. Pugh (Maesteg), J. Gore (Blaina), and Cliff Williams (Llanelly).
New Zealand: G. Nepia; K. S. Svenson, A. E. Cooke, J. Steel; N. P. McGregor, M. F. Nicholls, J. H. Parker, J. J. Mill, Q. Donald, W. R. Irvine, M. J. Brownlie, C. J. Brownlie, J. Richardson (capt.), L. F. Cupples and R. H. Masters.
Referee: Col. Brunton, Northern Ireland.

3 January 1925 England 11 New Zealand 17

- **Fourteen All Blacks Win**
- **Remarkable Ending to a Wonderful Tour**
- **Giant Forward Sent Off by the Referee**
- **New Zealand 2 3 17 England 2 1 11**

A great game, a surprisingly close finish, a desperate final rally by England and an incident unparalleled in the history of international Rugby football these were the chief incidents in the meeting of England and the New Zealanders at Twickenham.

Let me deal with the 'record' incident first, because it is possible that the game will long be remembered as the "match in which Brownlie was ordered off the field".

Such events, fortunately, are rare enough in club football; in national games, while it is true that there have been men who have run perilously near the line, no-one has hitherto incurred the most drastic penalty which lies within the province of a referee.

Any referee, naturally, would hesitate a long while before he brought disgrace (for that unquestionably is what it amounts to) upon a player, and yet, when the full facts are known, it is doubtful whether anyone will deny that drastic action of some kind was needed.

The first few minutes of the game were marked by incidents which could only be described as danger signals. England set off at a tremendous pace; their men, stung up to the knowledge of how much depended upon them, all the keener, perhaps, because they had been told in so many quarters that they had but a forlorn hope, started in a 'do-or-die' spirit.

The New Zealanders, on the other hand, seemed nervous. The vision of an unbeaten certificate probably weighed upon them. Their machinery, which usually works so smoothly, was a little out of gear, and individuals sought, by sheer force, to right the balance.

Warning, Then Action

Thus the stage was set for trouble. Mr Freethy quickly realised that stern measures had to be taken or the players would have been out of hand. Three times in the first ten minutes he warned both sides impartially that the 'rough stuff' had to stop.

Then when the game was just ten minutes old he saw he declares, C. J., Brownlie kicks one of the three English forwards who were lying on the ground. He decided that it was no question of an accident and he also decided that he had no option but to order Brownlie off.

Those are the simple facts; what the full effect was it is, of course, impossible to say.

The loss of one of their heaviest and best forwards naturally made a tremendous difference to the All Blacks. It had a serious moral effect and it disorganised their formation.

For, as it was obviously impossible to expect the six remaining forwards to hold eight Englishmen, Parker, who had been designed for the role of wing forward, had, instead, to take his place in the scrum.

Up to that point, nothing had been scored. Six minutes later, England got their first try but then, in the next hour and ten minutes, the All Blacks scored five times before England got another point.

To all intents and purposes, then, 14 New Zealanders beat England and that, in itself, is a significant and a remarkably fine performance.

I dare say that there will be considerable discussion as to the legitimacy of some of the New Zealand points. There was nothing controversial about the first try, which came, as so many of their tries have come during this tour, through a breakdown on the part of their opponents.

Kittermaster could not field a pass from Young and, characteristically, the All Blacks were on the attack in a flash the ball sped out to the right, it was checked, back it went to the left and a long throw-out to Svenson gave the wing man a clear course over the line.

But second try was considered by a section of the crowd to have been scored after Steel had gone into touch. The wing man had not far to run, but he was so near the touchline that there was those who thought he had stepped over the line at least twice. The certainty, I think, must have been shared by some of the Englishmen near him for no real effort was made to tackle him.

England's Points

The referee questioned the New Zealand touch judge, Mr Simpson, but the latter had no hesitation in saying the player had not gone out of bounds.

The third point came when Hilliard was offside so near the goal that Nicholls had no difficulty in sending the ball over the bar.

This brings us to half-time with the New Zealanders leading by nine points to three.

Their next try came ten minutes after the restart when M. Brownlie forced his way over and Nicholls kicked a great goal from the touchline, and their last, which fell to Parker, was not altogether clear because several players knocked the corner flag over.

It will be seen then that all the New Zealand points were not altogether free from doubt. None of the tries, except the first, perhaps, had the clear-cut stamp about them.

In that respect they differed from the two tries scored by England; the first a triumph of forward play, the second a glorious effort almost the full length of the field, and which ended in such a complete piercing of the All Blacks' ranks that there was not a man within twenty yards of Kittermaster when he ran over.

The first try, scored sixteen minutes from the start, followed an English wheel. Voyce steered the ball past Nepia, and then there was a great race for the line. It seemed that one of the two New Zealanders were bound to get the touch, but while they stooped Cove-Smith, just behind, threw himself on the ball and beat them by a fraction of a second.

Point number two fell to Corbett, who made a penalty kick in a somewhat awkward position look delightfully simple by the coolest of dropped kicks and point number three came when the All Blacks were almost on the English line. But England, with fine courage, passed instead of kicking for safety. Hamilton-Wickes raced up the field, swerved inwards instead of as expected outwards, and then passed to Kitterminster, who outpaced an opposition that was already well-beaten and scored a glorious try under the posts for Conway to kick the goal.

This was quite the most picturesque movement of the match. There were others, notably some tremendously fast or rather the most successfully completed, runs by Gibbs along the left touchline in the second half, indeed the match was replete with thrills.

The most curious and certainly unexpected feature about the whole game was the fact that the polish of execution was mostly on the English side; the New Zealanders won, not by combination or by brilliant individualism, but by opportunism.

Gibbs the Flier

Brownlie's disappearance made a big difference, and to add to their troubles, Steel was damaged so that he was unable to look after the flying Gibbs.

The Harlequin player took full advantage of this fact to make a spectacular first appearance in an international. Two of his runs in the second half roused the vast crowd - some 60,000 strong and including the Prince of Wales and the Prime Minister - to great enthusiasm.

For sheer speed Gibbs stands alone in English football. Hamilton-Wickes was not particularly well-served, but the New Zealand tactics were not designed to give the English backs much room to move. Their anxiety to lie up as close as they dared, cost them a penalty goal, but it had the effect of cramping the English centres.

Corbett was distinctly good and Davies' defence was sound. But Davies was not a great success. Hamilton-Wickes, with limited opportunity, showed the possession of all those finer points of the game which Gibbs lacks so.

Kittermaster's hands, as usual, were safe but Young was not often in the picture. The New Zealanders watched him pretty closely and the Cambridge captain hardly every was allowed to get far.

Brough was brilliant. He was, perhaps, overshadowed a little by Nepia who capped an extraordinary record of playing in every match with a wonderful exhibition of sure fielding, lengthy and accurate touch finding and kicking and great daring in saving but the Cumberland lad played as well as any full-back England has had for many a long day. Such a display ensures England her full back for a long while, provided always he can steer clear of accident and a temptation to forsake the amateur code.

The English pack lasted a fierce and fast game in great style. Blakiston, started as a front-rank Forward, but finished in his more accustomed role of winger. England's, preference, natural under the circumstances, for scrummages rather than line-outs, led to over eighty scrummages and the Englishmen got the ball, wheeled or rushed 19 of these in the first half to 11 claimed by the All Blacks. In the second half, the reckoning was more even, a score of times apiece.

Those who like statistics may also be interested to know that England had eight free kicks given against her and the New Zealanders seven.

As for the New Zealanders, Nepia has been dealt with; Cooke was invariably uncertain with his hands in attack, but good in defence; Nicholls shared with Nepia the honours behind.

The forwards worked heroically to atone for the loss of C. Brownlie and I thought the new-comer, White, as good as any.

Weary Vigil Rewarded

The conditions were unexpectedly good. The ground surprised everybody by its state and the rain held off until an hour after it was all over. So great was the crowd that the gates had to be closed half an hour before the kick-off.

Not one of those luckless persons without tickets could have regretted their long wait: some were at the gates soon after dawn broke.

Chilled blood was quickly warmed by the fervour of the start, and from the time of the kick-off until the final whistle, there was enough thrills to make the most hardened individual forget physical discomfort.

For once in a while the expectations of a great struggle were realised but after all is said and done, the battle was waged on more even lines because England had to face fourteen instead of fifteen men.

In golf language, England were given a bisque, but could not make quite enough use of it.

England: J. Brough (Silloth), R. H. Hamilton-Wickes (Harlequins), V. G. Davies (Harlequins), L. J. Corbett (Bristol), J. C. Gibbs (Harlequins), H. J. Kittermaster (Oxford), A. T. Young (Cambridge), A. F. Blakiston (Liverpool), G. S. Conway (Manchester), R. Edwards (Newport), R. J. Hillard (Oxford), A. T. Voyce (Gloucester), R. Cove-Smith (Old Merchant Taylors), J. S. Tucker (Bristol), W. W. Wakefield (Harlequins) (capt).
New Zealand: G. Nepia (Hawke's Bay), J. Steel (West Coast), A. E. Cooke (Auckland), K. S. Svenson (Wellington), M. F. Nicholls (Wellington), N. P. McGregor (Canterbury), J. Mill (Hawke's Bay), J. H. Parker (Canterbury), J. Richardson (Southland) (capt), A. White (Southlands), C. Brownlie (Hawke's Bay), R. R. Masters (Canterbury), M. J. Brownlie (Hawkes Bay), W. R. Irvine (Hawke's Bay), O. Donald (Wairarapa).
Referee: Mr A. E. Freethy (Welsh RU).

The "All Blacks" and Their Methods

The extracts from this article, from the *Illustrated London News* of 3 January 1925, examines the All Blacks' tactics and formation. It is by Major Leonard R. Tosswill (an English international).

"... the New Zealand team consists of seven forwards and eight backs, while teams in Great Britain are composed of eight forwards and seven backs. At first sight this does not appear to be an important variation, but that extra back enables the New Zealand men to adopt an arrow-head formation, which they consider is the most suitable for either attack or defence. To determine the advantages - and the weakness of such a formation, it is necessary to compare it with that of our own teams.

In our case, when the ball is "heeled" out of the scrummage, it passes to the scrum-half, who sends it out to his colleague, the stand-off half, who, in turn, passes it out to the line of four three-quarters behind him. In other words, behind the scrummage there are, excluding the full-back, three groups of players at different levels, and arranged one (scrum-half), one (stand-off half), four (three-quarters). In the New Zealand formation there are also three groups of players behind the scrummage, and arranged *one* (half), *two* (five-eighths), *three* (three-quarters).

The extra back in a New Zealand team, generally called a "wing-forward", is a general utility man with a variety of functions, one of the most important being that of putting the ball into the scrummage. This leaves the half-back free to receive the ball as soon as it is heeled; the English half-back puts the ball into the scrummage and then has to hurry back :to the base of the scrum to receive it, and, if his forwards heel too quickly, he may be too late to pass it out before he is collared.

It is clear that the New Zealand formation is more compact than our own, and enables an attack to be opened up on either side more speedily. On the other hand, when a passing run is initiated by our three-quarters, there are four of them opposed by three New Zealand three-quarters. In fact, there is a man over, and this overlapping is a danger to the New Zealand defence. This point was illustrated in a practical manner in the London v. New Zealand match, when R. K. Millar, the London wing three-quarter, was able to score two tries by this very overlapping.

Apart from putting the ball into the scrummage, the New Zealand "Wing-forward," or "rover," is used to strengthen the defence by pouncing on the opposing half-back if he gets the ball, by breaking up a wheel by the opposing forwards, by drawing the attention of the opposing backs to himself and so enabling his own half-back to have a few extra seconds in which to run or pass the ball out.

The principal weakness of the New Zealand formation is that they have only seven forwards to face eight in the scrummages. This disadvantage has not always been evident during the present tour, because the All Blacks' forwards are heavy enough to discount their inferiority in numbers when opposed 'by a light pack; but in every instance when they have been pitted against a heavy pack, they have failed get their share of the ball in the scrummages which means, of course, that their backs have had fewer chances of attacking..."

Reflections on the first tour match
"...there was certainly far less cohesion today on the New Zealand side than was the case in the same match in 1905... I believe they will train on into a very useful team indeed, with far more victories than defeats to their credit..."
D. R. Gent (Rugby International) in *The Sunday Times*

"I frankly think they are going to be very good indeed... Nepia, the full-back, quite justified his reputation."
Colonel Philip Trevor CBE in *The Daily Telegraph*

Victory in Cornwall
"All the afternoon we had continual illustrations of this brilliant and very up-to-date form of play"
Colonel Philip Trevor CBE in *The Daily Telegraph*

Cambridge University 0 All Blacks 5
"The inevitable try came at last, after 15 minutes play in the second half... from some loose play Mill got possession and by a quick swerving cut through the unprepared and disorganised Varsity attack and scored under the posts... After this reverse the University attacked and by fierce forward fighting they got the All Blacks on the defensive, but Nepia upheld his wonderful reputation in upholding the Varsity attacks. His gathering and catching was faultless, whilst his kicking was sure and of a beautiful length."
From the *Cambridge Daily News*, 12 November 1924.

7. *Rugby Every Time*

In 1937, Nepia wrote a weekly series of articles for the Halifax Evening Courier and Guardian, 'Rugby Every Time', *on his life story. The earlier ones cover similar material to that in his autobiography. However, the final four, reproduced below, cover his views at the time of switching codes and life in England.*

As Maori Captain in Australia 24 July 1937

I had failed to gain selection in the 1935 All Blacks and with it the honour of making a second international tour of Great Britain and Ireland. After an interval of eleven years it would surely have been a record in rugby history.

My disappointment was keen indeed, yet I had to admit that my playing form in the trials, which necessarily took place in the early part of the New Zealand season, had not been up to my best, and that the young West Coast fullback Gilbert, who had been chosen in my stead, would certainly prove a worthy successor.

Disappointment forgotten

There was some resentment among the Maori people that, of the twenty-nine players chosen, 'Tori' Reid was our only representative, fine forward though he certainly was. Our general disappointment was, however, forgotten when, a few weeks before the All Blacks sailed for England, the Rugby Union announced that a Maori team was to be selected immediately to tour Australia.

More than enough Maori players of talent had come to light during the All Black trials to make selection easy and I was appointed captain - this, as some commentators observed, being by way of a 'consolation prize'. Anyway, it was a position which I took great pride and enjoyment in filling, and with the redoubtable Billy Wallace, fullback of the 1905 All Blacks, and Kingi Tahiwi, the Maori selector, as co-managers, we set sail in high hopes for Sydney.

Up to standard

It had been reported that the Australian Rugby fans were disappointed that the 1935 All Blacks were not making a preliminary tour of the Commonwealth before sailing for England and that a Maori team was being sent across the Tasman Sea in their stead. I therefore take particular pleasure in saying that we gave the Aussies plenty to think about, and that they, in turn, greatly enjoyed the fast, bright football, which we, in typical Maori fashion, were able to hand out to them.

We won nine of the eleven games played, including two out of three tests against New South Wales. The critics were unanimous in stating that our football was well up to All Black standard and I myself succeeded in impressing them favourably (a thing I had failed to do in 1924 and 1929) by playing up to top form.

In great demand

Of the rest of the team, I though at the time that Jack McDonald and George Harrison (forwards) and Charlie Smith (wing threequarter) would have greatly strengthened the 1935 All Blacks and today I am more convinced of this than ever. Our team was in great demand on the field and off. Like all Maori, we (or most of us) had good singing voices and we were giving choruses of Maori songs on the field after games, over the radio, at dances, sing-songs and all manner of functions.

Our favourite was 'Maori Moon', the song I had sung so often at school. Within a week every dance band in Sydney was playing it, for the chorus has a catchy waltz-time.

Invited to join Rugby League

Soon after our return to New Zealand came the startling news that the several players who had just missed places in the All Black side had been invited to join the newly-formed Streatham & Mitcham Rugby League Club in London. The opportunity to visit the other side of the world was a great temptation and Charlie Smith, one of the first players approached, came over from his home at Walroa to ask my advice.

"Go by all means" I told him. "This will probably be your only opportunity to see the world and you're going to be paid for doing it". Little did I then think that within a few weeks I too would be following the trail of the All Blacks to England!

A sensation

So three of our Maori side set sail for London - Smith, George Harrison and Jack McDonald, accompanied by Eddie Holder, the speedy young wing threequarter who had won All Black honours in 1934, but had just failed to do so a year later.

Their change-over to the professional code caused a national sensation and all kinds of attempts were made to dissuade them from sailing - especially in the case of the three Maoris.

Then suddenly came a telegram from the New Zealand agent of the Streatham club asking whether I would consider too! The offer was a substantial one but it was not the first I had received.

Big offer

During our tour of Britain in 1924, both Cooke and I had been approached by Rugby League agents and a year or two later, I received an offer of £1,500 to sign on for the Huddersfield club. I had been unable to avail myself of the opportunity then, but this time, conditions were different.

I had no quarrel with the Rugby Union code, in which I had gained the highest possible honours. Here, however, was the opportunity to go abroad again, take up residence for two years in the world's greatest and most interesting Metropolis, to join a club in company with three good friends, Maoris like myself with a substantial cash sum and good pay at the end of the offer.

The cash would, I knew, come most opportunely for investment in my farm which I had found a hard job to keep going and develop during the blizzard of the world depression.

Back to England to play Rugby League 31 July 1937

Lately, moreover, I had become more interested in the Rugby League game. Bert Cooke, the only other member of the 1924 All Blacks still playing football, and undoubtedly one of the greatest centre threequarters the world has ever seen, had joined the Richmond Rugby League club in Auckland in 1932 and had taken well to the code: He had several times written to me expressing his liking for the game.

Everything was in favour of my changing over, so I accepted the offer. The news raised a second furore in the New Zealand press. Rugby Union officials, old friends of the 1924 side and hosts of others, protested against my decision, but the Maori people generally, who were still critical of the 1935 All Black selections and were becoming increasingly interested in the faster type of Rugby offered by the League code, were all in my support.

Increased confidence

So, amid another din of controversy, I left by the 'Akaroa' - by the very route I had followed in 1924 - via Pitcairn Island and Panama. A few hours before sailing, I received a cable of reassurance from Charlie Smith who had just arrived in England. "Kai te pai ahau" it said. "Everything's OK" is the English of it, and my confidence went up 100 percent.

My ship had excellent gymnasium facilities and I trained hard on the way over. At Panama I received a letter from my new club, Streatham & Mitcham, advising me that I would be required to play, if possible, two days after my arrival in England against the Wigan team. The opposing fullback would be none other that Jim Sullivan, the greatest custodian in the League game.

Great reunion

Here was the setting for a historic duel and I felt I must rise to the occasion, difficult as the conditions were. The message also contained ample information that my change-over to the League had 'hit the headlines' in Britain as well.

When I arrived at Tilbury, I felt it was great to be back in England, chill December day though it was. There too were my friends in voluntary exile - Smith, Harrison, McDonald. It was a great reunion.

Duel with Sullivan

There followed one day's intensive training and instruction in League rules and tactics and I took the field at Streatham with a little more confidence than I had expected I would.

In my duel with the redoubtable Jim Sullivan, I acquitted myself tolerably well, I believe, under the circumstances, although the offside rule of Rugby League, which generally required me to stay back after I had cleared the ball, bothered me a little. Sullivan is truly a great fullback, and I closely studied the way he placed his kicks for follow-up play by his forwards. The two of us exchanged opinions that evening in an "In Town Tonight" dialogue which was broadcast by the BBC.

Strengthened conviction

I left the field that day with the impression that I was going to like the new code, and my experiences since then have strengthened that conviction.

Games against sides like Wigan, Leeds, Salford, Warrington, Oldham, Barrow and Liverpool Stanley have taught me a great deal and I have been pleased to find that, as a League fullback, I have ample opportunity to start those sudden attacking movements which are typical of the unorthodox Rugby Union game played by the Maori.

The League game is undoubtedly very fast and I find that I need to keep even fitter for it than for Rugby Union. It cannot help but be faster with four men off the field just as seven-a-side Rugby is faster still..

Excellent rule

Extra speed in the game also results from the 'ball back' rule, which bars kicking into touch. This, I think, is an excellent law. It is, in fact, greatly favoured in the New Zealand Rugby Union game. They have just started to play it out there, after having been forbidden to do so for six years by the English Union.

When last season opened, it seemed the Streatham team would go close to winning the RL Championship and the Cup as well. A succession of victories brought us up into the third place in the league table and we were developing into a first-class combination. Things were not going so well, however, with the management of the club and financial considerations eventually compelled the directors to disband the side.

A Real Home from Home 7 August 1937

Sad as it was to see one of the best teams in the League sacrificed in this way, the outcome was not a surprise to us. So It came about that Charlie Smith and I joined the Halifax Club while our friends Holder and Harrison went to Wigan. Other members of the side were transferred to Leeds, Huddersfield, Castleford, Swinton, Rochdale and Dewsbury.

Playing in our original positions - Charlie at centre threequarter and myself at fullback - we have been able to combine in many of our old-time movements to pave the way for tries by Halifax, and once or twice I have scored one myself besides kicking goals. With its excellent management and well-organised Supporters' Club of several thousand members, Halifax Club has provided us with a real home away from home and I am now well satisfied with the turn of events that brought me to live in Yorkshire. It has been pleasant in my games against rival teams to meet fellow New Zealanders who have also come over to play for English League clubs. Hargreaves of York, Mason of Keighley, Innes of Wigan and French of Barrow are all members of our colony over here. I have also renewed acquaintance with many old friends whom I first met during the All Black tour of 1924 or in later years.

Interesting duels

In a match with Wigan , for example, I had the job of pulling down J. C. Morley, whom I knew in the British Rugby Union side that toured New Zealand in 1930 and a cup tie game with Leeds last season provided an interesting fullback duel between myself and Jim Brough. My last encounter with him was in the memorable All Blacks v. England game at Twickenham in January 1925. Yet Brough hardly looked a day older.

I find I have "contacts" in all kinds of places. The other day I received a message of good wishes from a wine merchant living near Dubrovnik, Yugoslavia. He had seen me playing in New Zealand in 1923. And a few days later I had news of a Maori cousin of mine who is leading a dance band in Shanghai. It certainly is a small world.

My games in this country as a fullback in both codes have enabled me to make comparison between the English Rugby Union and League crowds. The League crowd is, I find, by far the more volatile and outspoken of the two, more like our own Union crowds in New Zealand, though in this respect, the Welsh or French Rugby Union crowd is equal to either of them.

Critical enthusiasts

I should describe English RL enthusiasts as being highly critical of both home and visiting teams, very much alive to every point in the game and ever ready to do a little barracking now and then – all in good part, of course. Good sportsmanship is the rule among players and crowds in both codes.

Some of our critics can be caustic enough in their remarks as on one occasion when we visited Hull Kingston Rovers. I had fielded the ball, and running up the side-line, inpassed to Charlie Smith, who galloped the remaining thirty yards to touch down, knocking three opponents sprawling as he did so. The crowd was in an uproar - but not because Charlie scored. Two of them rushed to the side-line, shaking their fists and shouting "Go back to New Zealand, ye dirty foreigners. Play decent or don't play at all." Yet, when the final whistle blew, no-one seemed to be upset. I gathered later that the idea in denouncing us was merely to encourage the others to "play oop a bit".

Strapped in corsets

Charlie Smith very nearly provided the crowd with something else to talk about in a match with Barrow early this season. He had badly bruised three ribs in his previous game and they needed special protection if he was to play at all. We tried cotton wool but that wouldn't 'stay out' on his chest. Suddenly I got an inspiration, and we both hopped into a neighbouring draper's shop to buy a pair of women pink corsets. You know the old-fashioned type: braced with bone and laced up in the front. We strapped them tightly round Charlie's ribs - under his jersey, of course - and there they stayed by whalebone and the grace of God for the rest of the game.

"I'd like to see your jersey torn off" I told him as we took the field. But our opponents were merciful and the picture papers missed a first-class story.

Referees' rulings

When I was over here in 1924 I noticed how differently the laws of Rugby Union are interpreted by referees in different countries and I have come across the same trouble in the Rugby League code. A Lancashire referee will often give a decision exactly opposite to a Yorkshire official's ruling. Some referees too, I find, are a bit on the elderly side to control adequately the fast professional game. "Too old at 45" is the general rule in New Zealand. How can an elderly gentlemen, struggling painfully along 50 or 60 yards behind possibly say whether a flying winger has properly grounded the ball over the goal-line or not? There is only one answer: He cannot.

Captain H. B. T. Wakelam, I noticed recently, has suggested that two referees, one for each half of the game, might be employed for Rugby Union matches. The Soccer people are toying with the idea and the same innovation might be considered by the Rugby League. I suggest that a Lancashire referee for the first half and a Yorkshire referee for the second half of the game, might just about even up regional differences of opinion.

Supporters Clubs Commended **14 August 1937**

Different as English life is from our own style in sunny New Zealand, I can say that I have enjoyed every moment of my stay in this country. It has been packed with interest. In particular, I commend the work of the Supporters' Clubs. Members have gone out of their way to make us New Zealanders feel at home in a strange country and when I return to the Dominion, I propose launching a supporters' club movement to serve both rugby codes. I see that Blackheath, first of the Rugby Union clubs, is considering forming one. Clubs like these do valuable work, among other things, in smoothing out those little misunderstandings that arise in the best football circles.

Name will still be heard

This brings me to the point where there is little left to recall from a long innings not yet closed. It is very unlikely, however, that when I have finished with Rugby playing, the name of Nepia will no longer be heard of in the football world.

I have two sons and a daughter in New Zealand, and the elder boy, aged six, has been crazy about rugby ever since he has been big enough to kick a football.

I have always prized the ball used in the All Blacks v. England International at Twickenham in 1925. Again and again, I have told my lad the story of that historic match, showing him the ball in evidence of it and answering his oft-repeated questions about the speed of Cooke and Gibbs, the strength of the Brownlies and Wakefield and the size of the crowd. It is little wonder that, with such souvenirs to interest him, and in a great football district like my home province, the boy should have already become 'rugby mad'.

Missing football

I noticed one day that one of the footballs which I used for team practice was missing and my wife remarked that for a week our son had been taking extra large lunches to school – enough for three boys. I questioned him about the missing ball but he seemed to know nothing about it.

The next afternoon I was working on my farm, when, from a hay-field nearby, which was surrounded by tall pines, I heard boyish shouts of "mark!" and "on the wing" followed by the resounding punt of a football. Walking over to the pine trees I was amazed to see my son racing hotfoot for an imaginary goal-line with two schoolmates after him - all this at an hour when they should have been swotting spelling or arithmetic!

Provided rations

For a whole week, they had been "playing the wag" from school in the greater cause of rugby - in my own field with my own football while my son had been providing rations so that his team could play on, uninterrupted.

I gave him a spanking but had to admit that I had done much the same thing myself twenty-four years before him. If genius is "an infinite capacity for taking pains", my son will be wearing the All Black jersey before he is out of teens.

Happy memories

The next All Black team to visit England will be selected in 1948. My son will be getting on for 19 then - the age I was when I was picked to tour this country. If my boy isn't among the crowd when they arrive I'll be here myself to give an explanation. So much for the future. Days ahead are problems and days gone by memories, through every one of which I should like to live again.

I can look back on 25 years active participation in the only game I have really loved. I have not finished playing. Like all Rugby men, when playing days are over I shall put boots and togs aside with regret, but only when Old Man Time calls the tune.

In the words of our New Zealand football song, I can say:

"Oh, some talk of cricket and some of lacrosse
Some long for the huntsman's loud call
But where can be found such a musical sound
As the old rugby cry "On the ball!"

Remember then, boys, as we journey through life
There's a goal to be reached by and by
And he who runs true, why, he's bound to get through
And perhaps kick a goal from his try.

The chorus is in itself a lesson on the game:

"On the ball! On the ball! On the ball!
Through scrummage, threequarters and all
Sticking together
We keep on the leather
And shout as we go "On the ball!"".

The end

Rugby League international: Nepia stops Australian full-back Les Ward in the test match at Carlaw Park on 14 August 1937. New Zealand won 16-15. (Photo: Courtesy Bernard Wood)

8. Streatham & Mitcham RLFC

"I am now in the great Rugby League game and feel happier for it. My opinion is also that it has great possibilities among the Maori people...". So said George Nepia on the eve of his departure from New Zealand to play Rugby League for Streatham & Mitcham. He also told the reporter: "I hope to make good, not only as a Maori player, but also as one of many New Zealanders who have proved successful as Rugby League exponents on English soil... I have had a desire to play the 13-a-side game for a number of years and wish I had turned over six or seven years ago."

Nepia also said that he had no regrets about leaving Rugby Union, although he was sorry to be leaving his family behind, and said that Mrs Nepia took his departure "very bravely". He had been given a "popular send off" at Rangitukia, and been presented with "a well-filled wallet and other gifts".

It is clear from his autobiography that Nepia's primary reason for joining Rugby League was financial, as with many recruits to League from Union before and since. Unlike today, when players can play both codes as professionals, in those days there were huge barriers between Union and League. The great split of 1895 was still in living memory, and to sign for League as a professional was to cut any links with Union forever. Union in those days was solely amateur, and there was enormous hostility to League from the Union hierarchy. When London Highfield, the first professional Rugby League club in London, was set up in 1933, the Union authorities tried to dissuade their players from even going to watch the matches.

In these days of high-speed aeroplane travel, it is easy to forget what a journey it was from New Zealand to England in the 1930s. Instead of the 24-hour trip today, then it was a six-week sea journey. In the series of articles on his life story for the *Halifax Courier & Guardian* in 1937, Nepia recalled that he took the same route to England as in 1924, via Pitcairn Island and Panama. He trained hard on the journey, using the ship's "excellent gymnasium facilities". At Panama, he got a letter from the Streatham & Mitcham club saying that they hoped he could play two days after his arrival, against Wigan, who were led by the legendary League fullback Jim Sullivan. Nepia wrote: "Here was the setting for a historic duel, and I felt I must rise to the occasion, difficult as the conditions were."

Controversial switch

Nepia's decision to switch codes had caused controversy in New Zealand. He wrote in the *Halifax Courier & Guardian*: "The news raised a second furore in the New Zealand Press. Rugby Union officials, old friends of the 1924 side and hosts of others protested against my decision, but the Maori people... were all in my support". Streatham & Mitcham had previously signed four other New Zealanders, and Nepia recalled: "Their change-over to the professional code caused a national sensation, and all kinds of attempts were made to dissuade them from sailing - especially the three Maoris."

In England, the recruitment of Nepia by Streatham & Mitcham made headlines. Interestingly, one writer, George M. Thompson, speculated whether Nepia was young enough to last two years in Rugby League, and whether his best days were behind him, although he did conclude that Nepia would be a "box office draw in this country".

Although Nepia was now aged 30, he was far from retirement. He had toured Australia with the Maori team the year before, and was still playing club Rugby Union. In fact, George M. Thompson's doubts about his ability to thrive in Rugby League were proved to be wrong, as he made a successful conversion to the code. There are still some Union followers in New Zealand who try to ignore Nepia's time in Rugby League. There are many players who were eminent in Union but not could adjust to League after changing codes, and nowadays when players can go from League to Union, some League players are finding it equally hard to change codes. It is a tribute to Nepia's natural skill and ability as a Rugby footballer in the widest sense that he did make the adjustment successfully, as the record shows.

London Rugby League

Nepia had been recruited to Rugby League not by one of the game's traditional giants, such as Wigan, but by a new club which had been set up by the entrepreneur Sydney Parkes, based in London, far away from the game's heartlands in the north of England.

Since the split with the RFU in 1895, the Northern Union, which became the Rugby Football League in 1922, had faced the problem of how to expand its geographical base. The code's rules had changed in the first decade of the century, with the reduction to 13 players, abolition of line-outs, and the introduction of 'play the ball' being the key features that distinguished it from Union. To support professional clubs, the sport had to offer a product that would draw in spectators, and the new rules were designed to encourage more open and attractive play. But the game was still very different from League as it is played today. Scrums were fiercely competitive, with the hookers fighting for the ball. Also, there was no restriction on the number of tackles. One team could keep possession, so the role of the forwards was more important than today. For fullbacks, kicking was also an important skill.

Rugby League had tried various measures to expand the game. International matches were taken to different areas, including the south-west, the midlands and Scotland. The game had achieved some support in Wales before the First World War, but the last club collapsed in 1912, although the Welsh international team was strong, based on players from the Principality who had 'gone north'. A further attempt to develop a club in Wales, at Pontypridd in 1926, had lasted less than two years.

But the RFL's Secretary at this time, John Wilson, was keen on expansion. He had advocated the successful move of the Challenge Cup Final from the north to Wembley in 1929, and Wales had also played two matches against Australia at the stadium. This interest in expansion was linked with new stadiums developing in different areas for two sports that had grown in popularity from the mid 1920s: greyhound racing and speedway.

With no competition from floodlit football or television, these mainly evening events attracted thousands of followers, the thrills being added to by the effect of the floodlit tracks. Historian Stephen G. Jones outlines that in 1932, nine million people attended greyhound racing at London's 17 tracks, while in 1933, over a million had attended speedway meetings at the capital's five venues.

Unlike football, either rugby code, or county cricket, these new sports were clearly business ventures, aiming to produce profits for their owners. As Fulham Football Club chairman Ernie Clay was to realise over 40 years later, the more a stadium can be used, the more revenue it can produce. He collaborated with Harold Genders to launch Fulham RLFC in 1980, from his point of view "to make some brass". Similarly, some of the new stadium owners of the 1930s saw Rugby League as a possible source of income.

League's first professional club venture into the capital was London Highfield in 1933. Wigan Highfield had struggled for some years, competing with their more illustrious Central Park neighbours. Faced with continual economic problems, the club moved in 1933 to London's White City Stadium, then owned by the Greyhound Racing Association, run by Brigadier-General Critchley. He purchased the struggling Rugby League club, renamed it London Highfield, and staged matches on Wednesday evenings under floodlights. The players remained based in Wigan, travelling down by train on Wednesday afternoons, and returning home on the midnight train after the games.

The venture started reasonably well. The staging of the matches was spectacular for the time - the teams would come onto the pitch illuminated by a single spotlight, with the full floodlights coming on as they walked out. But although 14,500 came to watch London lose 20-5 to the Australian tourists, at the end of the season the club had lost £8,000 and the London experiment was abandoned. The club moved back north, became Liverpool Stanley, and had some success in the next four seasons, showing what might have been possible had the club's owners shown more perseverance with their London experiment.

In December 1934, Sydney Parkes wrote to John Wilson, saying: "I am interested in forming a Rugby League for the south. I have grounds for two teams in London". He also asked for a book of rules and raised the idea of a London team playing other counties. John Wilson replied the next day, explaining that the League's existing members had to approve a new club, but if accepted "your fixture list would of course be assured". A meeting was arranged, and there was speculation in the press in February 1935 about six London based teams to join the RFL, followed by reports of two new teams, based at the Wandsworth Greyhound Stadium and a new stadium at Mitcham. However, on 9 March 1935, following a meeting between Mr Parkes and the League Management Committee, an application was submitted on behalf of Streatham & Mitcham RLFC and Acton & Willesden RLFC to join the RFL.

Parkes' strategy was different from London Highfield. Matches would be played on Saturday afternoons, in line with the rest of the league, but competing with Association Football and Rugby Union. However, establishing two clubs in

London would create a local rivalry, and he recognised that London is a diverse area with more then enough potential supporters for two teams.

However, as events proved, Parkes also knew the financial potential of greyhound racing, and undoubtedly part of his motive for building the new stadiums was to try to secure greyhound racing licences for them. This was a politically contentious matter at this time, with much opposition by the church and others to the growth of gambling associated with the new sport.

Both clubs were accepted into membership of the RFL, with Acton & Willesden being put in the Yorkshire League and Streatham & Mitcham in the Lancashire League. At this time, Rugby League had two county leagues, with the results being integrated into one national table. Teams played all the clubs in their county, and some from the other. There were too many teams for them all to play each other.

Acton & Willesden recruited mainly Welsh players, and started reasonably well. But Parkes got a greyhound licence for the Acton Stadium, and at the end of the first season abandoned Rugby League there. The team had not been successful in the second half of the season, and attendances had declined. Many of the players joined Streatham & Mitcham.

The Streatham & Mitcham team, which became known as 'The Hams' fared more successfully. The club had recruited more established Rugby League players, although there was a feeling that Parkes had paid transfer fees higher than the players' value, a problem that also faced Fulham 45 years later when launching a new club. The signing of the New Zealanders started a tradition of Australasians providing the backbone - and the glamour - for London Rugby League teams, a tradition that would continue in modern times, with All Black (and Londoner) John Gallagher and Richie Barnett following George Nepia by playing full-back for London clubs at Rugby League.

The club's first home match, against Oldham on 7 September 1935, attracted 24,000 fans. 'Cherry-White', the *Oldham Evening Chronicle*'s reporter, said that Streatham & Mitcham "won admiration of their new supporters", despite losing 10-5. He quoted his "little Cockney messenger boy" saying "Lummy, Guv'ner, worra gime" in appreciation of the spectacle. He described the stadium as "having a classical look about its huge stands and magnificent stretch of turf", and that this was a "stimulating experience" for any Rugby League follower. The *Mitcham News* had photos of the teams being presented to the Mayor of Mitcham, who also kicked off the match. The caption for a photo of the action said it showed the "manly vigour" of the game. The paper also carried an article explaining the difference between "Rugby League and Rugby Football".

The impact of the new code could be seen when the *Mitcham News* reported that 173 boys from local schools had attended a special training session in Rugby League at the beginning of October. The Streatham & Mitcham team struggled early on, although a victory against Bradford Northern in their third home game attracted over 20,000 supporters. However, the gradual arrival of the New Zealanders saw the team's fortunes improve. In the *South London Press*'s report of an 18-2 victory over Rochdale in November, when All Black Maori Charlie Smith made his debut, he is said to have "scored a magnificent try, a well-deserved reward for a sustained exhibition of constructive, brainy play". The report also commends the play of Barnes at fullback, saying that "even Nepia, world-famous Maori back, now on the high seas en route for Streatham, could not have put up a better performance."

Nepia's debut

As Nepia outlines in his autobiography, two days after arriving at Tilbury, he played against Wigan, whose team included Jim Sullivan. The *South London Press*'s match preview was headlined "World's finest Rugby full-backs clash at Streatham", and anticipated the "Rugby treat of the year". It went on: "To see Nepia in action was an education in full-back play; and now, at the age of 30, the man who has been so often hailed as the world's greatest full-back is said to be playing better than ever."

Writing in the *Halifax Courier & Guardian*, Nepia recalls that after "one day's intensive training and instruction in League rules and tactics… I took the field at Streatham with a little more confidence than I had expected I would. In my duel with the redoubtable Jim Sullivan I acquitted myself tolerably well, I believe, under the circumstances, though the offside rule of Rugby League, which generally required me to stay back after I had cleared the ball, bothered me a little."

The *Mitcham News* report was headed: "Nepia's first Game - Wigan's "Star" Man Outclassed". It said that the two fullbacks "had repeated exchanges during the game, but the honours went to Nepia". It also said that Nepia "had not quite grasped the rules of the Rugby League code, but the referee always pointed out to him the mistake, and his appearance in every way was a great success". The *South London Press* headlined their report "Nepia shines on RL debut", and said that Sullivan "was out-kicked on four occasions… he was never able to pass the Streatham player". The two fullbacks left the field arm in arm, and that evening were heard on the BBC radio programme *In Town Tonight*.

Reflecting on his experiences in the *South London Press* the next week, Nepia said that he needed to adjust to League's rules: "The natural instinct of a defending full-back in the Union game is to clear to touch and then feels he has got himself out of trouble… I have to keep reminding myself that I have to land the ball inside touch now, but that will soon come, and I like the way it helps keep the game open. As a League player too, I find I shall have to open up the game more - run with the ball and try to get the threes moving. And here again the fact that there are only 26 players on the field gives one much more opportunity for enterprise."

The strengthening of the Streatham team over the previous three months, completed by Nepia's presence, paid dividends in the second half of the season. Nine more league and cup matches were won, with Nepia scoring 29 goals. But his goal-kicking alone does not reflect the impact he made. At the end of December, with less than a month's experience in this new code, he was made captain and acting manager. He held the latter position until the following September, when he reverted solely to being a player as it was felt that the additional responsibility was having a detrimental effect on his play. And ever the entrepreneur, Sydney Parkes started asking clubs Streatham visited for 25 per cent of the gate receipts to guarantee Nepia's appearance in the team.

Reports of the team's matches in the second half of the season were dominated by Nepia - whether he played well or not, or even if he was not playing. The week following his debut, The Hams' win at Liverpool Stanley was reported as being "in the main due to the fine play of the New Zealanders, Macdonald and Harrison, leading the pack, and Nepia at full-back". On 28 December, the *South London Press* report of the 3-3 draw with St Helens was headlined: "Nepia holds out to save a point" and said that he gave "another masterly display at full-back, especially towards the end when the Saints were working hard to get a winning score". At Batley in early January, where Streatham lost by a point, the *Mitcham News* said he "did brilliantly in defence and also helped in the two unconverted tries", although in the return match two weeks later, "he was not given much chance to shine, but... kicked two goals", according to the *South London Press*.

The same paper reported that there were plans to form a London Major Baseball League in the summer, and that Nepia was expected to play, as he "had a lengthy connection with the baseball game in America". In fact, he had played the game in New Zealand. At Salford, where Streatham lost 35-11 after losing their hooker injured after 10 minutes, he played in the pack for half an hour. He contributed two goals to Streatham's victory over Bramley, but apparently "was not as good as usual", although he "would achieve some smart piece of work to show what a grand player he really is". In early February, the Rugby League players played baseball as part of their training, and also to prepare for the competition that summer.

The Challenge Cup is always an eagerly anticipated part of the Rugby League season. Streatham had won their first cup match at Hull KR 18-5, and two weeks later, faced the mighty Leeds, who included Jim Brough at full-back, who had played against Nepia for England on the 1924-5 tour. 'Olympian', in the *South London Press*, said that "the Streatham & Mitcham team of stars has been welded together into a fighting force" and their "supporters are in a cup fever". Despite this, Leeds won 13-3, although the paper said that both fullbacks gave "a fine exhibition".

Streatham finished the season in 24th place, three places behind London rivals Acton. Two highlights at the end of the season were visits to France. Nepia played for a Dominions XIII against France, which was founder of French Rugby League Jean Galia's last match, and for a combined London side on tour. Nepia had last played in France at the end of the 1924-5 tour.

Sadly, in June, Streatham's threequarter Harry Berry died from lockjaw as the result of an injury sustained in the match at Warrington towards the end of the season. The jury at the Coroner's court returned a verdict of "accidental death".

However, events over the summer off the pitch would cast doubt over the future of the Streatham & Mitcham club.

Greyhound licence

In June and July, there were two hearings by the Surrey County Licensing Justices about Mr Parkes' application for a betting licence for Mitcham Stadium, to allow greyhound racing to take place. A referendum of local residents run by the Mitcham Borough Council had found in favour of greyhound racing by 691 to 421, although opponents of greyhound racing argued that people only voted for the dogs to stop speedway, with greater noise and disruption, being staged. There were arguments familiar today, about the value of property prices, noise and traffic. One opponent pointed out that the Stadium had been built for Rugby football, but then Mr Parkes had applied twice for a greyhound licence and been turned down.

The application was unanimously rejected, and this decision by local magistrates was the first nail in the coffin for the club's future. A couple of weeks after this decision, Ivor Halstead, the club's general manager, assured a Supporters Club meeting that the club would fulfil its fixtures, and pointed out that the Borough Council had approved the application, although he also said that Mr Parkes was putting the stadium up for sale. A report in the *Empire News*, however, quoted a club official as saying that without greyhound racing, the business position was "absolutely hopeless" and the gates from Rugby League did not even cover the rates.

The new season

Acton & Willesden had withdrawn from the League after one season, and 10 of their players joined Streatham & Mitcham. Two of the new recruits were Welshmen Dai Jenkins and Con Murphy, who would go on to greater things with Leeds and win international honours.

The new season, described in the *South London Press* as "particularly promising" and "of vital importance to the club" opened with two victories over Bramley. But after defeats against Broughton Rangers, and Barrow in the Lancashire Cup, Nepia was replaced as manager by Harold Ashton, as it was said that the additional responsibility was affecting his play. He moved to play centre against Hull KR, which the *Mitcham News* reported as a "great success" and said his play was of a "high standard". The *South London Press* said he was "outstanding" in Streatham's 39-3 victory over League new boys Newcastle, while the next week the same paper said he was "the star" in a 19-12 defeat at Halifax, where he scored all Streatham's points. He sustained a shoulder injury in an 8-5 home defeat against Warrington on 10 October, but recovered to play the next week at St Helens.

The quality of the Streatham team was shown as they now embarked on a run of seven consecutive victories. On 30 October, the *Mitcham News* was speculating that they could be Rugby League's Champions after a 33-3 demolition of Hull KR.

The visit of Rochdale Hornets to Mitcham Stadium on 14 November saw popular singer Gracie Fields, who was from the Lancashire town, kick off the game. The *Mitcham News* reported that she "appeared in football togs in the Rochdale colours and she received quite an ovation." Streatham won 15-0 in front of the club's biggest attendance of the season so far. However, despite the team's success, there were reports in the local press that this would be the club's last season in Rugby League.

The unbeaten run ended at Barrow at the beginning of December. The next week saw a 15-0 home defeat against Swinton, with the *Mitcham News* saying that "Nepia and his men seemed off form and disappointed the home crowd". Perhaps the speculation about the club's future was affecting the players - although they beat Dewsbury the following week, two defeats followed over Christmas against Liverpool Stanley.

Nepia was the team's star and driving force throughout this period. He featured in almost every headline in the match reports and had clearly adapted well to his new code.

At the beginning of December Charlie Smith had been sold to Halifax for a reported four-figure fee. The *South London Press* commented: "His departure is sad, for he is an extraordinarily attractive player, but the club is not doing well financially and so something must be done. The South London public is to blame entirely, for Streatham play the very best type of Rugby League football which would draw crowds of something like 20,000 every week were their headquarters in the north."

The end

The club management now started selling more players to raise funds, and departures included Con Murphy and Dai Jenkins to Leeds for £600, and then George Nepia to Halifax for £300, which Halifax recouped from the enormous crowd that saw his first game. The club drifted on for a few more weeks, even managing victories against Featherstone and Leigh. But after a 35-5 defeat at Swinton on 20 February 1937, the club withdrew from the League.

And as far as Rugby League having a professional base in London, that was the end until Fulham RLFC was launched in 1980. As happened so often in the sport's development outside the heartlands, it was undermined by events over which it had no control, although whether Sydney Parkes would have continued with his Rugby League operation had he been awarded his greyhound licence is open to speculation. The club had shown it could attract crowds on occasions, and had they been able to retain the players who did so well in October and November, could have challenged for honours. But maybe the task of taking on London's established sports, especially football, proved too much. The option of playing professional sport on Sundays was not open to clubs in those days, and the Stadium did not have floodlights for midweek floodlit matches. Of course, the number of actual Londoners in the team was very few, and maybe this contributed to the club's failure to win enough followers. Also, constant changes of manager and among the playing staff, problems that would haunt professional Rugby League in London in a later era, did not help retain support.

However, Rugby League was played again at Mitcham Stadium, when the amateur game had a short revival in London in the late 1940s, a Mitcham team played there. Greyhound racing never was staged at the Stadium, which became home to a football team, Croydon Rovers, but was only filled for Gaelic Games, until it was demolished in 1956. The main stand was sold to Leyton Orient Football Club, and is still at its Brisbane Road ground. So one piece of London's Rugby League heritage from Streatham & Mitcham survives to this day.

9. Halifax RLFC

On Monday, 28 December, 1936, the *Halifax Daily Courier & Guardian* reported to its readers: "Rumour has been persistent during the holidays concerning George Nepia, the famous New Zealand and Streatham player, and the Halifax club. The Halifax followers are naturally interested in the rumours, but Mr. Arthur Archbell [the Halifax secretary] made a statement yesterday that Nepia has not yet been signed by Halifax, but that negotiations are proceeding with this end in view. The clubs have come to terms respecting the transfer fee."

Nepia signed the following day, Halifax paying Streatham £300. The *Courier & Guardian* ran the good news on Wednesday, 30 December under the headlines:

- Nepia Signs for Halifax
- Famous All-Black to Partner Smith
- Remarkable Record Recalled
- First Appearance in Blue-and-White on New Year's Day

The article praised Nepia's performances on the 1924-25 tour, described Nepia as an accurate catcher and a brilliant place and touch kicker, emphasised his adeptness at taking the ball from the feet of onrushing forwards and lauded his immense strength in taking the ball through the strongest of packs. It declared that he was an attraction wherever he appeared on Rugby League grounds in the north of England.

Nepia arrived in Halifax on the Wednesday having travelled up from London with two Halifax directors, Mr. A. Wade and Mr. H. Webster. They were met at the town railway station by George's cousin Charlie Smith, who had signed for Halifax less than a month previously, and club secretary Arthur Archbell.

Halifax had had designs on both Smith and Nepia for some time. They were particularly keen on the powerful, high-stepping Smith, whose play in the centres for Streatham had been especially eye-catching. The reported fee for Smith had been £1,250. That was a massive amount and, if true, was a world record transfer fee, exceeding the £1,200 paid to Huddersfield by Leeds for spring-heeled centre/wing Stan Brogden in March 1934.

The performance of the New Zealand cousins in Streatham's 19-12 defeat by Halifax at Thrum Hall on 3 October, 1936 had really whetted the appetite of the Halifax directors. The pair had played all over the Halifax centres, Norman Foster and Jack Treen, who were two excellent players. Nepia, the star of the game, had scored all Streatham's points with three goals and two tries, one of which had been brilliant. The other had just been strange. Nepia had attempted a penalty goal and failed. However, some Halifax players had held up their hands to stop the ball and referee Albert Harding ordered the penalty to be taken again. Nepia fooled everyone by kicking the ball along the ground. All the Halifax men remained rooted on the goal-line as Nepia nipped along after the ball and touched down.

George Nepia had joined an ambitious club with roots stretching back to 1873. Halifax had won the Challenge Cup in 1931, their most recent trophy in an illustrious history. Since then, however, they had become a middle-of-the-table team. To restore its fortunes the club had become a limited company earlier in

1936 and the directors had shown they meant business by signing Hunslet's Yorkshire and England stand-off George Todd for £700 and Welsh winger Jim Bevan from Cwmavon. The signings of Smith and Nepia were further proof that the club was serious about returning to the sport's elite.

Halifax followers knew all about good full-back play and Nepia had a lot to live up to. Three hundred pounds was still a lot of money in 1936, especially for an ex-Rugby Unionist with less than two years experience of League and who had now passed the age of 30. The Halifax number one jersey had been worn by some great players. For several years before and after the Great Split the position had been held by former Kendal Hornet, Alf Chorley. Chorley later played for Swinton and Rochdale, but ultimately emigrated to New Zealand. Remarkably he played for New Zealand against the first Northern Union tourists in the only test of 1910, 18 years after his first game for Halifax. He was followed in the Edwardian era by the great Cumbrian Billy Little, an England International with a monster kick and a personality to match. From 1913 to 1925 Clem Garforth, who had also played soccer for Halifax Town, had been among the very best full-backs in the Northern Union and he was succeeded by the unflappable, match-winning drop-goaler from Swansea, Dick Davies. Davies had played almost 300 games before retiring, like Nepia would, to his farm in his native country.

If Nepia turned out to be as good as these men, the £300 would have been well spent. Some Halifax fans suspected that Nepia's arrival could be contentious, however. Halifax already had a very fine full-back in Hubert Lockwood, the club captain. Lockwood, stylish in everything he did and one of the game's top goal-kickers, was the current Yorkshire full-back and one of the most popular players Halifax ever had.

Interviewed at the age of 92 in 2001, Lockwood admitted that he was "a bit sloughed" (despondent, taken aback) when he heard that Nepia had been signed. However, when he learned that Nepia was probably not going to be staying beyond the season's end, he took it philosophically, realising that the publicity value would be considerable for the club. Anyway, it appeared that Nepia might actually be destined for a centre spot alongside Charlie Smith. Hubert was noted for his impeccable sportsmanship and never contemplated taking his bat home. He thought a lot of Nepia, considering him sound in every aspect of full-back play, if lacking in pace. Like most others, Hubert believed that Nepia had come to League too late but found him a delightful companion, a man who provoked a lot of fun.

Nepia's debut was set for New Year's Day 1937 when Halifax were to meet the Cup holders and current league leaders, Leeds, at Thrum Hall. Halifax had just beaten Huddersfield twice over Christmas before a combined crowd total of 37,000 and were confident of victory. The *Courier & Guardian* carried a huge advert announcing that Noel Coward was writing his serialised life story in the *Sunday Express*, while in Melbourne a record 78,000 people attended the first day's play of the third Ashes test. Australia had reached 181-6 with Don Bradman dismissed for 13, bowled by Hedley Verity's first delivery of the match. Around Halifax, however, Coward, Bradman and even Yorkshire's own sainted Verity were mere side-shows. George Nepia was the name on all lips as he took his place in the Halifax centres with Smith as his winger. Before the game George was photographed with Sydney Howard, the famous film comedian.

Despite a pretty grim afternoon Nepia's appearance helped to swell the crowd to 16,500 and the £797 taken at the gate probably paid off a large chunk of George's transfer fee. Halifax lost 20-5, but it was not as bad as it sounded, 10 of Leeds's points being gifted to them. Leeds came in for a great deal of criticism for their spoiling and obstructionist tactics, a style totally out of keeping with their usual game. George Nepia had a difficult time. George M. Thompson wrote in the *Yorkshire Observer* that "Neither Treen nor Nepia had sufficient speed to carve openings, and though the Maori excelled with some second half tackling, his first display for Halifax was not as convincing as one could have desired."

George had another indifferent game the following day when Halifax went down 9-2 at Widnes. Frank Williams, a former Swansea Rugby Union winger and a 1914 Rugby League Lion, was the local Halifax reporter. He wrote: "The constant attention that has been paid to Nepia and Smith appears to have unbalanced the side for the time being". The ball was reaching them slowly and they were being "mauled". Nepia was entrusted with a few penalty kicks and, on the whole, used the touch-line accurately. Williams was sure that "The New Zealander will provide skill to the backs when he becomes more accustomed to his colleagues and the runnings are better".

Things brightened up when Halifax entertained Broughton Rangers on 9 January. Hubert Lockwood was rested and George was drafted to full-back. It was evident that he was more comfortable than in the centre. Halifax won a tough game 16-7 before around 9,000 spectators and George was the star turn, scoring a try and four goals. 'Forward' wrote in the *Yorkshire Observer*, "Opinion will vary about Nepia as full-back, but he was so lively and followed up so keenly that he was like an extra three-quarter''. In the 55th minute, according to 'Forward', "Smith was barging his way through when up came Nepia from full-back, took a pass and found a way through half a dozen players for a try, and set the crowd laughing by kicking the goal without taking a run at the ball or even looking to see whether it went over the bar" .

Frank Williams was highly impressed, writing, "Nepia, 10 years ago, would have challenged the great Jimmy Sullivan for the supremacy he has held in the Rugby League as the leading full-back. Nepia joined the professional code much too late. He realises the fact himself but he showed against Broughton that he is far from a spent force. The try Nepia scored stamped him as a footballer of the highest class. Another feature about the score was the value of brilliant anticipation and understanding. So remarkably accurately and quickly done was the movement between Nepia and Smith that for a moment the crowd seemed to gasp in wonderment at the audacity and cleverness of the two New Zealanders. When, however, it was realised who had scored the try, bedlam was let loose."

On 16 January Halifax played the return fixture at Broughton and won 16-7. George was again impressive and landed two goals, the second his 50th of the season. Frank Williams was high in his praise: "In respect to unorthodox play, Nepia reminds me very much of Gwyn Thomas, the one-time Wigan and Huddersfield full-back. It is not difficult to understand how Nepia gained fame and popularity in his younger days. He is a 'personality' footballer". Of two spectacular tackles on Rangers' winger Turton, Williams wrote: "The way he encircled the home wingman was really thrilling for those Rugby followers who admire the full-blooded tackle. Nepia also positioned himself well in kicking duels and once or twice beat Howells for length. He also appeared to be continually giving encouragement".

A third successive victory was gained at Rochdale Hornets with a 6-2 verdict in a game dominated by wonderful defence. Frank Williams reported: "A happy spirit exists among the Halifax players at the moment. Smith and Nepia have settled down remarkably well and they are likeable fellows amongst their colleagues. I have never seen two new men taken into a side with such delightful friendship as Nepia and Smith have been by the Halifax players. Nepia has been of greater service to the team as a full-back. He gives his colleagues confidence by his determination in defence and attack. The Rochdale crowd did not take kindly to some of Nepia's ways, but he is merely robust, and in Rugby this is possible. Nepia is a powerful runner and opponents find him a difficult player to stop. The Halifax full-back exhibited cleverness when he ran to a rival, standing offside, within the five yards limit, touched him and gained many yards thereby, which is a feature in Nepia's make-up. This was intelligent play."

BBC broadcast

On 30 January Halifax beat Barrow 12-2 at Thrum Hall. The highlight was a stunning try by Nepia just at the half-time whistle, a rather inopportune time to score as the second half of the game was broadcast by the BBC. Taking a clearing kick from Fred French, Barrow's own full-back from New Zealand, Nepia skirted along a snow-speckled touch-line for 35 yards before launching himself over the line. For grit and determination his effort had seldom been seen on the ground. He paid the penalty, however, suffering slight concussion, a damaged finger, bruised ribs and abrasions to his nose. He missed the first 10 minutes of the second half and on the following Monday was surprised to find that his main trouble was a bruised back.

There was more pain for him in the next match at Headingley where 17,000 saw Leeds beat Halifax 17-4. George landed a great penalty goal off a post after two minutes and hit another from half-way after 39 minutes. He injured his knee just before the break, however, and the strapping on it hampered his movements throughout the second period.

On 13 February, Halifax met Barrow in the first round of the Challenge Cup at Thrum Hall. It was a big game for both clubs, Barrow overnighting in Leeds. A special dining car train brought close on 1,000 Barrow fans down from Furness and the crowd was 11,082, a remarkable figure in the circumstances. Overnight snow had been taken off the surface and a thaw had set in, leaving a quagmire. To make things worse, a fog descended. Halifax withstood a terrific barrage from Barrow in the first half hour, but finally broke away to score through scrum-half Les Sowden after 32 minutes. Nepia, who had been a doubtful starter and who was clearly uncomfortable for much of the match, added the conversion. It was remarked that his doggedness noticeably inspired his team-mates. It was Nepia too who started the move which sent Jim Bevan in for the match-clinching try late in the second half. An 8-2 victory had earned Halifax a home tie against Wakefield Trinity.

Before that, however, Wigan had to be faced twice at Central Park on Wednesday, 17 February and at Thrum Hall the following Saturday. Halifax sent a weak team to Wigan. Nepia was rested to allow his injuries to clear and Lockwood was down with 'flu. Jim Sullivan had a field day, kicking eight goals as Wigan won 37-7. Nine thousand Wiganers were reported to have been sorely disappointed with Nepia's non-appearance. He was back for the return match, however, when conditions were even worse than for the Barrow Cup-tie. Despite the harrowing conditions, a truly wonderful game was contested before a crowd of 10,500. George gave Halifax an 8-7 lead just before the interval with a well-struck penalty. In the snow storm which gathered for the second half he converted winger Jack Watson's try from the touch-line to give Halifax a decisive 13-7 advantage, although Wigan did add a late try. In view of the weight of the saturated ball and his damaged knee, this kick must have been one of the best he ever landed.

Frank Williams reported: "The anticipated full-back duel was interesting for the crowd. Sullivan's fielding and positional play were fine, and probably on the day, he was the more prominent, yet Nepia did many smart things, while his conversion of Watson's second try was a master-piece in the circumstances. In the first half the toe-cap of Nepia's boot was torn off and affected his kicking until he made a change."

On 27 February, Halifax faced the most important game of their season, the second round cup tie against Wakefield Trinity. Thrum Hall was heaving with 20,000 fans jammed inside. Halifax were expected to win, but expectations went unfulfilled and Nepia got most of the blame. True, he kicked two penalties but he made a calamitous mistake in the 15th minute when he short-kicked, followed up and left an open field. Trinity gathered and their winger Watson went away for an easy try, the only one of the game. Trinity led 5-0 and Nepia's goals could only narrow the final score to 5-4. Frank Williams moaned: "There are times when Nepia gives himself too much running about. The reason for this is that the New Zealander is always looking for an opening to attack, which is why I constantly refer to [the need for] absolutely perfect covering. Trinity kicked well to where Nepia wasn't and he hadn't the pace to cover... His short kick in the try was disastrous."

George's propensity for the short kick and follow up added a certain excitement to games, but there was a general feeling that he overdid it. He could get away with it in Union where formations were looser, but in League the consequences could be dire. There was also a feeling that his pace was failing him. Nepia was said to be 13st 5lbs while at Halifax. That was as heavy as most of the forwards. His season was on a downward spiral although he remained a popular figure. On 13 March, Halifax went down 19-0 at St Helens, who were one of the basement clubs. Nepia was really off colour and completely outplayed by Butler, the Saints full-back. He missed Halifax's 6-5 home defeat by Swinton on 20 March, a game played for a change in pleasant conditions. Nepia was in action the following day in Lyons, where a new municipal stadium was opened. He figured in a Dominions XIII which defeated France 6-3 before a crowd of

16,000. Ironically, the game was played on a morass - the bad weather was following him about. Still, the jaunt must have taken his mind off his fading form at Halifax and the £6 winning match fee would have been welcome.

On his return, Nepia was left out of Halifax's team for the next three games. Hubert Lockwood had been playing beautifully in the reserves and was again flavour of the month with the selectors. It was now Nepia's turn for a couple of games with the 'A' team and he turned out for them in a 10-0 home win against Castleford 'A' and an 8-8 draw at Rochdale. There were 3,000 present at the Castleford 'A' game, so Nepia was still putting money in the bank for the club.

On 3 April Halifax were at home to Leigh, who were propping up the league. It was a sure thing for the Thrum Hallers, who rested Lockwood and brought back Nepia. The game was a relentlessly tame affair and Halifax scraped a 5-5 draw, Nepia landing a penalty. The best entertainment came from the band of the Duke of Wellington's Regiment and there were dark mutterings about why a team which had cost £3,000 to build could not beat one which had barely cost £100.

Sullivan again

Lockwood was back for the next two games and shone in victories at Hunslet and at home to Batley. Neither Lockwood (injured) nor Nepia were available for the trip to Salford on 17 April, however, a game which also served as the great Gus Risman's benefit match. George was again playing representative rugby. This time he was at Brough Park, Newcastle in the Northern RL XIII which took on Wales, the international champions, in a match to raise funds for the ailing Newcastle club. Unbelievably, Nepia found himself playing on another quagmire. Opposite him was Jim Sullivan, captaining the Welsh. It was to be the last time the two icons would meet. Honours ended even, both men landing three goals, although Jim was the happier after his side won 15-12 and his pay was £5 compared to the losers' £4.

By now Nepia had been placed on the transfer list by Halifax at a fee of £300. The club stated that it was just procedural as they knew that Nepia would be returning home soon. However, Leigh and Newcastle were both said to be interested, with Newcastle wanting him as player-manager. Nepia himself announced on 21 April that he would "return to New Zealand for a holiday some time next month and his present intention is to return to England in time for the next football season". He was perhaps just keeping his options open, although everyone expected him to go back home for good.

On the same day that Nepia made his announcement he returned to Halifax's first team for the last league game of the season at Swinton. Halifax lost 7-0 but the game was exceptionally good. It was reported that there was only one regrettable incident. That was when Nepia went racing down the touch-line in the second half only to be struck violently in the face by a defender, who was immediately pulled out by a touch-judge and cautioned. Even the home fans were said to be upset because he was a popular attraction and had played an excellent all-round game. Hubert Lockwood had pulled out of the game at short notice with a septic finger and was replaced by the Maori. Swinton secretary Sam Jones stated that the gate-takings would have been £50 higher if only they had known Nepia was to play. He had never played at Station Road before.

On 24 April, the day before his 31st birthday, George Nepia played his last game in the blue and white hoops of Halifax and made his last appearance in any form of rugby in England. He was selected in the centre along with Charlie Smith for a game against Barrow in Whitehaven. The game was a friendly in aid of the Whitehaven and West Cumberland Hospital and was played at the Recreation Ground, a venue which had hosted many county and tour fixtures but had never staged a match between two professional club sides.

It was a splendid and successful affair. There was a crowd of 7,000, around £400 being raised for the hospital. A 50 guinea trophy for the winners had been donated and John Wilson, secretary of the Rugby Football League, was one of the touch-judges. The Mayor of Whitehaven, the town clerks of Barrow and Halifax and hospital dignitaries were present and attended the post-match dinner. It was a strange, but fitting finale for George Nepia. The game itself was excellent, clever, clean and robust, not at all of the exhibition order. Barrow won 16-7 and Hubert Lockwood showed his sportsmanship during the second half by swapping places with George, so that the crowd could see the great Maori playing at full-back, as he was getting few chances in the centre.

And that was that. Nepia's flirtation with English Rugby League came to an end. His Halifax career had consisted of 15 first team games, in which he had scored 34 points (two tries, 14 goals), and two games for the 'A' team (three goals). At £20 per first team game his £300 transfer fee might at first sight seem expensive. There is no doubt, however, that his presence in the team more than made up for the outlay in terms of raised attendances. In his four months at Thrum Hall he won many friends and admirers, who enjoyed the warmth of his personality and the fun and spectacle he brought to the game.

George Nepia's name continued to figure in the local Halifax paper for months after he left the country. His serialised life story, *Rugby Every Time*, in 18 parts, finally concluded on 14 August, 1937, by a strange coincidence, the very day on which he helped New Zealand to beat Australia 16-15 at Carlaw Park in the only Rugby League test match he ever played.

Nepia meeting local Rugby Union officials in Swansea on the Maori tour in 1982.
He received a standing ovation before the match when walking across the pitch.
He was also given a great reception at other matches on the tour.
(Photo: Western Mail)

10. George Nepia Double International

Why is it that rugby union people and those associated with their New Zealand Halls of Fame cannot bring themselves to call their beloved son, their player of the century George Nepia, a double international. Nepia played both rugby union and rugby league for New Zealand.

The two pictures on display here, and the autographed extract from the Canterbury Rugby League's programme, dated Saturday 31 July, 1937 clearly testify to the fact that George Nepia played rugby league in New Zealand after returning from England, where he had gone in 1935, enticed to the professional code by the payment of five hundred pounds. Nepia ventured to England to play for a new club, established by a greyhound entrepreneur on the outskirts of London, Streatham and Mitcham. The club pulled in 22,000 for their first home fixture on 7 September, 1935, when beaten by Oldham 10-5 but never succeeded, financially or on the football field, finishing 24th in the 30-team English competition at the end of the 1935-36 season, and one place better the following season in 23rd place. The club lasted only two seasons before being wound up. Not long into the club's second season Nepia transferred to the Yorkshire club Halifax, where he played 13 games before returning to New Zealand in 1937.

Nepia, now 32 years, captained the New Zealand Maori team on its short tour to Australia and on return guested in Christchurch for two weeks for the Canterbury Rugby League. He turned out for the Hornby club on Saturday 31 July, kicking two goals in the club's 21-12 loss to Addington. The Christchurch Press reported that Nepia, who kicked two goals, defended well and kicked prodigiously before 3,000 spectators.

The following Saturday 7 August, Nepia played his second game, this time for Canterbury against the West Coast side Inangahua, a game which attracted 7,000 spectators to Monica Park, the Canterbury Rugby League's headquarters.

In what became a hectic schedule, by today's standards and given slow transport, he was then whisked away to Auckland where just four days later on 11 August he played for the New Zealand Maoris in their dramatic 16-5 win over the visiting Australian Rugby League side, Nepia kicking four goals.

The newspaper report suggested that Nepia "gave one of his glorious displays. He never put a foot wrong. His tackling, fielding and kicking was a revelation".

That was not the end of Nepia's flirtation with rugby league because three days later on Saturday 14 August, he ran onto Carlaw Park for New Zealand in the second of a two-test series against the Kangaroos. The 'Professional All Blacks' had lost the first test the previous Saturday 8-12 but squared the series with a 16-15 win. Nepia converted one of New Zealand's four tries and kicked a penalty.

George Nepia was selected for the New Zealand tour of Australia in 1938 but made himself unavailable. So backed by the reality of a solitary successful appearance for the 'Professional All Blacks' as they were known at the time, George Nepia is a double international.

From the *1999 New Zealand Rugby League Annual*
Courtesy of the editor, Bernard Wood

The stamp of George Nepia issued in 1990 in support of children's health.
(By permission of the New Zealand Post Office,
image supplied by the Museum of Rugby)

11. Rugby League internationals

In 1937, on his return home from England, Nepia played two Rugby League international matches. The reports below are from the New Zealand Herald.

11 August 1937 New Zealand Maoris 16 Australia 5

Australia Beaten - League Visitors - Surprise By Maoris - Sixteen Points To Five - Fine Display By Nepia - Penalties Assist Winners

The Australian League football Team, which is en route to England, suffered a surprise defeat yesterday afternoon at Carlaw Park by a New Zealand Maori side by 16 points to 5. The Maoris scored two tries, one converted, and four penalty goals to one converted try.

The day was beautifully fine, the ground was in fair condition, and there was an attendance estimated at between 10,000 and 12,000. Undoubtedly, the attraction was the first appearance of a Maori side under the League banner, while there was the curiosity among the public as to the capabilities of the former famous All Black full-back, George Nepia.

Nepia's all round display stamped him as still being a fine full-back. In the early stages of the game he gave an exhibition of line-kicking the equal of which has not been witnessed for some years. Later on Nepia showed inconsistency in his line-kicking, but taken all round, it was an excellent display.

Added to his ability in this respect, Nepia proved himself a great defensive player, and not a single attacker was able to pass him during the match. On one or two occasions he was faced with a couple of opponents, and it was then he demonstrated that he still retained his ability to drive the attack in the direction in which he desired to make it ineffective.

Hemi's Injury

The Maori team put up a highly creditable performance. Hemi, playing at centre-threequarter, was more or less a passenger throughout the match. He was limping from a leg injury when he went on the field, and he was compelled to retire about midway through the first spell. After receiving treatment during the interval he returned to the field, but he was still unable to run and took little part in the play.

In addition to Hemi's indisposition the Maoris were also unfortunate that J. Cootes, one of the front row forwards, received a severe cut over the right eyebrow early in the second spell, and he to retire, much against his will, for medical attention. He came back later with his eyebrow thickly plastered, but was eventually persuaded by the referee to return to the dressing room.

Under the circumstances the victory of the Maoris was distinctly creditable. Their fine tackling was one of the deciding factors, both backs and forwards doing excellent work in this respect. The forwards deserve much praise for their exhibition, especially when the pack was depleted. McLeod's hooking of the ball was first class, and Watene, Brodick, Mitchell and the Cootes brothers all played solidly.

Puzzled by Rulings

Apart from Nepia, the Maori backs all did well. Mahima and the two Chase brothers combining nicely behind the scrum, while Broughton and Rata, on the wings, both handicapped by want of the ball, tackled and defended soundly.

As for the Australians, it must be stated in all fairness that it was not their first team. Some of the players had not had a game for four weeks, and since their arrival had been called upon to accept hospitality for two days at Rotorua and again on Tuesday at Ngaruawahia. They arrived back in Auckland early yesterday morning, and, with their lack of training, they did as well as could be expected.

The visitors were undoubtedly puzzled by the referee's interpretations of the rules, and in fact, seemed bewildered by the number of penalties awarded against them. These were in a proportion of just on eight to one. Both English and Australian teams of late years have invariably been unable to understand the interpretations of New Zealand referees, more especially in regard to scrum breaches and playing-the-ball rule.

Poor Sportsmanship

The attendance was a record for a mid-week League match played in Auckland. The spectators obviously favoured the Maoris from the start, but this did not excuse the poor sportsmanship displayed by a section of the crowd which hooted the visitors when they scored their only try. The calls of "put him off " which followed the awarding of penalties for scrum and other infringements were also in bad taste.

Early in the game Australia was penalised on three occasions, but Hemi failed to open the score, although two of the shots were from easy positions. The home team rushed the ball over the visitor's line and R. Chase scored, Hemi converting. Maoris, 5; Australia, 0.

After missing a penalty shot Nepia was applauded for a smothering tackle of Dawson, and his fine line-kicking gained 60 yards a few minutes later. The visitors were penalised for the eleventh time and Nepia kicked a goal.

Maoris, 7; Australia, 0.

Further penalties

On resuming Hemi reappeared, but still limped badly. The Maoris continued to play with great dash, and Watene was pulled down a few yards from the visitors' goal. There were several more penalties against the visitors, and from a kick in front Nepia missed at goal. Then came the finest try of the match, and the home team, passing brilliantly, changed direction twice and L. Cootes sent a high pass to Brodrick, who raced over. Nepia just missed with a great kick from the sideline. Maoris, 10; Australia, 0.

J. Cootes received a knock on the head and retired. With the home team depleted, the visitors made the most of the position, and Curran scored, Thompson converting. Maoris, 10; Australia, 5.

The tackling now became very solid and the Maoris more than held their own. The visitors were penalised five yards from half-way and Nepia kicked a fine goal. Maoris 12; Australia 5.

From another penalty, 40 yards out, Nepia kicked a great goal. Maoris, 14; Australia, 5.

McLeod and Mitchell led the Maori forwards, who pressed on the visitors' line. Once again Nepia's great kicking powers sent over a penalty from near the touchline and the game ended:- Maoris, 16; Australia, 5.

Mr P. Rogers was referee.

Maori Team Entertained - Dinner Tendered by Visitors

Members of the Maori team and officials of the New Zealand Rugby League were the guests of the Australian players at dinner at the Hotel Auckland last evening. In congratulating the Maori team on its victory, Mr R. Savage, joint manager of the visiting side, said that the Australians had been fully tested. He was sure that every encouragement would be given Maori teams to visit the Commonwealth.

On behalf of the Maori Board of Control, the Rev. Panapa wished the Australian team every success in England. Other speakers were Messrs J. Redwood, president of the New Zealand League, S. Watene, captain of the Maori team, and J. Rukutai.

14 August 1937 New Zealand 16 Australia 15

Second League Test - Fast Encounter - New Zealand Wins -
Australian Team Beaten - Margin of One Point - Visiting Players Injured

Carlaw Park was packed on Saturday for the second Rugby League test match between Australia and New Zealand, which was won by New Zealand by 16 points to 15. Weather and ground conditions were excellent.

The honours, however, were with the Australians, for it was their unlucky day. Early in the game S. Pearce, one of their best forwards, broke his leg, and later J. Gibbs had the misfortune to break several ribs. R. Stehr and W. Prigg were each off for a time and Australia then played three short for several minutes. The visitors put up a gallant fight, but found the odds too great. In the closing stages of play Norman and McKinnon made a brilliant but fruitless effort to save the game and the crowd was provided with a thrilling finish.

New Zealand can be credited with an even better display than in the first test. The tackling of the forwards rattled the visitors, and the general play showed improvement. Nepia was in great form and saved the home team by solid tackling. New Zealand's score comprised four tries and two goals, while Australia secured three tries and three goals.

Prime Minister Kicks Off

Among those present were the Prime Minister, the Rt. Hon M. J. Savage, and the Minister of Finance, the Hon. W. Nash. Mr J. E. Redwood, president of the New Zealand Rugby League Council, introduced the Ministers, who briefly spoke to the crowd through loud speakers, and extended a welcome and best wishes to the Australians. Messrs R. E. Savage and H. Sunderland, co-managers, responded on behalf of the Australians.

The Prime Minister, who received a hearty ovation, then shook hands with the layers and kicked off.

Australia won the ball from the ensuing scrum and Norman badly beat the defence, but Dawson was pulled down a few yards from the New Zealand line. The home team was penalised and Beaton kicked a fine goal. Australia, 2; New Zealand, 0.

Williams smartly sent Prigg away and Dawson beat Kay, but the home forwards worked their way back and Halloran cut-in and transferred to Tittleton, for Davison to take the final pass and dive over at the corner. Dawson's kick at goal just missed.

New Zealand, 3; Australia, 2.

The visitors continued to hold the upper hand, and Pearce passed out to Beaton and Prigg, who easily beat Kay and sent the ball to McLean. Tittleton just missed the speedy winger, who scored a fine try. Beaton failed to convert.

Australia, 5; New Zealand, 3.

Pearce Breaks His Leg

Australia was getting the ball from the scrums and McLean made another fine dash, until he was caught by Brodrick. Then Pearce suffered a broken leg. Nepia snapped up from the fast-raiding Australian forwards, went down low, and Pearce crashed over him.

Ward started McKinnon and Norman on attack, but smart cover defence held up the movement. Brodrick was again prominent, and, getting the ball from Bickerton, he raced 40 yards before passing to Glyn, Tetley and Davison completing the movement for another try at the corner. Davison again failed to convert.

New Zealand, 6; Australia, 5.

Stehr was injured and retired for a few minutes. The visitors were playing well, and Norman followed a kick and, obtaining possession, beat Nepia, who chased and caught him near the goal. Gibbs and Nolan were handy, however, and the latter scored near the posts. Beaton missed an easy kick. Australia, 8; New Zealand, 6.

The visitors then staged a brilliant offensive. Prigg and Stehr handled well and McLean took the ball at top speed to outpace the home backs for a fine try. Williams converted, and half time came with the scores:- Australia, 15; New Zealand, 6.

The Second Spell

Soon after the kick-off Davison had an unsuccessful shot at goal from a penalty. Twice Nepia saved with excellent kicking. Gibbs was forced to retire with rib injuries. Tetley opened up the game for New Zealand and a nice passing bout between Cootes, Glynn and Satherley enabled the last-named to score. Nepia converted.

Australia, 15; New Zealand, 11.

The home forwards now dominated the game and Brodrick and Cootes broke away. Tetley, however, missed badly and New Zealand lost a try. From two penalties Nepia gained 60 yards and several strong forward rushes were checked by Australia, both Williams and Norman proving very elusive. Halloran nearly scored a try, and Brodrick was pushed into touch.

New Zealand in the Lead

Brodrick thrilled the crowd with a great dash. His final pass to Glynn, however, was knocked on. From a penalty Nepia kicked a splendid goal from 40 yards out on the touch line. Australia, 15; New Zealand, 13.

New Zealand attacked vigorously and good work by Cootes and Brodrick improved the position. Halloran cut in nicely and passed to Tittleton and Kay, who drew the defence cleverly and sent Bickerton over for a try. Nepia failed to convert.

New Zealand, 16; Australia, 15.

Prigg was forced to retire with an injured shoulder, but came back to assist his team. The visitors were now faced with an uphill battle and only splendid defence kept the home team out. Brodrick went close to scoring, but a scrum was ordered on the visitors' line. A few minutes before time Norman made a brilliant opening and the crowd had anxious moments when McKinnon burst through. However, Nepia saved splendidly and the game ended:- New Zealand 16; Australia 15.
Mr M. Wetherill was referee.

Nepia's Day - A Great Fullback - Visitors' Bad Luck - Thrills For Large Crowd

Although the Australians lost by a single point, they were perhaps greater in defeat than in victory, for injuries reduced their strength to twelve players in the latter part of the first spell and then to eleven shortly after the interval. For brief periods in the second half they were left with ten men, but in spite of the fact that only three forwards were left in the scrum, they still provided strenuous opposition to the full strength of the New Zealand side. Whenever the visitors' backs had the ball they were a menace to the defence right to the finish of play.

It is safe to say that had New Zealand fielded any other fullback than Nepia, the visitors would have won handsomely, even allowing for their misfortune. Nepia was responsible for saving at least four certain tries with his deadly tackling, twice when Beaton was well clear of the rest of the field, and also when Gibbs and McLean each attempted to beat the Maori custodian.

It was exceedingly unfortunate for Pearce, the big versatile Australian forward, to be carried off with a broken leg left early in the gam. Pearce charged down on Nepia, who kept low to the ground and rose, just as the Australian reached him with the result that the latter crashed heavily over him. Australia suffered a further temporary misfortune when Stehr fell heavily on his left shoulder and had to retire for a time.

Loss of Gibbs

At this period of play, however, Australia's twelve representatives showed what they were capable of, and the bad luck appeared to inspire them to brilliant efforts. Assisted by weak tackling on the part of the New Zealand backs, the visitors were seen in clever passing bouts which had the defence rattled, and with nine points in their favour at half-time, the result appeared to be a foregone conclusion.

However, the retirement with rib injuries five minutes after the interval, of Gibbs, who had been the outstanding forward among the Australians, placed a totally different complexion on the game. Gibbs had been playing brilliantly, with repeated dashes for the line, and participating in nearly every attack, and his loss was keenly felt. Prigg, the Australian captain, had adopted the role of rover to harass the New Zealand inside backs, but later he, too, met with an injury to his right shoulder and had to leave the field for attention. He returned in a few minutes, determined to help his remaining ten men in their desperate efforts to keep the New Zealanders at bay.

Crowd Rushes Players

By this time the New Zealand backs had stiffened up their defence with more resolute tackling and their forwards were obtaining possession of the ball from their three opponents in the scrums. The result was that the visitors were repeatedly called upon to stop bright passing movements which swept toward their line. When the final bell sounded a wildly enthusiastic crowd rushed the ground to congratulate the players as they exchanged jerseys on their way to the dressing rooms.

Nepia is justly entitled to the credit for staving off defeat. His defence and positional play were very sound, his kicking brilliant and his tackling deadly. Only once was he bluffed, when Norman broke away with two men in support and only Nepia to beat. The nippy Australian five-eighths dummied his way past Nepia, who quickly gave chase and brought him down with a flying tackle from the rear, though unable to prevent the ball being tossed back to Gibbs and Nolan for a try.

Tittleton was the best of the threequarter line, his tackling being an outstanding feature and an object lesson to his fellow-players who were prone to attempt the high collaring so futile against the heavy Australian forwards.

Davison's Two Tries

Davison scored two good tries, using his pace effectively, but his defence was weak, and failure to tackle let his opponents away repeatedly. Kay was also weak in this respect and missed a certain try through hesitating. Chase made the most of his opportunities, although he had not the pace to get clear. Bickerton was overshadowed by the versatile Norman at five-eighths, and was several times left standing. However, he was always handy ion attacking movements. Halloran tackled well and sent out good passes, but the transfers of all the backs lacked the snap and precision which characterised the work of the Australians, and there is room for considerable improvement in this department.

Brodrick, Glynn and Gault were a trio of determined, hard-working forwards, with the first-named most prominent. Brodrick made a number of brilliant dashes, but should learn to drop his one handed style of passing and dangerous hurdling tactics. Cootes and Satherley gave valuable support and the latter's try was a fine effort. Tetley, however, was inclined to play too much in the back line and several times spoil promising movements through faulty handling and being caught in possession.

Ward and Norman Shine

Ward, for Australia, was almost equally as good at fullback as Nepia was for New Zealand. His fielding of the ball was perfect, and in the second half he made an extra man in the three-quarter line with bursts of speed after obtaining possession. McLean played his best game and confirmed the impression that he is a worthy successor to the brilliant Horder of former tours. He showed much better positional play than on his first appearance and has plenty of pace. Beaton and McKinnon were well watched by Tittleton, and the former's clever runs were frustrated by Nepia. He was off colour at kicking, otherwise Australia might have won. Dawson, who took Hazelton's place on the wing, was safe and speedy, although he was allowed few chances.

Norman was undoubtedly the brains of the Australian attack and his understanding with Williams behind the scrum made the pair a dangerous combination. Williams was handicapped after the forward losses, but came to light as a splendid goal-kicker. Individually Williams and Norman were responsible for clever openings and good running, while their defence was very sound.

Gibbs and Pearce, until their retirement, played great football and Prigg was little inferior, although he was allowed a good deal of latitude as rover by the referee. Stehr, Nolan and Lewis stuck manfully to their task of holding the scrums and were always on hand to open up the play from the ruck.

12. Manukau Rugby League 1938 and 1939

On his return to New Zealand in 1937, Nepia had played a couple of games for Hornby in the Canterbury Rugby League, in preparation for his sole international Rugby League appearance against Australia. But in April 1938, he joined Manukau, who competed in the nine-team Auckland Rugby League.

The Auckland Rugby league was covered by the *New Zealand Herald*, and the reports in this chapter are from that paper. They were headed "The League Code", and featured regularly in the paper. Most matches were played at Carlaw Park.

He missed Manukau's first match - a pre-season game against Ponsonby when they won 19-11, but on 6 April the paper reported on the Auckland Rugby League: "The most discussed team is Manukau, which created a very favourable impression against Ponsonby. Nepia and Hemi are doubtful players, but even their absence will not weaken the team to any great extent." Manukau lost their first game, but the paper was still saying that "Manukau [are] considered by many to be the strongest team in the competition." Manukau won their next three games, without Nepia playing. But on 16 May, in a report headed "Appearance of G. Nepia" - a testimony to his status - the paper said in the report of Manukau's 18-16 victory over Richmond: "Undoubtedly a great attraction was the appearance of G. Nepia, New Zealand representative at both codes of Rugby. Nepia played full-back for Manukau". The report went on: "Considerable attention was focussed on G. Nepia. He played a sound game without doing anything brilliant except for a great save in the second spell when Devine was injured. Nepia did not appear fit."

Tour selection

The New Zealand Rugby League were preparing for a tour of Australia at this time. Despite his lack of appearances, on 23 May, it was reported that Nepia had been selected for squad for Australia tour. The report went on: "From games seen in Auckland Nepia has not yet struck form and he appears to have passed his best. A repetition, however, of his form against the Australians last season would be welcomed in Sydney. His wide experience is an asset to the team."

In a tour trial, Nepia played full-back for the 'Probables' against the Possibles. The report showed that some of his form was returning: "While his defence was good, Nepia still appears to be unfit. His tackling in the second half, however, was very deadly." However, a couple of days later, it was said that: "Nepia has not shown anything like the form he revealed last season, but it is expected solid training will make a great difference in his play before the first game in Sydney on June 11."

As outlined in his autobiography, Nepia withdrew from the tour party - and there are no reports of his playing again for Manukau that season. Manukau had a fairly successful season, winning the Phelan Shield, and losing 16-7 to Australian visitors East Sydney in an end-of-season tour match.

1939 - a return to action

Despite a period of inactivity, on 5 April 1939, the *Herald* said : "It is reported that Manukau will be strengthened on Saturday week by the inclusion of G. Nepia and J. Hemi." The next week, in the paper's preview of Manukau's match against Easts, it reported: "Considerable interest will be taken in the appearance of G. Nepia. He has been training for some weeks and is reported to be fit...His appearance with Manukau should prove a big attraction." Four players in the Manukau team: G. Nepia, T. Chase, J. Hemi and J. Brodrick had all represented New Zealand at Rugby Union and Rugby League.

Easts won 23-10. The match report said: "Play was always interesting although it was not a high class exhibition of the code. There was too much kicking by Manukau." It went on: "The appearance of G. Nepia at fullback for Manukau was a popular attraction and he did some very solid tackling." Nepia stopped a break by Easts' Manson in the second half "with a fine tackle", but his kick was charged down which led to an Easts' try.

On 22 April, Manukau beat Papakura 20-0. Nepia was now clearly back to full fitness and having more impact on the matches. The report said: "Nepia made a brilliant run from fullback and Panapa scored." It added: "Nepia played a splendid game at fullback and was a thorn in the side of the opposition. His ability to make plays for the threequarters was a feature of the game." Later that week, the paper's Rugby League column said that: "The presence in the [Manukau] team of G. Nepia made a great difference, especially as he showed good form."

The next week, Manukau beat North Shore 23-7. Nepia again made a contribution to the victory. The paper reported that: "Nepia at full back was very solid. His fine defence and strong kicking with either foot were invaluable to the side while at times he started attacking moves cleverly." It went on: "Manukau has a good and elusive set of backs… Nepia, although he has lost some of his pace, is still very sound and a strong kicker with either foot."

The next week, Manukau faced Mount Albert in a key match. The Herald's preview said: "Mount Albert is the only unbeaten team to date, while Manukau has suffered one defeat. The result will therefore have considerable bearing on the championship honours and under fine conditions a fine exhibition of the code is anticipated" Mount Albert proved too strong for Nepia's side, winning 38-15. However, his try took the headlines, as the report proclaimed: "An early Try - Nepia's Fine Movement"

Mount Albert scored early in the match. Then: "...following up rewarded Nepia with a try. He kicked high and when several players jumped for the ball, including the Mount Albert fullback, it rebounded several yards and went over the line. Nepia raced on to score unopposed… Shortly afterward Nepia was again prominent in a fine movement which led to a try. Gaining the ball about 40 yards out from the drop-out Nepia ran up and feinted to kick. Suddenly he swung a long over-arm pass across the field. T. Chase gained possession and beat three opponents to score a spectacular try." But Mount Albert fought back to lead 20-8 at half-time. In the second half: "Nepia did some sound kicking at fullback and started some nice movements, but he was twice well beaten, once by Donaldson with the "dummy."

A couple of days later, the paper was more critical of Manukau: "The exhibition given by Manukau when faced with solid all round opposition last Saturday was disappointing. Its defence wilted on several occasions while support for an attacking player was also lacking… G. Nepia, the Manukau fullback, still does some clever work on the field, the benefit of experience gained during his long career being often shown during the progress of a match. His defence on Saturday against Mount Albert, however, was found wanting. By allowing a player to come inside him and on another occasion taking the "dummy" Nepia cost his team two converted tries."

The next Saturday, Manukau lost again, this time 15-5 against Richmond. However, it was reported that Nepia was back towards his best: "Faulty handling by the Manukau backs checked a promising movement in which N was prominent… "Nepia showed vast improvement on his form last Saturday and rarely made a mistake. His quick return kicking when pressed was a feature of the game."

Nepia missed the club's next match, a 21-0 victory over City, due to an injury to his arm. Hemi played at fullback. But a further representative honour came Nepia's way when he was selected at fullback for the Auckland Maori Rugby League team to play South Auckland. However, South Auckland beat the Maoris 19-8.

Now the New Zealand Rugby League was preparing for the forthcoming ill-fated tour of England. On 30 May, it was reported that a representative League match was to be played at Carlaw Park next Monday between Maori and Pakeha teams. Nepia selected at fullback for the Maoris. The match was then reported as an Auckland team versus the Maoris, and an important trial match for forthcoming tour of England. The paper said: "In the selection of fullback, J Smith of North Shore was the first choice for the Auckland team, and he will be opposed by George Nepia, who is fit again after an injury to his arm some weeks ago. Against South Auckland last Sunday, Nepia played a brilliant game and Smith will need to be right on his game to overshadow the famous Maori fullback.

In a separate article headed: "Maori Players – Nepia and Hemi", the *Herald* added: "The Maori selectors are confident that Nepia has no peer as a fullback and his many followers expect a great game from their popular star. Nepia has on many occasions proved his ability to rise to great heights in big football."

On 3 June, Manukau won again, beating Marist 26-11. Nepia started at five-eighth, but then the backs were rearranged, with Hemi moving to centre. The Herald reported that "Good tackling by Nepia was a feature of the game." Nepia converted three tries and kicked a penalty

On 6 June, the paper outlined that Nepia was a serious prospect for the tour. It outlined on the Auckland versus Maori match: "Spectacular football at Carlaw Park … an Auckland team played the Maoris in the first serious trial game for selection of the NZ team to tour England in July this year… Nepia at fullback, also played a fine game. His defence was perfect, and on his present form he must be considered a possibility for the trip to England… Petersen headed the Auckland forwards in a sweeping offensive, but Nepia made a great save and kicked well back past halfway… Nepia was in his best form, racing along the touchline before passing to Mataira and Tukere who almost scored." At half-time, the Maori team were 14-2 ahead. Nepia continued to play a vital defensive role in the second half, and "...tackled McInnarney when the winger looked certain to score." Towards the end of the match: "Herring, Gunning and Leatherbarrow were associated in a thrilling passing movement which Nepia stopped on the goal-line." The Maori team hung on to win 19-15.

A review of the match published the next day said: "Nepia was a little superior to Scott and on the day, Nepia played a great game, showing his ability to rise to the occasion in big football."

Nepia missed Manukau's next match, a 10-6 victory over Ponsonby. The next week, there was no league fixture for Manukau. The team played Huntly, the champion South Auckland team and won 9-8. It was "...a fast open game before a large crowd at Onehunga... Nepia gave a fine display at fullback for Manukau and saved his side from a possible defeat. His safe fielding relieved many anxious moments and his well placed kicks often turned defence into attack."

On 23 June 1939, despite war on the horizon, the programme of the New Zealand's Rugby League tour to England was announced. It was to start on 2 September at St Helens, and end on 16 Dec with the third test. The players were to leave Wellington on 27 July. Consideration was also being given to playing six matches in France.

Nepia missed Manukau's next couple of matches through injury, but on Saturday 1 July, the *Herald* reported: "Manukau will be strengthened by having Nepia, Hemi and Brodrick back in its ranks." Despite the return of these three players, North Shore won 19-5. The report was headed: "Fine Forward Play – G. Nepia's strong defence." It said: "The North Shore forwards had been raiding the defence determinedly, but found Nepia a stumbling block, the veteran showing all his old guile and generalship and claiming a distinct advantage in duels of range-kicking with Smith, the opposing full-back... Nepia and Broderick took the ball right downfield with inter-passing and Mahima worked the blindside from a scrum to enable Winberg to score." The report concluded: "Nepia was his old self at fullback for Manukau and repeatedly saved his side."

On 5 July, it was reported that further trials for the tour were being held. The *Herald* said that: "G. Nepia evidently was not considered for the fullback position. It is understood that Nepia was available. J. Hemi has been preferred in the North Island team to J. Smith, who will play for the Possibles." Cec Mountford, who would have an illustrious career in British Rugby League after the War, was playing fullback for South Island. North Island won 35-13, and the report said. "Hemi is the best player in this position (fullback) in New Zealand"

For Manukau's next match, a 21-19 defeat by Mount Albert, Nepia was selected at five-eighths. He soon made an impact: "Within a minute of the kick-off, Nepia, at five-eighths, dashed in between several Mount Albert players, knocked the ball over the goal line and recovered it before touching the ground to score a spectacular try." However, he was injured and left the game just before half-time.

The next week, Manukau returned to winning ways with a 23-14 victory over Richmond: "A feature of the game was the splendid form of Nepia, who was hurt early in the game, but pluckily carried on. One of his runs was a really brilliant effort."

A couple of days later, the *Herald* reported a proposal that Nepia join the tour party as player-coach. The headline read: "Player-coach offer - Suggestion for Nepia - Council rejects proposal." The report outlined: "An offer of £200 was made to the New Zealand Rugby League Council yesterday through Mr J Rukutai, a member of that body, by a keen supporter of the code, for the purpose of sending G. Nepia to England as player-coach of the New Zealand team. Mr Rukutai stated that Nepia was still playing good football and his knowledge of both English and New Zealand conditions would be very valuable to the team. The New Zealand Council considered the matter yesterday and decided that at such a late hour, it was unable to accept the offer."

Whether Nepia would have been able to leave his family and his farm for six months is debatable. However, it shows that even at the age of 34, he could still attract this level of attention.

The tourists left without Nepia, for what was to be a tour of only two matches before the team were forced to return home due to the outbreak of war. At the end of July, Manukau drew 9-all with City: "..Manukau backs got going early, and Nepia, playing at centre, made a nice opening for Brodrick to score a try." "Nepia started another passing movement in which Rata, Brimble and Awhitu joined, the last named scoring." In the second half, the report commented on: "Nepia's solid work at fullback". A hailstorm made the pitch a quagmire. But "Nepia, as usual, was invaluable… particularly when he dropped back to fullback in the second spell."

He was then selected for an Auckland team to play South Auckland on 5 August, but did not play in the match. He missed Manukau's next match, but returned for a 15-2 defeat by Newtown. The Herald previewed the match: "Newton has been drawn to meet Manukau in the principal attraction on No.1 ground… Manukau will be greatly strengthened by the inclusion of G. Nepia who has returned to Auckland and will captain the side." The report said: "it was very interesting to compare the tactics of Dempsey and Nepia, the respective fullbacks. Both players kicked altogether too often, where a smart run would have opened up scoring movements… Nepia was not so prominent as usual, although his defence was very sound." However, he did kick a penalty goal.

On 28 August, it was announced that Nepia was in the squad for an Auckland team to play Taranaki next Thursday. For Manukau, his next appearance was on 2 September in the Roope Rooster (knock out) competition, in a 27-12 victory over Papakura. He played at five eighths again: "A nice opening by Nepia from five eighths gave Hapi a good try." He also converted three tries

The next week, Manukau lost 31-15 to Marist, and Nepia does not seem to have played.

Tangi for Legendary Nepia

A Giant Kauri Has Fallen

The headlines from the *New Zealand Herald* about Nepia's death.
The top one was on the front page the day after he died.
The lower one was on the funeral report.
(Courtesy *New Zealand Herald*)

13. A Legend remembered

George Nepia's death was major news in New Zealand. This chapter includes some of the tributes and obituaries that were published. Statistics are not included in the obituaries, but can be found in the statistics section of this book.

The *New Zealand Herald* reported his death on the front page. In an article headed "Tangi for Legendary Nepia", it said how he had just attended a test match in Dunedin, and recalled playing there against the Lions in 1930. The report also said that "The Government also paid tribute to Mr Nepia. The Minister of Internal Affairs, Mr Tapsell, described him as a 'dignified gentleman' and 'a leader of all Maoridom.' Mr Tapsell said all members of the Government were greatly saddened at the passing of such a great New Zealander."

On 30 August, *The Herald's* report of the funeral was headed "A Giant Kauri has Fallen," quoting NZRU Councillor Ivan Vodanovich who was one of the speakers to the "many hundreds" of people present. He also said: "Who could put a price on what he meant to New Zealand society? He was a great man."

The Dominion reported the reaction of some of Nepia's former team-mates. Brent Reid's report quoted Bert Grenside, who played with Nepia for Hawke's Bay saying that "He was an inspiration whose wonderful play saved his forwards a lot of running about. There has never been a fullback as good as George Nepia. Jackie Blake, who also played with Nepia for Hawke's Bay, added: "He was a full-back who stayed back and who was never out of position. He was the last line of defence, totally dependable."

In London, *The Times* also carried an obituary of Nepia, praising him as an "outstanding" member of the 1924-5 team, and recalling his "brilliant displays of kicking, tackling and fielding of the ball and he was nominated as one of the five players of the year by the *Wisden Rugby Almanack*"

'Boy Wonder' Became Invincible Sporting Hero from the *New Zealand Herald*

T. P. McLean, doyen of New Zealand sports writers, pays this tribute to George Nepia, doyen of rugby fullbacks.

The legendary Maori fullback George Nepia, who died yesterday aged eighty-one, thought that the ultimate distinction of his life was to be appointed a few months ago an honorary life vice-president of the South African rugby board.

Politics and racism put aside, the gesture was extraordinary. No non-white had been remotely considered for the post.

In fact, the ultimate tribute was paid within a week or two after the election when Mr Nepia starred in one of television's *This Is Your Life*'s cameos.

The compere, Bob Parker, was supposed to limit the piece to 30 minutes. It ran for 42 and so successfully that all subsequent portraits of personalities have been taken at a more leisurely pace.

The programme caught on so much that its rating soared to well above one million viewers - a staggering number midweek.

So it was shown conclusively that the boy wonder of the 1924 All Blacks, who beat all comers in 30 matches in England, Ireland, Wales and France (Scotland, being in dispute with the international board declined a fixture with Cliff Porter's team) had remained, for the rest of his life, a treasure amongst New Zealand's sporting heroes.

He deserved the place. From end to end of a life not unaffected by personal tragedy, he was a warm, modest man of high principles and ultimate sincerity.

These last few years, you could have walked the streets of towns, cities and country places and enquired casually about Mark Nicholls, Cliff Porter, Maurice Brownlie, Bert Cooke and Karl Ifwersen.

Clothed In Legend

A few among those you asked might have mumbled, grasping for the identity. The rest would have marched on.

But "Nepia?". Ah, but of course. That young Maori who played every match of that All Blacks tour that was never beaten. It came out pat; and that, in life is as close as you may reach to immortality.

The man was soon clothed in legend. Against strong opposition, he won the hand of Huinga Kohere, whose father had been killed in action as padre of the Pioneer or Maori Battalion of the First World War. Huinga was beautiful. She was also Ngati-porou and Nepia was Kahungunu.

On the Kohere side, there was resistance as long as two years to the marriage of one of high birth and the son of a farmer.

At about the time that consent for the marriage was given in 1926, a memorial church for the Maori dead of the Great War was on the point of commissioning on a tall hill at Tikitiki, near Ruatoria.

Pine Taiapa, the famous carver, had done wonders, personally and in acquainting the Maori people with the significance of the church. As one example, women of the Arawa dispatched the pulpit from Rotorua covered in £5 notes as a gesture to the wellbeing of the church.

Taiapa, a fine footballer and a proud man, declared that his reward for his services would be that he and his fiancee would be the first to wed in it.

Somewhere in what was then a wilderness, a voice spoke, crying "George Nepia is to marry Huinga Kohere. They are taking up a farm at Rangitukia"

First Trial At 16

Years later, telling the story, Taiapa, smiling, spread his hands. "Mine was the second marriage in the church" he said. "How could I possibly dare to step in before George Nepia?"

The main facts as to Nepia's playing career in both rugby and league are soon ascertained.

He was aged sixteen years and one month when, in 1921, he played in a trial match for a New Zealand Maori team to tour Australia.

Two years later, he played regularly for the Hawke's Bay at the beginning of its record-breaking hold on the Ranfurly Shield which did not end until 1927.

Chucked In As Fullback

He played as five-eighths in a trial at Eden Park for the 1924 All Blacks. By some selectorial aberration or inspiration, for the next match he was chucked in at the deep end at fullback.

He knew nothing of the position. He knew little else than that, as a non-Mormon pupil at the Maori Agricultural College at Hastings, he had, through tutelage and natural gifts, acquired amazing power and precision on the punt, a tackle of deadly, American gridiron-style strength and accuracy from a Mormon teacher, Elder Moser, as well as an infallible skill in catching and fielding the ball.

These turned out to be the skills anyone would dream of playing at fullback. George passed his first test; he past his second at Wellington. He was chosen at nineteen in the team which was to make a preliminary canter in Australia.

He had an uneasy time in those four matches. Homeward-bound to England, the hierarchy of the team - S. S. Deans, the manager, Porter the captain and Mark Nicholls the captain of backs - seriously doubted that he should be played in the first match.

'Never Let Us Down'

The place could be entrusted to Nicholls, now a sound, experienced player.

The die was cast. Nepia played. The All Blacks won by only 11 to nil where their predecessors of 1905 had won by 55 to 4.

No other selection for the position was considered for the rest of the tour. Backs and forwards told me over the years: "Whenever the ball was kicked over our heads, we never troubled to turn around. 'Hori' was there. All would be well. We could be sure he would never let us down."

So Nepia passed on to a career of 46 matches for New Zealand, nine of them internationals and many other first-class fixtures.

In 1935, heaving led New Zealand Maori in Australia, he felt compelled, because of impoverishment caused by farming at Rangitukia - "You were a good farmer, George" said his neighbour Victor Rickard on *This Is Your Life* - to switch to rugby league.

Returned to New Zealand, he often filled Carlaw Park for a couple of seasons before the onset of the Second World War drove him back to his farm on the coast.

Wartime Amnesty

By wartime amnesty, he was reinstated to rugby. He served the game faithfully as a referee, and night after night, coached his eldest son, George, in the arts of fullback play.

Young George was shaping up well, too, when he was called up into the army and a posting in Malaya as a sergeant in the Fiji battalion. He was killed. He was only 22.

Years later, I handed George the first copy of *I, George Nepia*, which I had helped him to write.

He flicked over the pages until he came to the story of young George and, in particular, of young George's death. Old George wept. We wept with him.

One marches back almost into prehistory to one's first sight of George Nepia elsewhere than on a rugby field. It was the stage of the Municipal Theatre, Hastings, from which he sang his theme song of the 1924 tour, the theme song of his life, *Beneath The Maori Moon.*

He retained that lovely singing voice, not much affected by advanced age, and in the commercial break of *This Is Your Life*, sang it for the studio audience so well that later TVNZ featured it.

By the post-war years, he had shifted from Rangitukia to a five thousand acre farm near Wairoa, which he was managing for its multiple Maori owners. It was not, I understood, an easy assignment.

His beloved daughter, Kiwi, called and he and Huinga settled with her, her husband Bert - a stalwart of the Maori battalion - and their family in Masterton.

In Masterton, George worked as a refrigeration engineer. He and Huinga were happy with their family. One day, Huinga and a woman friend of about the same age set off to walk into Masterton to shop.

Along the way they spotted a mobile x-ray caravan run by the Cancer Society. "For a lark" said Huinga, "why don't we hop in and have ourselves tested?".

Call Of Coast

Within a few weeks, she was dead of lung cancer. In his suffering - for theirs had been a marriage made in heaven - George, at 70, suffered a heart attack.

Numbed, he felt the call of the coast. Huinga's body was carried for the tangi and burial at Rangitukia. George settled for the last, rather lonely, years of his life with his son, Winston, a police constable in Ruatoria.

Things were not as before for George, or Ruatoria. "This used to be a paradise" he said at the time of his *Life* programme. " Now, it is a place of distrust and fear".

I mentioned to the secretary of the East Coast Rugby Union, which is based in Ruatoria, that I hoped at a convenient time to call upon George.

"I think you had better hurry" said Mrs Kath McLean. "He is, I am afraid, beginning to wear".

That was not apparent on the television appearance. Naturally, later, there was a party. It thinned down to George and another champion fullback, Fergi McCormick. They quietly drank beer for beer, small ones, and talked.

George stood as straight as a guardsman, joyful at all the experiences of the show. New Zealand that night (or morning) knew no happier man.

McCormick, who is a publican, at last exclaimed "George, I must go to bed, I really must".

"One more, Fergi" George smiled. "Just one more".

It was three in the morning. George mounted the stairs with the spring of a man 30 or 40 years younger. It had been a night of his life, when he was uplifted, lionised, memorialised and placed forever in front of the greatest audience of his career, in the pantheon of the truly great of sport.

Here was a man who in life, in sport, embodied perfect simplicity. No wonder he was known as 'The Nonpareil".

The *1987 Rugby Almanack of New Zealand* (Edited by R. H. Chester & N. A. C. McMillan) obituary is below:

GEORGE NEPIA *(Hawke's Bay and East Coast)* was probably New Zealand's most famous rugby player. As a fullback on the 1924-25 All Black tour of Britain he was widely acclaimed for his outstanding play in all 30 matches. A strong kicker, a fearless fielder of the ball and a devastating tackler he maintained a wonderfully consistent form through the tour and his later career.

It is generally understood that he was born at Wairoa on 25 April, 1905 the date given in the book *I George Nepia* written in partnership with Terry McLean. Some doubt has been thrown on this date in recent years by Nepia himself who claimed his date of birth was in 1907 and by his school records. The Nuhaka Native School records that he was aged 10-years and three months on the school register dated 8 June, 1914 and at the Mormon Agricultural College, Hastings when he registered there in 1921 his date of birth is given as 4 April, 1904.

He made his first-class debut while a student at M.A.C. on 25 May, 1921 on the wing for an East Coast (N. I.) Districts team in a trial match to assist the selection of the New Zealand Maori side of that year. The next season he won a place in the Hawke's Bay team against Wairarapa on 3 June on the wing, scoring a try in the Bay's 14-12 victory. He played the next match as a five-eighth against a New Zealand Maori side and later in the season appeared for the Hawke's Bay 'B' team against Poverty Bay. Although still a student at M. A. C. he played 11 matches for Hawkes Bay in 1923, all at five-eighth and also represented a Hawke's Bay-Poverty Bay-East Coast team against the visiting New South Wales side. For Hawke's Bay he scored 39 points from three tries, nine conversions, three penalty goals and a goal from a mark. He added a further 11 points for the combined team, all from the boot.

In 1924 he appeared at second five-eighths in a regional trial match at Auckland and two days later played his first first-class match at fullback for a Southern Maori XV against the Northern counterparts at Eden Park. The following week he made a further appearance at fullback in a North Island trial at Wellington landing nine points from kicks. From this match he proceeded to the North Island team that met the South Island. Nepia scored 17 points in a North Island 39-8 rout.

That night he was included amongst the first 16 players named for the New Zealand team to tour Britain. Four days later he appeared in the final trial. Before the New Zealand side left for Australia he had time to play a sole match for Hawke's Bay in their Ranfurly Shield defence against Poverty Bay. He played in all four matches in Australia and later in two in New Zealand before the side left for Britain where he played in 30 consecutive matches and a further two in Canada on the way home, winning lavish praise for his fine displays.

The 1925 domestic season saw him again playing with the Aotea club in Dannevirke. His first match for Hawke's Bay was at second five-eighth in partnership with his 1924 All Black team mate Lui Paewai. His other eight matches for Hawke's Bay were all at fullback as were his appearances for the North Island and for New Zealand against New South Wales at Auckland. By 1926 he had shifted to Nuhaka and was playing with the local club. He appeared in four matches for Hawke's Bay - all Ranfurly Shield challenges in the season.

The four were momentous matches with the Bay defeating Wairarapa 77-14, Wanganui 36-3, Wellington 58-8 and Auckland 41-11. His only other first-class match that season was a Maori trial at Gisborne. He was mysteriously left out of the 1926-27 New Zealand Maori side that toured to Europe and by 1927 was living at Rangitukia and playing for the local club. He played in both of East Coast's matches that year at five-eighth. The following year he appeared in the away game against Poverty Bay, for Tai Rawhiti and for the New Zealand Maori team against the touring New South Wales side. For New Zealand Maoris he landed three penalty goals to win the match 9-8. It was strange on reflection to understand why he was not called on to play for New Zealand in the three-match series with New South Wales earlier in their tour.

He returned to the New Zealand team in 1929 when after appearing in a trial match he was included in the touring team to Australia. This was the first occasion that an

East Coast player had won selection for New Zealand. However the tour was a disappointment for Nepia who suffered a back injury after the first match. He played in the first test against Australia but was forced to retire in the second half and was replaced by Stringfellow. He took no further active part on the tour.

After his return home he recovered to play twice for East Coast, and after an appearance in the Prince of Wales Cup match played for the New Zealand Maoris against a New Zealand XV at Wellington.

In 1930 he again played for New Zealand in all four tests against the visiting British side as well as the warm-up match against North Otago. Early in the season he represented East Coast and then appeared in a national trial match at Wellington. As well as the tests he also appeared against the British side for the New Zealand Maoris and for the Poverty Bay-Bay of Plenty-East Coast combination.

Two matches for East Coast in an unbeaten season and a Prince of Wales Cup match were his only games in 1931 with three matches for his union in 1932 and a further two in 1933. At the end of the 1933 season he appeared for the North Island at Wellington.

His only match in 1934 was the Prince of Wales Cup match at Rotorua. This match is remembered with great sadness for the fatal injuries suffered by Jack Ruru who was captain of the Tai Hauauru team in this match.

With the selection for the New Zealand team to tour Britain dominating rugby players' thoughts in 1935 Nepia took part in four of the long series of trials to select the team. He played in the final match but was passed over in the final selection. However he won selection in the New Zealand Maori side that toured Australia. As in 1924-25 he showed his great stamina and consistency by playing in the first 10 of the tour matches missing only the final fixture against Newcastle. He scored 37 points including two tries from fullback on tour and enjoyed a successful tour. On the team's return home he appeared in both matches played against Wellington and Auckland before the team disbanded. Shortly after this tour George Nepia accepted an offer to play rugby league in Britain.

(He played initially for Streatham & Mitcham, then transferred to Halifax during the 1936-37 season. In N Z he played in 1937 for the Manukau club and represented N Z v Australia at league. He had one further season in club league.)

Following the Second World War he was reinstated to rugby and in 1947 played two further matches for East Coast, 13 years after his previous appearance for the union. He landed a penalty goal in both matches. His final first-class match came in 1950 when he captained the Olympians club team against Poverty Bay. Apart from being his last first-class match the game had great significance for Nepia as his son played at fullback for Poverty Bay, This was the first occasion that a father and son had appeared together in a first-class match in New Zealand.

In subsequent years this charming and modest man gave service as a referee.
At Ruatoria, 27 August, 1986.

Rugby league historian Robert Gate contributed the following to Code XIII

George Nepia **A Leader of all Maoridom**
Born Wairoa, 25 April, 1905 Died Ruatoria, 27 August, 1986

George Nepia's career in English rugby league covered only one-and-a-half seasons during which he played in 54 first-class fixtures and scored 210 points. In statistical terms it was unremarkable but his defection from the rugby union ranks to the fledgling London league club Streatham and Mitcham in 1935 was a sporting sensation. Nepia was then 30 years old and perhaps past his prime.

His fame as arguably the greatest full-back the union game has ever spawned lives on to this day. In spite of his league connections he remains New Zealand's most celebrated and revered player. He was the archetypal living legend. A Maori from an impoverished farming community, Nepia had displayed a precocious talent for rugby making his first-class debut as a winger for Fast Coast District in a New Zealand Maori trial just a month after his sixteenth birthday. By the time he was eighteen he was playing Ranfurly Shield football as a five-eighth for Hawke's Bay and was only nineteen when he won selection for the All Blacks tour of Great Britain and France in 1924-25 as a novice full-back.

History shows that that All Black team went through the tour winning all 30 games to earn the title of "Invincibles". Amazingly Nepia played in every match, His international debut was made in a 6-0 victory over Ireland at the tender age of 19 years 190 days.

Within 13 months he had played 39 consecutive games for the All Blacks. The next ten years would see him add only seven games to that total as injuries, selection blunders and apartheid politics conspired to deprive New Zealand of the services of this undoubted genius. Nepia made 129 representative appearances but his tests were limited to a mere nine, and, as a Maori, he was excluded from the 1928 South African tour,

As a full-back Nepia was a paragon. Sturdily built at 5' 9" and a few pounds over 13 stones, his defence was rock-like and he had the uncanny ability to mesmerise ball-carriers into running exactly where he wanted them to run. Agile as a monkey, fearless against the fiercest footrushes and a sure handler, Nepia had the priceless ability to extricate himself from the most hopeless of situations.

An excellent kicker both from hand and ground, Nepia became a master of the torpedo spiral punt which he used to gain prodigious amounts of ground in his touch-finding. With New Zealand operating under local dispensation rules on direct kicking to touch, he also perfected the art of dropping the ball into touch on the first bounce, league fashion, It was no wonder that he was a magnet for ambitious league clubs.

As early as 1925 it was reported that his signing by Hull was imminent and that clearance had been obtained from the New Zealand Rugby League Council, which was necessary under an agreement between the English and New Zealand rugby league authorities, In the event it was to be another decade before the great man turned professional. He had not wanted to but dire necessity forced his hand as the £500 he received from Streatham was the means by which he preserved his depression-hit farm at Rangitukia on New Zealand's North Island.,

George found his new game exhilarating but soon realised that the pace and fitness required was much greater, Like the champion he was, he soon buckled down and met the demands. His reputation apart, Nepia pulled in the crowds for as a league player he was a natural. Indeed so great was his pulling power that Mr S. E. Parkes, Streatham's supremo, actually charged opposing clubs 25 percent of their gates to ensure an appearance by Nepia. 20,000 are reported to have turned up for George's debut on 14 December, 1935. The opposition was Wigan and Nepia was pitted against the league's own legend, Jim Sullivan. Streatham lost 11-3, but *The Daily Despatch* ran: "The rugby league game owes a great deal of gratitude to its two greatest full-backs, Jim Sullivan and George Nepia, not only for an epic display of football but also for a fine exhibition of sportsmanship. For 80 minutes they hammered away at each other with almost cut-throat rivalry. At the end, they left the field arm in arm, What did it matter if 20,000 people almost completely forgot the rest of the players?"

Streatham must have seemed like a home from home to George for the team contained other notable New Zealanders in Charlie Smith, Eddie Holder, Jack McDonald and George Harrison. Within a fortnight Nepia was appointed captain and acting manager. His first season saw him establish himself as the club's goalkicker and full-back, although he was pressed into a game at loose-forward in the game at Salford.

His second season, however, saw him relieved of his managerial responsibilities, and playing at centre in the majority of his games. Having won seven successive games in 1936-7 and climbed to second in the league, Streatham began to wane. Charlie Smith was sold to Halifax for a record fee (reportedly £1,250) and a month later in December, 1936, George followed his half-cousin to Thrum Hall for a fee of £300.

George had played a superb game against Halifax in October scoring all twelve points in a 12-19 defeat, including an extraordinary impudent try. He had just taken a penalty at goal and missed, but was ordered to take the kick again as the Halifax players had moved. This time the Halifax players stood stock-still on the goal-line whilst George tapped the ball forward to touch down! It was probably some consolation for the three kicks at goal which had bounced off the posts!

Nepia's first game in Halifax's colours was the New Year's Day clash with Leeds at Thrum Hall. The weather was foul but 17,000 hardy souls came to see the great Maori and the gate of £797 must have paid off the transfer fee at a stroke. Nepia only played 13 games for Halifax before returning to New Zealand at the end of the 1936-37 season. His final game in England, oddly enough, was at Whitehaven in a Hospital Cup match when Halifax went down to Barrow 7-16 on 24 April, 1937. Even though a veteran, Nepia won selection twice for a Dominions XIII in France and represented a Northern Rugby League XIII in Wales.

On returning to New Zealand he played league for Manukau and was still good enough to inspire his country to a momentous 16-15 victory over Wally Prigg's Australia at Carlaw Park on 14 August, 1937.

Such was his stature, however, that the New Zealand Rugby Union actually reinstated him, their rules, of course, being very flexible when it suits them. In 1947 he represented East Coast at the age of 42 and three years later he became the oldest man to play first class rugby in New Zealand when he captained the Olympian Bay club against Poverty Bay whose skipper was his own son, George Nepia jnr - the only occasion that such an occurrence has taken place. He later became a noted referee.

The final measure of Nepia's greatness followed his death when the New Zealand Government officially acknowledged the passing of "... a great rugby player and a great New Zealander... a dignified gentleman... and a leader of all Maoridom." Rugby league in Britain will know that it is truly recognised when the death of one of its great players is acknowledged by the Government. At least rugby league had George Nepia for his twilight years.

Appendix: Statistics

Rugby Union

First-class record:

For	*Matches*
Hawke's Bay	28
East Coast	15
Tai Rawhiti.	6
North Island	3
New Zealand Maoris	15
New Zealand trial teams	9
Hawkes Bay-Poverty Bay -East Coast	1
Poverty Bay-Bay of Plenty-East Coast	2
Maori trial teams	2
Olympians club	1
North Island XV (Canada)	1
New Zealand	46
Total	**129**

Tries:	8	Conversions:	117
Penalties:	37	Drop-goals:	6
Goal from Mark:	1	Points:	396

A comparison of the four great full backs: Appearances for New Zealand

Billy Wallace:	51	George Nepia:	46
Bob Scott:	52	Don Clarke:	89

Note: Nepia was the oldest New Zealander to appear in a first class match when he captained Olympians against Poverty Bay, who were captained by his son George.

Rugby League

In Britain:

		App	T	G	P
Streatham & Mitcham	1935-6	20	0	29	58
	1936-37	18	8	44	112
Halifax	1936-37	13	2	14	34
Representative games		3	0	3	6
Totals		54	10	90	210

In New Zealand:

New Zealand:	1
New Zealand Maori:	1
Hornby (1937)	1
Canterbury (1937)	1
Manukau (1938)	1
Possibles (1938 - tour trial)	1
Manukau (1939)	13
Maori (vs Auckland 1939)	1

N.B. Figures for 1938 and 1939 are taken from newspaper reports and not official club records.

Rugby Union statistics provided by Clive Akers (official record keeper NZRFU)
British Rugby League statistics provided by Robert Gate
New Zealand Rugby League statistics provided by Peter Lush

Bibliography

Books

New Zealand Rugby Legends: 15 reflections by T. P. McLean (Moa Beckett, 1987)
1987 Rugby Almanack of New Zealand edited by R. H. Chester & N. A. C. McMillan (Moa Beckett 1987)
Sky Television New Zealand Rugby League Annual 1999 edited by Bernard Wood (NZRFL, 1999)
Touch and Go - A History of professional Rugby League in London by Dave Farrar and Peter Lush with Michael O'Hare (London League Publications, 1995)

Newspapers and journals

Athletic News
Code XIII
Halifax Evening Courier
Hawke's Bay Herald
Illustrated London News
Mitcham News
New Zealand Herald
South London Press
The Dominion
The Times (London)

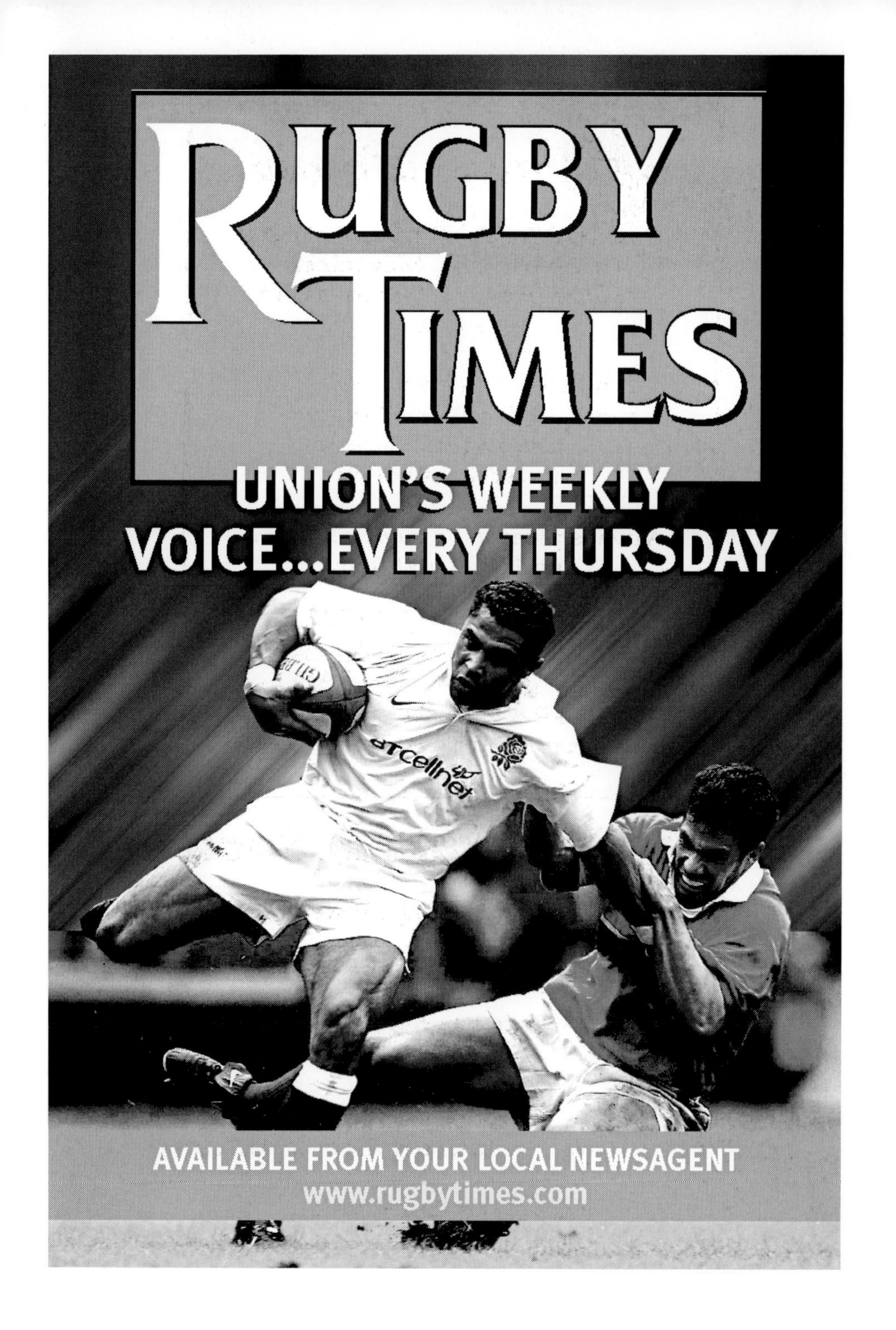
RUGBY TIMES
UNION'S WEEKLY
VOICE...EVERY THURSDAY
AVAILABLE FROM YOUR LOCAL NEWSAGENT
www.rugbytimes.com

A national Rugby League magazine published twice a year

Our Game covers the history of the game, international reports, current issues, book reviews, 'changing the rules', fiction, poetry, obituaries and much more.

Regular contributors include Robert Gate, Tony Collins, Huw Richards, Michael O'Hare, Phil Melling and Craig Wilson.

Subscribe

Four issue subscription: £7.00
Special £10.00 offer:
Three issue subscription plus a copy of **one** of the following books:

- *Tries in the Valleys - A history of Rugby League in Wales*
- *From Fulham to Wembley - 20 years of Rugby League in London*
- *The Fulham Dream - Rugby League tackles London*

Back numbers available:
No. 1: Brian Bevan, Central Park, Melbourne Storm;
No. 2: 1954 World Cup, Lebanon, North America, Alex Murphy;
No. 3: 1985 Challenge Cup Final, Cumbria, Andy Gregory,
No. 4: Jim Sullivan, Ashes 1988, Hull FC.
No. 5: Bev Risman on Wembley '68, Yugoslavia, Hawaii and Salford.
£1.50 each or special offer: £6 for all five

- To subscribe, please write to London League Publications Ltd, PO Box 10441, London E14 0SB.
- Please indicate the length of subscription, book chosen if taking the £10 special offer, any back-numbers ordered and your name and address.
- Please indicate which issue you want you subscription to start with.

Cheques payable to London League Publications Ltd, no credit card orders.

Or: to order a copy post free, send a cheque for £2.00 to: London League Publications, PO Box 10441, London E14 0SB. (no credit card orders).

Our Game is also available from Sportspages (London & Manchester), Smiths of Wigan, and is on sale at all London Broncos home matches

Rugby League Bravehearts
The History of Scottish Rugby League
By Gavin Willacy
Foreword by Alan Tait

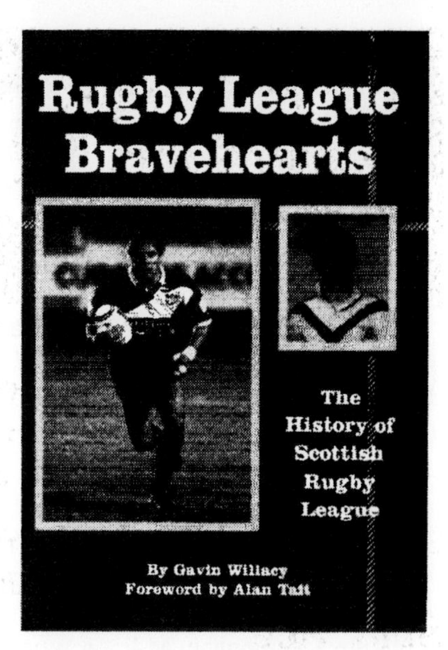

Despite never having a professional club, Scotland has a rich Rugby League history. From the sport's earliest years, there have been Scottish players in British Rugby League, including Great Britain internationals such as Dave Valentine, George Fairbairn and Alan Tait.

Since 1995, Scotland have competed on the international stage, including in the 2000 Rugby League World Cup. Since the barriers between Union and League came down in 1995, League in Scotland has developed tremendously, and the amateur, student and development parts of the game are fully covered in Rugby League Bravehearts. The book includes:

- A full record of Scotland's international matches
- Interviews with key Scottish players
- Profiles of Scottish Rugby League professionals
- Scottish players' participation in representative matches
- Scottish Students and amateur Rugby League

Lavishly illustrated, this book will be of interest to all Rugby League supporters and those interested in the development of sport in Scotland.

Published in June 2002

£9.95 net in the United Kingdom. ISBN: 1903659-05-1

To order the book at a special offer price of £9.00 post free in the UK, (add £2.00 for overseas orders) please write to:
London League Publications Ltd, PO Box 10441, London E14 0SB

(Cheques payable to London League Publications Ltd. No credit cards. Sterling cheques only)

The Rugby League Grounds Guide

By Peter Lush and Dave Farrar

Foreword by David Hinchliffe M.P.

Travelling to watch your team play away, and visiting new grounds is one of the best experiences in rugby league. Equally enjoyable is going to watch an amateur game or a big match at a ground you have never visited before. This book will help you get to the match and use the ground's facilities when you get there.

The book includes for all the British professional clubs:

- History and description of the ground
- Telephone numbers, websites and email details
- Information on price reductions, catering and facilities for people with disabilities
- Public transport details and road directions, with a local map
- Local tourist information

It also has basic details of:

- The Australian National Rugby League clubs
- French professional clubs
- BARLA National Conference clubs
- Summer Rugby League Conference clubs

Published in April 2001. If ordered by post, includes a 2002 supplement.

Every Rugby League supporter will find this book very useful.

Special offer price for readers of this book: Order your copy for £7.00 post free in UK - add £2.00 for overseas orders (cover price £7.95) from London League Publications Ltd, PO Box 10441, London E14 0SB

(Cheques payable to London League Publications Ltd, no credit cards. Sterling cheques only)

ISBN: 1-903659-02-7

Knowsley Road
Memories of St Helens Rugby League Football Club

By Andrew Quirke

Foreword by **Mal Meninga**

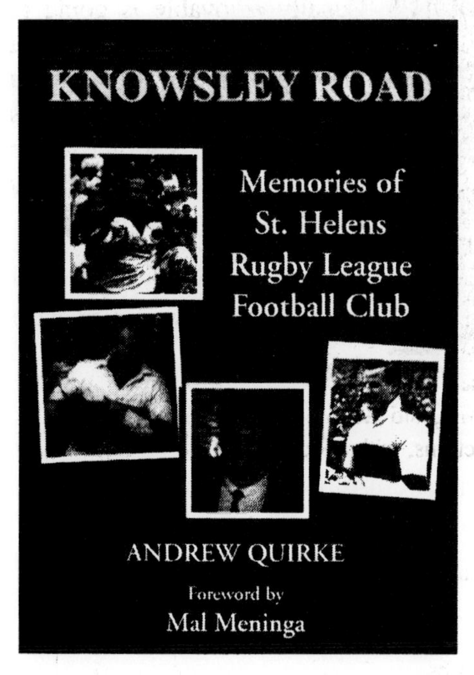

Published in September 2001, this book has memories about one of Rugby League's most successful clubs.
It includes interviews with **Duggie Greenall, Tom van Vollenhoven, Alex Murphy, Kel Coslett, John Mantle, Harry Pinner, Bobbie Goulding, Keiron Cunningham, Chris Joynt** and many other Saints stars of the past 70 years along with recollections from coaches, supporters and other people involved with Saints.

Published at £9.95, the book is available to readers of this book for £9.00 post free in the UK, add £2.00 for overseas orders. Order from London League Publications Ltd, PO Box 10441, London E14 0SB.

(Cheques payable to London League Publications Ltd, no credit cards. Sterling cheques only)

ISBN: 1-903659-04-3

Sports Books available from London League Publications:

Rugby League:

From Fulham to Wembley - 20 years of Rugby League in London
Edited by Dave Farrar and Peter Lush
Published in June 2000 to celebrate the London Broncos' 20th anniversary, the book includes profiles of key players and coaches, supporters' memories, and reports of key matches.
Published at £8.75, special offer £8.00 post free in the UK, add £2.00 for overseas orders.

The Fulham Dream - Rugby League tackles London
By Harold Genders
The inside story of how Harold Genders set up Fulham RLFC and won promotion in the club's historic first season. Fully illustrated with full records of that great campaign.
Published in September 2000 at £6.95, special offer £6.00 post free in the UK, add £1.00 for overseas orders.

London books special offer: The two books for £12.00 post free in the UK, £14.00 overseas.

Tries in the Valleys - A History of Rugby League in Wales
Edited by Peter Lush and Dave Farrar
Foreword by Jonathan Davies
Covers the Welsh international team, clubs in Wales and interviews with key people involved in the game in Wales.
Published in 1998 at £14.95, special offer £8.00 post free in the UK, add £2.00 for overseas orders.

Cricket:

Buns, Bails and Banter - A Season watching County Cricket
By David Spiller
Foreword by Vince Wells
The author followed Leicestershire home and away in the 2000 season. Captures the unique atmosphere of county cricket today.
Published in 2001 at £8.95, special offer £5.00 post free in the UK. Add £2.00 for overseas orders.

Order from: London League Publications Ltd, PO Box 10441, London E14 0SB
(Cheques payable to London League Publications Ltd, no credit cards. Sterling cheques only)